Our Changing Journey
to the End

Volume 1
New Paths of Engagement

Volume 2
New Venues in the Search for Dignity and Grace

Our Changing Journey to the End

Reshaping Death, Dying, and Grief in America

Volume I

New Paths of Engagement

**Christina Staudt, PhD and
J. Harold Ellens, PhD, Editors**

 PRAEGER

AN IMPRINT OF ABC-CLIO, LLC
Santa Barbara, California • Denver, Colorado • Oxford, England

Library of Congress Cataloging-in-Publication Data

Our changing journey to the end : reshaping death, dying, and grief in America /
Christina Staudt, PhD and J. Harold Ellens, PhD, editors.

    volumes cm

  Includes bibliographical references and index.

   ISBN 978-1-4408-2845-4 (hardcopy : alk. paper) — ISBN 978-1-4408-2846-1 (ebook)
1. Terminal care—United States.   2. Right to die—United States.   3. Death—Social
aspects—United States.   4. Grief—Social aspects—United States.   I. Staudt, Christina,
editor of compilation.   II. Ellens, J. Harold, 1932– editor of compilation.

  R726.8.O87   2014

  179.7—dc23   2013024633

ISBN: 978-1-4408-2845-4
EISBN: 978-1-4408-2846-1

18   17   16   15   14   1   2   3   4   5

This book is also available on the World Wide Web as an eBook.
Visit www.abc-clio.com for details.

Praeger
An Imprint of ABC-CLIO, LLC

ABC-CLIO, LLC
130 Cremona Drive, P.O. Box 1911
Santa Barbara, California 93116-1911

This book is printed on acid-free paper ∞

Manufactured in the United States of America

Contents

SECTION II: SPEAKING IN A NEW LANGUAGE

SECTION III: TRANSFORMING THE AFTERMATH

Foreword

Robert Pollack

Director, University Seminars
Professor, Department of Biological Sciences

Director, Center for the Study of Science and Religion
Columbia University

In accepting the challenge to write this Foreword to *Our Changing Journey to the End,* I have had the chance to reconsider my own thoughts and strategies for dealing with matter of death, dying, and bereavement. At the end of the last millennium, I attempted to lay out these thoughts in an essay on the place of science along that journey. Here, I am sharing them with you, but in the sharper light shed by them after another dozen years of life. I hope these reflections will serve to provide a new and useful context for the astounding diversity of contributions to these two new volumes. Also, as the current Director of the University Seminars at Columbia, writing this Foreword allows me to properly thank my colleagues and predecessors for their wisdom and foresight in preserving this remarkable institution over many lifetimes.

In 1905, Columbia University built a magnificent brick and limestone palace of science, Schermerhorn Hall, for its new and expanding departments of geology, botany, and zoology. Carved on its facade is the inscription "Speak to the Earth and it will teach you." To someone who has studied the Bible, whether the Jewish Tanakh or the Christian Old Testament, this line from the Book of Job is clearly not the motto of science that it appears to be. It is Job himself, in pain, telling his friends that neither he nor they can possibly understand the ways of Heaven and that he therefore wants to die on the spot.

Appropriately enough, Schermerhorn Hall is the site of the discovery that closed for all time the chance that death could be transcended by science. The ninth floor of Schermerhorn is now shared by the departments of biology and art history; rooms full of slides of paintings and sculptures spill into rooms full of slides of tissues and organs. In a room here in 1910, Thomas Hunt Morgan established the physical reality of a half-dozen genes, showing that a number of different genes were actually different pieces of a fly's chromosome. In this first demonstration that genes were chemicals, Morgan opened a line of research that led, in only a few decades, to our current understanding of DNA-based, chromosomal inheritance as the chemical mechanism for the inheritance of variation from generation to generation on which Darwinian natural selection depends. Speaking to the Earth after the fashion of science, these followers of Morgan have unexpectedly converged on Job's vision of the natural world. Because life is chemical in its deepest essence and random in its origins, they have shown that it need have no purpose beyond its own propagation; in studying the details of the history of life, they have found that the survival of life on this planet has always depended on, and always will depend on, the death of individual living things.

It is not merely that the death of any individual organism hardly matters. It is that individual deaths are essential: random variations in DNA that arise in one generation can enter the competition for survival only through succeeding generations. Each individual death means the loss of a singular version of DNA, to be sure, but for a species to survive, the individual members of the species must die. Science claims to control what it can understand, yet death is one aspect of life we can understand all too well without any experiments and the one over which we will never gain an iota of control. Faced with these facts, both biology and medicine have become stuck in a long series of persistent, clever, but useless attempts to ignore them: medicine, by insisting that death is its failure, and biology, by insisting that death is not interesting.

We may know how to counter the effects of aging within a few years or a few decades or never. People dying in very old age after having been successfully kept from the slow decline of aging will still want—as we do even now—any assurance they can get that the quality of their remaining lives, however short, will be preserved until the very moment of death. In *these volumes,* we see that there are indeed physicians and scientists who consider that last task to be of scientific interest and worth the work. We see as well, many strategies for getting past giving false promises that every condition is curable in principle, that impending death is the failure of a cure, to instead concentrate on the medical and scientific aspects of the very last stage of life—that is, on dying.

Today, with the majority of people dying before 80 of infectious, environmental, behavioral, and inherited problems we cannot yet solve, this issue may seem premature. But there is a risk involved in not confronting it now: silence means we will see biomedical research continue to use each successful reduction in premature death as an excuse to avoid dealing with death's inevitability. The old people who today suffer avoidable disease, unnecessary isolation, and pain in their dying are the major victims of this avoidance of the link between aging and death. They deserve a better deal than the one they are getting from today's medical science. Not for them alone, but also for today's children who will be the aged of 2050 and beyond, science and medicine have to learn how to attend to the problems of the dying.

The medical treatment of the dying is almost invisible today, an embarrassing situation that can only get worse as the rest of medical science succeeds in allowing a greater fraction of the population to live into old age with sufficient residual mental and physical capacity to understand their situation. For the sake of these lucky people—may we all be among them—medical science is obligated now to begin a research effort focused on making dying itself as brief, and as healthy, as possible. This is no joke: the hospice movement—not a product of scientific medicine but a reaction to it—has shown that a dying accompanied by a minimum of pain and a maximum of social interaction is healthier and better by far than the typical dying of today, accompanied as it so often is by prolonged agony and isolation.

For most of my life, and for all of my thirty years as an experimental scientist, I scrupulously avoided my own personal and professional responsibility to attend to the dying. It is not that I had no chances to make the connection between science and dying; I simply chose not to take them. In my own confusion, I lost sight of the fundamental truth that dying is as distant from death as any other stage in life is.

The deaths of my parents bracketed the period in which I came to see how a failure to acknowledge death properly distorts the practice of medical science. My father died of a respiratory infection acquired in the hospital a decade after he had lost his senses to Alzheimer's disease. During his last years I did not see him at all, and I did not understand that he was dying, for I already imagined him as dead. He lived for many years in a home for the demented, his body kept alive by strangers because his family—myself included—could not carry the burden of caring for him after he ceased to know who we—or anyone else—were. He was allowed to die at last, of pneumonia, because my parents had signed papers in advance, asking that their lives not be extended by heroic measures once they had crossed an irreversible threshold of pain or dementia.

My mother survived him, and in her last months, and even in her last days, she gave me and my family ample evidence of the difference between dying and being dead. She became stronger as she became weaker, became increasingly generous and wise with me and my relatives, and with a host of new and old friends, in ways that she could not while she was more fully alive. This stunning emergence of a kinder and wiser person from the dying body of my mother came to a halt only in her last few days, when the pain of her tumor began to require such high doses of morphine that she was unable to speak with any lucidity. Even then, she clearly accepted her death, said good-bye, and, with the help of hospice care at home, died peacefully.

Hospice care is still controversial at many major medical centers today, for its goal is not to provide curative treatment for the dying but to provide a good death. At their best, hospices excel at delivering what they promise: control over pain, dignity to the end, and the assurance that no one need spend their last moments alone.

When I wrote my essay in 1999, the hospital response of science to the dying reflected my own attitudes during those decades I worked in my lab. It went something like this: "You have had the misfortune to be born too soon to benefit from science's ever deeper comprehension of nature. That is too bad, but since we can know how everything works, certainly one day we will know how to keep a death like yours from happening. Until then, you will understand if we do not spend much time on the relatively uninteresting matter of how it is to die." This attitude has certainly not disappeared and is in evidence in many places, especially in large research hospitals in major metropolitan areas, but *Our Changing Journey to the End* shows how these attitudes are being undermined by two primary forces: the baby boomers who demand good care of their dying parents and soon themselves, and the cost of futile interventions in a time when health care costs are zooming. Other chapters in these volumes suggest how change could take place and how some changes are already under way in spite of the many remaining obstacles, which are also discussed.

Today, medical scientists treat very old age, dying, and death with equally fastidious disdain, as if they were all somehow intrinsically uninteresting. If they are as frightened of death as everyone else, then their disdain for aging, death, and dying is a prophecy that keeps them from confronting their fears. A good deal of interesting science lies waiting to be done by scientists able to admit their fears of death and look beyond them to study dying on its own terms.

The questions to be asked are familiar: which parts are painful and may therefore be made better by the easing of emotional, existential and physical pain; which parts are inherited through the genome and may therefore be made better by the manipulation of the genome or the addition or subtraction of a gene or a protein; which parts are conscious, and which are unconscious, so that we may better understand how it feels to be dying and learn how to alleviate the worst of those feelings. Those questions would form a minimal agenda for research on the dying stage of life.

Beginning with Elisabeth Kübler-Ross's 1969 classic, *On Death and Dying,* many serious studies of dying have been built around interviews with people in the last days of their lives. A doctor herself, Kübler-Ross broke many rules at her hospital by insisting that the dying be given a chance to describe their feelings directly; simply allowing the dying a voice was a major accomplishment. From their narratives, she produced an anatomy of the physical and emotional stages of dying: denial, anger, bargaining, depression, and acceptance. As she points out, all but the last of these five stages express a deeper and more fundamental denial, attitudes that allow one nevertheless to have some hope. Hope in the face of certain death may seem absurd, and perhaps it is, but nevertheless the dying showed her—and many studies since have confirmed—that a dying person often does not lose hope until just before death, and sometimes not even then.

A person's last days can be the most remarkable example of dying as an aspect of living: when the end is near, a dying person begins to pull away from the world, sleeping a lot, not seeing anyone, not interested in anyone. At best, and without pain, the end of life seems quite remarkably like the beginning, the clock of internal time run backward one last time, to the earliest days of infancy. Kübler-Ross counseled that hope should never be denied, that the dying should not be burdened with facts that would remove all hope before the person was ready to set it aside, and that the enemy of the dying is not unavoidable death so much as avoidable physical and mental pain. In the decades since Kübler-Ross's book came out, about a third of her readers have passed through her five stages and died. In all that time, precious little has been added to, or taken from, her five stage formulation of dying, and almost nothing has been done in science to carry out any of her prescriptions.

There is, then, a realistic scientific agenda for the period from the moment when there is nothing that medical science can do to stop death from coming until the moment of death. It is to understand the mind and the body well enough to keep both as free of pain, and as free of isolation, as possible. Science can complement the work of a hospice by providing it with new tools to accomplish these ends.

Much dying today happens poorly, with unnecessary pain. It is time for medicine to acknowledge what torturers have always known: pain is a pathological state that mocks any pretense to health. To uncover the underlying mechanisms of pain, it is useful first to recall that no matter what part of the body is in pain, the hurt is, of course, in the head. Pain is a brain state, and as such it ought to be as understandable, and treatable, as other unwanted brain states are turning out to be. The most effective painkillers we use today work only by dulling the senses, and all are highly addictive when taken by people whose lives are not almost at an end. Doctors who try to prescribe large enough doses of these compounds—morphine and its derivatives—are often suspected of inducing a dying patient's addictive craving.

This is a cruel joke to anyone who is dying with intractable pain and who may reasonably argue that one cannot be addicted when one is dead. A civilized medicine that fully accepted the reality of death would also recognize that the pain itself is as damaging as any addictive state. There is another, equally ironic barrier to the straightforward study of the proper pharmacology for intractable pain: the fear that an overdose of morphine might be used intentionally to shorten the life of a dying person, with or without the person's consent. It is ironic because the most frequent reason for requesting an early death is precisely unbearable pain.

Beyond the tragedy of dying people having to hasten their death with the same compounds that might have given them a reason to live longer, the denial of proper painkillers damages a person's body. A person in pain suffers from a reduction in the efficiency of the immune system and usually cannot actively participate in any other courses of treatment. We need a major effort to find or synthesize—and then to distribute openly—a new generation of more effective painkillers. Such research would need strong government support, since the political problems of such research and development make these studies as uneconomical as vaccine production for today's pharmaceutical firms.

The "how" of mental life—the mechanisms of gene expression, protein synthesis, and cellular communication that work so well for a century in some brains but not well at all in others—are at the intersection of basic biomedical science and the right of a dying person to full membership in society until the last moment of life. It may take decades or longer to fully understand the molecular biology of mental life, but it is not too early to say with confidence that whatever the molecular mechanisms involved, people need the touch of other people's hands—those soft touches that let them know they are not alone—all their lives, to the very end. The cruelest of the paradoxical consequences of the denial of death in modern medicine is the insistence on treating a dying person in ways that destroy all chance of privacy and dignity, that deny the person the ancient right to the continued presence of friends and family.

The usual argument for leaving the dying person alone in a cold room with tubes and monitors blocking all human interaction, for allowing the rarest and sometimes the richest of words to go unheard or unsaid, is that this regimen is necessary to extend the person's life, albeit only for the shortest of times. But to extend external time by so little while removing all chance of the person's sharing any of the little internal time left with anyone else is surely another form of *de facto* torture, equal to withholding painkillers.

With this short Foreword, I welcome you to *Our Changing Journey to the End.*

Preface and Acknowledgments

Death, as thanatologists like to emphasize, is not the opposite of life but its extension; and dying is not the reverse of living but is life's final chapter. Whether articulated or silenced, mortal concerns shape everyone's journey from birth onward. In the scholarly world, aspects of death insert themselves into every discipline and can be addressed from the loftiest of abstract heights, as well as from the level of somatic functions, operational experiences "down on the ground" so to speak, and the sanitary disposal of remains. Regardless of the scope or the details, when the discourse is about death, the subject is never trivial.

The two volumes of *Our Changing Journey to the End: Reshaping Death, Dying, and Grief in America* cover a broad range of death-related topics on the theme of change and evolution since the 1990s and also project how the current direction will be—and needs to be—reshaped to meet the challenges facing America in the 21st century. The volumes have their origin in a call for papers for the third biennial Austin H. Kutscher Memorial conference, organized by the Columbia University Seminar on Death and held in March 2012. Most of the chapters gathered here were presented at this conference, entitled *Reshaping Our Journey to the End: Death, Dying, and Bereavement in 21st Century America,* or at regular monthly meetings of the Columbia University Seminar on Death during the academic years 2011–2013. Their substance has been honed in the collegial discussions that characterize the Seminar's conferences and meetings and they have been revised for publication here. Additional contributors were invited to supplement the core group of chapters and ensure a broad coverage of the theme.

This final product is the work of many, and I acknowledge their roles in this endeavor with great respect and appreciation. First and foremost, I want to thank all of the authors who have contributed their vast expertise to the individual chapters. These volumes belong to them. An eclectic group of dedicated scholars, their vision and knowledge have enriched me profoundly. The diversity of styles and approaches they bring to the theme ensures that the reader is exposed to the many ways that the journey to the end can be viewed and traveled.

The Columbia University Seminar members have contributed importantly to this project by considering and selecting the individual papers among the many proposals submitted to the conference and refining the content in their roles as facilitators and participants of the panel discussions. Furthermore, I am very grateful to them for their comments on a preliminary draft of the content and organization of these volumes. I thank them all: Michael Bartalos, Thomas Caffrey, Nathan Ionascu, Kevin Keith, John Kiernan, Jerry Nessel, Maureen O'Reilly-Landry, Jerry Piven, Karla Maria Rothstein, Sherry Schachter, and Margaret Souza. While they have provided helpful suggestions, they cannot be held responsible for any omissions or mistakes.

Among others, notably, my enormous gratitude goes to J. Harold Ellens, coeditor of these volumes, for his generous encouragement and support during every phase of the development, assembly, and editing of these publications. I could not have asked for more gracious guidance. Debbie Carvalko's patience and experience, as Acquisition Editor for Praeger Publishers, have been indispensable, as she has shepherded this project through the publication process with good cheer and careful attention to details. Marcelline Block holds a special place in my heart for her unfailing willingness to apply her intelligence and many skills to different facets of this project, be they probing suggestions to my own chapters, clarifying the language of another contributor, or formatting the bibliographies. I am grateful to Catherine Rogers, whose insightful and poetic vignettes add a fresh dimension to the sections they introduce.

The Columbia University Seminar Office has been enormously helpful in many ways. Bob Pollack, Director, has offered intellectual stimulus and support for the concept of this project from the start. I also want to thank him, the Advisory Board of the Columbia University Seminars and its Associate Director, Alice Newton, for the generous approval of a grant from the Schoff Fund. Pamela Guardia assisted in making the conference run smoothly, as did the Seminar's conscientious rapporteur, William Gassaway, who was also immensely helpful throughout the planning process of the conference.

Finally, but not least, I want to recognize my husband and family. I am indebted to them for their patience and continued expressions of love while I have been preoccupied with this project.

Christina Staudt

Our Changing Journey
to the End

Time

Mean Time
Time isn't nice to us.
It wrinkles us and forgets to iron, pinches us, steals our money,
our brain cells, our boyfriends.
Time isn't very nice.
Mean time

Catherine Rogers

Chapter 1

Introduction: A Bird's Eye View of the Territory

Christina Staudt

*T*he *first part of this introduction is a summary of the history of death and dying in the United States. It gives a telescopic view of the last 400 years, merely touching on the period before the mid-20th century and following more closely the development since then. A review of the literature on death since the mid-1950s helps us understand how we have arrived at the approach to and perception of death that we experience in the 21st century. Different models of death are presented to illustrate how death can be managed and constructed, ending with a sketch of the neo-modern model that shows the dominant trend in the early teens of the 21st century and suggesting that "death engaged" has become a suitable label for our death system. The second part of this introduction, entitled "New Paths of Engagement," briefly reviews the chapters in this volume, placing them in the following groupings: The Changing Landscape, Speaking in a New Language, and Transforming the Aftermath.*

THE PANORAMA[1]

Ideas about death, practices around dying persons, and the rituals of mourning vary among people based on the traditions and beliefs of the group. In some societies, they are stable, fixed by religious dogma and rigid societal patterns. In the 21st-century United States, they are amorphous and in flux. *Our*

Changing Journey to the End: Reshaping Death, Dying, and Grief in America can be considered a guidebook, of sorts, to help the reader navigate this territory: a Baedeker for a very particular journey, not our individual journeys to the end, but rather, a journey through a landscape where we meet death, dying, and grief in different guises.

This overview and brief history merely touches on the first 400 years. The focus is on the pioneers of the 20th century who attempted to bring death into the public range of vision at a time when it had disappeared from view. Their work paved the way for the shifts in attitudes and practices that take form in the 21st century. The second part of this introduction, "New Paths of Engagement," presents the chapters of Volume I of *Our Changing Journey to the End: Reshaping Death, Dying, and Grief in America.* The chapters represent important ways that we engage with death in the 21st century. They are, so to speak, the major monuments and worthwhile excursions on our journey through the death system.

"Death system," is used here as a catch-all phrase for everything related to death in a society; more formally, it has been defined as "the sum total of the persons, places, ideas, traditions, acts, omissions, emotions, and statements that we make or think about death"[2] and as "the interpersonal, sociophysical, and symbolic network through which an individual's relationship to mortality is mediated by society."[3] Other words that cover much the same collection of meanings are "episteme of death" or "paradigm of death." In this volume, these concepts are used more or less interchangeably, while respecting the word choice of a cited author.

A caveat is needed about "American." In this book, it is used in its standard definitions to mean "of or relating to the United States." Given the growing ethnical, religious, and cultural diversity of the United States, such a definition becomes less and less meaningful. Cultural differences are critical in many arenas but perhaps nowhere more so than, when we speak about what, literally, is a matter of life and death. Social, cultural, and spiritual traditions and values are deeply entrenched in some communities, and also individual and rapidly changing in other quarters—and nuances are essential for meeting individual needs at the end of life. Because this is an overview, this is not the place to account for the many variables and properly differentiate among the groups in a meaningful way. Therefore, regrettably, when reference is made to the "American public" or "American mainstream," the statement may not be applicable to large swathes of the American population but only to the dominant, traditionally Euro-American majority.

Death System Models

The definitive history of death and dying in America has not yet been written, so for the big picture I turn to Philippe Ariès's *The Hour of Our Death,* a broad historical survey of the attitude to death in Western civilization. Ariès uses literary, liturgical, testamentary, epigraphic, and iconographic documentation to categorize Western death cultures over the past two millennia as "tame death," "death of the self," "death of the other," and "invisible death."[4] With minor adaptations, these categories are applicable to North American circumstances.

The "tame death," characterized by tacit acceptance, was the prevailing death system during the first millennium of the Common Era. In the period when the "tame death" dominated, prescribed, ritualized roles controlled the conduct of the dying and their surrounding community. Belief in an afterlife connected earthly life with a mystical universe in one cosmology. This death system characterized the native populations encountered by the colonizers of the New World.

The new settlers brought with them from Europe the model of "death of the self," a label Ariès uses to signify the individual's desire to play an active role in the course of his or her own death. Unfolding first among the rich, educated, and powerful around the turn of the first millennium, this approach to death spread into the growing merchant class and then into what would become the bourgeoisie and professional class in the 18th century in Europe and America. European *transi* figures represent this idea by portraying the "self" divided into its two natures on the deathbed: the immortal, idealized person bound for heaven on top of the casket and the decomposing body below. *Ars moriendi*, treatises and illustrations describing the art of dying well, placed the burden of an appropriate ending of life on the individual person. "The Day of Doom," a popular poem by the minister Michael Wigglesworth (1631–1705), exemplifies such a text in 17th-century Colonial New England. Handbooks for living well within the confines of Protestant dogma were also common in America in the 18th and 19th centuries.[5] The practice of writing a last will and testament was carried over from Europe to the New World and, like there, was a sign that the individual—the self—wanted to control what happened around the time of death.

In the 19th century, Romantic currents and the emergence of the nuclear family as the heart of society placed close family members and loved ones at the center of the encounter with death, introducing the approach that Ariès calls the "death of the other." The "other" in Ariès's phrase stands opposite to, but in close relationship with, the speaking "self" and is wholly different from the postmodern "Other" which designates a group or person alien to the dominant group in society. The focus on loved ones gave rise to affectionate, cult-like practices, such as displays of photographs and memorabilia of the dead in the home, personalized graves, and visits to the cemetery on All Saints' Day and other holidays. *Ars moriendi* changed character, with an eye to making death a beautiful experience for the family as well as the dying person. The afterlife became popularly reconstructed as a place where loved ones would be united. The United States was in line with European customs of "the death of the other," as can be seen in numerous post-mortem photographs from this period and in cemetery decorations of 19th-century graves.

Characterized by advanced, impersonally applied medical technology, the end of life began to retreat from view after World War I in the United States as well as Europe. The era of the "invisible death" began. In this model, the dying are increasingly hidden from view, while physicians marshal their resources to prolong life, no matter at what cost to the dying person and his family. The inability to overcome death was seen as a failure, making repression, isolation, and denial normative responses. Some of these responses continue into the 21st century.

Ariès identifies death denial as a phenomenon of modern industrial times and the paramount attitude to death in the 20th century. He sees it as negligible during the periods when "tame death," the "death of the self," and the "death of the other" were the dominant attitudes toward the end of life. In those death systems, the dying and the dead were present among the living; religious and social rituals imparted meaning to the end-of-life experience and helped the dying and the bereaved manage the passage; and belief in an afterlife and the immortal soul softened the cruelty of death and the suffering that accompanied it.

Similar to Ariès, Mervyn F. Bendle argues that the shift in the culture of death from the 19th to the 20th century marks the arrival of a new episteme of death. While the 19th century derived its concepts and perceptions of death and dying from religion, mythology, and tradition, the 20th century looked to utilitarianism, neoliberalism, and bureaucratic calculations. Bendle sees the 20th-century experience of death as dominated by two institution-based processes: "medicalization" and "militarization." Militarization was the main influence in the first half of the century. Two world wars with enormous casualties defined how death became perceived and processed by society. Medicalization overshadowed militarization in the second half of the 20th century. The dying process became so closely identifiable with the medical prognosis that it left scant room for the value of the patient as an individual and for the needs of the surrounding family and community. The dying and everything to do with their management were removed as far as possible from the living and the normalcy of quotidian life.[6] In the 1950s and 1960s, the concealment of death, which marked the entire 20th century in the United States and Western Europe, reached its nadir.

The Arduous Climb Back into the Light

Mid-century, a handful of notable scholars in different disciplines expressed their concerns about society's lack of attention to issues of death and dying in Western society, but for many years their work had minimal impact on practices in ordinary life. In his article "The Concept of Death," published in 1955, the political historian Franz Borkenau looked into the future and perceived an increasingly secular society living under the threat of the atomic bomb. He feared the emergence of a culture that might reject immortality and embrace death. Classifying different civilizations as predominantly "death denying," "death defying," "death accepting," or "death transcending," he expressed concern that modern Western society might increasingly turn to death denial as its primary coping mechanism.[7] The same year, Geoffrey Gorer, a social anthropologist, observed in his essay "The Pornography of Death" that death had become taboo in the Western world; it was denied with the same vehemence as was sex in the Victorian era—neither had a place in polite society. Gorer originally commented on the state of affairs in mid-20th-century Britain but found his observations equally applicable to the United States a decade later.[8]

In *The Meaning of Death,* published in 1959, the American psychologist and death study pioneer Herman Feifel sounded an alarm about our ingrained tendency to avert our eyes from mortal matters. His introduction noted that "denial and avoidance of the countenance of death" constituted one of the three leitmotifs among the range of approaches to death presented by the philosophers, religionists, and scientists writing for his volume, and that "this has implications not only for the individual but for society as well." His anthology was a concerted attempt to break the prevailing taboo. In gathering reflections from experts representing different disciplines, Feifel sought fresh insights and attempted to stimulate explorations in new directions. He believed that "our science-conscious culture . . . does not furnish us with all the necessary parameters for investigating and understanding death" and saw "a pressing need for more reliable and systematic, controlled study in the field."[9] While Feifel's work was noted in some academic circles, his message did not penetrate into society as a whole and did not lead to change among the general public.

Death was not a common scholarly subject in the 1950s and 1960s, not even in anthropology and art history, disciplines that could point to long traditions of works related to burial and death prior to the topic becoming taboo.[10] Archeological articles on mortuary practices and funeral monuments appeared with some frequency in specialized journals, but the list of books published by academic presses on death-related subjects remained sparse throughout the decade. Among the exceptions are *Death and Western Thought* (1963) by Jacques Choron, who demonstrated a close connection between philosophical traditions and the traditions surrounding death and dying; and *Man's Concern with Death* (1968), with the British historian Arnold Joseph Toynbee as the editor and principal contributor, a major attempt to cover every aspect of death from its definition to philosophical and cultural matters.

A review in 1968 of the American edition of Gorer's *Death, Grief and Mourning* sounded an optimistic note: "this book is one of a half-dozen or more social science investigations of mortality that have appeared in the past two years—a welcome indication that the cover of repression on this taboo topic is being increasingly lifted."[11] The first book with broad appeal that began to lift the veil in the United States was *The American Way of Death*, a scathing account of the exploitive pursuits of funeral directors, by the British-born activist Jessica Mitford published in 1963. The public took notice when it discovered that placing a muzzle on death can have financial consequences. Congressional hearings on the practices of the funeral industry ensued as a result of the attention this book engendered.

The second book that caught the imagination and attention of the public was *On Death and Dying* (1969) by Elisabeth Kübler-Ross. During the 1960s and early 1970s, television and photojournalists reported in vivid images on the Cuban missile crisis, the Vietnam War, the assassinations of President Kennedy, Robert Kennedy, and Martin Luther King Jr., as well as on the shootings at Kent State University and the deadly urban riots. Yet the deaths of our relatives and friends that occurred due to aging or illness remained largely invisible and unaddressed in mainstream American communities. The publication of *On Death and Dying* began to change the *status quo* and move the subject of ordinary death and dying into the public arena.

Dr. Kübler-Ross—a Swiss-born psychiatrist who had worked with the terminally ill since her arrival in the United States in 1958 and had educated medical students on the special needs of the dying—posited that people's attitudes after receiving a terminal diagnosis or losing a loved one followed five consecutive steps. The stages she set forth—denial, anger, bargaining, depression, and finally, acceptance—have since lost their dogmatic status among clinicians, but resonated with the public. *On Death and Dying* became an international bestseller and is arguably both the turning point in bringing the needs of the dying into public discourse and the seed of what we now refer to as the death awareness movement.

The road was long and hard for those who sought to wrest dying and death from the medical establishment and back under the control of the individual and her family. Kübler-Ross testified, at the first national hearings on the subject of death with dignity, conducted by the United States Senate Special Committee on Aging, in 1972: "We live in a very particular death-denying society. We isolate both the dying and the old, and it serves a purpose. They are reminders of our own mortality."[12] In spite of the prominence of the forum, her words took time to penetrate the general consciousness to any meaningful degree.

Other attempts in the 1970s to bring interest and attention to death and dying and educate people about these topics include the launching of the *Omega Journal* in 1970 followed by *Death Studies* (formerly *Death Education*) in 1977, but the readership was small and specialized. In *The Tyranny of Survival and Other Pathologies of Civilized Life* (1973) Daniel Callahan, a philosopher and ethicist, tried to bring attention to the problem of unrestricted use of all-out technologies to keep a person alive: "If the price of survival is human degradation, then there is no moral reason why an effort should be made to ensure that survival."[13] (In Chapter 5 of this volume, "Prognosis, Costs, and End-of-Life Care," Daniel Callahan addresses this issue, 40 years later.) Callahan was one of the pioneers in the field of bioethics, a discipline originating in the 1960s as a response to the need for thoughtful contemplation of difficult moral issues in the face of medical and biological advances. In 1969, he cofounded The Hastings Center, an independent, nonpartisan, and nonprofit bioethics research institute in Garrison, New York. Robert Fulton, another pioneer in the field of bioethics edited the anthology *Death and Identity* (1965) and became the first Director of the Center for Death Education and Bioethics (CDEB) in 1969. Prescient as these scholars were about the need to find ethical answers to questions surfacing at the intersection of health care and individual rights, their ideas only slowly gained traction beyond the emerging professional bioethics community.

Nevertheless, the compass was pointing in a new direction. When Feifel, in *New Meanings of Death* (1977)—almost two decades after publishing his first volume—laid out the issues that focused the contemporary discussion on death, he noticed that "surface considerations of death . . . have become more lively," although "Americans still approach dying and death warily and gingerly."[14] Feifel remained concerned that a waning of belief in personal immortality might complicate the public's ability to cope. He wrote that death had changed from traditionally being "a door" to "becoming a wall."[15] The social scientist and philosopher Erich Fromm shared Feifel's concern about a science-focused society's ability to make sense of death. Fromm postulated that since at least the Renaissance the haughty ambition of Western civilization had been to conquer and dominate nature and that death is irrefutable evidence that we have failed in our task, contributing to our urge to deny death.[16]

When death began to remove its cloak and became more apparent in the culture in the last quarter of the 20th century, denial emerged as a defense against its presence and a theme in the discourse on death and dying. In 1973, *The Denial of Death* by cultural anthropologist Ernest Becker was published. It came to deeply influence the debate on death among psychologists and psychoanalysts as well as among a broader public. The crux of Becker's thesis is that the fear of death ultimately determines all our actions and experiences as individuals and communities. His argument starts with the premise that awareness of our own mortality gives our lives unique meaning and drives the human spirit. According to Becker, denial is the human being's instinctive and universal way to cope with the fear produced by an awareness of death. From this, he infers that all of our physical, cultural, and symbolic systems and productions are founded in the fear of death, and that our need for religious rituals and communal ceremonies, as well as our construction of heroes and monuments, grows out of our death anxiety.

Among those who countered Becker and saw life-affirming solutions to the problem of denial was Erich Fromm. He did not find the denial of death intrinsic to the human being but rather a sign of a person's inability to love life well. In his manifesto *To Have or to Be?* (1976), Fromm argued for the cultivation of the joy of life, productivity, creativity, self-expression, and humanistic religiousness as means of transforming a person. He saw denial as a consequence of the individual's focus on "having" rather than "being."

In *The Broken Connection* (1979), Robert Jay Lifton, a post-Freudian psychiatrist, who has treated the topic of death from several historic and psychological vantage points, also argues from a more life-affirming perspective than Becker that "while the denial of death is universal, the inner life-experience of a sense of immortality, rather than reflecting such denial, may well be the most authentic psychological alternative to that denial."[17] Lifton sees a sense of immortality as "an appropriate symbolization of our biological and historical connectedness."[18] To Lifton, it is the awareness of the end of life—not the denial of death—that underlies "whatever additional constructs or gaps we call forth in our symbolizing activity."[19] Lifton's view of death, as one component of our psychological makeup that drives us to seek meaning, was echoed by scholars in other disciplines in the 1970s and first years of the 1980s. Mostly employing traditional methods of data collection and research in their respective fields, they addressed matters of mortality at considerable geographic or temporal distance.[20] As the taboo of death was beginning to lift, historical and ethnographic studies allowed the authors and readers to approach the topic without treading too close to home.

The outbreak of the AIDS epidemic in the United States in the early 1980s made it difficult to keep death and dying at a distance. After the disease was recognized by the U.S. Centers for Disease Control and Prevention in 1981, AIDS education became a feature in school curricula, billboards, and public service broadcast announcements. Finding a cure for AIDS, or at least, life-prolonging treatment, became a *cause célèbre*. Descriptions of victims and the brutal course of the devastating deadly disease became commonplace, not just in medical journals and the mainstream press, but AIDS and its victims also became central characters in plays, films, novels, stories, and musicals.[21]

Simultaneous with the private and public debates among clinicians, patients, and families to achieve fair and comfortable treatment for AIDS victims, and others at the end of life, academia became increasingly engaged in the phenomenon of death. During the 1980s and into the 1990s, studies of death were highly theorized with scholars of English, linguistics, and cultural studies drawing on French post-structuralists such as Michel Foucault, Roland Barthes, Georges Bataille, and Jean Baudillard. They turned to and expanded on theories of Marxism, feminism, psychoanalysis, and semiotics (including deconstruction) for their cultural and literary criticism courses and books. The plethora of books with death in the title and a focus on identity politics—race, gender, ethnicity, and sexual orientation[22]—was closely aligned with fashionable literary and cultural theories.

The sophisticated exercises expanded the theoretical horizon in the ivory towers but had limited consequence beyond their walls. In the broad public and intimate private sphere away from the academy, people battled the problems of daily life in hospitals, nursing homes, and clinics: how to make decisions about removing ventilators, allowing artificial hydration and nutrition, and extending dialysis treatments to give themselves or their loved ones additional time with a heartbeat but possibly scant quality of remaining life. A major breakthrough for those who were concerned with the practical aspects of managing these issues was the inclusion of the Medicare Hospice Benefit in the Tax Equity and Fiscal Responsibility Act of 1982, and Congress subsequently, in 1986, making the provision permanent. With this step, a vehicle was created to reimburse a health care agency (a hospice) for offering terminally ill patients the services of teams of professionals consisting of doctors, nurses, social workers, chaplains, personal care aides, and volunteers. These specialists and other complementary therapists treated pain and symptoms, as well as addressed psycho-spiritual matters and practical caregiving quandaries that occupied the patient and her family. The Hospice Benefit was a big stride forward for the death awareness movement. (For a detailed description of hospice and palliative care, see Chapter 8 of Volume II.)

The movement to establish by law the right of patients to state their choices about health care decisions, including the right to refuse or cease treatments, and have their choices followed ran parallel with the hospice awareness movement. A complicated legislative history was brought about, in part, by the attention given to some challenging court cases, notably those of the comatose young women Karen Ann Quinlan and Nancy Cruzan.[23] After much debate, the Patient Self-Determination Act was signed by Congress in 1990, effective December 1991. It gives patients the right to participate in and direct health care decisions pertaining to their own health, to accept or refuse medical treatments, and to make advance directives for health care in case of incapacity. In the decades that followed, all 50 states passed legislation that enables an individual to appoint someone to make medical decisions for him or her, should he or she not have capacity to do so.

In the 1990s, the work to promote the hospice movement and achieve medical self-determination at the end of life began to bear fruit, not just in the legislative arena but also among the general public. With Congressional attention to these issues, people began to look for information to better understand what happens when we die. Among those who responded with books that spread into popular literature were Sherwin Nuland with *How We Die—Reflections of Life's Last Chapters* (1994) and Cedric Mims with *When We Die—The Science, Culture, and Rituals of Death* (1998). A physician and a microbiologist, respectively, Nuland and Mims describe scientifically what happens to the body as it goes through the four most common ways of dying and what happens to the body in its state as a corpse. They include cultural and sociological information, together with personal comments and illustrative narratives from their clinical experience, bringing the dying process and its aftermath into the realm of commonplace occurrences and within reach of the layperson.

Notable media events moved the general public closer to the recognition that death is amidst us when in September 2000, *Time* magazine published a feature story entitled "A Kinder Gentler Death," billed on the cover as "Dying on Our Own Terms," with photographs of contemporary dying Americans and interviews with them and their families. The same year on public television, Bill Moyers's series *On Your Own Terms* promoted acceptance of the natural course of death and openness among professional caregivers, families, and the dying persons.[24]

A New Model: Awareness and Control

Arguably, Ariès's descriptive labels for the Western death system, "death denied" and "invisible death," definitively expired on September 11, 2001. Although the actual corpses resulting from the terrorist attack were barely shown on television that day, there were images of people jumping from the buildings, and all the news media were filled with reminders and memorials of this new "day of infamy" in American history for weeks and months afterward. A force seems to have been set in motion that brought us across an imaginary line, and in short order we were flooded with images of war, famine, and pestilence from around the world, a trend that would continue.

Via new and traditional media the dead and dying entered our homes in unprecedented numbers and forms, in vivid technicolor around the clock: a journalist pleading for his life at gunpoint; Iraqi women bent over their husbands' corpses; starving refugee children in Darfur; corpses floating in the Mississippi River after Hurricane Katrina; students mourning their dead classmates after a school shooting; and cyclone victims in Burma. We were also exposed to harrowing reports about insidious threats to our well-being from pandemics and poisonous Chinese toys and pharmaceuticals to childhood obesity, which may result in the current generation of young people being the first in national history to die younger than their parents.[25] Popular television shows featured undertakers and organized crime families with strong killing instincts. Although the average life expectancy at birth in America in 2006 was 78, as compared with 49 in 1906,[26] the world—as presented in the media —seemed a more deadly place than the one we envision existed a century ago.

However, we were not only exposed to gore and shocking images that assaulted our senses; the media also instructed us how to better manage the ordinary deaths of our friends and family members. *A Lion in the House* (2006), a two-part documentary, followed the lives and deaths of children diagnosed with terminal cancer and the lives of their families.[27] Numerous handbooks on how to die well appeared in the bookstores, building on work such as Ira Byocks's *Dying Well—Peace and Possibility at the End of Life* (1997) and *The Four Things That Matter Most—A Book about Living* (2004).[28]

From the political arena, we were exposed to arguments between the press and the Bush administration about the photographing of coffins that returned with the war dead, as well as Congressional hearings about the case of Terri Schiavo. The latter included lengthy discussions in Congress about the definition and meaning of life and death, as well as a bizarre scene of Schiavo being examined on a video monitor by members of the House of Representatives, who scrutinized her vacant face for signs of life.

Death emerged from its hiding place—or rather, as people started to engage with the issues facing the dying, the paradigm of the hidden, invisible death shifted. The tendency toward denial lingered, especially when death appeared close to home, with oneself or a loved one diagnosed with a terminal illness, but "death denied" and the "invisible death" were no longer signature marks of the American death system. In the 21st century, the movements pushing back against these labels had become so forceful that we can justifiably say that a new episteme of death emerged.

Part of the story toward a new American death system around the turn of the millennium was that American society in general had become—and continued to become—more and more diverse, and the social and cultural identities of minority groups were at the forefront of 21st-century sociopolitical discourse. American society was not a cohesive system sharing one death system. Some groups were in tune with the mainstream, and others more open or closed to confronting matters of mortality. America was not a melting pot where different ethnicities, religions, and cultures blended together and cohered; nor was it a static mosaic where each group held isolated practices and ideas. Rather, the landscape resembled a kaleidoscope, a "complex and varied, changing form . . . continually shifting from one set of relations to another . . . an endless variety of variegated patterns."[29] People with origins from around the world share neighborhoods, work places, schools and civic organizations, and communicate their ideas and practices in word and by example. The media creates communities shared by all who watch the same programs. What once may have appeared strange becomes interesting, and soon commonplace. Those who are not deeply entrenched in their own cultural rituals adopt, or absorb by osmosis, the conduct and habits of those around them. In the kaleidoscopic society, shifts in the attitude and approach to death are not only fostered by groups of different heritage rubbing up against each other but also by different, simultaneously present, overlapping paradigms of death.

Currently, three behavioral models, each spawned by different *zeitgeists,* co-exist and are interspersed: the **traditional,** the **modern,** and the **neo-modern.**

I have borrowed these labels from concepts framed by the British thanatologist Tony Walter;[30] I have also drawn from the work of James W. Green[31] in making adjustments to American 21st-century circumstances and substantially from my own introduction to a 2009 anthology.[32] Most American communities have aspects, to a greater or lesser degree, of all three models. Some people will identify exclusively with one of the three paradigms, but most individuals probably recognize something of themselves, their families, and their surroundings in more than just a single model.

In the **traditional** model, which dominated in America until around 1920, a familiar and trusted "village" provides the social context for death and dying. Norms and practices are usually not perceived as choices but rather as god-given, absolute truths and "natural" responses. Sacred texts and religious leaders are invested with authority and those who die embrace time-honored practices. They accept their fates with equanimity and die convinced that their souls will have a place in eternity and their families will find comfort in established rituals and congregational life.

Fragmented, transient communities where people shy away from death are characteristic of the **modern** model. Urbanization and the breakup of traditional family structures as well as advances in medical technologies, which require specialized health care providers and clinical settings, contribute to this behavioral model and place those at the end of life out of public view in hospitals and nursing homes. The dying and their loved ones are often isolated from a wider support system, lack the tools to manage their situation, and are uncertain of their ability or the preferred direction to navigate the final journey. They turn to the medical and legal professions as the primary arbiters and authorities on available options. Belief in "the beyond" is seen as a choice rather than an unshakable absolute.

Adherents of the **neo-modern** model, based on the ideals of the death awareness movement emerging in the 1980s, assert the importance of acknowledging death as part of life. High value is placed on the individual's right to self-determination and personal control. The dying and their families are expected to take charge of the journey toward death. The dying person is seen as the primary authority, with his appointed agents acting as informed surrogates in case he is incapacitated. Guided by therapists, "end-of-life counselors," and nondenominational chaplains, the person's inner spirituality replaces a native or chosen religion. Hope, meaning, and transcendence are individually defined and can be found in relationships with others as much as in connections to a deity. To cope with his situation, the dying person subscribing to the **neo-modern** model resorts to personal expression and not to established rituals or stoic silence, as in the **traditional** and **modern** models, respectively. The worst sin among those who adopt the **neo-modern** model is neither unbelief, as in the **traditional** model, nor intrusion, as in the **modern** model, but isolation and denial.

In everyday life these theoretical constructs overlap and crisscross, collide, and blend in our kaleidoscopic society. **Neo-modern** practices can be seen as "still informed by an ancient, persistent, and religiously inspired ethos which shapes how we understand the value of life and solemnize its ending."[33] Clashes between the models may occur in immigrant families where the (grand)parent generation holds fast to traditional practices from "the old country," while the younger, American-born family members embrace the power of modern medicine and technology. The **modern** and **neo-modern** approaches may come into conflict in the care of a terminally ill patient with adult children who have adopted different outlooks on life (and death) from their parents.

The **neo-modern** model of "death awareness" and "controlled dying" is the fastest growing of the models in the 21st century. The findings of a survey on issues related to death and dying conducted among mature residents in Massachusetts in 2005[34] suggests that death—at least in "The Bay State"—can no longer be viewed as a taboo subject: 8 in 10 respondents indicated that they are very or somewhat comfortable talking about death. In all, 85 percent of the respondents considered it very important to get honest answers from doctors and to understand their treatment options. A concern about quality of life at the end of life emerged as a consistent theme. People expressed their desire for "communication, connection, comfort and control."[35]

The **neo-modern model** is still in development and does not have clear contours. Not until we have gained historical perspective will we be able to see its form more clearly. It is the model adopted by the adherents of the movements promoting self-determination and hospice care. Yet, by 2013, we realize that for many, the desire for "communication, connection and comfort" may be as important as having control. It is hard to measure which of the factors have grew the most between 2005 and 2013, but in that period, we have seen the original hospice movement increasingly embrace palliative care, blurring the line between chronic and terminal care; and with increasing acceptance that not all patients need or want to be aware of fatal diagnosis. Further, we are seeing the self-determination movement expanding the idea of patient-centered decision making to include loved ones as well as health care providers who are likely to be in the patient's circle of trusted advisors. The National Health care Decision Date was inaugurated in 2008 "to inspire, educate & empower the public & providers about the importance of advance care planning."[36] The initiative has grown into a large network promoting advance care planning. The emphasis is on holding conversations with loved ones and physicians about treatment wishes and appointing a trusted surrogate in advance of a serious health event that may lead to incapacity to speak for oneself. As a result, on one day in mid-April (April 16, in 2013 and most years), a growing number of people are involved in talking about their choices for end-of-life care.

Yes, in 2013 there is still denial and anxiety about death. But the winds are blowing away from the idea that speaking about death is as inappropriate as pornography. In retrospect, we may find that the new tagline for the 21st century's death system will be "death engaged."

NEW PATHS OF ENGAGEMENT

Projecting that "death engaged" will be an appropriate label for our death system in the early decades of the 21st century, this first volume of *Our Changing Journey to the End: Reshaping Death, Dying, and Grief in America* is entitled *New Paths of Engagement*. It contains chapters showing the new ways that we currently engage with death as well as proposals for how we could do this better to meet the challenges of the new millennium.

Multifarious forces outside the control of the ordinary citizen are shaping the engagement with death, but two stimuli—crosswinds, really—appear of particular influence in the chapters that follow here: namely, changes in the demographics of the U.S. population and advances in science and biotechnology that give us new ways to look at the human body and treat it. We will see how these trends play out in different contexts in the individual chapters, organized in three groupings: The Changing Landscape, Speaking in a New Language, and Transforming the Aftermath, with a concluding chapter pointing out issues around life expectancy, global threats, and environmental health hazard that are not specifically covered elsewhere. Several of the authors state outright or imply the ethical consequences of not contending with the changing outlook but the chapters addressing the complexities around improving the end-of-life experience for the dying and their families are concentrated in Volume II—*New Venues in the Search for Dignity and Grace*.

The Changing Landscape

The greatest challenges in the management and care of the population at the end of life in the 21st century will the large number of aging baby boomers and the high cost of medical technologies that allow us to prolong the dying process as well as the length of life. These issues are addressed in this section with a focus on attitudes of the baby-boom generation to death, the problems of long-term care facilities, and new neurological evidence questioning the validity of the idea of rational decision making.

The number of travelers approaching the end of the journey is increasing rapidly. The demographic bulge representing the baby boomers is about to clog the roadways. In 2011, 2.5 million people died in the United States out of a total population of 312 million; among them, 1.8 million (73%) were older than 65 years.[37] In 2005, 12 percent of the population was older than 65 years; by 2050, that cohort is projected to be 19 percent of the population and would be doubled in absolute numbers.[38] How this dominant group approaches death and its challenges will be a strong determinant in how society as a whole manages the end of life. In this volume, J. Harold Ellens looks at the characteristics of the baby boomers and how we can expect them to handle death and its rituals, in "From Death Denial to Death Control: The New Baby-Boomer Approach."

A growing group of elders is spending time on the road to the end in a frail state. They have greater life expectancy than their parents but not always good quality in the years that they have gained. In the 1980s, someone who was diagnosed with cancer or organ failure lived an average of six months. In 2013—because of medical advances—some of those struck by these formerly fatal diseases can be cured, and although a few still die, more and more often, they end up with long-term, debilitating conditions. Some people live well with, rather than tragically die from, AIDS, cancer, heart disease, and kidney failure. However, many are too incapacitated to remain in the communities where they were active and end up in nursing homes, not yet ready to die but not quite among the living. This pre-mortem state is considered by Donald Joralemon in "Dying While Living: The Problem of Social Death."

Among the enormous advances in biological research are strides in neuroscience. Research in this field has produced evidence that suggests that human beings do not have the capacity to make rational—analytically reasoned—decisions but react instinctively and then rationalize their "gut reaction." In presenting these findings in "The Biology of Decision: Implications of Neuroscientific Research for End-of-Life Care," Daniel Liechty and Bruce Hiebert place in question the principle of self-determination, one of the foundational pillars of advance care planning and a corner stone in the neo-modern death system.

In his chapter, Daniel Callahan revisits issues he first presented in 1973, outlining the three areas of greatest concern in health care: the high cost of caring for patients at the end of life, the search for ways to make death more peaceful, and managing inefficiencies in caring for long-term chronically ill patients. He argues that we will incur untenable financial costs if we continue down the current path. If we are to gain hope for a better experience in the future for those at the end of life and their families, our attitude needs to be reshaped. We need to be willing to rethink current practices and make the best possible use of our resources without losing sight of the fact that our resources are limited and some form of rationing of the care as well as willingness to confront the viability of our most entrenched values may be necessary. Callahan concludes his chapter, "Prognosis, Costs, and End-of-Life Care," by questioning whether our premise for decision making and costs should be revised and, thereby, also points to some of the ethical considerations that will be addressed in Volume II.

Speaking in a New Language

When culture changes, so do the connections between representation and ideas relating to death and dying. Scholars and artists of the 1990s focused much of their attention on analyzing death through the theoretical constructs of post-structuralism and identity politics. In the new millennium, the trends of engagement are breaking new ground. In *This Republic of Suffering—Death and the American Civil War* (2008), Drew Gilpin Faust demonstrates how the experience of death during the Civil War does the work of "creat[ing] the modern American union—not just by ensuring national survival, but by shaping national structures and commitments."[39] To Faust, death and the dead is the prism for her investigation, the generator and agents for the changes that formed the future American nation. She notes: "We still seek to use our deaths to create meaning when we are not sure any exists."[40]

Melinda Hunt is a 21st-century artist who engages directly with the resting place of disposed corpses. On Hart Island, a "potter's field" for the indigenous in New York City, her Hart Island Project aims to make "the largest cemetery in the United States visible and accessible so that no one is omitted from history."[41] Her work is to rescue the unmourned from anonymity—as do other art movements in the new millennium that bring attention to forgotten groups, most notably slaves and repressed Native Americans. Hunt has turned her work into a not-for-profit mission. Without rationalizing the death anxiety and loss at the core of her project, Hunt demonstrates an engagement with mortality by bringing attention to it. Unlike the Civil War dead in Faust's treatise, those buried at Hart Island are not the medium or prism for looking at society as much as the aesthetic project itself, blurring lines between art and life, and ethics and aesthetics.

The chapters in this section offer other examples of how we engage in new ways with death in images and words. They show how we can employ narratives about death and dying to improve the care of those at the end of life, how age-old fixations on death anxiety are seemingly difficult to banish, as well as how contemporary ideas of feminism and visual culture can impact the spectator in new ways, to make us look at mortality with fresh eyes.

Marsha Hurst and Craig Irvine begin their chapter, "Stories of the End: A Narrative Medicine Curriculum to Reframe Death and Dying" by acknowledging that medical professionals commonly avoid the dying for whom they cannot provide further treatment and deny that death is a possible outcome for the patients they treat. To mitigate this state of discomfort, Hurst and Irvine argue for medical professionals' close reading of, and deep engagement with, narratives centered on dying. Such exercises aim for—and result in—a greater ability to be present at the bedside of the dying and better understand their needs. They ask for "an openness to immersion in possibly the most profound of human experiences—dying, caring for the dying, and death itself . . . this immersion will deepen compassion, enable a new or renewed affiliation with human suffering, and open the capacity for caring to include facing death itself—one's own or the death of another."

In "What Rational Philosophy Cannot Tell Us about Death in the 21st Century," Jerry S. Piven observes that no matter how much we speak about death we are still rooted in our death anxiety. He argues that we cannot reason away our death-denying fantasies, "a process of relentless existential engagement to fathom the elusiveness of death, for obliviousness toward our own dark motives allows us to inflict our own fears, emotional wounds, and irrationality on others." Perhaps such existential engagement is what is sought in the program Hurst and Irvine direct.

"Grim Discoveries: Agnès Varda's *Vagabond* (1985) and Karen Moncrieff's *The Dead Girl* (2006)" by Marcelline Block considers the engagement with death in cinematic and televisual texts centered on the idea and figure of the "beautiful dying woman." The aggressive destructive behavior that occupy humankind—especially males according to Piven, as the result of repressing our death anxiety—manifests itself in these films at the intersection of gender, politics, ethics, and aesthetics. As art always has, this work tests boundaries and searches for culturally appropriate forms of expression for its time and place.

Kathryn Beattie's chapter, "Unveiling the Corpse in 21st Century," examines an art form that attempts to reignite our engagement with the body, distanced by the masses of images that bombard us. She shows how Sally Mann's photography offers a new way to bring into operation the subject of the corpse at the intersection of art and document. Her images are not necessarily pre-infused with meaning that she seeks to communicate but rather allow for the possibility that the viewer will, in her word, "exhume" their own meaning when they confront the images. Without directly responding to Piven, Beattie argues for the possibility that a 21st-century aesthetic presents a new relationship between art and society that may help us face death—uproot our death anxiety. As Beattie writes, quoting Julia Kristeva, "What good is Art if it does not help us face death?"

Transforming the Aftermath

For fellow travelers of those who are approaching the end, the journey does not terminate with the demise of the person who is dying. The road through the land of the grieving follows: reshaping the demands and needs of memorializing the growing and diverse population of the deceased—coping with grief and keeping loved ones' memory—is the theme of this section.

Increases in the number of people who will be dying in the forthcoming decades and projected changes in their ethnicity and religious affiliation or non-affiliation will reshape the way we manage corporeal remains and comfort survivors. The Pew Research Institute projects that 82 percent of the population growth between 2005 and 2050 will be due to first- and second-generation immigrants. The kaleidoscope is being shaken and we need to adjust to the new patterns that emerge. Caucasians will be the largest minority group with an estimated 47 percent. Latinos, 14 percent of the population in 2005, will increase to 29 percent, the black population will rise less than 1 percent and remain around 13 percent, and Asians will account for 9 percent.[42] The most important aspect of these projections is not the specifics of race and ethnicity. After all, why would we assume commonalities among natives of Calcutta, Shanghai, the Philippines, and Japan, on the basis that they are all Asian? Rather, what is essential about this survey is that we are in the midst of movement and change.

What appears to remain strong and high on the list of identifiers is to be "American" and the content and meaning of that signifier is being reshaped by the influx of people and continued mobility of much of the population. Poverty ghettos—in urban areas in the Northeast, "hollers" in Appalachia, on reservations in the South West or the Mississippi delta—experience practically no in-migration and limited exodus. Mostly racially and religiously unified, these population pockets preserve faith and cultural traditions and by their static nature remain at the edges of kaleidoscope. In areas of greater dynamism, the trend is toward flexible rituals that permit individual and family specific choices—much as self-determination has been the mantra in the care of the terminally ill. It is also true that those who live in multicultural areas tend to hold on to traditions around death, burial, and mourning to a greater extent than other cultural expressions. Nevertheless, rituals are changing—and need to be reshaped—to accommodate families and individuals who do not fit traditional molds.

As a composite, lifestyle choices, education, occupation, income, personal interests, residential locale, and religious affiliation (or lack of it) is increasingly more relevant than race and ethnicity alone in defining and determining the groups with which we identify. The most marked and important change in the American population as it relates to death and grief is the change in religious affiliation. With a third of adults under the age of 30 and a fifth of all adults not identifying with any religion,[43] the need for recreating our end-of-life rituals is growing. These numbers are even higher in large metropolitan areas and have an upward trend. How to create secular rituals and dignified spaces outside churches, temples, and mosques to honor the dead and serve the survivors are challenges that begin to find answers.

Sherry R. Schachter's and Kristen M. Finneran's chapter, "Expansion of New Rituals for the Dying and Bereaved" broadens the definition of rituals to include all rites and customs created to maintain and continue our relationship with the deceased who were once part of our lives. They offer specific examples of how these new practices help sustain us and provide a roadmap for our journey of grief, as well as point to future needs and possibilities as we meet new social and cultural realities.

Creative expressions and new space for memorializing are spawned by Internet technology. Articulation of grief and memory is growing rapidly in virtual space and finding new forms suitable for digital media. The most recent developments are outlined by Candi K. Cann in "Virtual Memorials: Bereavement and the Internet." The complex relationship between mourners and the virtual space in which they mourn is explored in "Strange Eternity:

Virtual Memorials, Grief, and Entertainment," by Angela Riechers, who also shows how personal mourning objects can "morph" into virtual "objects" and images—and be exploited for entertainment value.

In "Roadside Memorials: A 21st-Century Development," George E. Dickinson and Heath C. Hoffmann explore a particular aspect of seemingly traditional memorializing—the literally changing landscape along our roads, where a growing number of roadside memorials are cropping up. Although seemingly a traditional and established gesture, the rural roadside memorials break with established customs: they move the veneration of the dead into our public thoroughfares and they are designed for the most part by the grieving survivors to meet individual needs.

Karla Maria Rothstein also proposes moving memorializing into the public sphere. She takes the concept one step further by examining not just innovative ways of memorializing in the communal arena but also new methods and spaces for corpse disposal within the urban landscape. When we talk about the frail and elderly consuming unprecedented resources on their final journey, depriving future generations of resources, we are not exclusively referring to health care. Rothstein's proposed projects address the shortage of land for traditional earth burials and the damage that our traditional burial and cremation methods have on the environment. In "Reconfiguring Urban Spaces of Disposal, Sanctuary, and Remembrance," she and her students in an advance studio at Columbia University School of Architecture explore—in her words— "architecture in dialog with impermanence, urban archives and our unsettled relationships with memory and identity."

* * *

No guidebook covers every aspect of a land. Some important pathways have not been explored here. Looking down those other roads and contemplating the prospects may present us with hope of longevity and healthy aging. It may also contribute to fear and anxiety. Pandemics and cyber warfare are uncomfortable to consider for the neo-modern person whose death system is defined by control and self-determination. In the conclusion of this volume, "Additional Vistas," I look briefly at some of this territory, which my imaginary bird, viewing the scenery from high above the ground cannot completely ignore.

NOTES

1. Portions of this Introduction have previously been published as "From Concealment to Recognition: The Discourse on Death, Dying and Grief," in *Speaking of Death, America's New Sense of Mortality,* ed. Michael K. Bartalos (Westport, CT: Praeger, 2009).

2. John Morgan, "Living Our Dying and Our Grieving: Historical and Cultural Attitudes," in *Readings in Thanatology,* ed. J. D. Morgan (Amityville, NY: Baywood, 1997), 12.

3. Robert J. Kastenbaum, *Death, Society, and Human Experience* (Boston: Pearson, 2007), 104.

4. Philippe Ariès, *The Hour of Our Death,* trans. Helen Weaver (Oxford: Oxford University Press, 1981). Orig. *L'homme devant la mort* (Paris: Editions du Seuil, 1977).

5. An example is Johan Friedrich Starcks's "Tägliche Hand-Buch in guten and bösen Tagen" which was published in many editions for the German-speaking population in Pennsylvania in the early 19th century.

6. Mervyn F. Bendle, "The Contemporary Episteme of Death," *Cultural Values* 5, 13 (July 2001): 349–67.

7. Franz Borkenau, "The Concept of Death," in *Death and Identity,* ed. Robert Lester Fulton (New York: John Wiley & Co, 1965), 42–56.

8. Geoffrey Gorer, "Introduction," *Death, Grief and Mourning* (New York: Arno Press, 1967). Geoffrey Gorer, "The Pornography of Death," *Death, Grief, and Mourning in Contemporary Britain* (London: The Cresset Press, 1965). U.S. Edition: *Death, Grief, and Mourning* (Garden City, NY: Doubleday, 1965). Paperback Edition (Garden City, NY: Doubleday-Anchor, 1967), 192–99.

9. Herman Feifel, ed., "Introduction," in *The Meaning of Death* (New York: McGraw-Hill, 1959), xv–xvi.

10. For example, *The Golden Bough* (1890) by a founder of the field of anthropology, James George Frazer and Erwin Panofsky, *Tomb Sculpture. Four Lectures on Its Changing Aspect from Ancient Egypt to Bernini* (New York: Harry N. Abrams), 1924.

11. Robert Blauner, "Review of Death, Grief, and Mourning. Geoffrey Gorer. London: The Cresset Press, 1965," *Psychoanalytical Review* 55 (1968): 521–22.

12. "History of Hospice Care," National Hospice and Palliative Care Organization, accessed March 29, 2013, http://www.nhpco.org/history-hospice-care

13. Daniel Callahan, *The Tyranny of Survival and Other Pathologies of Civilized Life* (New York: MacMillan, 1973), 93.

14. Herman Feifel, ed. "Death in Contemporary America," in *New Meanings of Death,* 4.

15. Ibid., 4.

16. Erich Fromm, *To Have or to Be?* (New York: Harper & Row, 1976), excerpted in Rainer Funk, ed., *The Essential Fromm, Life between Having and Being* (New York: Continuum, 1995), 103.

17. Robert Jay Lifton, *The Broken Connection—On Death and the Continuity of Life* (New York: Simon and Schuster, 1979), 13.

18. Ibid., 17.

19. Ibid., 47.

20. Examples of texts from different disciplines that are frequently cited include the following: in archeology, J.M.C. Toynbee, *Death and Burial in the Roman World* (New York: Cornell University Press, 1971); in American Studies, David Stannard, *The Puritan Way of Death—A Study in Religion, Culture and Social change* (New York: Oxford University Press, 1977); in anthropology, Richard Huntington and Peter Metcalf, eds., *Celebrations of Death: The Anthropology of Mortuary Ritual* (Cambridge:

Cambridge University Press, 1979); and in social history, Joachim Whaley, ed. *Mirrors of Mortality: Studies in the Social History of Death* (New York: St. Martin's Press, 1981).

21. See Andrea R. Vaucher, *Muses from Chaos and Ash: AIDS, Artists, and Art* (New York: Grove Press, 1993) and Edmund White, "Journals of the Plague Years," *The Nation,* May 12, 1997, 13–18.

22. A representative list of studies on death, which employs one or more of these tools, would likely include the following: Maurice Bloch and Jonathan Parry, *Death and the Regeneration of Life* (Cambridge University Press, 1982); Garrett Stewart, *Death Sentences: Styles of Dying in British Fiction* (Cambridge, MA: Harvard University Press, 1984); Ronald Schleifer's *Rhetoric of Death: The Language of Modernism and Postmodern Discourse Theory* (Urbana: University of Illinois Press, 1990); Regina Barreca's anthology, *Sex and Death in Victorian Literature* (New York: Macmillan, 1990); Elizabeth Bronfen's *Over Her Dead Body: Death, Femininity and the Aesthetic* (New York: Routledge, 1992); and Sarah Webster Goodwin's and Elisabeth Bronfen's anthology *Death and Representation* (Baltimore: Johns Hopkins University Press, 1993).

23. A summary of the history is available in Joseph J. Fins, *A Palliative Ethic of Care—Clinical Wisdom at Life's End* (Sudbury, MA: Jones and Bartlett, 2006).

24. Bill Moyers, "On Our Own Terms: Moyers on Dying," produced by Public Affairs Television, Inc. and presented on PBS by Thirteen/WNET New York, Broadcast, September 10–13, 2004.

25. Stephen R Daniels, "The Consequences of Childhood Overweight and Obesity," *The Future of Children* 16, 1, Childhood Obesity (Spring 2006): 47–67.

26. Elizabeth Arias, U.S. Department of Health and Human Services, Centers for Disease Control and Prevention, *National Vital Statistics Report,* Vol. 58, No. 21, June 28, 2010, Table 12. Estimated life expectancy at birth in years, by race and sex: Death-registration states, 1900-1928 and United States, 1929–2006, 33–34.

27. Steven Bognar and Julia Reichert, "A Lion in the House," independent film premiered on PBS, June 21 and 22, 2006.

28. Ira Byock, *Dying Well—Peace and Possibility at the End of Life* (New York: Riverhead Books, 1997). Ira Byock, *The Four Things That Matter Most—A Book about Living* (New York: Free Press, 2004).

29. Lawrence H. Fuchs, *The American Kaleidoscope: Race, Ethnicity, and the Civic Culture* (Hanover, NH: University Press of New England, c1990, 1995), 276.

30. Tony Walter, *The Revival of Death* (London: Routledge, 1993), 47–60.

31. James W. Green, *Beyond the Good Death—The Anthropology of Modern Dying* (Philadelphia: University of Pennsylvania Press, 2008).

32. Some of this text is adapted from Christina Staudt, "Introduction," in *The Many Ways We Talk About Death in Contemporary Society: Interdisciplinary Studies in Portrayal and Classification,* ed. Christina Staudt and Margaret Souza (Lewiston, NY: Edwin Mellen Press, 2009), 1–42. Used by permission of Edwin Mellen Press.

33. Green, *Beyond the Good Death,* 30.

34. Massachusetts Commission on End of Life Care Survey Project 2005— (conducted in March/April 2005 and published in September 2005).

35. Ibid., 9.

36. National Health care Decisions Day, http://www.nhdd.org/

37. Donna L. Hoyert and Jiaquan Xu, Division of Vital Statistics, National Vital Statistics Reports, Volume 61, Number 6, October 10, 2012, Deaths: Preliminary Data for 2011, 3. http://www.cdc.gov/nchs/data/nvsr/nvsr61/nvsr61_06.pdf

38. Jeffrey S. Passel and D'Vera Cohn, "U.S. Population Projections: 2005–2050," Washington, DC: Pew Research Center, February 11, 2008.

39. Drew Gilpin Faust, *This Republic of Suffering—Death and the American Civil War* (New York: Alfred A. Knopf, 2008), xiv.

40. Ibid., 271.

41. The Hart Island Project, http://hartisland.net/.

42. Pew Research Institute, Pew Research Social & Demographic Trends, Second Generation Americans—A Portrait of the Adult Children of Immigrants. http://www.pewsocialtrends.org/2013/02/07/second-generation-americans/

43. Pew Research Center, "'Nones' on the Rise: One-in Five Adults Have No Religious Affiliation," Poll released October 9, 2012, http://www.pewforum.org/Unaffiliated/nones-on-the-rise.aspx

Coney Island

I suppose I miss Coney Island as much as the next guy. There's not really an island in the old folks home. They don't call it "old folks home" any more but that's what it is with the pink and purple handrails to settle down the suburban daughters with puff jackets and kids in blue and red windbreakers who come out here in the vehicle. There's a man who sings with an electric loudspeaker "Fly Me to the Moon" so we won't forget how to tie our white shoes. The kids just Velcro their shoes these days. And they carry little gameboxes where they press the buttons and you hear the beeps.

Catherine Rogers

Section I

The Changing Landscape

Chapter 2

From Death Denial to Death Control: The New Baby-Boomer Approach

J. Harold Ellens

*F*reud *thought the main human problem with coping with reality was neurotic anxiety and Becker thought it was simply the unconscious fear of death. The baby-boomer generation behaves in a surprising new way with regard to dying, reducing its idealization, its transcendent mythology, and its financial cost. Becker was sure that our fear of death produces a denial of death that drives the idealization of its transcendent meaning for pre-boomer generations. This chapter addresses the apparent open-faced realism about death expressed by the boomer cohort, which is now approaching its declining years and radically changing the human journey to life's end. How does this new approach to the way of handling death and its rituals relate to the uncalculating and antihistorical independence and individuality that defined the boomers' self-styled identity? How are the boomers solving the problem of the diminished sense of meaning inherent in the social isolation and psychological unconnectedness their early choices have now produced; and what does their style of dying say about this?*

INTRODUCTION

In his Pulitzer Prize–winning book about death, *The Denial of Death* (1974), Ernest Becker proposed that our universal denial of death is the lie that makes it possible for humans to handle the essential questions of our existence. His thesis is interesting:

> The fear of death is a universal that unites data from several disciplines of the human sciences, and makes wonderfully clear and intelligible human actions that we have buried under mountains of fact, and have obscured with endless . . . arguments about the 'true' human motives.[1]

Launching his volume on Samuel Johnson's observation that the prospect of death wonderfully concentrates the mind, Becker observes that we used to think that if we could get a good grasp of the truth about life and the world, we would relieve our sense of burden about this tragic adventure of life and death. However, he continues, we now find ourselves at a point at which we are laboring under a burden of such an enormous volume of data about everything in the world that we cannot consume it at the rate it is hatched in our scientific world. We have more truth than we can handle and are noticing that the actual data may not be as important or valuable as its interpretation—the way it shapes our worldview.

There may be reason to believe that the impasse Becker suggests is less burdensome and less controlling of the current state of mind in our world than he thought. The baby-boomer generation, a popular but inexact term for folks born between 1946 and 1964 in the United States, seems to be cutting through the psychological blockade against facing death head on and is moving the culture from the denial of death to control of death. For example, they are signing up by the thousands to MyWonderfulLife.com and taking positive initiative to plan their own style of celebrative funerals. This has already had a strong impact upon the nature of our changing journey to the end of life. Boomers have been accused of or commended for taking innovative and even system-changing approaches toward almost every traditional or established pattern in the North American culture, and perhaps the worldwide social systems. Now they are applying their nonconformist approach to the management of their own dying (boomers' notions of death).

CONTROL OF LIFE AND DEATH

This new open-faced approach to managing one's own death has surprisingly large social and economic implications. Reduction of costs of the end of the journey include the options of cremation, prepaid personalized commemorative ceremonies, shared electronic recording of simple tributes, online funerals instead of formal rituals, and the like. The funeral industry has made radical changes to meet the new and unusual approaches that the boomers now generally require.

These innovations seem to be driven by a desire to radically reduce expenses that may fall to estates or descendants, as well as provide direct personal control over the nature of the ritual processes for managing the final require-ments death brings. Having done their own thing in life, boomers now intend to do their own thing in death. There is an underlying acknowledgment that drives this perspective, that is, that living longer may not mean living better. Taking charge of the nature and timing of one's own death seems to be a factor also at play here.

This attitude is now also seeping into the older generation just preceding the boomers and currently at the long end of *its* life. My brother, who died in the summer of 2012 at 78 years of age, illustrates this fact. He was born with a minor pulmonary deficiency that did not really affect him until the last five years of his life. However, in these last years he was increasingly plagued with various kinds of suffering, mainly recurrent pneumonia. As this affliction closed in on him with more and more frequent exotic intravenous antibiotics and frequent hospitalizations, he finally came to a crisis in which he was on a ventilator for an extended time. He recovered from that, put his affairs in order by some very wise and momentous decisions, was attacked again by the afflic-tion, and hospitalized once more.

At last he was clearly near the end of his fight for meaningful life, spent three days in a coma, awakened brightly one morning, called his family to him, took his leave of each of them in an intensely personal goodbye, motioned for the nurse to take off his oxygen mask, and in three minutes was gone. He died as he lived: wisely, decisively, courageously, and in control. That is not a new way to die. In the third century BC, Eratosthenes, the wisest man of his generation and the preeminent scientist at the Ancient Library of Alexandria, reached 80 years, found himself going blind from old age, decided not to eat any more, and died intentionally within a short time. The difference is that Eratosthenes and my brother, Stanley, used to be the exception. Their approach seems now to be increasingly the standard for the generation of baby boomers.

According to the online essay entitled "How Baby Boomers May Change the Notion of 'Death' in Society," their move from denial of death to control of death is leading to an increased interest in and innovative thought regarding assisted suicide.[2] New challenges are being raised about humane euthanasia as an alternative to the erosive process of the end-of-life suffering that deperson-alizes and dehumanizes us and uselessly eats away estates that could provide increased quality of life for their progeny.

It may be that Dr. Jack Kevorkian was a generation ahead of his time in promoting assisted suicide and pushing the political structures of our society to face the issue of a person's right to determine the how and when of his or her own death, with all the implications that it has for family and loved ones. Three states in the United States (Oregon, Washington, and Montana) and three countries (the Netherlands, Belgium, and Switzerland) now allow human eu-thanasia and Japan has no law against it. I suspect that Dr. Kevorkian's ideas would have been more amicably received if he had gone about his crusade in a more humane and less belligerent manner. He always looked and behaved like such a ghoul that psychologically he became his own worst enemy in the advance of his ideas. The mindset of the American populous seemed much more supportive of his exploration of new possibilities than it was of him, personally, as the very unappealing man he proved in the end to be.

Frequently I have seen an interesting sign in funeral parlors where I have conducted funerals of close acquaintances. It claims that the quality of a civilization can be discerned best from the manner in which it treats and memorializes its dead. I believe that is an accurate observation. A century ago, in the culture of my childhood, that would have implied forthrightly that the only civilized way to conduct the journey to our end is to celebrate the life of the deceased in a heroic commemoration and a solemn but dramatic funeral. Any suggestion at that time that the entire matter might be significantly truncated by a cremation and brief memorial service with only the nuclear family attending would have been consider uncivilized and disrespectful. That is no longer the case and it is now difficult to find believable social or spiritual reasons to value negatively such an abbreviated completion of our attention to our dead loved ones. Boomers in general do not see that such an efficient and cost-saving approach would be inadequately loving or estimable for themselves. More practical is apparently more perfect for that generation now coming to the point of thinking about their own demise in a decade or two. Apparently it is becoming preferable to die than to become psychologically or economically burdensome to loved ones.

This is a particularly poignant issue now in view of the current reports from the CDC in Atlanta indicating that the boomer generation (age 45–64) has the highest number and percentage of infections and deaths from hepatitis C and HIV (AIDS). Indeed, hepatitis C is more prominent in that generation as well as in the general population in the United States than is HIV. Annually, around 12,500 U.S. deaths are caused by HIV and approximately 15,500 from hepatitis C. This is a low percentage of the total boomer cohort, of course, but illustrates the vulnerability to early demise on the part of that group.[3]

Based upon 22 million death cases examined (1999–2007), John W. Ward, MD, and his team reported that 1 in every 33 boomers has hepatitis C. He called it a silent epidemic and declared that to bring down the death rate as radically as we have brought down the death rate from HIV will require a completely new national policy initiative for detecting, diagnosing, and treating this pernicious disease. It is little wonder, I suppose, that the boomers are conscious and intentional about their address to the issue of death—that of their progenitors and particularly of themselves. They do not seem to fit into Becker's set of rubrics.

FREUD, BECKER, AND UNIVERSAL HUMAN NEUROSIS

Becker puts much stock in Freud's notion that an inherent human narcissism makes us all feel immortal and this is an unconscious level drive prompting our denial of our inevitable death. Becker declares, for example, that

This narcissism is what keeps men marching into point-blank fire in wars: at heart one doesn't feel that *he* will die, he only feels sorry for the man next to him. Freud's explanation for this was that the unconscious does not know death or time: in man's physiochemical, inner organic recesses he feels immortal.[4]

As a veteran of eight wars, twice wounded, I can personally testify to the fact that quite obviously neither Freud nor Becker ever served in the military or experienced combat. They are both wrong on both counts. Men do put their lives on the line for principle and for the mission for which they were trained, and they do it often with the full awareness that they are likely to die doing it. Moreover, it is common for soldiers to have a stark and vivid premonition that they will be killed in the next battle and the premonition usually proves precisely accurate. Indeed, many Medal of Honor winners are celebrated for their having come to the conclusion that they were already as good as dead, suffering from multiple wounds and unlikely to survive, and for that very reason undertook heroic action to protect and preserve their comrades, their unit, or the objective of the specific military action to which they were committed at that moment.

The boomer generations seems to have decimated Freud's claim and Becker's argument that of all the things that drive human nature and shape our destiny, one of the principal forces is our terror of death. Indeed, Becker stated that upon the framework of this claim is strung the argumentation of his entire book. Perhaps, Freud unwittingly sowed the seed of the graphic and open-faced confrontation of death that seems now to characterize the boomer generation. Freud wisely asked,

> Is it not for us to confess that in our civilized attitude towards death we are once more living psychologically beyond our means, and must reform and give truth its due? Would it not be better to give death the place in actuality and in our thoughts which properly belongs to it, and to yield a little more prominence to that unconscious attitude towards death which we have hitherto so carefully suppressed? This hardly seems, indeed, a greater achievement, but rather a backward step . . . but it has the merit of taking somewhat more into account the true state of affairs. . . .[5]

The baby boomers seem to have taken up his enjoinder and incarnated it in a pragmatic new perspective on life and death.

THREE BOOMER SCENARIOS

What does this tell us regarding the psychological and spiritual direction our North American social culture seems to be taking? There are, of course, a number of possible answers to that question. Firstly, the boomer's view of death may suggest, for example, that our current cultural course is toward a kind of secular society that denies the possibility or at least the certainty of a destiny reaching beyond death and, therefore, the management of death is merely the rather trivial matter of disposal of the worthless remains of a life that is already erased. In that case, the elaborate funeral enterprise that has been developed in the Americas over the last three centuries is likely to be seriously at risk. Death merely brings the problem of a decent removal of a useless carcass.

A second possibility, of course, might be exactly the opposite. Is it possible that the baby-boomer generation is so spiritually attuned and secure that its sense of the transcendent leaves it with a radically decreased interest in or preoccupation with the final disposition of physical remains? Certainly that must be true for as large a percentage of them as is true of the rest of the population, perhaps larger.

There are two great difficulties in assessing any aspect of an entire generation such as the Greatest generation, boomers, Generation X, or the Millennial generation, of course. First of all, people are so individual and varied that global generalizations are almost always misleading at best and wholly inapplicable at worst. Labels are easily and cavalierly assigned in sociological studies and probably apply more to that minority that makes a lot of noise in each generation rather than to any approximation of a majority of that cohort. Second, the internal consistency of any person regarding his or her transcendent faith perspective, on the one hand, and psychosocial operation such as funeral requirements, on the other, is largely unpredictable, inconsistent, and uneven across any general population.

A third possibility for interpreting the boomers' innovative posture, however, might simply be that the boomer generation is not nearly so fraught as were previous generations with the historic human struggle with neurosis. Hence it is more clearheaded and self-confident regarding life and afterlife. That could lead to their having no particular anxiety or sense of obligation regarding rituals of farewell. That is, after all, the generation that started early to act in an antiestablishment style, defying the constraints of ideal social decorum, repudiating the heroic traditions of their parents, and generally revolting against all restraints on their radical individual freedom and narcissism. Insofar as that worked for them, it may well have given them a sense of self-confidence that also removes all historic notions about traditional styles of death rituals as well as traditional notions of eternity.

THREE ENDOGENOUS AND ENDEMIC SOURCES OF HUMAN NEUROSIS

Such a disposition would relate to Becker's perspective on the general state of neurosis that naturally influences, indeed shapes, most humans.[6] In line with classic psychoanalysis, Becker argues that neurosis is an endemic and inevitable condition of human existence. Neurosis may be defined as an exaggerated state of anxiety about circumstances or experience which should induce moderate or normal range worry or caution.[7] Becker asserts that there are three aspects and sources of neurosis that can be identified in humans generally. They are those that result from character formation, those that are a consequence of aberrations in one's perception of reality and illusion, and those that result from historical circumstances. One might argue cogently, it seems to me, that the baby-boomer generation has very little interest in traditional rituals for processing the experience of death, their own and that of their loved ones, because they have lived their lives in assertive forms of exploration and freedom from the historic boundaries of psychosocial decorum. So they are largely free from the nostalgia or anxiety-driven management of life and death. Thus they are largely free from the historic human neurosis about these things.

THE CHARACTER SOURCE

Neurosis devolving from the process in which human character is formed has mainly to do with the fact that every human experiences as a challenging burden just living with the truth of existence. We must protect ourselves from the world while we explore how to live and die in the world. Each of us, no matter what our character or belief system may be, is in the world but in a crucial sense not of the world. We are individual and distinctive. Becker thinks that the neurosis this induces is mainly caused by the fact that humans are animals without instinct. We must find some mechanism for managing our life quest that takes the place of instinct in other animals. What we do, therefore, is to narrow our exposure to the world and focus upon the things that immediately count for survival, growth, and understanding day by day.

"Gods can take in the whole of creation because they alone can make sense of it, know what it is all about and for."[8] However, as soon as humans start exploring the ultimate issues beyond daily survival imperatives and ask the questions of the meaning of life and death, "the meaning of a rose or of a star cluster," we are in trouble because we are reaching beyond our scope of control and management. Kierkegaard thought that most humans, therefore, "tranquilize themselves with the trivial."[9]

To function with some degree of success in our personal worlds of experience, we need to try from birth on to fashion a concept of ourselves and our context that is psychologically and physically manageable. Becker says that inevitably narrows our focus upon our immediate surroundings and the coping requirements of each day so as to create a normal operation of life. That means we shut out a wide range of the world of potential experience and perception, or to put it differently, we engage in a denial of reality:

What we call neurosis enters precisely at this point: Some people have more trouble with their lies [denial of reality] than others. The world is too much with them, and the techniques that they have developed for holding it at bay and cutting it down to size finally begin to choke the person himself [or herself]. This is neurosis in a nutshell: the miscarriage of clumsy lies about reality. But we can also see at once that there is no line between normal and neurotic, as we all lie and are all bound in some way by lies. Neurosis is, then, something we all share, it is universal.[10]

Becker concludes that we call a person neurotic when his denial of reality becomes counterproductive for him or others. His or her view of life is so narrow that most of reality is not in view. Such a person is dragged down or wallows in the dysfunctional nature of a closed-minded blindness to the full scope of reality.

When a person's management of reality produces no evident problems, however, we call that person normal. His or her heroic self-assertion and self-confidence within a narrowed vision of reality serves that chosen lifestyle effectively within its limited boundaries. That sounds a lot like many boomers, particularly regarding their constructs about life and death.

THE FUNCTION AND DYSFUNCTION OF ILLUSION

Becker's second source that produces our universal neurosis is our common human illusion that we can take in our whole world and manage it effectively. That prompts some folks to be so open to all the possibilities and stimuli of the world we encounter outside ourselves that their view of reality is scattered, unfocused, and chaotic. This illusion that reality is fully known and effectively managed overwhelms humans with the inability to take it all in and control it. The product of such megalomania is a need to create a nearly delusional belief that one is actually succeeding in such control despite the fact that it is not so. The tension between the illusion and the reality induces a depth psychology neurosis around the feeling of need for global control and the unworkability of the illusion that one has it when the world does not oblige one with complying:

> The *causa-sui* project is a pretense that one is invulnerable because protected by the power of others and of culture, that one is important in nature and can do something about the world. But in back of the *causa-sui* project whispers the voice of possible truth: that human life may not be more than a meaningless interlude in a vicious drama of flesh and bones that we call evolution; that the Creator may not care any more for the destiny of man or the self-perpetuation of individual men than He seems to have cared for the dinosaurs. . . . The whisper is the same one that slips incongruously out of the Bible in the voice of Ecclesiastes: that all is vanity . . . [and vexation of spirit].[11]

It is a psychosocial and cultural lie that reality is manageable and we are secure. That lie drives us into the neurotic tension between cultural illusion and natural reality, on the one hand, and the creeping suspicion about our inadequate selves, on the other. This pushes us to adopt the illusion of control and security as our reality. Rank thought that the more we embrace appearance as essence and our illusion about reality as truth the better adjusted and comfortable we will be. "This constantly effective process of self-deceiving, pretending and blundering, is no psychopathological mechanism."[12] Our cultural illusion is "a necessary ideology of self-justification, a heroic dimension that is life itself to the symbolic animal"—the lively, creative person.[13]

HISTORIC IDEALISM AND ITS FAILURE

Becker's third source or dimension of our inevitable and universal cultural neurosis is what he describes as historical. He means that throughout history humans coped with the complexities of life and death by remembering their progenitors as heroic figures. They accentuated the positive memories and downplayed the negative much of the time. Moreover, the more often the heroic stories were retold, the more they were filled out with larger than life "memories." This created an historic ideology of generations of immortally heroic antecedents: parents, grandparents, earlier ancestors, going back to famous figures of history.

"If history is a succession of immortality ideologies, then the problems of men [and women] can be read directly against those ideologies—how embracing they are, how convincing, how easy they make it for men [and women] to be confident and secure in their personal heroism."[14] For the boomers, traditional immortality ideologies have failed. They have set aside the values and ideologies of their forebears and struck out on their own to cut a new swath in life. Thus they have lost their grip on the historic "self-perpetuation and heroism." Our cultural neurosis has slid into pathological neurosis and this is now a widespread mental health problem "because of the disappearance of convincing dramas of heroic apotheosis of man" [and woman].[15]

"It begins to look like modern man [and woman] cannot find his [or her] heroism in everyday life any more, as men [and women] did in traditional societies just by doing their daily duty of raising children, working, and worshipping. He [and she] needs revolutions and wars" and needs them to perpetuate a spirit of such violent heroism so they can continue to seem to have meaning when the revolutions and wars end.[16] Becker likes to cite the case of the Salpêtrière Mental Hospital at the time of the French Revolution. The revolutionaries began their march to the barricades. The hospital was opened and all the patients were turned loose. "All the neurotics found a ready-made drama of self-transcending action and heroic identity. It was as simple as that."[17]

I suppose that is precisely descriptive of the 1960s–1970s boomer revolution in the United States and many other parts of the world, and also the explanation of the surge of violent rebellion first known as the Arab Spring and now seen more clearly as an irrational lunge of terrorist agency and affect. This is a rejection of any notion of how complex is the matter of managing reality and an arrogant ignorance about fashioning a rational world by means of irrational change. Becker is sure that all this begins with the dethronement of God and the rejection of the divine dimension of reality.

I think that may be the logical fallacy of confusing the part with the whole. Perhaps ignorance and a loss of quest for the divine dimension may be related to the posture of the boomers, but I think that is simply one aspect of a larger problem of their consciously and intentionally setting aside historic values, ideals, and methods in a generational attempt to seek the gratification of personal happiness, freedom from obligations set by others than themselves individually, and assertive legitimation of narcissism as a productive worldview, as well as a workable ethical philosophy and style.

THE BOOMER LABEL AND BOOMER IDENTITY

Despite the difficulty in globally labeling any generation or generalizing about all its individual members as having a unique character, the distinctive contrasts between the psychosocial patterns of the boomers and their antecedent generation are sufficiently remarkable as to afford them a palpable group identity. Mary Vander Goot has examined that fact in a useful way in her erudite but highly readable recent study of the early development of the boomer generation and the way in which boomers are maturing as they negotiate midlife and face their personal journeys to the end.[18]

Vander Goot points out that boomers now populate the 50- to 65-year-old cohort of the human sociocultural community. They started out in the 1960s with the intent of remaining forever young. Now they are wondering what it means to grow old. They are trying to figure out how such a generation grows old sensibly and whether there is any point in growing old. From the outset they were certain, to the point of narcissism, that they were special in wisdom, insight, courage, and invention. They were sure in the 1960s–1970s, for example, that *they* had invented sex. They believed they could improve on the world of their progenitors by throwing caution to the winds and pursuing freedom in every way, at all cost.

What the boomers thought were unique visions of freedom have now become culturally standard, for better or for worse. However, Vander Goot asks the existential question whether the freedoms achieved are real or illusory, constructive or self-defeating, and do they matter more than historic notions of virtue and character. Were they merely another, not very successful, form of illusion for coping with reality by denying it? Can we be certain or confident that in our now secularized world we have the kind of life left in which we can recover respect for the cherished or sacred? "The time is ripe for Boomers to reconsider those good things in the past they refused to honor, to voice their blessings for generations who will shape the future, and to reclaim conviction as they stand firm and dare to say in a secular age, 'This I believe.'"[19]

The issue at stake here for the boomers is the same as it has always been for every human generation: the search for meaning in and about their lives. Each of us has many stories to tell about life's experiences. As we progress in life we massage each of these stories into a master story of our individual and intensely personal lives. These stories grow, unfold, change, and interpret themselves as they develop over time. In the end, the master story is not as much about accurately remembered data as it is about the way we have massaged our experience and memory into interpreted meaning.

Vander Goot, who is a boomer herself, declares that,

> The bold pursuit of dogmatic freedom unseated the foundations of our sense of meaning. Cultural transformation over the last forty years has tangled up our collective views of freedom, truth, and power. Rather than being exhilarated by our freedom we have become anxious and cynical . . . but despite the pervasive skepticism of the Boomer era, the way we construct our personal stories has everything to do with whether the meaning of our lives deepens or whether the haunts of meaninglessness increasingly overtakes us.[20]

The composite narrative of the last two decades records the ascendancy of the boomer generation. It is not a pretty picture. As in every generation, there are cultural strengths and weaknesses evident, constructive and destructive forces at work, and functional and dysfunctional styles for the game of life. Unfortunately, the individualism of the original quest for freedom seems to have matured into what Christopher Lasch called *The Culture of Narcissism* (1991).

Lasch thought that starting with the late 1960s the culture of the United States had moved in such a self-preoccupied and arbitrary individualist direction that the narrowly clinical term of narcissism could be used appropriately to diagnose the pathology "that seemed to have spread to all corners of American life."[21] In line with Freud's model, Lasch perceived that the narcissistic boomer society was driven by "repressed rage and self-hatred."[22] This had prompted a flight into a grandiose self-conception that saw the world as fodder to be devoured for one's own gratification. Other people became useful objects to be chewed up and spit out. This was manifest in "the fascination with fame and celebrity, the fear of competition, the inability to suspend disbelief, the shallowness and transitory quality of personal relations, the horror of death,"[23] in which the Happy Hooker is more idealized than our founding fathers or the paragons of virtue in American history. Vander Goot agrees:

> The last forty years have been a time of unimaginable progress and at the same time an era of deep cynicism that cut to the taproot of

our convictions. The most popular writers include the most negative. The most powerful leaders have been some of the most undisciplined, and some of the most successful financiers have been the least ethical. Each generation engages the search for meaning in its own way, but in the Boomer generation . . . the results . . . are not what we imagined.[24]

She wonders whether boomers can disentangle themselves from the enmeshments of triviality and meaninglessness into which their rejection of the past and their abandonment of themselves to the innovative pursuit of radical freedom have led them. Are they able to come to terms with what Lasch called their horror of death?

Can we take Vander Goot's brilliantly expressed analysis seriously? Is it on track in terms of its substance as well as in its pleasing and articulate style? Is Lasch correct in his proposal that the boomer's perception of death as a horror explains the manner in which their generation is reshaping our cultural style in the remarkably changing journey to our individual and communal ends? Is their new style really a denial of death or control of the death culture as both inevitable and of no particular or heroic account?

Vander Goot thinks the measure of the truth may be taken in terms of a few interconnected considerations. The Greatest Generation tended to create community out of mutually held deeply grounded ethical and spiritual values that operated as principles for their thought and behavior. For the boomer generation spiritual grounding became less a shaper of public life. This trivialization of values made principal living all but impossible for many boomers. The burgeoning of technological power made it possible to do and have anything and everything that seemed to please. Consequently the suspicion grew that living without firm assumptions could be disorienting rather than exciting. Unfocused freedom produces anxiety. Cynicism easily slides into a pooling of mutual ignorance. Many boomers seem to have moved from freedom to scattered thinking as they found themselves overloaded with technology and the multiblasts of information, ready-made without any analytical thought under it. Thus, many boomers suffer from information overload, cease thinking vigorously and deeply, loosen their grip on the quest for life's deep meanings, turn into spectators rather than agents in culture and society, and move on to the ennui of disinterest.

Vander Goot's perspective rings true to cultural experience of the last four decades in the United States and may suggest a general process of trivialization of personality development as well as a remarkable superficiality in the quality of life for much of her generation. Is this the clue to the substantial change evident in the manner in which the boomers manage the culture of dying and death? A recent Pew Research Forum assessed them as the gloomiest generation.[25] Vander Goot quotes Saul Bellow as one of the outstanding literary voices of the boomer generation:[26]

> This generations thinks . . . that nothing faithful, vulnerable, fragile can be durable or have any true power. Death waits for these things as a cement floor waits for a dropping light bulb. The brittle shell of glass loses its tiny vacuum with a burst and that is it.[27]

As Rollo May declared, this generation is without "I believe" statements about the historic idealizing traditions of the past, without the hopeful visions of the future, without informing myths of time or eternity.[28] How can they appreciate the weighty import of the transition of death to a quality of life beyond life and that which transcends imagination? Vander Goot quotes him, *"The loneliness of mythlessness is the deepest and least assuageable of all. Unrelated to the past, unconnected with the future, we hang as if in mid-air."*[29] Little wonder that many boomers generally have no profound interest in the culture and ritual of celebrating death as a transition from life to life. With no mythic perspective of hope, it is probably impossible to generate a sense of meaning about death or about a usable future. Moreover, if there is nothing of heroic adulation about life and nothing of the past that is ideal, there is little to celebrate or commemorate, so why spend time, money, and emotion on death?

SUMMARY

How are we to interpret this picture, particularly the perspectives and patterns of the boomers' influence on our culture's changing journey to the end of life? Is this cultural shift we are experiencing in the style of our journey to our end a product of the secularization of society, its trivialization of death with no eternity, and the view that funerary ritual has nothing to celebrate so it is reduced to the mere disposal of a useless carcass? Or, are Boomers sufficiently spiritual in their orientation and secure in their sense of the transcendent that they experience a decreased interest in or preoccupation with the burial of "the physical remains"? Is the third option suggested above a real possibility, that is, boomers are not greatly troubled by the historic human struggle with neurosis and thus more clearheaded and self-confident about life and afterlife, having no particular anxiety or sense of obligation regarding commemorative rituals of farewell?

It is possible, in Vander Goot's terms, that their quest for freedom, which was quite arbitrary and individualistic, has cut many boomers loose from social moorings and responsible connection to other persons and causes, aside from their own comfort and ambition. It is possible that their hard-won sociocultural innovation has landed them in the degree of narcissism of which Lasch alerted us. It is possible, that is, this is the boomer generation's new type of illusion, called to our attention by Freud and Becker. Has it narrowed their vision to the pragmatics of individual existential sensations and survival, resulting in a sense that when that fails or terminates all meaning is lost?

If there is little or no meaning in death because it has no transcendent reach, its rituals of idealization, commemoration, celebration, and emotive leave-taking hardly call for costly dramas of reflection or mythic visions of life after life. Then endless care of the aged and infirm and the funerary processes at their demise are more a ritual of dismissal than a liturgy of farewell.

Vander Goot's challenge to the boomers is a worthy one. She urges her colleagues of that generation to try to identify a purpose for their temporal and eternal existence that goes beyond their self-preoccupation and transcends their limited illusion of reality. She suggests that reflections upon the gains and losses of their lives may suggest that aging is a gift and a time for a more blessed vision of things temporal and eternal.[30] "If we cannot relinquish this attachment to our own importance the passing of time will turn us into meddlesome, resentful old people. Or if all else fails and we weary of asserting our own importance we may be reduced to indifference. Both prospects are grim."[31]

She asks whether, as boomers complete their individual narratives of unfolding life, they will be "drawn back to the wisdom of the ages to sustain [them] in facing the limits and the mystery of life?" Having forged their freedoms with aggressive independence, the boomers are now in "a stage of life after freedom that requires more than freedom."[32] Vander Goot closes her excellent volume poignantly with Longfellow's pensive poem, "Morituri Salutamus":

> For age is opportunity no less
> Than youth itself, though in another dress,
> And as the evening fades away,
> The sky is filled with stars, invisible by day.[33]

NOTES

1. Ernest Becker, *The Denial of Death* (New York: Free Press, 1974; New York: Simon and Schuster, 1997), ix–x.

2. "How Baby Boomers May Change the Notion of 'Death' in Society," US Funerals Oneline, accessed November 16, 2012, http://www.us-funerals.com/funeral-articles/how-baby-boomers-may-change-the-notion-of-death-in-society.html#.UKbRvOOe_zM

3. John W. Ward, *Sources of Hepatitis C Infection* (Atlanta, GA: CDC, 2008).

4. Ibid., 2.

5. Sigmund Freud, "Thoughts for the Times on War and Death (1915)," in *Collected Papers,* eds., Ernest Jones and James Strachey, Vol. 4 (New York: Basic Books), 316–17.

6. Becker, *The Denial of Death,* 198.

7. Karen Horney, *The Neurotic Personality of our Time* (New York: Norton, 1937).

8. Becker, *The Denial of Death,* 178.

9. Ibid.

10. Ibid., 178–9.

11. Ibid., 187.

12. Otto Rank, *Will Therapy and Truth and Reality* (New York: Knopf 1936, 1945), 251–2.

13. Ibid., 251–2

14. Becker, *The Denial of Death,* 190.

15. Ibid.

16. Ibid.

17. Ibid.

18. Mary Vander Goot, *After Freedom, How Boomers Pursued Freedom, Questioned Virtue, and Still Search for Meaning* (Eugene, OR: Wipf and Stock—Cascade, 2012).

19. Ibid., cover.

20. Ibid., 13–14.

21. Christopher Lasch, *The Culture of Narcissism, American Life in An Age of Diminishing Expectations* (New York: Norton, 1991), 53.

22. Ibid., 59–61.

23. Ibid.

24. Vander Goot, *After Freedom,* 15.

25. Pew Forum on Religion and Public Life, "Statistics on Religion in America," *Pew Forum,* 66, last accessed November 11, 2012, http://religions.pewforum.org/reports

26. Vander Goot, *After Freedom,* 71.

27. Saul Bellow, *Herzog* (New York: Viking, 1964), 289–90.

28. Rollo May, *The Cry for Myth* (New York: Norton, 1991).

29. May cited in Vander Goot, *After Freedom,* 73.

30. Vander Goot, *After Freedom,* 155.

31. Ibid., 158.

32. Ibid., 159.

33. "Longfellow: Morituri Salutamus," Henry Wadsworth Longfellow: A Maine Historical Society Website, accessed November 16, 2012, http://www.hwlongfellow.org/poems.php?pid=275

Chapter 3

Dying while Living:
The Problem of Social Death

Donald Joralemon

*F*or most of human history, a large proportion of people died quickly of acute *diseases or accidents. The sociocultural processing of a death—"social death" in language familiar to death studies—followed the biological end of life and served the purpose of restructuring the social order in the aftermath of loss. By contrast, death in contemporary America typically comes late in life and after a prolonged period of chronic disease. In conceptual terms, social death now precedes biological death. This means that most Americans will experience a state of pre-mortem liminality, when they are caught between fully engaged social life and final biological death. This chapter contrasts the traditional significance of social death to the mixed messages of contemporary dying that demand we simultaneously struggle to survive and prepare to die.*

There is an advanced stage of our lives that bristles with an ambiguity that we have never named and that most of us will go through for differing lengths of time. We need to acknowledge, or better, define, carve out, and name the living-and-dying stage that precedes the about-to-die stage of our life. This prefinal stage of life might be called "dying, with a small 'd,'" or, for short, "small-d-dying."[1]

CAUGHT BETWEEN: MIXED MESSAGES IN SOCIAL DEATH

Life's transitions are often marked by a period of ambiguity, when we have effectively departed from one status but have yet to fully inhabit the identity we are soon to adopt. The great 20th-century anthropologist Victor Turner explored this potentially complicated time, elaborating on the analysis of rites of passage offered by the French scholar Arnold van Gennep and introducing the concept of liminality to capture the "betwixt and between" of important life changes.[2] Caffrey's "small-d-dying" is just such a liminal period.

The question for this chapter is: How does dying in contemporary North America confound the cultural space between life and death? After all, anthropologists are accustomed to charting the symbolic power of funerals as classic liminal periods, with the goal of moving the deceased on to the afterlife, however that is conceived, and returning the mourners to the social life of their community. So, why should the circumstances of 21st-century dying be any different, any more ambiguous, or hard to define?

The novelty of contemporary dying is the length of the liminal period—"social death" is the term I will use—and the mixed messages we convey to those experiencing it. Biomedicine stretches the time to death, sometimes by many years, and thereby promotes the illusion that the passage has yet to begin. All sorts of social institutions and culturally sanctioned scripts conspire to cushion the fact that the transition is actually underway. At the same time, and in the name of self-determination and concern for our loved ones, we ask the dying to prepare for the inevitable, by completing advanced directives for health care and last wills and testaments. Preplan your funeral and order your casket online! The result is a contradictory message: You aren't dying, but prepare to die. I want to explore this confusing terrain, beginning with a visit to a peculiar liminal space, the assisted living facility.

THE LIMINALITY OF "ASSISTED LIVING"[3]

Wander into a contemporary American assisted living facility and you enter a world of walkers and wellness centers, memory lapses and hearing impairment, inconspicuous surveillance, and the mirage of independent quarters. There are activities—lots of activities—and leather menus at meals. There are more women than men, by a factor of three to one. The sudden disappearance of a resident occasions the hushed question: Will she be coming back?

Sit for a dinner in the dining room and one sweet lady confuses how many children she has while another tries her best to share pieces of her chicken dinner. The quiet one across the table shows no facial expression, but occasionally offers a biographical bit that suggests she is still with you. The waiter, an elderly African American with an unexpected French accent and a crisp white shirt with bow tie, is admirably patient with the royal demands coming from his predominantly white clients, and this with no tips in the offing.

At breakfast two men sit by themselves in a corner, both with wedding rings on their fingers. One is fully sociable and quick to answer the standard questions about prior residence and career. The other either can't hear or doesn't care. Are they happy to have the company of an outsider, someone still able to claim the relative advantage of youth, or is this an unwanted disruption of the routine?

This isn't a nursing home, that's for sure; too many reminders of normality and not enough signs of imminent demise. The medical tools are here, but kept in the background, part of a subtle dance that encourages a false sense that one is still in control. Few are residents by choice; most have been coerced by their loving family who were worried but unable to do the work of caring. Assisted living really means risk reduction and support nearly to the end of life.

It is expensive to assist in living. Around $7,000 per month for a one bedroom apartment in a small, high-quality facility in New Jersey (prices vary by region of the country),[4] but that includes three squares a day and room service. They do your laundry, take your blood pressure, transport you to the mall and, for a little extra, someone will make sure you take your meds as prescribed. The social director says it is like a cruise ship that never leaves port.

You may get turfed out if your condition worsens—maybe a bit too aggressive in your Alzheimer's or too needy in your habits of daily living.? Then it's off to the real final station, the place where nurses rule and technology hums, the last stop before the end of the line. That's when assisted living looks pretty good!

We have some ground to cover to understand this liminal zone for those no longer able to be, in the language of elder care, independently living. I start with concepts common in the thanatology literature: social and biological death.

SOCIAL AND BIOLOGICAL DEATH

Biological death refers to the process by which critical organ systems permanently cease to function and physical decay begins. Life-support technology has made it more difficult than ever to determine with certainty when biological death has occurred, but the concept is at least intuitively sensible because it is based on observable facts.[5] The notion of social death is more abstract, less familiar, and equally complicated. It refers to the disintegration and disappearance of a person's social identity.

Think of yourself as a thread in a network of social relations, linked to others by connections of varying intensity and duration. Taken together these bonds constitute your social identity and have a profound effect on your own self-image. When you die, there is a tear in the web to which you were connected. The repair of the network requires a reorganization of the bonds without you, or at least without your ongoing engagement. A person with minimal connections—a hermit would be an example—poses little difficulty to the social system, but people with far-reaching bonds pose a greater recuperative challenge. In either case, the concept of social death refers to the process by which the deceased is taken out of the social network altogether, or reconfigured so as to perpetuate at least some of the importance of the decedent to the still living, for example, through memorials, annual death recognitions, and beliefs in ghosts.

Throughout most of human history, biological death preceded social death because most people died young and quickly. Funerals were elaborate rituals in part because they bore the burden of repairing the social fabric when an unanticipated death ruptured the network of social relations. But the pattern of longer lives and slower deaths that evolved over the 20th century in wealthy countries reversed the order: social death first, biological death some time later. This trend is affecting our rapidly aging population. As the post–World War II babies enter their final decades in increasing numbers, they bring attention to the problem of experiencing one's own social death and demand attention to the issues it raises. Prolonged dying at advanced ages results in the separation of people from their social networks well in advance of biological death. Retirement parties start the process: to retire, after all, means to withdraw, or go away or apart. Eventual moves to assisted living facilities and then full care nursing homes nearly complete a person's segregation from society before death. Our social universe narrows in an inexorable movement toward complete detachment.

The active elderly may protest that they remain fully engaged in life, and aging baby boomers are not likely to go quietly off to seclusion in old-age ghettos. Some manage to preserve their professional life well into their later years, but these are notable exceptions precisely because the culturally scripted paths available even to the most energetic seniors—volunteer work, travel, age-adjusted sports, and continuing education—are still steps away from the world of younger people. More time is spent in the exclusive company of persons similarly situated in the life cycle. Social Security, Medicare, and senior discounts increasingly define daily life. For those who survive beyond the statistical mean for their gender and ethnicity, the sense of a shrinking social universe is intensified by the progressive loss of close friends and relatives.

Since so much of the societal work of recuperation from a person's demise is now accomplished before biological death, there is often an anticlimactic character to life's final end. The throttling back of funeral customs evident in some sectors of modern society[6] may be, at least partially, explained by the simple fact that funerals have less to accomplish when the dead have already been written out of the social script. Rather than considering this development as an impoverishment of culture, we should stop searching for traditionally elaborate funeral rituals and explore what is taking their place.

THE LIMINALITY OF SOCIAL DEATH

As mentioned above, anthropologists pay a great deal of attention to rituals of dying and death, as they do to all passages that mark an individual's life, such as birth, puberty, and marriage. Studies of these rites of passage conclude that they invariably include a period of liminality, when the individual undergoing the transition from one status to another is, in the memorable words of the anthropologist Victor Turner, "betwixt and between." No longer of the former status, but not yet fully situated in the new position, the ritual subject stands temporarily outside the social system. As Turner shows, it is common for this liminal period to include the seclusion of the ritual subject, a leveling of social distinctions, a temporary suspension of time, and restrictions on behavior that underscore the ambiguous condition of the person undergoing the transition. In the case of death rituals it is often both the deceased and his or her close kin who are taken through a passage, the former toward the world of the dead and the latter back into the social world after the stigma of association with death—or the comforting attention bestowed on the bereaved—is diminished.

In traditional death studies the notion of liminality is used to explain practices that occur between biological death and the final disposition of the corpse—the time period when the deceased has yet to be definitively removed from the world of the living. However, modern mortality patterns, which put social death ahead of biological death, require us to reconsider this analysis. There is now, to coin a phrase, a pre-mortem liminality. Sometimes it starts at a precise moment in time, as when a person hears a terminal diagnosis or suffers a near fatal blow from which recovery is unlikely. In other cases the liminal state begins at some indeterminate point when physical and/or mental decline tip the balance between being fully alive and embarking on the process of dying. A prime example for the 21st century is the gradual development of liminality that accompanies chronic conditions such as Alzheimer's disease, in which engagement in the world diminishes slowly over time. At some, often-disputed, point family and friends sense that the person they once knew is no longer there, even if the physical form remains.[7]

When the onset of pre-mortem liminality is sudden, it can be experienced as an odd feeling of being a spectator in a world that seems unfazed by a death prediction that changes everything for the subject. For example, it is not uncommon for someone receiving a cancer diagnosis, with the doctor rattling off survival statistics, to feel a rupture in his or her taken-for-granted world, which is exacerbated by the discovery that everyone else seems to be carrying on as usual. The delusion of self-importance that protects us from having to admit our insignificance is shattered by the realization that our death may be closer than we expected and that this isn't exactly headline news.

Gradual onset pre-mortem liminality creates complications in a social world that depends on a degree of stability and predictability in human relations. A person afflicted with a progressive disease requires us to continually adjust our expectations of social interaction as new limitations and deficits appear. This is expertly described by Columbia University anthropologist Robert Murphy in *The Body Silent,* which documents the discomfort of friends and family who were forced to adapt to the author's changing social identity as a spinal cord tumor left him ever more paralyzed.[8] Murphy reflects on the increasingly awkward interactions with friends as he advances to a state of quadriplegia, noting that his identity is progressively spoiled by his physical restrictions and by the closeness to death they portend. Despite the fact that his mind is unaffected, there comes a point when he is all but declared dead by everyone save closest relations. He is uncomfortably betwixt and between, too close to biological death to postpone social death any longer.

Whether sudden or gradual, the pre-mortem liminality of social death brings with it some of the same conditions as other liminal states. The person is often secluded—either in a medical institution or in a home transformed by the requirements of nursing care—and the limitations on behavior (e.g., mobility, eating, and bathing) underscore his or her in-between status just as they do for neophytes in many rites of passage (e.g., male puberty rites in many traditional societies). Time can seem frozen or redefined as a futureless present. Status differences evaporate among those who share the liminal condition, as Murphy noticed when hospital staff treated patients without concern for distinctions of gender, age, education, or ethnicity. This leveling of identity markers was especially striking for someone trained to pay attention to the structures of social relations.

Liminal periods in rites of passage typically include an educational component, when the subject undergoing transition is instructed about the role he or she is about to occupy. Think of the classes that lead up to Christian confirmation, Jewish Bar and Bat Mitzvahs, or the pastoral counseling that precedes marriage. The liminality of contemporary social death has its own instructional dimension as well, represented in the volumes of self-help books and death-related websites, counseling sessions with religious figures and psychologists, and appointments with medical specialists. There is a push/ pull in the messages conveyed by these sources of instruction. On the one hand, there are prescriptions for better dying that set out tasks to accomplish and stages to pass through on the way to a "good death." There are step-by-step accounts of what one can expect as biological death approaches and even how-to manuals for arranging your own departure. Your local funeral home will be glad to assist you in preplanning your final arrangements. All of this constitutes forward-looking instruction, designed to promote full understanding of an impending biological death.

On the other hand, a vast medical effort is directed at discouraging the person from accepting or even acknowledging that biological death is the natural end point of the transition. Far from facilitating the passage, many doctors routinely treat the possibility of death as an avoidable, or at least deferrable, reality, even after the point that their patient's quality of life has so deteriorated that the patient, were he or she able to take charge of treatment decisions, might choose to forgo further interventions. As a result, the pre-mortem liminality of social death is sometimes replaced with another form of liminality: a depersonalized patient tethered to medical instruments and subject to instructions inscribed on a chart. This is the in-between space that Margaret Edson explores with such power in her play *W;t* (1995).

It's difficult for a person to experience the in-between condition of pre-mortem social death when there are contradictory messages at the end of life: *struggle to live and prepare to die.* The impulse to treat that dominates medicine, supported by what Helen Stanton Chapple calls the "ideology of rescue"—the conviction that giving up is not an option—resists a smooth transition to biological death.[9] Pulling in the opposite direction are the hospice and right-to-die or physician-assisted death movements—the expansion of palliative care medicine—and economic disincentives for futile medical treatments. Liminality is tough to take when the direction of the impending transition is a matter of cultural contention.

RETURN TO "ASSISTED LIVING"

It is not just during the last days and weeks of life that the contradictory guidance of pre-mortem liminality shapes the experience of those on the long course of social dying. Consider the public relations narrative of assisted living versus the implicit mission of the institutions.

Vernon Home in Vermont promises that its residents "can live life to the fullest in one of [their] 39 modern, comfortable one- and two-room apartments, each with a private bath."[10] The Arbors in Amherst, Massachusetts, boasts of "New friends! New possibilities!"[11] Bella Terra in Jackson, New Jersey, offers "a stimulating environment with a hospitality-centered staff . . . senior living that complements the best of Living Life. Relax. It's time to Live Life to its fullest."[12] Juniper Village in Chatham, New Jersey, "strives to nurture the spirit of life in each individual by providing an environment and programs that encourage an active body, an engaged mind and a fulfilled spirit"[13]

A different view emerges if you spend time talking to the residents. As I visited facilities in northern New Jersey, I found a pragmatic attitude among those I had a chance to meet. Even those who are content with their situation know why they have been relocated and it isn't to "live life to its fullest." They understand that the brochure talk is aimed at reassuring the relatives. They experience at a visceral level the gap between "the best of living life" and the requirement that they complete detailed advanced directives before moving in. Such are the mixed messages of our pre-mortem liminality.

REIMAGINING SOCIAL DEATH

It is easy to envy the clarity of social death rituals in traditional societies. When someone dies on the South Pacific Trobriand Islands, everyone knows what is expected based on kinship ties to the deceased: close matrilineal kin begin a well-orchestrated period of intense mourning, while those from other lineages carry out the work related to extended funeral ceremonies.[14] In the Sierra Nevada de Santa Marta of Columbia, the death of a Kogi is met with powerful rituals that symbolically return the dead to a fetal state before being placed in a grave conceived as the uterus of the Great Mother, where he or she will gestate anew to be reborn into the ancestral world.[15] When social death follows biological death, the only ambiguity is whether the spirit of the deceased will insist on lingering behind.

By contrast, uncertainty reigns when the work of removing a person from the fabric of social relations must begin at some indeterminate point before that person has biologically died. Like the proverbial horse before the cart, it is hard to treat a living person as though he or she were dead. It is no wonder that the script for this new way of dying is still under revision, with competing visions of the timing and meaning of the transition. In a highly individualistic culture like America, it would perhaps be fitting if each person could exercise some degree of control over the narrative of his or her own social death, balancing struggle and acceptance in a way that reflects the values they share with their loved ones.

NOTES

1. Thomas A. Caffrey, "When the Time is Ripe for Acceptance: Dying, with a Small 'd,'" in *Speaking of Death: America's New Sense of Mortality,* ed. Michael K. Bartalos (Westport, CT: Praeger, 2009), 227–36.

2. Victor W. Turner, "Betwixt and Between: The Liminal Period in Rites of Passage," in *The Forest of Symbols: Aspects of Ndembu Ritual*(Ithaca, NY: Cornell University Press, 1967), 93–111; *The Ritual Process: Structure and Anti-Structure* (London: Routledge and Kegan Paul, 1969); *Dramas, Fields and Metaphors* (Ithaca, NY: Cornell University Press, 1974). Arnold Van Gennep, *The Rites of Passage,* English Trans M. B. Vizedom and G. L. Caffee. See also, Graham St. John, ed., *Victor Turner and Contemporary Cultural Performance* (New York: Berghahn Books, 2008).

3. Based on observations in a New Jersey facility in January 2012.

4. For national averages and state comparisons see http://www.assistedlivingfacilities.org/articles/assisted-living-costs.php

5. For a review of the complications of biological death see Robert J. Kastenbaum, *Death, Society, and Human Experience* (New York: Pearson, 2011), 11th edition.

6. For a review of changes in death rituals see Jenny Hockey, "Changing Death Rituals," in *Grief, Mourning and Death Ritual,* ed. J. Hockey, J. Katz, and Neil Small (Philadelphia: Open University Press, 2001), 185–211. Crouch, Mira. "Last Matters: The Latent Meanings of Contemporary Funeral Rites," in *Making Sense of Dying and Death,* ed. A. Fagan, (Amsterdam: Editions Rodapi B. V., 2004), 125–40.

7. Michael Castleman, D. Gallagher-Thompson, and M. Naythons, *There's Still a Person in There: The Complete Guide to Treating and Coping with Alzheimer's* (New York: Penguin Putman, 1999).

8. Robert F. Murphy, *The Body Silent: The Different World of the Disabled* (New York: W. W. Norton, 1990).

9. Helen Stanton Chapple, *No Place for Dying: Hospitals and the Ideology of Rescue* (Walnut Creek, CA: Left Coast Press, 2010).

10. http://www.vernonhome.org/

11. http://www.arborsassistedliving.com/

12. http://www.seniorlifestyle.com/senior_living/Jackson_NJ/zip_08527/senior_lifestyle_corporation/5022.

13. http://www.junipercommunities.com/CHsignature.php

14. Annette Weiner, *Women of Value, Men of Renown* (Austin TX: University of Texas Press, 1983).

15. Gerado Reichel-Dolmatoff, "Funerary Customs and Religious Symbolism among the Kogi," in *Native South Americans,* ed. P. Lyon (Long Grove, IL: Waveland Press, 1985), 289–301.

Chapter 4

The Biology of Decision: Implications of Neuroscientific Research for End-of-Life Care

Daniel Liechty and Bruce Hiebert

A convergence of material from a number of sources indicates that decisions are made in the unconscious mind before the conscious mind is even alerted to the need for a decision. The role of conscious reasoning is to provide rationalizations for decisions that are already made in other processes of the brain, in accord with strongly emotional recall, interpreting present situations in light of previous emotionally charged experiences. Following the insights of social anthropologist Ernest Becker and subsequent extension of Becker's ideas in experimental social psychology under the rubric of terror management theory (TMT), we suggest that the most basic fear, perhaps even the root of all other fears, is the fear of death. We conclude that techniques coming mainly from religious traditions for bringing unconscious fear of death forward into consciousness—techniques such as silent meditation, guided visualization, contemplative prayer, and others— should be employed as a first step in the process of making end-of-life decisions. These techniques, in their religious or secular versions, do not guarantee satisfying outcomes. Nevertheless, the findings of the new research suggest that these techniques deserve to, and likely will, participate in reshaping the traditional process and practice of important decision making regarding options at the end of life in the 21st century.

Shaped by thinkers as diverse as Aristotle, Thomas Aquinas, Rene Descartes, and Max Weber, Western thinking about rational decision making is essentially grounded in the idea of mind-body dualism. Reasoned decisions are fundamentally understood to be in the realm of independent rational minds. This is central to the doctrine of informed consent and a key assumption of the European Convention on Human Rights and Biomedicine of 1997 ("Oviedo Convention") and the UNESCO Universal Declaration on Bioethics and Human Rights of 2005. The assumption of these legal instruments is that a sound decision is arrived at by a rational mind, aware of all the relevant, available information and possible outcomes, on the basis of internal preferences. The right to such autonomous thinking is seen as inherent to universal human dignity and well-being.

The grounding of decision making in rational thinking has been criticized in the Universal Declaration on Cultural Diversity of 2001 as culturally inappropriate in some circumstances, which argues that the personal autonomy implied by this approach to decision making violates the essential well-being and values of some groups and, in addition, places an undue and inappropriate burden on individual decision makers.[1] What has remained unchallenged until recently is the legitimacy of the underlying mind-body dualism, specifically the assumed irrelevance of the mind-brain connection, and especially the impact of emotion on decision making.

Contrary to the traditional doctrines of a mind-body distinction, contemporary neuroscience indicates that human minds and brains cannot be separated. This finding, a new reality, argues for a concomitant need, among other things, to integrate emotionally triggered brain functioning into moral decision-making theory.[2] Neuroscientists have begun to develop models of brain functioning that call into question key components of the Western model of decision making, specifically human autonomy and reasoned thought. Human brains, the research indicates, are social creations; they are the independent results of a personal chain of experience.[3] They are nonrational in their fundamental operations, typically turning to conscious reasoned processes only when habitual or intuitive patterns are felt to be inadequate, and then usually to support a weakly felt previous solution. In particular, no decisions are made that are not rooted in an emotional encounter: emotion drives the fundamental structure of decision making.

The most intense emotions are those of most significance in shaping decision making. Few experiences are more emotionally intense than those related to death. Although we like to pretend that humans are the direct descendants of powerful hunters and warriors, the fact is that for most of our species' history, we were a relatively weak and timid species, hiding out of range of the big cats in hopes that they would leave some scraps of meat and bone behind from their kill that we could scavenge. Our evolutionary development, including our psychology, was shaped much more by the millennia of being preyed upon than by the much shorter and more recent history of being powerful hunters and warriors. This transition from prey to predator was made possible by harnessing weapons technology. The residue of this history is not only our continued love of and fascination with technology, but probably also many of the images of danger and evil that haunt our nightmares are those of large cats and snakes.[4]

Much as we would like to flatter ourselves to the contrary, we are fundamentally a nervous and cautious species, driven at least as directly by avoidance of real and imagined dangers, the ultimate form of which is death, as we are by noble desires and ambitions. As will be argued later in this chapter, drawing from the empirical studies of TMT, if we are hardwired at all in a cognitive and emotional sense, it is to avoid death and to symbolize life in a death-denying fashion.

This view of human motivation has implications for many areas of human endeavor, and nowhere more certain than when we consider the social conditions surrounding end-of-life decision making in clinical settings. This was true even when we conceived of end-of-life decisions as based on rational processes of moral and personal calculation. Even then we had a good idea that in many instances, the psycho-emotional need to deny and defy death often intervened to muddy the waters of clear and rational mental processes. A new understanding of the decision-making process is emerging from cognitive brain research and is leading us to assume that strong emotions do not so much intervene to muddy the waters of rationality as to constitute the original basis of the decision itself, which then is passed on to our reasoning faculties for confirmation and rationalization.

Because the impact of emotions on decision making has not been well understood, rational reasoning has been assumed to be relevant in end-of-life decision making and the concept of informed consent has, as a consequence, become legitimized. Given the intensely emotional conditions surrounding end-of-life situations, assumptions of rational behavior must be rethought and new strategies for making end-of-life decisions must be considered. Resources for developing new strategies can be found in religious and spiritual traditions. All religious and spiritual practices are deeply concerned with the experience of death and have developed techniques for assisting adherents to face death with relative calm. These practices, such as silent meditation, guided visualization, and contemplative prayer, among others, produce conditions permitting those human beings who are terrified of death to face it with relative equanimity, and they can help foster relatively reasoned decisions about how to proceed toward that end.

NEUROPSYCHOLOGICAL ANALYSES RELEVANT TO DECISION MAKING

The body of work exploring issues of neuropsychology and decision making is expanding rapidly, and professionals are recognizing the profound moral implications it contains. As an example, MIT Press recently released a three-volume set of explorations devoted exclusively to the relationship between brain neuropsychology and the morality of decision making.[5] This collection cumulatively suggests at least four aspects of brain functioning that critically impact decision making: emotion precedes decision; every brain is unique; all decisions are social and often unconscious; and schemas and heuristics determine informational relevance and application. While significant debate remains over the exact meaning of these aspects, they can be taken in their broad outlines as the contemporary scientific consensus on the relationship between the brain and moral decision making. We elaborate on each in more detail in the following.

Emotion Precedes Decision

According to magnetic resonance imaging, positron emission tomography, and other brain scanning studies, stimuli interpreted as requiring a decision cause a number of parts of the brain to activate in a timed sequence. Emotional centers of the brain, especially the amygdalae—the four almond-shaped masses of gray matter in the anterior extremity of the temporal lobe—are activated prior to the prefrontal cortex, the center of conscious decision making, thus indicating that all decisions emerge out of an emotional framework.[6]

The consequence for decision-making theory of this emotional substrate is that all decisions must be recognized as nonrational in their origins and related to the satisfaction of the emotional conditions that generated the initial response. Typically this means that the decision is designed to help the decision maker feel better The normal result is a quick decision that meets the emotional criteria without the person taking the time to more fully process the decision. This will be especially true when the emotions are intense and the time to make a decision constrained.

Every Brain Is Unique

Studies show highly variant levels of all aspects of brain functioning among individuals, from differing levels of stimulation required to trigger specific brain effects to wide variations in the pattern of brain response to any specific stimulation. Since emotional response is one of the points of high variability in brain functioning, the manner in which any specific individual will approach a decision cannot be predicted. While skilled observers and developers of decision processes may know that most minds will approach a decision within an anticipated range, some individuals will approach a decision in an unexpected manner. They will react based on their own brain patterns and thus may respond more or less emotionally than expected to any specific trigger context. Such extreme responses, in the context of a required decision mediated by professional caregivers, are not responsive to rational decision cues. Instead, these individuals are more likely to make rational decisions after a process in which respondents are encouraged to reflect upon their feelings and mental processes.

All Decisions Are Social and Often Unconscious

Perhaps the most radical challenge posed by neurological research to the Western ideal of informed individual decision making is the emerging picture of the brain as fundamentally social in its functioning. Human social patterns are etched into brain systems from the earliest stages of life through adulthood. Individuals continually react unconsciously to social cues generated by others in order to assess their surroundings and develop adequate responses. Neurons referred to by some scientists as *mirror* neurons trigger in response to the behavior of others, and a rapid assessment of socially generated stimuli leads to our quick understandings of what constitutes approved or desired behavior in a particular situation.

In decision making, this means that the expectation of authorities and contextual cultural traditions powerfully shape the decisions that emerge. People react without giving the matter conscious thought, following what they perceive as a socially desirably norm, in accord with collective patterns of action. When the emotional intensity increases, so does the reliance on the sociocultural environment and its patterns of perceived accepted responses. Under extremely high stress, the brain overloads its conscious processing centers and comes to rely in large measure on direct external cues for correct understanding of a situation and guidance for responses.

Schemas and Heuristics Determine Informational Relevance and Application

The human brain does not accumulate and assess information. It responds to general patterns abstracted quickly from the torrent of incoming stimuli. Using memory and habit, the human brain looks for what it perceives to be the most similar experience or habit of behavior with which to respond to the newly perceived stimuli. These schemas and habits comprise a whole field of emotions, thoughts, and behaviors that may join together in complex strings to produce sophisticated responses. They may also be relatively simple. In the midst of these schemas there are often heuristics, decision-making algorithms, and assessment trees that are oriented toward specific types of decisions and outcomes.

Emotionally charged situations reduce the brain's ability to assess circumstances and typically, but not always, lead to closer dependence on habits and heuristics in decision making. However, if the brain cannot find an appropriate schema, then the emotional stress level can be expected to rise while the respondent becomes more actively engaged in the situation.

MORAL DECISION MAKING BY THE SOCIAL BRAIN

We can diagram these four factors as they relate to moral decisions (see Figure 4.1). Every decision event emerges in the space between brain structures and social structures, once they are triggered by an initial event (left side of chart). The diagram process shows how complex, and both situationally and experientially unique, each decision is. It also illustrates the two distinct phases to the decision, an unconscious decision process and a subsequent conscious decision process.

A moral event emerges in the brain through a process of event framing in which the initial reaction based on memory and unconscious social perception determines the meaning of the event. The production of this frame of reference is an extremely rapid one where surface associations and emotional reactions guide the process of creating the perspective. How others in the environment appear to respond to the stimuli is critical to how the brain responds, as it carries out its rapid search for clues to the meaning of the event. This initial response is always unconscious. The precise framework will emerge, as memory and emotion combine with the perceived social cues to create an appropriate decision schema. The schema is unique to the individual, but typically similar to schemas developed by others raised in the same culture with roughly similar life experiences. There is no way of predicting

Figure 4.1
Moral decision making and the social brain

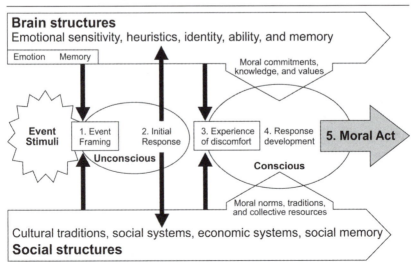

how much similarity there will be. The unique characteristics of each brain, based as it is on variant genetics, developmental experiences, and life histories, lead to inherent and unstable uniqueness of response to a given stimulus. The result is a socially and historically constructed but individually unique moral intuition regarding how an event should be understood and reacted to.

Every frame of reference has implied decision-solution heuristics, sets of rules, and associated tactics that the individual applies. These heuristics generate an initial response to the situation, which is immediately ready for application. These heuristics are often of the fast and frugal variety enabling a speedy and relatively simple and internally consistent decision that is formed by restricting information available and applying tactics that are relatively well developed from similar previous situations.[7] Under most circumstances this initial solution is good enough, and the individual can act without the need for a conscious decision. However, this is not always true. Every solution faces the test of personal and social responsibility—to what extent is it congruent with the individual's general identity and social existence, and what are the social cues the proposed solution is generating in the existing social context are the two questions. How these two linked questions are answered leads to what might be identified formally as a moral decision.

If the initial response creates a feeling of discomfort or dissonance in the person making the decision, then a period of conscious moral or value analysis follows. The source of the discomfort may be either inner, a sense of unfitness between some part of individual perception and the idealized or remembered self, or it may be a perceived conflict with an aspect of the social environment. The responses generated earlier by the unconscious do not fit the conscious parameters for acceptance. Once there is some source of discomfort, the brain "bumps up" the problem to the next level in the decision process, that of conscious decision making.

It is essential to note here that the conscious moral decision-making process is not the beginning point, but a subsequent development of an already found solution. As Marquardt demonstrates, the initial event schema is the critical step in the decision process.[8] While the decision maker may use complex reasoning to develop his or her final position, the initial frame of reference will be central to the way the evidence is evaluated and other social and personal information brought to bear. The initial frame of reference is more likely to determine the outcome than is the moral reasoning that follows, even if the response does not follow the earlier unconscious heuristic.

Because of the complex nature of the relationship between reasoning and other brain processes, it is likely that only at the point of actively considering the issue does the agent become aware of entering into a decision. The earlier unconscious analysis and resulting tactics are usually only of peripheral awareness, and may only precede the conscious activity by milliseconds. *This is a primary reason that formal systems of decision making break down. They presume that the conscious effort is the first run at the problem, when it is in fact the second run at the problem, and comes only after the first has failed.* In all problem-solving situations the first step is to determine the nature of the problem; if that first step is unconscious then it means that the individual has constrained the subsequent decision without awareness that any restriction has taken place (see Figure 4.2). The direction of inquiry, including a general sense of the socially acceptable solutions, has been established without any conscious analysis, moral or otherwise.

In the moral decision-making process that emerges after the breakdown of the earlier fast and frugal decision, the individual undertakes a personal and evidential interrogation of the situation based on his or her value system. This is the typical course of a logical moral analysis. In undertaking this interrogation, the person is aware of the social environment and of the presumed or actual actors in that environment, some of whom may be perceived carriers of high levels of moral influence and power. The individual projects how the existing social cues indicate the likely response of the actors in the social environment to the anticipated, or internally evaluated, new response. It is in this complex personal and social interaction that the moral response is developed and subsequently initiated. The social brain has come to a conclusion based first on the unconscious framing, and only later, in a follow-up interrogation, which may be quite complex and sophisticated, develops what is perceived to be a socially appropriate response.

Current approaches to end-of-life decision making continue to emphasize rational responsiveness to issues and procedures based on informed consent. Following the model of decision making described above, however, it is not hard to see that the concept of rational actors and informed consent is not adequate for framing decisions of significance, especially for emotionally charged

Figure 4.2
Framing effects on conscious decision results

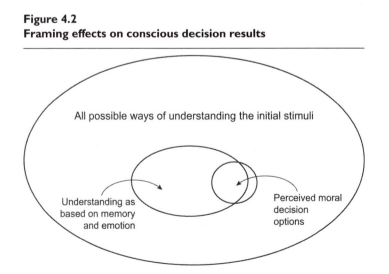

decisions related to end-of-life issues. Conceptualization, and subsequent operationalization, of effective social contexts for personal and family decision making regarding end-of-life issues requires quite a different model. The social brain is not the neutral decision maker required by existing models. In this reappraisal of decision-making frameworks, we suggest that traditional religious practices may become important tools for many decision makers.

EMOTION IN THE FACE OF DEATH

Although philosophers have posited that our rational faculties are what characterize our species as human, it is now increasingly established that our rationality itself is strongly rooted in emotions.[9] Furthermore, as our emotions emerge from a complex and preconscious feedback loop of the central nervous system, recent neurological research is gradually but strongly confirming a view of the mind-body relationship that reaches back at least as far as the theorizing of William James,[10] and is now associated with the work of Joseph LeDoux.[11] This view underlines the idea that in sequence, bodily/emotional states are prior to the employment of our rationality to interpret such states. We are, in short, already *in motion* before our rational faculties are called into function. Thus, especially in circumstances in which strong emotions are elicited, our rational faculties are employed mainly to rationalize actions and decisions sparked in the unconscious areas of the brain that are sequentially already in progress.[12]

This suggests, then, that the more strongly emotions are sparked by circumstances, the more we must assume that subsequent actions emerge from the unconscious mind, unchecked by rational thought. Of the basic human emotions, one of the strongest is fear. Anthropologist Ernest Becker, synthesizing an enormous volume of psychological and sociological literature, theorized that a basic and unconscious fear of death—death anxiety—lay just beneath the surface of most of human activity.[13] Becker suggested that humans, the only species, as far as we know, able to conceptualize death as an inevitable future condition, are largely motivated by the need to create cultural forms, beliefs, and institutions that function to quell the rumble of underlying death anxiety endemic to our nature as a species capable of abstract thought. Although developed independently, drawing from quite different source material, Becker's general understanding of the functioning of cultural institutions to quell anxiety and facilitate equanimity in human social action dovetails neatly with the theoretical perspective of Berger and Luckmann in their influential formulation of the sociology of knowledge.[14] Their theories were subsequently extended by Berger into a model of religious ideology providing for society what he characterized as a protective sacred canopy, shielding social life from a potentially disruptive upsurge of confrontations with the chasm of the unknowable.[15]

Although, as he presented them, Becker's ideas can be seen as speculative, lacking the hard empirical support increasingly valued in social sciences, over the last two decades, significant aspects of Becker's central ideas have been subjected to careful laboratory experimentation and scrutiny by a growing team of social psychologists. Pursued under the rubric of TMT—referring to psychological terror, terror of death, not political terror, although the mechanism of political terror may be seen as a special case in point of the larger theory—this extension of Becker's thesis concerning the impact of deep-rooted mortality anxiety on human behavior has become one of the most widely accepted theoretical perspectives in current social psychology.[16] Furthermore, much of this work correlates well with areas of cognitive brain research exploring the relationship between human religiosity and psychology.[17]

Basic to TMT research is the mortality salience hypothesis, which states that stimulation of underlying death anxiety provokes in some measure the fight/flight response to danger humans share with other species, and results in predictable patterns of behavioral reactions very different from the reactions of control groups. Furthermore, such altered responses remain largely outside of test subjects' conscious awareness. A number of modes and methods have been used in this research to achieve the mortality salient condition, from inserting questions about death into test questionnaires, to subliminal priming on a visual screen. One experiment carried out by a group of German researchers found significantly different responses to street poll questions between randomly selected people who were questioned either before or after having passed a funeral parlor. The differences conformed to the pattern predicted in the theory.

TMT, a theory of social psychology, zeroes in particularly on the anxiety-allaying function of cultural beliefs, practices, and institutions suggested by Becker's synthesis. The pattern of response this theory predicts is that people in the mortality salient condition, that is, those whose unconscious death anxiety has been stimulated, will react with measurably stronger levels of xenophobic defensiveness than will control groups who are not placed in the mortality salient state. This is measured both intellectually—for example, by answers to questions concerning cultural beliefs or degree of preference for characters depicted as sharing one's own cultural values—and behaviorally—for example, how far from a foreigner one sits in a waiting room or one's degree of reluctance to desecrate cultural symbols such as a flag in the course of assigned tasks. The differences elicited by this research are statistically sound and significant, replicable and heavily scrutinized in peer reviews.

It must be granted that social psychology is not mathematics, and thus plausible alternative explanations could be posed to account for the results of any one of the TMT experiments. However, the sheer number of positive experimental results now being reported in the literature, combined with the consistency of the results across age groups, educational levels, nationalities, and socioeconomic levels among the test subjects, has now established TMT as one of the most well-investigated and well-established theories in social psychology.[18]

If, as this research suggests, fear of death prompts strong and unconscious emotional reactions in response to reminders of death, then this has profound implications for the process of end-of-life decision making. We might go so far as to suggest that being faced with end-of-life decisions is the prime example of being placed in the mortality salient condition. To the extent that this is true, we have to assume that rationality *per se,* weighing alternatives according to the measured rules of rational choice theory, plays a much more diminished role in the process of end-of-life decision making than is generally imagined. Unconscious heuristics and social cues will dominate decision processes under these conditions. When dealing with end-of-life issues, we are engaged in a deeply emotional and unconscious process, in which our rational faculties are likely to become employed in *post hoc* rationalization of decisions already made.

Yet, while recognizing and acknowledging the complexity of the decision-making process, we cannot as counselors and professionals simply abandon the notion that this decision-making process can be improved. Furthermore, at least presently, it still appears that employment of our rational faculties has to be an integral and fundamental aspect of any improvements we might achieve. As we follow the results of contemporary cognitive and neural sciences, we find ourselves in the paradoxical position of seeking rational approaches to improving what all of this research suggests is essentially an unconscious, prerational, nonrational process.

Is there a direction out of this paradox? Fortunately, at least some TMT research suggests so. Although the largest body of TMT research leads rather inexorably to the conclusion that we are predictably puppets of manipulated unconscious death anxiety, as advertising executives and demagogical politicians have long understood, this research also suggests that exposure to the mechanism of manipulation strongly neutralizes the results.[19] To put this in a context most applicable to our concerns here, this research suggests that it is not the conscious acknowledgment of death's inevitability that sparks the defensive reaction, but rather its unconscious repression. Bringing awareness of death's inevitability into consciousness effectively cancels the negative impact of unconscious death anxiety, at least for a period of time. This has implications for end-of-life decision making well worth exploring.

PRACTICES TO ORDER A SOCIO-EMOTIONAL MIND

TMT brings us to the tentative conclusion that a central and necessary task for psychological care and counseling is to assist the patient in moving anxiously unconscious thoughts and emotions about death into conscious awareness, there to be sustained and befriended rather than denied and repressed. This is no easy matter and given the parameters of human psychology outlined earlier in this chapter, it may not even be possible on a permanent basis. It would require ongoing attention and cultivation, taking on the character of a lifestyle quest rather than a once-for-all achievement.

As this last sentence implies, ongoing cultivation of conscious death awareness does take on the contours of a religious commitment, and it is not surprising that we find in our great religious and spiritual traditions, and traditions of contemplative philosophy, a pool of techniques and advice for doing so. The core of our many great religious and spiritual traditions has been formed by the human confrontation with death and mortality.[20] Although it is true that the largely cultural function of religion has been to bless, sanctify, and provide the transcending symbols for society's ongoing battle to deny human mortality, it is also true that this describes only one side of the religious coin. There is another side of all major religions pushing us toward acknowledgment and acceptance of our mortal condition, and it is on this side that the trove we seek may be found.[21] Following are some of the better-known examples found across the manifold religious traditions and spiritual practices of our species that have been employed in counseling for anxiety and end-of-life care with at least some success.

MEDITATION

Meditation is a broad category including a variety of practices drawn from many religious and spiritual traditions. What each of these practices has in common, however, is the goal of what is often referred to as quieting the mind. The thought process works by interjecting an inner voice into our ongoing experience that acts as an "interpreter" of that experience.[22] This inner voice gives expression to the many worries, concerns, and anxieties that are contained in a person's life experience. Meditation techniques have emerged as avenues for noticing that voice and allowing it to speak, but to increasingly distance oneself from the immediacy of the voice. For example, one may be encouraged to understand this inner voice as giving expression to the "little" self, while cultivating a larger sense of a "true" self that chooses to accept or reject the immediate promptings of the voice to be anxious, fearful, or agitated. Practitioners have noticed that the inner voice tends to dwell constantly on past events, usually characterized by negative experiences, and can be preoccupied with warnings about the present and future. This is exactly what would be predicted by TMT to be the general content of the mind of a self-aware but mortal species. Though necessary for survival, these anxious, fearful, and angry thoughts do not actually provide protection from mortality, and such primitive defenses interfere fundamentally with accommodating to our mortal condition. Practitioners report that meditation is a key technique in the process of quieting the mind and creating a space of respite from the mind's chatter.

The longest standing and most thoroughly researched clinical program of meditation is that of Herbert Benson and his colleagues at Harvard Medical School and the Benson Henry Institute at Massachusetts General Hospital.[23] Characterized as the relaxation response, this approach stemmed directly from experimentation in applying techniques of Transcendental Meditation (TM) to clinical practice. Benson and others quickly demonstrated and documented the benefits of meditation to alleviate diverse problems such as high blood pressure and other circulatory problems, chronic pain, and stress reduction. Subsequent research and experience have proven that the same response can be elicited from many different approaches to meditative practice beyond TM. Significantly, on the Benson Henry Institute website (massgeneral.org/bhi), Benson specifically states that this research demonstrates that meditation circumvents the fight/flight stress response, which is the predominant response TMT research suggests is elicited in the mortality salient condition.[24]

GUIDED VISUALIZATION

Guided visualization, also called guided imagery, intends to harness the imagination in the process of stress reduction and anxiety reduction. Although examples are found across cultures, much of the contemporary use of guided imagery emerged as an attempt to bring the wisdom associated with Native Americans, for example, vision quest ceremonies, into the practice of psychotherapy. In sessions of guided visualization, practitioners are invited to listen quietly to sounds and stories and are encouraged to imagine themselves entering into the images these sounds and stories create in the mind. Although the mind tends to think in words, it is reasonable to assume that imagery precedes even use of language.[25]

Whereas meditation is generally a solitary practice, guided visualization assumes the presence of a leader, a guide, to give direction to the imagery of the session. However, through recordings and other such technology, guided visualization has become an individual practice as well. Use of guided visualization is widespread in psychotherapeutic practices, and is also advocated by specialists in grief counseling and end-of-life care.[26] In reaction to uses of various forms of guided visualization in once-popular and highly controversial repressed memory therapy, much of the empirical research literature emphasizes that its therapeutic value should be treated with extreme caution and even downright skepticism.[27] But its positive benefits in areas of stress reduction are also being noted and this is most relevant to end-of-life care and counseling.[28]

CONTEMPLATIVE PRAYER

Contemplative prayer is a practice most closely associated with the Christian tradition, although many religions contain similar practices by other names.[29] Contemplative prayer has been taught for centuries in various monastic traditions, and interest in this practice was boosted considerably in contemporary society by Christian monks and priests, such as Thomas Merton and Matthew Fox, whose writings, retreats, and workshops focused on contemplative prayer have created wide attention for the contemplative style of life.[30]

Contemplative prayer is usually defined as prayer focused exclusively on the Being of God as the object of prayer, and progressively assuming an open, passive, and nondefensive stance toward the object of prayer. It might be thought of as the exact opposite of petitionary prayer, the common type of public prayer in which the focus in on making requests to the prayer object. Practitioners of contemplative prayer report that experientially it is much like meditation. One experiences how difficult it is to silence the mind and focus attention exclusively on the object of prayer.[31] Quickly the anxieties, fearfulness, and agitation of the mind interfere to keep attention focused on past events and current or future concerns. As the contemplative process continues, practitioners report that entering the state of the quieted mind becomes easier, and eventually in the contemplation of God a "true" self emerges that is experienced as more authentic than the chattering mind that precedes it.[32]

MINDFULNESS

The concept of mindfulness is associated most closely with traditions of Buddhist practice and in Buddhist teaching; it is one of the pillars of the Eightfold Path to enlightenment. Mindfulness has come into the realm of therapeutic practice through therapists who were explicit about their own involvement in exploring Buddhist meditation techniques.[33] Although mindfulness in psychotherapy is defined in a number of ways, all converge on the basic concepts of heightened awareness of self and surroundings, and learning to encounter self and surroundings in an attitude of phenomenological acceptance.

The practice of mindfulness seeks to notice both the positive and negative elements of living as they are encountered, to acknowledge the existence of these elements, and to accept these elements for what they are in a nonjudgmental attitude. Clearly, there is significant overlap between mindfulness and meditation, and visualization and contemplative prayer. It would be fair to suggest, however, that mindfulness is distinguished from the other practices in that it is understood more as a state of living rather than as any particular technique. Meditation and other techniques may contribute to achieving a mindful attitude in living, but mindfulness is an achievement in itself, and is not defined by the particular techniques employed to foster it.

RITUAL PARTICIPATION

Rituals are part of all religions, and many people have rituals for infusing daily life with transcendence, such as saying the Catholic Rosary or daily prayer cycles associated with meals or other routine activities. Religious rituals are not arbitrary behaviors, but develop in the context of intellectual, social, or personal sites of anxiety.[34] Religious rituals flood the brain with calming memories while at the same time directing thoughts to transcendent sources of identity and significance. They carry the individual through moments of difficulty, providing a point of orientation that integrates difficult circumstances and can reduce stress.

Integrating religious rituals into human experience paradoxically raises awareness of the stressors even while reducing the associated stress. Since religious rituals often include symbolic references to death, such practices typically present death-related thoughts and conditions, as, for example, a funeral, with a stress-calming source of transcendent meaning. Encouraging ritual participation during times of high stress may contribute to a reduction in stress and a corresponding increase in the ability to focus on appropriate strategies for coping with trauma. This is highly speculative and not yet supported by research, but suggests another avenue by which religious and spiritual techniques may contribute to effective practice.

CONCLUSION

Until very recently, techniques such as those outlined here have been outside of the professional therapeutic mainstream. This is changing, although older suspicions remain.[35] Clearly a larger accumulation of empirical research will need to be amassed on the clinical effects of such approaches before they will gain full acceptance in the practice of clinical care. Several obstacles to this continue. One of the most important of these is simply the problem of definition. If clinical effects are to be measured empirically, more attention needs to be given by therapeutic practitioners to clear definitions of what they are doing. All of these practices originate in spiritual and religious traditions, and need yet to be translated into the functional language of behavior science if the goal of clinical verification is going to be met. Although advocates of such practices are generally friendly and cooperative, and understand the need to translate their work into functional terms, this accepting attitude is by no means universal. Practitioners of contemplative prayer have been particularly resistant to viewing their practice in purely functional terms.[36]

While there are acknowledged barriers of a mainstream embrace of the alternative approaches outlined above and based on the model of brain/mind functioning emerging from the field of cognitive neuroscience, growing evidence supports the contention that increased employment of such techniques is particularly relevant in counseling for end-of-life care and decision making.

NOTES

1. Violete Besirevic, "End-of-Life Care in the 21st Century: Advance Directives in Universal Rights Discourse," *Bioethics* 24 (2010): 105–12.

2. David Pizarro, "Nothing More Than Feelings? The Role of Emotions in Moral Judgment," *Journal for the Theory of Social Behavior* 30 (2000): 355–75.

3. Charles Nelson, Michelle de Haan, and Kathleen Thomas. *Neuroscience of Cognitive Development: The Role of Experience and the Developing Brain* (New York: John Wiley and Sons, 2006).

4. Barbara Ehrenreich, *Blood Rites: Origins and History of the Passions of War* (New York: Henry Holt, 2007).

5. Walter Sinnott-Armstrong, ed., *Moral Psychology*, 3 Volumes (Cambridge, MA: MIT Press, 2008).

6. Daniel Kahneman, *Thinking, Fast and Slow* (New York: Farrar, Straus and Giroux, 2011).

7. Gerd Gigerenzer, "Moral Intuition=Fast and Frugal Heuristics?" in *Moral Psychology*, Vol. 2, *The Cognitive Science of Morality: Intuition and Diversity*, ed. W. Sinnott-Armstrong (Cambridge, MA: MIT Press, 2008), 1–15.

8. Nicki Marquardt, "Implicit Mental Processes in Ethical Management Behavior," *Ethics & Behavior* 20 (2010): 128–48.

9. Antonio Damasio, *Descartes' Error: Emotion, Reason and the Human Brain* (New York: Putnam, 1994); *The Feeling of What Happens: Body and Emotion in the Making of Consciousness* (New York: Harcourt Brace, 1999).

10. William James, *The Varieties of Religious Experience: A Study in Human Nature* (New York: Longmans, Green & Co., 1902).

11. Joseph Ledoux, *The Emotional Brain: The Mysterious Underpinnings of Emotional Life* (New York: Simon and Schuster, 1996).

12. An interesting correlate to this view is found in Robert K. Adair's *The Physics of Baseball* (San Francisco: HarperCollins Perennial, 2002), in which he demonstrates that, given the speed at which current major league pitchers throw and the speed at which the central nervous system executes conscious decisions in action, the "decision" by a batter to swing or take a pitch has to be made even before the ball has fully left the pitcher's hand; thus any reasons a batter would give for his "decision" in any particular instance would be clearly a *post hoc* rationalization.

13. Ernest Becker, *The Denial of Death* (New York: Free Press, 1974).

14. Peter L. Berger and Thomas Luckmann, *The Social Construction of Reality: A Treatise in the Sociology of Knowledge* (New York: Doubleday, 1966).

15. Peter L. Berger, *The Sacred Canopy: Elements of a Sociological Theory of Religion* (New York: Doubleday, 1967).

16. Sheldon Solomon, Jeff Greenberg, and Tom Pyszczynski, "Tales from the Crypt: On the Role of Death in Life," *Zygon: The Journal of Religion & Science* 33 (1998):

9–44. Jeff Greenberg, Tom Pyszczynski, and Sheldon Solomon, "A Perilous Leap From Becker's Theorizing to Empirical Science," in *Death and Denial: Interdisciplinary Perspectives on the Legacy of Ernest Becker,* ed. Daniel Liechty (Westport, CT: Praeger Publishing, 2002), 3–16. Tom Pyszczynski, Sheldon Solomon, and Jeff Greenberg, *In the Wake of 9/11: The Psychology of Terror* (Washington, DC: American Psychological Association, 2003).

17. John J. McGraw, *Brain and Belief: An Exploration of the Human Soul* (Del Mar, CA: Aegis Press, 2004). Andrew Newberg and Eugene D'Aquila, eds., *Why God Won't Go Away* (New York: Ballantine Books, 2001). Andrew Newberg and Mark Robert Waldman, *Born to Believe* (New York: Free Press, 2007); *How God Changes Your Brain: Breakthrough Findings from a Leading Neuroscientist* (New York: Ballantine Books, 2010). James B. Ashbrook and Carol R. Albright, *The Humanizing Brain* (Cleveland: Pilgrim Press, 2003).

18. A periodically updated bibliography of TMT-related publications is maintained by Prof. J. Arndt at http://www.tmt.missouri.edu/publications.html

19. Jamie Arndt, Jeff Greenberg, Sheldon Solomon, Tom Pyszczynski, and Linda Simon, "Suppression, Accessibility of Death-Related Thoughts, and Cultural Worldview Defense," *Journal of Personality and Social Psychology* 73 (1997): 5–18. Jeff Greenberg, Tom Pyszczynski, Sheldon Solomon, Linda Simon, and Michael Breus, "The Role of Consciousness and Accessibility of Death-Related Thoughts on Mortality Salience Effects," *Journal of Personality and Social Psychology* 67 (1994): 627–37.

20. Kenneth Kramer, *The Sacred Art of Dying: How the World Religions Understand Death* (Mahwah, NJ: Paulist Press, 1988).

21. Richard Beck, "Defensive Versus Existential Religion: Is Religious Defensiveness Predictive of Worldview Defense?" *Journal of Psychology & Theology* 34 (2006): 143–53. Michael Friedman, "Religious Fundamentalism and Responses to Mortality Salience: A Quantitative Text Analysis," *International Journal for the Psychology of Religion* 18 (2008): 216–37. Kenneth Vail, Zachary Rothschild, David Weise, Sheldon Solomon, Tom Pyszczynski, and Jeff Greenberg, "A Terror Management Analysis of the Psychological Functions of Religion," *Personality and Social Psychology Review* 14 (2010): 84–94.

22. Michael Gazzaniga, *Nature's Mind: Biological Roots of Thinking, Emotions, Sexuality, Language, and Intelligence* (New York: Basic Books, 1994). Michael Gazzaniga, Richard Ivry, and George Mangun, *Cognitive Neuroscience: The Biology of the Mind* (New York: W. W. Norton, 2009).

23. Herbert Benson and Miriam Klipper, *The Relaxation Response* (New York: Wm. Morrow/HarperCollins, 2000; original 1975).

24. Tom Pyszczynski, Jeff Greenberg, and Sheldon Solomon, S., "A Dual-Process Model of Defense against Conscious and Unconscious Death-Related Thoughts: An Extension of Terror Management Theory," *Psychological Review* 106 (1999): 835–45.

25. Temple Grandin, *Thinking In Pictures: And Other Reports from My Life with Autism* (New York: Doubleday/Vintage, 2010). Temple Grandin and Catherine Johnson, *Animals in Translation: Using the Mysteries of Autism to Decode Animal Behavior* (New York: Scribner, 2005).

26. Sandra Salka, "Enlisting the Unconscious as an Ally in Grief Therapy: The Creative Use of Affirmations, Metaphors, and Guided Visualization," *Hospice Journal* 12 (1997): 17–31.

27. John R. Paddock, "Guided Visualization and Suggestibility: The Effect of Perceived Authority on Recall of Autobiographical Memories," *Journal of Genetic Psychology* 162 (2001): 347–56. John R. Paddock and Mark Noel, "Imagination Inflation and the Perils of Guided Visualization," Journal of Psychology 133 (1999): 581–95.

28. Michel Bedard and Melissa Felteau, "Pilot Evaluation of a Mindfulness-Based Intervention to Improve Quality of Life among Individuals Who Sustained Traumatic Brain Injuries," *Disability and Rehabilitation: An International, Multidisciplinary Journal* 25 (2003): 722–31.

29. For works by Thomas Merton, see Kathleen Deignan, *A Book of Hours* (Notre Dame, IN: Sorin Books, 2007) and Kathleen Deignan, *A Book of Hours: At Prayer with Thomas Merton* (Schola Ministries 2009, Audio CD set); Merton's own voluminous but scattered writings on the contemplative lifestyle have now been collected and edited by Christine M. Bochen, *Thomas Merton: Essential Writings* (Maryknoll, NY: Orbis Books, 2000). On Matthew Fox, see the website www.matthewfox.org

30. John R. Finney and H. Newton Maloney, "An Empirical Study of Contemplative Prayer as an Adjunct to Psychotherapy," *Journal of Psychology and Theology* 13 (1985): 284–90.

31. Peter Madsen Gubi, *Prayer in Counseling and Psychotherapy: Exploring a Hidden Meaningful Dimension* (Philadelphia: Jessica Kingsley Publishers, 2007).

32. Thomas G. Plante, *Contemplative Practices in Action: Spirituality, Meditation and Health* (Santa Barbara, CA: ABC-CLIO/Praeger, 2010).

33. Jon Kabat-Zinn, *Wherever You Go, There You Are: Mindfulness Meditation* (New York: Hyperion, 1994). Jon Kabat-Zinn, *Full Catastrophe Living: Using the Wisdom of Your Body and Mind to Face Stress, Pain and Illness* (New York: Bantam Dell, 2010).

34. Pascal Boyer and Pierre Lienard, "Why Ritualized Behavior? Precaution Systems and Action Parsing in Developmental, Pathological and Cultural Rituals," *Behavioral and Brain Sciences* 29 (2006): 595–650. Pierre Lienard and E. Thomas Lawson, "Evoked Culture, Ritualization and Religious Rituals," *Religion* 38 (2008): 157–71.

35. Barry Boyce, *The Mindfulness Revolution: Leading Scientists, Psychologists, Artists and Meditation Teachers on the Power of Mindfulness in Daily Life* (Boston: Shambala, 2011).

36. Jeff Astley and Leslie Francis, *Psychological perspectives on prayer* (Leominster, UK: Gracewing Publishing, 2001). Philip Zaleski and Carol Zaleski, *Prayer: A History* (New York: Houghton Mifflin, 2005).

Chapter 5

Prognosis, Costs, and End-of-Life Care[*]

Daniel Callahan

*H*ere *we consider the current state of American health care by looking at three different, often clashing "streams"—or aspects—of end-of-life care in order to shed light on them and to also propose ways of improving as well as integrating them for the future of health care in this country. The three streams are the following: end-of-life costs; how to make end-of-life clinical care as peaceful as possible; and how to effectively manage the care and treatment of chronically ill patients who are likely to die—but not in the near future. How much better off are we today when we frequently linger on the brink of death for years, and in this condition, become not only the beneficiaries but also the possible victims of expensive advances in medical technology, research, and treatment? In seeking answers to how to bring together these frequently disparate end-of-life care streams, I conclude by citing a recent personal experience with loss, although not that of a human being, but rather, that of my family's beloved dog Sunny. The example of Sunny's death offers some painful and yet potentially revealing and*

* This chapter makes use of large selections from two previous papers, with permission granted by both to reprint it. They are: Daniel Callahan, "The New Frontier: Prognosis and End-of-Life Care," *Journal of Health & Biomedical Law* (2012) VIII (1): 1–7; and "The Death of a Pet: A Glimpse into the Human Future," *Bioethics Forum,* April 25, 2012.

valuable insight into what the future holds for health care in terms of the thorny questions and streams discussed herewith, particularly about cost and decision making.

To use a metaphor, the confluence of three special streams in health care encapsulates much that is a major problem in American health care. Each is a strong stream in itself but, when they come together they are full of fury and confusion, both clashing and blending. One of them is the high cost of patients at the end of life, consuming a disproportionate share of overall national health care spending. Another is that of clinical care at life's end, a decades old search for ways to make death more peaceful, less vexed by assorted cultural forces that seem designed to work against it. Still another is the effective management of chronically ill patients with multi-organ failure, many likely to die but not certainly in the near future.

By and large, though these three streams converge, they are typically (to overgeneralize) dealt with in different ways by different kinds of skills and expertise. The costs of patients at the end of life are a major concern of health care economists and policy analysts. The quality of life at the end is heavily in the hands of palliative care and hospice experts. The efficiency of care of those with multi-organ failure is of particular concern to cost- and quality-effectiveness experts as well as those concerned with the effective coordination of care by teams of physicians.

My aim in this chapter is to look at each of the three streams, summarizing briefly what is known about each of them but also to propose ways of improving each of them, hoping to show in particular how they can be better integrated—managing some of the fury of their convergence in a more orderly way. I will end with a description of what was, for me, a vision of a fine blending of the streams—in the care of a pet, not a human.

THE COST OF CARE OF THE CHRONICALLY ILL

Few figures in American health care are more striking than the cost of care of the chronically ill. A recent study by the Agency for Health care Research and Quality found that "[i]n 2008, 1 percent of the population accounted for 20.2 percent of total health care expenditures, and in 2009, the top 1 percent accounted for 21.8 percent . . . with an annual mean expenditure of $90,061. The lower 50 percent of the population ranked by their expenditures accounted for only 3.1 percent and 2.9 percent of the total for 2008 and 2009 respectively."[1] Moreover, "while the elderly represented 13.2 percent of the overall population, they represented 42.9 percent of those individuals who remained in the top decile of spenders."

Many if not most of those patients are critically ill but not necessarily dying when they come to need hospital care. They fall into what I call the gray zone. If costs are to be better controlled as well as the quality of end-of-life care, then we must begin that effort before it becomes clear that a seriously ill patient is obviously dying. The aim of that examination would be to push the end-of-life discussion back into the chronic illness context in order to find ways of stopping aggressive life-sustaining treatment earlier for individual patients, thus leading to better deaths, but no less helping to reduce the costs of care of the chronically ill. One important result of expanding that new frontier would be that more chronically ill patients would die earlier than is presently the case, a benefit for them and for the economics of health care.

But are we not already making great progress in end-of-life care? Over a million people a year are dying in hospice programs, a trend that continues to rise, as do the number of those who have living wills and/or an appointed surrogate (about 25%). But it has been well recognized for years that a large percentage goes into hospice care much later than they should. While there has been some progress in recent years, from a national average of 12.4 to 18.3 days in hospice, there is also enormous (and inexplicable) variation in different parts of the country (6.1 for Elmira, New York and 35.2 for Lubbock, Texas).[2] Moreover, patients seeing 10 or more doctors during the last six months of life increased between 2003 and 2007, reflecting the complications of multi-organ failure from chronic disease (underscoring the need for better coordination among the physicians). Even if the costs of their dying (once that has been determined) can be reduced, it does not mean inexpensive care prior to that last phase. On the contrary, the odds are good that costly care was provided. It is exactly that combination of care prior to the dying phase and during it that is heavily responsible for the disproportionate costs of those patients.

We now have a fairly good picture why the costs of those critically ill with chronic disease are so expensive. They include a tradition in medicine of all-out treatment of the critically ill with medical technologies, considerable difficulty in discerning the line between living and dying (a function of the capacity of technologies to almost always make possible further life-sustaining treatment), hesitation on the part of physicians and patients to face up to the coming of death, and a strong and an enduring tradition of hope inspired by physicians and desired by patients. On the latter point, an important study by Allan S. Detsky found that "even if patients are in a health state for which cure is exceedingly unlikely, they want to have hope and be offered options that might help ... as well, patients and their families feel guilty if they do not try to get better."[3] In sum, almost everything in the culture of medicine, and imbibed by patients, pushes toward more, not fewer, curative life-sustaining efforts.

A large proportion of people, it seems, act (even if they had said otherwise earlier) as if it is better to be treated for too long a time than too short a time. And that is probably why, after all these years working to improve end-of-life care, sad stories about poor deaths are readily at hand. Atul Gawande noted a conversation with a critical care physician, who said "I'm running a warehouse for the dying." Out of some 10 patients, only two were likely to leave the hospital for any length of time.[4] Why, one must ask, were they even in an ICU, and were they given a chance to discuss their prognosis before being admitted?

MANAGEMENT AND COST REFORMS

I don't want to leave the impression that little is being done to better manage the chronically ill in the gray zone. On the contrary, the cost and complexity of that kind of care is now recognized. Three efforts are worth a brief mention. The first is the need for better coordination of care, finding ways to meld into an integrated system the variety of specialists who can be called upon to treat patients with multi-organ failure. Just who is in charge, many have asked over the years and a common answer was: no one. Efforts to remedy that situation are being pursued.

A second reform theme has been the need for much better evidence on quality- and cost-effective treatments. Ironically and perhaps oddly, while there have been many efforts in recent years to make use of technology assessment data, they have for the most part focused on technologies and treatments where just one procedure has been analyzed to treat one specific condition: the value of a particular drug for cancer, or a particular screening procedure for a particular disease (e.g., mammography for breast cancer). But combinations of procedures for dealing with the simultaneous failure of more than one organ are in short supply—if for no other reason than the complexity of carrying out such research. A protocol to carry out a research project involving simultaneous treatment of three potentially lethal conditions of three organs would be difficult to conceptualize and carry out. Nonetheless, efforts are being made to find out how to do that kind of thing.

A third stream of reform has been efforts to bundle payments for the varied costs of chronic illness or to deal with them by means of capitated payments. The traditional fee-for-service method is a particularly expensive way of treating chronic illness and multi-organ failure, rewarding the use of technology with little restraint on its costs. Bundling and capitation are ways of moving beyond that expensive tradition.

A RETURN TO PROGNOSIS

A 2012 study reported in *The Journal of the American Medical Association* (*JAMA*), by Dr. Lindsey C. Yourman et al., "Prognostic Indices for Older Adults: A Systematic Review," directly addressed itself to gray zone questions of that kind. "Failure to consider prognosis in the context of clinical decision making can lead to poor care . . . guidelines increasingly incorporate life expectancy as a central factor in weighing the benefits and burdens of tests and treatments."[5] Their own study, its authors reported, reviewed a large number of such studies, aiming to "assess the quality and limitations of prognostic indices for mortality in older adults through systematic review." They identified "some 16 validated non-disease specific indices," but immediately noted their limitations, concluding that "there is insufficient evidence at this time to recommend the widespread use of prognostic indices in clinical practice."[6] They note, however, that clinical decision making is most likely to be most influenced by a "very high or very low mortality risk . . . [and that] midrange probabilities may still be useful in clinical decisions in which life expectancy plays a role, allowing patient preferences to drive the physician's recommendation."[7]

A number of commentators responded with some skepticism, picking up on the limitations noted by the authors of the study. One comment said that physicians already rely too heavily on technological tests and strategies to deal with sick patients, opting for improved overall care of the terminally ill.[8] Others thought the indices could be useful for hospital patients or elderly patients in nursing homes or at home.[9] A website, designed by the authors of the *JAMA* article, eprognosis.org, drew a wary response, partly because the public could access it, but also out of a suspicion that patients may not be much helped or may not know how to apply the data to their own lives.[10]

My own reaction was to immediately recall the health reform debate about comparative effectiveness research that became part of the final ACA (Affordable Care Act) legislation, and the 2009 argument that ensued when the United States Public Health Service Task Force determined that mammography for women under the age of 50 should no longer be routinely prescribed. In both cases, a major line of criticism was that general probability data, often mockingly called "one size fits all," should be rejected. Physical variability, on the one hand, and psychological variability, on the other, militates against an uncritical use of such data. Even to have a solid probability that a sick patient has an 80 percent prognosis of death within a short time is no sure predictor of how his family and he, himself, will want to be treated or should be treated. A 10–20 percent possibility of survival will seem well worth the struggle to stay alive for some. It is axiomatic in my field of ethics that an "ought" cannot be derived from an "is"; that is, data on life expectancy does not entail how that life ought to be treated. Of course one might reply that if a patient has a 1 percent likelihood of survival at the cost of a miserable death, that would not be a wise choice. But for some patients 1 percent is better than 0 percent.

The combination of statistical uncertainty and the problem of what to do with solid prognostic data, even when one has it, serves to underscore the importance of the doctor-patient relationship. Just about the time the *JAMA* article came out, quite coincidentally some other articles appeared about the importance of sick patients discussing with their physician their prognosis. One article in *The New England Journal of Medicine* (*NEJM*), by Dr. Alexander

K. Smith et al., contended that "[t]o improve the quality of decision making for the very old, we believe we should radically alter the paradigm of clinician-patient communication: offering to discuss overall prognosis with very elderly patients should be the norm, not the exception . . . we would suggest that clinicians should routinely offer to discuss the overall prognosis for elderly patients with a life expectancy of less than 10 years, or at least by the time a patient reaches 85 years of age [in light of the fact that] the average life expectancy in the United States is six years."[11]

Another physician, Dr. S. R. Workman of Halifax, Nova Scotia, wrote that "asking permission to talk about prognosis can facilitate discussion while respecting patient autonomy."[12] In an interview Dr. Workman said that physicians should avoid circumlocutions and evasions, saying instead to a patient: "We're not winning. The treatment's not working. She's dying despite our best efforts."[13]

Neither article displays the kind of skepticism about the use of prognosis data found in response to the *JAMA* article, much less the reservations conceded by the authors of that article themselves. In fact, the *NEJM* article suggests a kind of middle ground: "to explain the patient's overall prognosis, the physician might say 'people in their mid-80s with health similar to yours live about 6 more years, on average. Some people live more than 6 years, others less.' In this way the physician would acknowledge uncertainty. He could then assess how the patient received and processed this information."[14] But that six-year figure does not, it appears, derive from prognosis studies about the course of a particular illness; it is a figure that applies to all persons in their mid-80s. If that is correct, then it might seem that the physician has not told the patient with any kind of precision the actual prognosis.

Clearly, Dr. Yourmans et al. seem to believe that much better prognosis data is necessary in order for it to be used effectively with large numbers of patients with different medical conditions in a reliable and fully useful way. Dr. Smith et al. appear willing to settle for far less specificity. Patient surveys, they note, show that they are open to talking about prognosis, and they conclude their article by saying that "we believe we should start talking about overall prognosis now, even as we carry out more research on patient preferences and ways of improving such discussions."[15] Not mentioned at all is the need for more and better prognosis data, something that Dr. Workman does not deal with either. Let me call this the informal way of using data.

Three questions emerge. Is the informal way of using prognosis data sufficient to inform a patient with enough information to make a meaningful choice and should a physician be willing to use such data? If research on prognosis continues, as it should, what level of specificity will be necessary to give a patient and his doctor enough information to act responsibly? And to further complicate matters how can such research be kept up to date in the face of new treatments or improved old treatments, shifting the prognosis? Comparative effectiveness research, if it is any good, could constantly change the prognosis-effective treatment equation.

I can offer no good answers to those questions. They can only be answered with more research, with the informal physician probably demanding less than the severe. Once again, then, we have a common enough situation these days: we need more good research and data to act responsibly, and that will take much time, perhaps years to be forthcoming—and we can't wait. In the meantime, the advice of the *NEJM* authors will probably be the best we have for the short run. Moreover, in light of the high costs of critical care for chronic illness and the possibility of increased costs in the years ahead, I would opt for the informal method, adding that those so inclined should at least look at the more specific data now available for some patients with some maladies. Whichever way one goes, the physician should openly and candidly inform the patient and family just what the criteria for presenting information to patients are. Uncertainty will always be part of the process, however good the data—if only because patient and doctors can respond differently to the same information. It has ever been so with medicine.

THE DEATH OF A PET: A GLIMPSE INTO THE HUMAN FUTURE

I recently had a painful but revealing insight into what the future might look like on both costs and decision making. It came about from an unexpected angle of vision, the care provided by a veterinarian in an emergency care center for pets.

Our much loved dog, Sunny, a six-year-old female Cavalier King Charles, otherwise in good health, began throwing up, ignoring her food, and displaying untoward lassitude. The symptoms got worse within a few days and we took her to a neighboring pet hospital, one that advertises a range of available technologies and treatments equal to that found in a hospital for humans.

We took her in the morning, left her there, and in the late afternoon were told that she had kidney failure, was unable to pass urine, and had other serious symptoms. The prognosis was not good, but it would take another day or so to see what difference treatment might make. She gradually went downhill the second day, a catheter failing to bring forth much urine, and with increased signs of distress.

At the end of that first day, we were given a detailed set of cost projections. We were required to put up, via credit card, $2,600 as part of an estimated cost of $5,000 or so for two days of intensive care—a treatment plan which could come to $9,000 if it went on for over three days. I had read about the high cost of upscale veterinarian care, but it had never occurred to us that we would have to face it. Yet if the projected costs were jolting, something else was no less arresting: the time and care the chief veterinarian in charge of Sunny's care took to explain exactly what was going on with her, what they were doing, what the prognosis was—and how rapidly the costs would continue to rise if Sunny survived. She was equally frank about the fact that Sunny was not likely to make it, but also what it would cost us if she did. The veterinarian told us in a way that beautifully integrated money, medical candor, and compassion. It was, I thought as she was doing so, just what we might hope for from a human doctor for our care, but by no means yet reliably available.

We agreed at the end of the second day that we would see how Sunny did overnight. If there was no improvement, we decided it would be best to put her to sleep (I don't believe her doctor ever used the phrase "put her down"). She did not improve, required oxygen during the night, and passed little urine. Sunny's doctor called us early the next morning to report the bad news, and I told them to stop. It was both a hard and an easy decision. Emotionally it was hard to say stop, but easy because it seemed the only reasonable decision, and the doctor readily assented.

What will stay in my mind in addition to the pleasure Sunny brought us in her relatively short life—she was always at our side or in our laps—was that doctor's combination of sensitivity and telling the truth. The veterinarian practiced the art of prognosis of just the kind we need with humans. Patients and families need to have some sense of what the future will bring, even if it is uncertain. They need to know the likelihood of death and also what may ensue if a very sick patient survives: what then? Our veterinarian said that, if Sunny were lucky enough to make it, she would likely remain in poor health, requiring considerable future medical care. Our doctors often fail to tell patients and families about just that disturbing likelihood. Seeing it well done by our vet underscored its value, for our pets and for us.

But my most telling glimpse into the human future came with the introduction of cost as an upfront consideration, something I believe will soon become common in our health care, perhaps routine. That's what it will be like for us with our loved ones. For us, the $5,000 charge for Sunny's care was bearable, but the prospect of the cost of successful treatment, had that been possible, would surely have given us pause. I am sure we would have said at some point that financially enough is enough, but I am not certain just when that might have been. I am convinced, however, that the future will force us directly to deal with high, and in many cases, insupportable human costs of end-of-life care and to stop treatment for that reason. Sunny's quick decline spared us that decision, which was a blessing in a way.

I was left with some troubling thoughts. Would it have been better if veterinarian medicine had not moved into the high technology realm once reserved for humans? My wife and I both had dogs (and sometime cats) as we grew up. When they got sick they just died or were put down to save them from misery. I don't recall anyone thinking that state of affairs was an evil. Are we better off now that our pets have access to expensive, high technology medicine—and are they? And how much better off are we as humans because of the way we now often die, sometimes lingering on for years, the beneficiaries, and sometimes victims, of a medicine equal to what our pets can now have? For me, those questions were left hanging in the air.

NOTES

1. Stephen B. Cohen and William Yu, "The Concentration and Persistence in the Level of Health Expenditures Over Time: Estimates for the U.S. Population 2008–2009," *Medical Expenditure Panel Survey, Statistical Brief #354* (January 2012): 1.

2. David C. Goodman, Amos R. Esty, Elliott S. Fisher, and Chiang-Hua Chang, "Trends and Variations in End-of-Life Care for Medicare Beneficiaries with Severe Chronic Illness," The Dartmouth Institute For Health Policy and Clinical Practice, August 12, 2011.

3. Alan S. Detsky, "What Patients Really Want from Health Care," *Journal of the American Medical Association* 306, 22 (2011): 2500.

4. Atul Gawande, "Letting Go," *New Yorker*, August 2, 2010, http://www.newyorker.com/reporting/2010/08/02/100802fa_fact_gawande?currentPage=all

5. Lindsey C. Yourman, Sei J. Lee, Mara S. Schonberg, Eric W. Widera, and Alexander K. Smith, "Prognostic Indices for Older Adults," *Journal of the American Medical Association* 307, 2 (2012): 190.

6. Ibid.

7. Ibid.

8. Manny Alvarez, "Doctors Should Not Rely on Computers for End-of-Life Decisions," *Fox News,* January 11, 2012.

9. Paula Span, "Plain Speaking at the End of Life," *The New Old Age Blog. New York Times,* December 14, 2011, http://newoldage.blogs.nytimes.com/2011/12/14/plain-speaking-at-the-end-of-life

10. Carol Levine, "Beware the Ides of March 2.0," *Bioethics Forum (the Hastings Center Blog)*, January 18, 2012, http://www.thehastingscenter.org/Bioethicsforum/Post.aspx?id=5711&blogid=140

11. Alexander K. Smith et al., "Discussing Overall Prognosis with the Very Elderly," *The New England Journal of Medicine* 365 (2011): 2149.

12. S.R. Workman, "Never Say Die? As Treatments Fail Doctors' Words Must Not," *The International Journal of Clinical Practice* 65, 2 (2011): 117.

13. Span, "Plain Speaking at the End of Life."

14. Smith et al., "Discussing Overall Prognosis with the Very Elderly," 2151.

15. Ibid.

In All These Hotels

In all these hotels there is music, slightly romantic, slightly playing. Behind the sinks. Under the bar glasses. Piano trills. Memory music. Without name. Just the soft illusion of something that was. Or never was.

The sweetness of a spring afternoon in Pangrati stays. It doesn't change. The futon dragged into the sun. The air through the double doors. The jungle on the balcony. The coffee later.

All of it will last with the Karyatides. A story in marble. Time will not tear it. No matter the Mongol hordes, the German troops, the kids from the university with their spray paint. None of that will take down that memory. And when one body leaves it in the air above Mets, its ghost will whisper to another girl. And she, I think, will climb Aeropagus as the one beside her carries up the red wine.

Catherine Rogers

Section II

Speaking in a New Language

Chapter 6

Stories of the End: A Narrative Medicine Curriculum to Reframe Death and Dying

Marsha Hurst and Craig Irvine

*T*raining *of health care professionals reflects and reinforces the denial of death prevalent throughout much of American culture. As a result, clinicians are ill-equipped to face the challenges of caring, empathically and ethically, for the dying. In a course we have devised for Columbia University's Master's Program in Narrative Medicine, we address the need to shift attitudes and alter the discourse on death by bringing together clinicians from multiple health care professions with writers, artists, and thinkers from the humanities and natural and social sciences. Experiential as well as conceptual in content, our course nurtures those moral attitudes toward death and dying that reinforce, or, if need be, reinstate, the humanity in end-of-life care. We teach the narrative competencies required to attend fully, to represent accurately, and to affiliate completely with patients approaching the end of life. We counter the hidden curriculum, which is based on foundational narratives about death as the failure of medicine, about dying and caring as someone else's work, about compassion as emotional interference with science, with narratives that grant permission to talk about death in all its awe and all its raw humanness. This curriculum is a model of the kind of educational initiative necessary if we are to better accompany one another on the journey to the end in coming decades.*

Pauline Chen, in the introduction to her book, *Final Exam,* writes:

> Twenty years ago when I was applying to medical school, I believed I was
> going to save lives. Like the heroic doctors of my imagination, I would
> spend my days in triumphant face-offs with death and watch the parade
> of saved patients return to my office full of life, smiles, and back-slapping
> gratitude. What I did not count on was how much death would be a part
> of my work.[1]

"Preparing for death may be the most difficult exam of all," Chen goes on
to say, but it is an exam that every medical clinician must take. "Few of us," she
notes, "ever adequately learn how to care for patients at the end of life."[2] Physician and writer Larry Cripe echoes this concern. The "personally demanding measure of a physician's compassion," he writes, is "the capacity to remain
present throughout *the lived experience of suffering* regardless of whether or
not we can provide remedy."[3]

In their study of the hidden curriculum, Elizabeth Gaufberg and colleagues
argue that the distance between ideal and real physician capacity for care and
compassion at the end of life begins as a "misalignment" between ideals of
medical practice as taught in the formal curriculum of medical school and
realities of clinical experience and mentoring that form the basis of the hidden
curriculum.[4] To illustrate this misalignment, they offer the following from a
medical student narrative:

> I always thought my first time would be different. I took extra time
> through first and second year to hear about what it was like to have dying
> patients, going to seminars, hearing from professors, even researching
> music in palliative care. But when a 42-year-old man with terminal
> Gardner syndrome was admitted to my surgery team, I followed every-
> one's lead and avoided him.[5]

The messages of the hidden curriculum shape what Dutch physicians Gert
Olthius and Wim Dekkers call "moral enculturation" into the medical community.[6] Of course, the medical community is part of a larger health care community that includes many other professions: nursing, social work, dentistry,
public health, physical and occupation therapy, and clinical and hospital administration, to name a few. All of these professions practice their own forms
of moral enculturation, and while there are significant differences among
them, they share an orientation that reflects and reinforces the denial of death
about which Chen and many other health care practitioners have written so
movingly. Denial by the health care community, in turn, reflects and reinforces attitudes toward death prevalent throughout much of American culture. To change the care of the dying requires more than a tweaking of the way

medical students are trained: it requires a shift in attitudes and understanding of death on a broad, cultural scale. In a course we have devised for Columbia University's Master's Program in Narrative Medicine, we address this need to shift attitudes and alter the discourse on death by bringing together clinicians from multiple health care professions with writers, artists, and thinkers from the humanities and natural and social sciences. Experiential as well as conceptual in content, our narrative curriculum nurtures those moral attitudes toward death and dying that reinforce, or, if need be, reinstate, the humanity in end-of-life care. We believe this curriculum is a model of the kind of educational initiative necessary if we are to better accompany one another on the journey to the end in coming decades.

NARRATIVE MEDICINE

In narrative medicine we argue that the competencies required to practice humanely, to attend fully to the patient's suffering, to represent that experience to others through reflection and narration, and thus to affiliate completely with that patient can and should be taught explicitly like any other set of competencies. A hidden curriculum that is based on foundational narratives about death as the failure of medicine, about dying and caring as someone else's work, and about compassion as emotional interference with science can itself be confronted with narratives: stories that give us permission to talk about death in all its awe and all its raw humanness.

As one of the routes toward educating clinicians of the future, we teach a course on "Narratives of Death: Living and Caring at the End of Life" to students in the Narrative Medicine Master's Program at Columbia University. If you were to imagine an ideal learning environment, it might look very much like our seminar—15 to 18 students gathered around a seminar table: practicing clinicians (physicians, social workers, nurses, psychologists, physical therapists), health care administrators, recent college graduates, writers, humanities scholars, and miscellaneous others whose clinical experience has often been as a patient and/or caregiver. We as faculty members also bring to the class our different disciplines, philosophy (Craig) and political science (Marsha), and different work and life experiences.

The challenge and the value of this course lie not only in its content or in its interdisciplinary narrative approach, but in its particular mix of students involved in a pedagogy of the intensely engaged. Not surprisingly, students are destabilized by a course that challenges entrenched ideas regarding death. Our physician students sometimes seem defensive. They have seen more death but have been trained to strive toward certainty, toward a clear answer, or at least a clear question. Yet the ambiguity that is at the heart of a narrative of death and dying is not something to be clarified, but to uncover, peel open, and nurture. "I thought I at least knew what death was," said one nonphysician clinician in the middle of the semester, "but now I am not even sure of that."

Sometimes tensions rise. One older physician announced that "young people don't know anything about death," which upset and angered a young student whose boyfriend had recently died. The course challenges assumptions about authority or expertise. Each narrative has its own authority, its own truth. Moreover, none of our disciplines, including medicine, gives us authority over the other.

Narrative medicine opens students to the potential of patient and clinician stories as cocreations of each other. This is especially true in teaching about death, which in our culture, and particularly in medicine, is a taboo topic disguised as a medical event. Our narrative-based approach enables us to be thrown into turmoil in our thinking about death and dying, while staying anchored by the structure of story. Stories bring coherence to an experience, particularly when the experience involves suffering, sadness, trauma, and often chaos or confusion. Narrative in all its voices has form, and we can learn by deepening our skills of narrative understanding even as we appreciate the form and the external frame within which the story rests.

THE NARRATIVE ARC OF THE COURSE

We begin the semester with *The Death of Ivan Ilyich* by Leo Tolstoy,[7] asking students to examine the novella's narrative arc. The first thing students notice is that the story begins after Ivan has already died. In the ways Ivan's friends and relatives react to his death, the students form a sense of the meaning of Ivan's life *for others*. Our discussion of the first chapter explores the inappropriateness of death for the living—(we sometimes show a clip from Monty Python's *Meaning of Life* called Social Death, in which the Grim Reaper rudely interrupts a pastoral dinner[8])—and the strategies survivors employ to deny death's inevitability, including stories they tell to blame or exceptionalize the deceased. By the end of this chapter, we begin to wonder what Ivan's life and death meant to the man himself, how his perspective might differ from that of his friends and family, and what sort of life he lived and death he faced, such that his survivors could respond to his suffering and death with so little empathy.

The rest of the novella is a flashback through Ivan's life, beginning with his childhood and continuing through the very moment of his death. Since we already know Ivan is doomed, there is no mystery, no chance of what Arthur Frank would call a "restitution narrative."[9] We are not allowed to dwell on *whether* death occurs, but rather forced to focus on how living and dying might be related. Our students note that, by removing any doubt regarding Ivan's fate, Tolstoy forces us to engage with the dying man: we must enter into the agonies of his dying itself, including seeing his life through eyes that face death.

We ask students what they notice about the narrative voice, particularly with respect to perspective, over the course of the narration of Ivan's life. Students observe that the narration moves increasingly inward, closer and closer to Ivan's inner voice. We ask students what this increasing personalization conveys about the meaning of Ivan's life for Ivan himself. In answering this question, students note that, as the perspective moves inward, time in the story becomes increasingly dense: chapter two moves from Ivan's childhood through the 17th year of his marriage; the following nine chapters cover just a few years, narrating through Ivan's temporary setback at work, his renewed success, the first signs of his illness, his worsening ill health, and his impending death. Most of the last chapter is devoted to the final few moments of Ivan's life.

We ask the students to explore the meaning of this temporality. How does it help the reader enter Ivan's perspective? In other words, what is the relation between the story's temporal configuration and its movement inward? What does this temporal perspective reveal about the way Ivan experiences and narrates his own life, his approaching death? What might it reveal about how one lives time in the shadow of death? We find the philosopher Emmanuel Levinas helpful here: "The death agony is precisely in this impossibility of ceasing, in the ambiguity of a time that has run out and of a mysterious time that yet remains. . . . Dying is agony because in dying a being does not come to an end while coming to an end; he has no more time, that is, can no longer wend his way anywhere, but thus goes where one cannot go, suffocates—how much longer."[10] Near the end of his life, Tolstoy tells us, Ivan feels as if he's being thrust into a "black sack," unable to breathe.

In the course, we mirror the movement of Tolstoy's novella. Like Tolstoy, we begin with death and move, as Ivan does, into a world of living with the knowledge of death. We work on making the interdisciplinarity explicit, integral, not incidental to the work. Some of this is done through framing the week's work. Craig will begin a class by sharing a philosophical text that we can consider as a commentary, or Marsha will talk about the policy or history that contextualizes that week's topic. Each week one or more students post framing questions on a Wikispace where work and ideas, pictures and links, videos and media can be shared by everyone in the group. Some years we have a required rotation of question and response. In this way we move through our narrative arc: from death to dying to the dead body and then out again to caring for the dying and remembering the dead.

Our students begin to think about this narrative arc even as the class itself begins its own journey. Stepping back from the experiential journey of a dying man, we discuss the historical trajectory of death in Western civilization as presented by cultural historian Philippe Ariès. There is an historical journey, he argues, that includes the acceptance of a "tamed" death, an externalization of death and fear of mortality, and a desire for immortality.[11] Returning to a personal narrative, this time to the memoir of writer Paul Zweig, we attend to his exploration of approaching death, and his passage through periods of fear, longing for immortality, and then reluctant acceptance of his own mortality.[12] We invite students to contribute visual images of death and dying, using these as Ariès does to help us understand our cultural narrative tropes. Students wonder about "the scientism of modern death" as they look at symbols, images, and signs of a medicalized death and then learn how palliative care is an effort to change this narrative.

As we explore what it is like to live with the knowledge of our death, considerations of culture and history help students find a wider and deeper meaning in narratives. Cultural difference in the process of dying and construction of death enters the course not as a topic to be separated out from or barricaded within the narrative arc of the course, but as a thematic thread, one that comes out of our engagement with particular stories. *Ikuru,* Kurosawa's 1949 film about a Japanese bureaucrat who learns he has untreatable and incurable stomach cancer and sets out to find the meaning of life before he dies,[13] asks questions about life and death we first heard from Ivan Ilyich, a late-19th-century Russian magistrate, and will talk about again when we read *The Plague.*[14] Can one life have meaning, even within the meaninglessness of the larger world? How do we find that meaning in our lives, or how do we make it?

Attention to the text requires engagement not only with its frame and form, but also with its "voice," the language, and the feel of the experience. In this way we consider what meaning is made of life when we know we are dying. Many of our narratives tell a kind of quest story of the dying who seek meaning and closure at the end of life. Filmmaker Tom Joslin dies knowing that *Silverlake Life,* his documentary of his own dying, will engage others in the experience of living and dying with AIDS.[15] A century and a half earlier in New England, Deborah Vinal Fiske dies of consumption knowing her carefully crafted letters will be guidelines for her motherless daughters to live by.[16] Paul Zweig has a burst of creative productivity that accompanies his knowledge that he is nearing his death. In *Ikuru,* Mr. Watanabe dies on a swing in the park whose construction gave his life—and his dying—meaning; and while the intertextuality of Kurosawa's film and Tolstoy's novel is clear, Watanabe dies with a song, not a scream.

The stories we discuss raise societal as well as personal questions and our students struggle with integrating the two. Facing death, Socrates teaches his students that they must not fear death, but neither may they choose it, raising questions regarding the limits of self-determination.[17] We complicate these questions by viewing *The Sea Inside,* a Spanish film based on the life and death of Ramon Sampedro, a quadriplegic who sought help in ending his life.[18] This narrative requires us to deal with death as relational: Do we have a moral obligation to stay alive for those who love us? To help someone die because we love them? Questions of moral liability arise from individual stories and connect us to our own experiences of illness and death. As one student wrote,

[N]o one would hold me even partially responsible for my father's death because my attempts to stop his lifelong habit of smoking were feeble or because I sat with him, year after year, in diner after diner, laughing and talking with him as he enjoyed the eggs, bacon and cheeseburgers that would contribute to his death from a heart attack at age 69.

In the narrative arc of our course we move from facing death, to the state of death, to being a dead body. The physician in training may well encounter death first in the anatomy lab, facing a cadaver. The first of the "great paradoxes" Christine Montross encountered in medicine was "that you begin to learn to heal the living by dismantling the dead." Her "meditations on mortality from the human anatomy lab," as she subtitles *Body of Work,* reflect on the dead body that harbors "the great mysteries of creation and humanity."[19]

Montross's narrative evokes "meditations" from students who have felt that connection to another's dead body. A student who is herself an organ recipient is struck by how the Thai people call donated bodies *ajarn yai,* or a "great teacher." A physical therapist remembers dissecting a body in his training. "I just took it as a matter of course," he said, but now he thinks about that dead body on which he trained in relation to the living bodies of his patients. Future medical students reflected on ways various medical schools have tried to connect the anatomy lab experience with the reality of personhood, mulling over approaches that emphasized thanking the family for its gift versus those that focused on literally and figuratively putting a face on the cadaver.

We ask students to question the physiological fact of death. Here we turn to ethnographic studies of death and organ donation in Japan and in the United States, as well as American narratives of negotiating definitions of death as a contingency in organ donation. Close reading leads one student to consider how the language of the transplant industry speaks of the gray area connecting death with organ donation: "We move from 'harvesting' (as in a crop?) to 'procurement' (as in sexual services?) to . . . 'retrieve' (as in a bird dog?) and 'recover' (as in to get back what's owed?)." An experienced physician distances herself from her classmates: "Death is a dead body," she says. "I know it when I see it." The idea that death is a social or sociomedical construction challenges the authority of her experiential knowledge.

In a class with both physicians and nurses, we sometimes get quite different clinical lenses. During one discussion, a nurse with many years of experience responded to questions posed by an attorney, who tended toward the concrete. What we think of as death, the nurse said, may be "a time range during which they are dying as opposed to the legal determination of a moment on a death certificate." She recalled discussions with families that often alluded to a "soul's journey" having begun, though the soul was still "tethered on by a thin filament." These discussions, she noted, were often reassuring to the bereaved, although they would not meet medical or legal standards of "validity." "I have heard nurses apologize," she continued, "for clumsy transfer from gurney to morgue slab. The care for the newly dead is a transition that rarely achieves a complete objectification." We think of Montross, who recalled the shock she felt confronting the humanness, the femaleness, of painted toenails on a cadaver. Could the actuality of death not only be contingent, but also a process? All of us in the classroom reexamine our feelings about facing death in light of these ambiguities and about caring for others who face death.

In the last two parts of the course we talk about caring for the dying and remembering the dead. Perhaps because we began the course with *The Death of Ivan Ilyich,* we have the Gerasim model of caregiving in mind: Gerasim, the peasant who cares for Ivan Ilyich, does so simply because Ivan is a sick man.[20] Caring for another is a fact of human existence, one that Ivan Ilyich, like all of us, needs. But our narratives and our individual experiences tell us otherwise: however straightforward the motivation to give care, the realities are not at all akin to the simple act of providing support for the legs of the sick person.

Like *The Death of Ivan Ilyich, The Best Day, the Worst Day,* Donald Hall's book about his wife, the poet Jane Kenyon, begins with her death. The book then moves back in time, to a day of ordinary life—life before illness, before dying—to a "best" day:

> What we did: We got up early in the morning. I brought Jane coffee in bed. She walked the dog as I started writing, then climbed the stairs to work at her own desk . . . We had lunch. We lay down together. We rose and worked at secondary things. I read aloud to Jane; we played scoreless ping-pong; we read the mail; we worked again. We ate supper, talked, read books sitting across from each other in the living room, and went to sleep. If we were lucky the phone didn't ring all day.[21]

When Jane gets sick there are no ordinary days.

We have a rich and sometimes heated discussion about Donald Hall's caregiver memoir. Some in the class are disturbed at what feels to them to be a boundary that Hall has crossed, telling not only the story he owns about himself as caregiver, but Jane's story as well. Others, including female physicians, admire the loving bodily care Hall gives and the evenness his prose conveys as he manages increasingly rough and changing terrain. The next week, when an admirer of Hall characterizes as "whiney," the essays by female caregivers that we read, her classmates wonder whether we would ever apply this term to a male caregiver. Women are expected to assume the role of caregiver and to do so without complaint. This is an area where personal narrative and policy writing can and should be read together, and we take advantage of the opportunity to do so. Carol Levine, an expert on family caregiving policy and practice, has written about this intersection of gender and caregiving, of policy and personal experience, in her own life. "To my chagrin," she wrote, about facing a new life after her husband was disabled in an accident, she found herself "back in a world dominated by gender stereotypes." Nurses, doctors, social workers, and even friends and colleagues assumed she would give up her work and devote herself full time to caring, without complaint or support, for her husband. In this world, old paradigms reigned. She tells her story and advocates for change to open the eyes of professionals and policy makers: "I will not be a poster wife for caregiving."[22]

The narratives of caregivers also allow the students to connect more directly with death and dying as they experience it in their lives. In some classes, the separation between those with clinical medical experience and those without gives way to a separation between older and younger students. Although, perhaps not surprisingly in a narrative medicine program, even many of our younger students have themselves been, or been close to, family caregivers.

What of the clinician as caregiver? How does the doctor face death? *The Plague* by Camus offers us an opportunity to speak from our respective disciplines, placing the book in the context not only of Camus' existential philosophy, but also of his political choices and purposes. The book resonates in our modern era, suggesting both the late-20th-century HIV/AIDS epidemic and the metaphor of social and personal destruction by any oppressive regime. (The filmmaker Puenzo chose to set his version of *The Plague* in Argentina during the dirt wars of the 1970s.[23]) The book brings our discussion directly to the role and responsibility of the physician when a community faces catastrophe. Dr. Rieux, the students note, just does what he has to do. There is no greater meaning. There is no heroism. There is only persistence. The connection of one person to another in *The Plague* is most caring when no grand principles or beliefs are at play: no church, no state, simply individuals. Craig raises questions of physician self-care, particularly when confronted with death,[24] and a student notes that despite his exhaustion, the only way Rieux can carry on is to "tighten the stranglehold on his feelings and harden his heart protectively." Is professional distance necessary in order to cope with sustained exposure to illness and suffering, the student continued? Is it ethical?

We next move to narratives in which clinicians are also family caregivers. Students in the class who are clinicians often echo the frustrations of the narrators we read: many have faced the question geriatrician Jerald Winakur confronts in his narrative, "What am I going to do with Dad?"[25] One student gives voice to a common response to the stories of these physician caregivers: "medical professionalism," she contends, "can lead to a presence without attention." And, because attention is the most fundamental competence we teach in narrative medicine, the student suggests, if we learn to practice the tools of reflection and close reading, we will begin to apply the "moral power" of attention to our clinical work.

The course ends with a unit on grief, mourning, and memorializing. Grief narratives are intensely personal, yet the turmoil, the "derangement," as Joan Didion says in *The Year of Magical Thinking*,[26] are a "chaos narrative"[27] familiar to all who have grieved. The face of that grief, and particularly the public face, is shaped by social and cultural tropes. We explore this interaction in various ways, including through short stories that frame grief and mourning within a context of culture and class. We choose stories that are on the borderland, that sit uneasily between cultures or culture and class. In Jhumpa Lahiri's story, "A Temporary Matter,"[28] grief is indeed that place that "none of us know until we reach it."[29] Grief, in this story, has no readily available expression, no ritual, no closure. That the young couple are Indian Americans does not give them or us a way to process the loss that isolates each of them from the other. The particular restitution narrative we expect of death, grief, and mourning does not happen, and culture does not rescue them or us. They move on with their lives, but alone.

Near the end of the course, two threads come together: One relates to the physicality of caring for the dying and of the dead body itself; the other to moving away from death, moving on, through ritual and memorializing and, perhaps, narrating. We go back and forth, figuratively touching the body and moving away. We watch *Departures,* a Japanese film about ritually preparing the body for cremation, and read about other cultures that incorporate the dead body into rituals of transition.[30] Our students begin to talk about their distance from dead bodies, which are taboo. Bodies are embalmed, medicalized, objectified—and whisked away after death. What would it be like, students ask each other, if we all participated in embodied rituals of death? We ask everyone to bring in stories of their own cultural rituals of death; sharing these rituals, there is no division between physicians and other clinicians, clinicians and others.

Our course ends, fittingly, with a focus on memorializing and new media. We ask whether memorializing in cyberspace distances us ever further from death and from the bedside of the dying, or whether it actually enables us to remain closer to the dead through a virtual and timeless connection.

STUDENT WORK

As part of our course, we incorporate the pedagogy of narrative medicine into our students' assigned work. Students pair up to prepare and give mini-lessons, putting together the kind of curriculum that might be used in workshops they may give or courses they might teach. Each mini-lesson includes a narrative in any genre, discussion questions, and a prompt for a short reflective writing. One lesson, for example, was based on William Carlos Williams' poem, "The Last Words of My English Grandmother:"

Gimme something to eat—
They're starving me—
I'm all right—I won't go
to the hospital. No, no, no[31]

The students asked their classmates to write to the following prompt: "De-scribe a time you refused help or someone refused your help." On a voluntary basis, reflective pieces are read aloud, and a question or prompt, such as "what do you make of the different perspectives found in the poem?," helps guide the discussion.

The final paper is a media or genre analysis, asking students to reflect on how different ways of telling stories of death shape the way we understand and face death. In the years he lived with lymphoma, for example, Paul Zweig wrote po-etry about living with dying. How does Zweig's poetry tell a different story—or a story differently—than his prose? In his prose, writes a student, Zweig tells a lin-ear story, "and explores the concept of time, as he lives with the knowledge of his impending death." Passages about playing in the sandbox with his three-year-old daughter, "trying to imitate my daughter's innocence of time," are poignant and direct: "[N]either of us had any time and the irony was terrible, for I had lost mine and she hadn't acquired hers yet. Therefore we had each other." Poetry, the student writes, "allows [Zweig] more immediate access to feelings or ideas cre-ated by images, rhythm, and flexible linguistic tropes." The sense of time, of the time his daughter will grow up without him, is present in Zweig's poetry, but he narrates the feeling of imagining his daughter's sense of his absence:

Genevieve, one day
You will remember someone: a glimpse,
A voice, telling you what I never told
—What the living never say—
Because the words ran backward in my breath.[32]

Both Zweig's prose and his lyrical voices deepen our students' under-standing of those who live with dying—and with leaving behind. Students can attend to these stories, represent them to us, and affiliate with a dying young father.

A student paper analyzing stories about dying patients posted on medical student and physician blogs has particular resonance for the goal of educating clinicians in a new culture of death and dying. To the medical student blog-gers, death was a sad and strange phenomenon, shared by "*all of humanity.*" To physicians, it was almost inverted: Death was "unstrange" and an experience "shared by a patient and *a single professional.*" Medical students wrote their sto-ries as "civilians" or "voyeurs" with no sense of agency: "all you can do is watch"; "life is fragile"; "death is universal." Physician bloggers see death as "actionable," an "avoidable event, an undesirable outcome, and a moral cause for action." Attending to the stories of these bloggers required our student to inquire of his or her own future, "Will I be able to maintain moral agency through medical school and personal connection with the human reality of a life ending?"

CONCLUSION

In this course we ask students for a great deal: not simply a heavy work load, but an openness to immersion in possibly the most profound of human experiences—dying, caring for the dying, and death itself. What we offer in return is the possibility that this immersion will deepen compassion, enable a new or renewed affiliation with human suffering, and open the capacity for caring to include facing death itself, one's own or of another. But how do we know whether these narratives we probe, these reflections we elicit and share, these weeks of facing and even welcoming the place of dying in our lives have an impact on our students?

Our student course evaluations, like most in this genre, are focused on faculty performance, on reading materials, on assignments, and on feedback. We found in reviewing even the students' qualitative remarks that they did not offer us any more substantive understanding of how our seminar participants felt about the impact of this work. So we asked them directly. In particular we asked that they share with us their thoughts about what it felt like talking about death and dying in a small seminar with clinicians and nonclinicians, young and middle-aged adults. We asked them what they thought the impact of the course might be on medical or clinical education in general, and, most personally, what they felt the impact had been on them.

At the core of the class experience was the "intimacy" of the seminar, and the "safety" of the space. The course, said one student, "unfolds in a relatively closed environment." This was particularly important because the different experiences and professional roles of the students were both exposed in class discussion and then, with attention and respectful discussion, became part of the learning experience. "This combination of careers, personal experiences, etc.," said one student, "helped me understand better how the same event can be experienced so differently and how death and illness and love and life can mean such different things to different people." For clinicians, it was helpful to "have the voices of others—patients, thoughtful physicians, and peers—in mind as I think forward to my own patients." The physician/nonphysician dualism so often felt in the classroom was challenged, "as no one has a monopoly on death, everyone has experiences with it, often quite closely, as caretakers, children, parents, people who live with their own illnesses, as living organisms who will die."

We asked our former students what they thought about offering a narrative-based course like this to medical students and other clinicians. "Of the courses I took, the class on death and dying has been without a doubt the one that I think back to most often," wrote a young man now studying medicine. "In medical school we discuss death mostly tangentially, but it is of course always in the background." Or, from another former student, "given its inevitability as part of their work, it strikes me as unethical *not* to present it to med students." Whether physician or nonphysician, asked one response, "Who doesn't have deep and probably unexplored fears about death?"

Yet our students were forthcoming about the contradiction perhaps inherent in the study of experiential narratives as a means to connect with the patient's nonmedical experience. A therapist in one of our classes perhaps expressed it best:

> [B]y taking death on as a subject of study, there was an inherent distancing at work, a bit of the distancing that we looked at happening to clinicians who are confronted by death. While narrative study might not be the same as experiencing death through the anatomy lab for a semester, I think there may be something similar at play: it brings us closer to it than we would otherwise be, but it also sets us apart from it. We analyze and theorize about death and dying, rather than directly empathize.

Other students welcomed this distancing, interpreting it not as something that removed them from the dying, but rather allowed them to connect with their own feelings and fears: "I felt somehow liberated from my personal questions, history, and fears and at the same time grounded, so that in the self-reflecting the class invited, I could visit my personal death/dying-demons and such with a kind of safety net."

These students' responses, written to us usually after graduating and moving on, after taking other classes and following other paths, also told of their frequent return to the subject, to the reflection, to the texts. As an example, a student reflecting on the poem "Grief" by Matthew Dickman[33] wrote:

> For whatever reason the moment where he writes "while she tells me how unreasonable I've been/crying in the checkout line/refusing to eat, refusing to shower/all the smoking and all the drinking" is a turning point in the poem that hits me every time I read it, despite being such a simple notion and image of grief, perhaps because of how it stands in contrast to the otherwise fantastical yet endearing metaphor he establishes of grief being a purple gorilla.

We write this as the semester nears an end, and the class, once again, turns to grief—its dailiness, its chaos, its simple pain. This year our purple gorilla is the brick carried in the pocket of a mother whose son has died many years ago,[34] always there, always a weight, but now also a part of life ongoing. We have been struck by how many students wrote about the continued "presence" of the course, of the reflection on death and dying, in their lives and in their work. It was almost as if a course that embraced the work of narrating death and dying, a subject that invites the silence of fear and failure in our society, came to embody the power of narrative itself. A student new to narrative medicine, and an attorney by profession, expressed her experience this way:

> I think I realized the power of narrative when a few weeks into the course I felt that the way I understood the material, viewed the patients we spoke about, and was able to contribute to the class, was as someone who had lived amongst people who had experienced illness, dying and caregiving.

Through narratives she entered the world of living with dying. Our students' responses spoke to that power of narrative to enable us to enter the world of the other, to "live amongst" the dying, and to deepen our ability and willingness to know, or to feel, that which is unknowable in another.

> [W]hat I had hoped to find in the course is some cure, if not for death, then for my own personal fear. What I got instead was a primer on how narrative functions to attempt to understand and know the unknowable. . . . So perhaps instead of leading me to an answer for how not to fear death, our course set me on a path for how to use art and narrative to makes sense of what we otherwise cannot understand.

NOTES

1. Pauline W. Chen, *Final Exam: A Surgeon's Reflections on Mortality* (New York: Vintage, 2008), xii–xiii.

2. Ibid., 61.

3. Larry D. Cripe, "The General," in *At the End of Life: True Stories about How We Die,* ed. Lee Gutkind (Pittsburgh: Creative Nonfiction Brooks, 2012), 49.

4. Elizabeth H. Gaufberg, Maren Batalden, Rebecca Sands, and Sigall K. Bell, "The Hidden Curriculum: What Can We Learn from Third-Year Medical Student Narrative Reflections?" *Academic Medicine* 85, 11 (2010): 1711.

5. Ibid., 1711.

6. Gert Olthius and Wim Dekkers, "Medical Education, Palliative Care and Moral Attitude: Some Objectives and Future Perspectives," *Medical Education* 37 (2003): 930.

7. Leo Tolstoy, *The Death of Ivan Ilyich,* trans. Lynn Solotaroff (New York: Bantam Books, 1981).

8. Monty Python, "Part VII—Death: The Grim Reaper," *The Meaning of Life,* film, directed by Terry Gilliam (North American release 1983).

9. Arthur Frank, *The Wounded Storyteller: Body, Illness, and Ethics* (Chicago: University of Chicago Press, 1997), 75–96.

10. Emmanuel Levinas, *Totality and Infinity: An Essay in Exteriority,* trans. Alphonso Lingis (Pittsburgh, PA: Duquesne University Press, 1969), 56.

11. Philippe Ariès, *Western Attitudes toward Death: From the Middle Ages to the Present,* trans. Patricia M. Ranum (Baltimore: Johns Hopkins University Press, 1975).

12. Paul Zweig, *Departures: Memoir* (New York: HarperCollins, 1986).

13. *Ikiru,* directed by Akira Kurosawa (1952; USA release date 1956).

14. Albert Camus, *The Plague,* trans. Stuart Gilbert (New York: Vintage International, 1991).

15. Tom Joslin, *Silverlake Life: The View from Here,* documentary film, directed by Peter Friedman and Tom Joslin (1993).

16. Sheila M. Rothman, "Part II—The Female Invalid: The Narrative of Deborah Vinal Fiske, 1806–44," *Living in the Shadow of Death: Tuberculosis and the Social Experience of Illness in American History* (New York: Basic Books, 1994), 77–127.

17. Plato, "Phaedo," in *Five Dialogues,* trans. G. M. A. Grube (Indianapolis: Hackett Publishing Company, Inc., 2002), 93–154.

18. *The Sea Inside,* directed by Alejandro Amenabar (2004).

19. Christine Montross, *Body of Work: Meditations on Mortality from the Human Anatomy Lab* (New York: Penguin, 2007), 2.

20. Susan Taylor, "Gerasim Model of Caregiving," *Death Studies* 21 (1997): 299–304.

21. Donald Hall, *The Best Day The Worst Day: Life with Jane Kenyon* (Boston: Houghton Mifflin, 2005), 108.

22. Carol Levine, "Night Shift," in *Stories of Illness and Healing: Women Write Their Bodies,* ed. Sayantani DasGupta and Marsha Hurst (Kent, OH: Kent State University Press), 241–6.

23. *La peste (The Plague),* film, directed by Luis Puenzo (1992).

24. Craig Irvine, "The Ethics of Self-Care," in *Faculty Health in Academic Medicine: Physicians, Scientists, and the Pressures of Success,* ed. Thomas R. Cole and Thelma Jean Goodrich (New York: Humana, 2009), 127–46.

25. Jerald Winakur, "What Are We Going to Do with Dad," *Health Affairs* 24; no. 4 (2005): 1064–72.

26. Joan Didion, *The Year of Magical Thinking* (New York: Vintage, 2007).

27. Frank, *The Wounded Storyteller,* 97–114.

28. Jhumpa Lahiri, "A Temporary Matter," *Interpreter of Maladies* (Boston: Houghton Mifflin, 2000), 1–22.

29. Didion, *Year of Magical Thinking,* 188.

30. *Okuribito (Departures),* film, directed by Yojiro Takita (2008)

31. One stanza from "The Last Words of My English Grandmother," by William Carlos Williams, from *The Collected Poems*: VOLUME I, 1909–1939, copyright ©1938 by New Directions Publishing Corp. Reprinted by permission of New Directions Publishing Corp.

32. "The River," *Eternity's Woods* by Paul Zweig, copyright © 1985 by Paul Zweig. Reprinted by permission of Georges Borchardt, Inc., on behalf of the Estate of Paul Zweig.

33. Matthew Dickman, "Grief," *The New Yorker,* May 5, 2008, accessed June 12, 20112, http://www.newyorker.com/fiction/poetry/2008/05/05/080505po_poem_dickman

34. *Rabbit Hole,* film, directed by John Cameron Mitchell (2010).

Chapter 7

What Rational Philosophy Cannot Tell Us about Death in the 21st Century

Jerry S. Piven

*T*his chapter argues that the massive cultural changes and global violence of the 20th century have led to epiphanies of darkness in the new millennium, pervasive ideological losses of meaning that have laid bare our fear and trembling before death. Some would argue that we've transcended the dread of death in the 21st century, having deprived it of its sting and mystery through cultural and scientific advances. Despite any self-congratulatory reassurances, however, we've barely scratched the surface of understanding or transcending the elusive complexities of death anxiety. Thus this chapter asks how we could fathom the intricacies of death and dispel our fears. Since Plato, philosophers have illuminated how our terror of death inspires us to conceive illusory gods, adversaries, hells, and disasters. Philosophy would tell us that our fears of death are irrational, and only the practice of reason can banish our dread without resorting to metaphysical consolations and sophistries. This chapter nevertheless debates whether philosophy is capable of dispelling our fear since rational modes of inquiry may not delve into the perplexing psychological depths of death. Further, death is a complex symbol, comprising innumerable nonrational ideas and surreal fantasies opaque to conscious self-understanding. One cannot merely reason away such trenchant, emotionally crucial, death-denying fantasies. Rather, we need a process of relentless existential engagement to fathom the elusiveness of

death, for obliviousness toward our own dark motives allows us to inflict our own
fears, emotional wounds, and irrationality on others.

The massive cultural changes and global violence of the 20th century have led to epiphanies of darkness in the new millennium, pervasive ideological losses of meaning that have laid bare our fear and trembling before death. We are haunted by the specter of death, and our traditional ideologies no longer provide certitude and solace. Some would argue that we've transcended the dread of death in the 21st century, having deprived it of its sting and mystery through cultural and scientific advances. In this chapter I argue that such notions are unfounded and naïve. Despite any self-congratulatory reassurances, we've barely scratched the surface of understanding or transcending the elusive complexities of death anxiety. Thus this chapter asks how we could fathom the intricacies of death and dispel our fears. Since Plato, philosophers have illuminated how our terror of death inspires us to conceive illusory gods, adversaries, hells, and disasters. We turn to all manner of distraction, consolation, and creed to blot out our horror and panic. Philosophy would tell us that our fears of death are irrational, and that there is no cogent reason to fear mortality and nonexistence. Philosophy is a lucid preparation for death, and only the practice of reason can banish our dread without resorting to metaphysical consolations and sophistries. This chapter nevertheless debates whether philosophy is capable of dispelling our fear since rational modes of inquiry may not delve into the perplexing psychological depths of death. The dread of death is obscure and bewilderingly convoluted. Further, death is a complex symbol, comprising innumerable nonrational ideas and surreal fantasies opaque to conscious self-understanding. One cannot merely unravel such psychological complexities by imparting philosophical enlightenment, much less reason away such trenchant, emotionally crucial, death-denying fantasies. Rather, we need a process of relentless existential engagement to fathom the elusiveness of death, not detached philosophical explanations on why we simply have no reason to fear death, for obliviousness toward our own dark motives allows us to inflict our own fears, emotional wounds, and irrationality on others. This oblivion has enabled us to wreak havoc on the ecology of our planet and its denizens as we ardently massacre and torture countless civilians, and still remain opaque to ourselves.

INTRODUCTION: EPIPHANIES OF DARKNESS
AND THE DREAD OF DEATH

> *what defines human life in our corner of the planet at the present time is not just a fear of death, but an overwhelming terror of annihilation.*
> *What we seem to seek is either the transitory consolation of momentary oblivion or a miraculous redemption in the afterlife.*

It is in stark contrast to our drunken desire for evasion and escape that the ideal of the philosophical death has such sobering power. . . . Possibly the most pernicious feature of contemporary society is the unwillingness to accept this reality and willingness to flee the fact of death.

—*Simon Critchley[1]*

an insistent sense of finitude . . . is the only credible sense of reality after serious reflection on the experience of what it means to be human.

—*Charles Winquist[2]*

without death there would hardly have been any philosophizing.
—*Arthur Schopenhauer[3]*

It was Nietzsche who famously proclaimed the death of God.[4] The context of this oft-misunderstood parable is important for us here in the 21st century. Nietzsche wrote of the man who went mad when he realized that God was dead, a metaphor for our own panic when our ideologies no longer comfort us in the face of death. Nietzsche was not saying that a living being called God had actually died. He was describing the psychological wound that leaves the soul empty, terrified, and panic-stricken when deprived of a cohesive worldview, and the crushing inability to sustain faith and certainty amid the anarchic flux of ideas and doubts.

To the contemporary mind perhaps this seems somewhat hyperbolic, a relic of history, since we culturally diverse, savvy, jaded individuals suffer no agony at the thought that there may be no God, immortality, or paradise. Our composure and indifference in the face of meaninglessness and death may not be the whole story, however. As Winquist writes, "We have experienced a progressive series of losses that has left us in a world of contingency and relativity."[5] This is why James Joyce could allude to God as "a shout in the street" in *Ulysses.* For many (though not all of us), religion has given way to chaos, uncertainty, randomness, and bewilderment.

The 20th century has ravaged us with losses and "epiphanies of darkness," as Winquist terms it. If technology and medicine have prolonged life and cured diseases, the horrific recurrence of desolation, the wars, purges, and genocides that have slaughtered hundreds of millions have rendered death an uncanny, ghostlike presence forever hovering at the dim periphery of consciousness. They have exposed the hollowness of our typical consolations, and rendered us susceptible to cheap sophistries, exploitive creeds, and volatile pieties that seduce us with the fantasy of transcending anomie and death. The ghastly globality of massacre has laid bare our fear and trembling before death, the human condition in its nakedness, stripped of our comforting chimeras. Hence in the closing decades of the 20th century, Becker could write that modern life is characterized by the failure of traditional immortality ideologies, and that a kind of "normal madness" emerges from the disappearance of convincing dramas of salvation and redemption. The fear of death haunts us like nothing else. It is the worm at the core of our being that impels our desires, ambitions, beliefs, and pandemic lunacy.[6]

In the 21st century we haven't stopped denying death. Despite the title of Becker's book—*The Denial of Death* (1973)—he is *not* suggesting that denial is the sole means of rendering ourselves oblivious. To assume such is an immensely facile, weak reading of Becker, who illustrates in extraordinary (and contemporaneously relevant) detail the complicated, diverse ways in which we avert and displace the dread of death. People can fully accept the reality and permanence of death while finding innumerable ways of dissociating their fears or dislocating them into various beliefs and behaviors. We are still haunted, we just don't realize it. We have blissfully succumbed to our own rigid defenses, which hide a massively wounding terror of death that lurks within us. Though we may console ourselves with the fantasy of being calm and rational, this dread of death rages and spurs us toward all sorts of ruses to keep that dread at bay so that we are not nauseated and paralyzed. Secularization, civilization, and education haven't eradicated the dread of death. We haven't transcended it intellectually, spiritually, or psychologically. We still barely fathom the copious ways death invisibly assails the mind. Nor do we perceive the way death worms its way into our *own* psyches, possesses our desires, permeates and deranges our perceptions, and inspires our beliefs, fantasies, and delusions. The dread seeps into our behaviors, our manic, frenzied, self-absorbed pursuits, into our laws, policies, and cultural activities. It leaches into the ways we behave toward the world, gobble its resources, and treat our indigent, sick, and dying. To quote Bamyeh: "a critique of the role of death in the cultures of governance is especially pressing today, precisely because it is easy to misapprehend such an unheroic, consumption- and gratification-oriented postmodernity as a condition of true forgetfulness of death."[7]

We may obscure our dread with ingenious strategies and self-esteem-boosting reassurances, but the notion that we could merely transcend that dread in our worldly sophistication is, sadly, rather naïve and shallow. Oblivion and narcissistic arrogance do not signal tranquility in the face of death; rather these are often symptoms of a psyche that refuses to dwell upon its own shrouded terrors. Absence isn't inherently a symptom either. It would be a circular argument to assume that the absence of fear signals the unconscious presence of fear. Instead, this chapter is arguing that absence of conscious fear is not sufficient to conclude that fear doesn't lurk somewhere in the psyche or express itself indirectly. Smugness in the face of death doesn't prove anything, and self-congratulations that we have transcended death are premature. We may believe that our obliviousness, or lack of any conscious fear, means that we understand ourselves and have no terror that secretly moves us, but this merely confuses that obliviousness for equanimity before death.

Our excesses and obsessions rather suggest consumption by death: the way our media and entertainment are saturated by murder, corpses, apocalyptic imagery, vengeance, and the relentless drive to extinguish evil; the ways we are driven to acquire, believe, ravage, and destroy in the real world. All these suggest relentless angst over death and annihilation, a fantasy of vanquishing death, not indifference. If religion has faded for many, fundamentalism and sanctimonious dogma also surge around the globe, and assorted multitudes massacre their enemies and themselves in the name of their holy truths. Others inflict sundry forms of violence, remain unmoved while people around the world are slaughtered, suck the life out of nature and litter it with debris, support the massacre of other nations, and dwell upon our own tragic suffering and desire for things. We still suffer from the void of meaning and certainty while the dread of death lingers, and we too struggle to forget, and deny, and shut out horror.

So how do we know ourselves, and penetrate that opaque oblivion we create for ourselves? How do we face death without panic, illusions, and destructiveness? How can we understand our own irrationality and blindness?

PHILOSOPHY, DEATH, AND REASON

For thousands of years, the pursuit of rational self-inquiry would seem to be the conduit to self-understanding, and teach us that the fear of death is irrational. Socrates reputedly faced death with serenity and soothingly elegant logic: If one dies, one is no longer alive to experience it and has nothing to fear. In Plato's *Apology,* Socrates argues that it would be foolish to fear the unknown, since indeed there is no knowledge of anything beyond death and no reason at all for trepidation. Death might even be likened to blissful eternal sleep. In the *Phaedo,* Socrates claims that philosophy is a preparation for death, and that wisdom and reason should purify us of any dread or anxiety. This has become a leitmotif in philosophy. Rationality must prevail, and reason must banish irrational thoughts and emotions from the mind. The fear of death would only impel nonsensical reactions and cloud the mind with inanity.

Philosophers after Socrates wrote of the irrational, violent deliria germinated by the dread of death. Cicero asseverated that the terror of death created the gods themselves.[8] Lucretius (ca. 55 BCE) wrote that affliction turns human beings devoutly toward superstition, and that greed, crime, and the blind lust for status are running sores fed by the fear of death. We suffer seething envy, hate life itself, and "heap carnage on carnage" as we revel "with heartless glee" in a brother's tragic death.[9] We are so haunted by the fear of punishment after death that we are easily manipulated and conned, and have little resistance to hocus pocus or intimidation.[10] Our own dread makes us susceptible to all manner of delirious figment that sends us deeper into terror and pain. For Lucretius only philosophy can remedy the dread of death and lead us from panic, despair, and the insanity of violence and worship, to sanity and serenity. For in his Epicurean philosophy, *death is nothing to us.*[11] Whereas "this dread and darkness of the mind cannot be dispelled by the sunbeams," it can only be banished "by an understanding of the outward form and inner workings of nature."[12]

The notion that reason can abolish the dread of death pervades the history of philosophy. In his essay "That to Think as a Philosopher is to Learn to Die," Montaigne observes that the dread of death hangs overhead like the rock of Tantalus, and asks how we can step forward without trembling. But he hardly advocates gross blindness and brutish thoughtlessness toward death, and instead exhorts us to deprive it of its unfamiliarity and habituate ourselves to mortality: "He who has learned to die has unlearned servitude. . . . To know how to die frees us from all subjection and compulsion. . . . He who should teach men how to die would teach them how to live." Montaigne continues: "Death is less to be feared than nothing." Hence he could calmly advise: "The same transition that you made from death to life, without suffering and without fear, make it again from life to death. Your death is one of the parts of the order of the universe; it is part of the life of the world." And Montaigne finally endeavors "To establish you in this moderate course, of neither flying from life nor shunning death."[13] This echoes the philosophy of Zen master Dogen, who counsels us neither to fear nor desire extinction but rather to accept the natural inevitability of death.[14] In his essay "On Physiognomy," Montaigne argues that *the whole life of philosophers is a contemplation of death.*[15] Reason would supplant the madness of irrationality, and the dread of death could be obliterated if one disciplined the mind with philosophy. Thus Spinoza could write "a man who lives according to the dictates of reason alone, is not led by fear of death."[16]

The notion that rationality and self-control could dispel the fear of death continues in contemporary philosophy, where prominent thinkers like Nagel, Murphy, and Critchley reiterate the conviction that there is ultimately nothing to fear, and hence one *should* not.[17] The recurring theme is that one actually has the capacity to *think* oneself out of irrationality and fear. Critchley writes, "I want to defend the ideal of the philosophical death. . . . it is my belief that philosophy can teach a readiness for death without which any conception of contentment, let alone happiness, is illusory."[18] Contemporary societies suffer agonizing gaps in meaning, and people embrace all sorts of sophistries that provide easy magical answers to the problem of death. "This is where the ideal of the philosophical death has such persuasive power in undermining the death-denying shibboleths of our age."[19]

However, Critchley elsewhere recognizes that death is more than just an irrational problem assuaged by rational philosophy, for he notes the angst that drives the philosophers themselves to discover meaning, master death, and "find a fulfillment for human finitude."[20] And Ricoeur too could write that "The whole philosophy of Spinoza is an effort to eliminate the negative—fear and pain—from the regulation of one's life under the guidance of reason."[21] To suggest that one is obsessed with something, that dread and desire motivate an intense need for mastery and fulfillment, already undermines any certainty that the thought process is rational. The drive to become rational is already weakened by its own irrational despair. It calls the rational process itself into question since thought itself is inherently infiltrated by irrationality, obsession, a void in meaning, and the terror of death. Hence Murphy could write that many of the philosophical arguments about why we need not fear death "are so far beside the point that they at most demonstrate only one thing—that the fear of death must be very terrible indeed for some people if they are willing to grab at such small straws and take comfort in such inanity."[22] And Davis could similarly write that "the apostles of Reason thereby disguise how deeply their position derives from psychological and emotional factors which they are careful to conceal from themselves."[23] Here in the 21st century, philosophers are still trying to think their way out of death, and still consoling themselves with the notion that rationality will magically make it all disappear.

THE OBSCURITY OF PERCEPTUAL CLARITY AND THE EXISTENTIAL ASPECT OF BELIEF

How much can one *think* one's way out of irrationality? This is both a psychological and philosophical problem, for a disciplined, analytic approach to ideas may disentangle threads of illogic, incoherence, and contradiction as it clarifies the thought process. Far beyond the popular notion of philosophy as a pedantic, bourgeois luxury enabling people to think about generally impractical, useless, lofty ideas, philosophy is (in addition) an immensely disciplined and critical approach to ideas that enables practitioners to identify crucial fallacies of logic and reasoning, to pursue and refine ideas with acumen and rigor, to advance thought through the construction of robust, sound arguments. So indeed one may be able to think analytically, see the light of reason, dispel confusion, and use the rational faculties to influence one's perceptions of the world. Reason may be able to quell anxiety, and replace trepidation with sobriety.

It is still a question whether one can be reasonable in the first place. A person beset by dread, panic, or other trenchant emotional conflict may not have control over one's thoughts, nor even the capacity to perceive whether they are rational. And here we return to one of the major issues in philosophy: whether one can be rational, whether one can recognize the way the mind distorts perceptions of the world (and oneself), and to what degree one really has control over such thoughts and perceptions. What intellectual faculty would enable a person to recognize if he or she were distorting perceptions of the world, or oneself? If someone were distorting things, the perceptual faculties evaluating one's thoughts and perspective would themselves already suffer those same distortions, and thus distort the sense of what might be real or rational. Imagine a person suffering paranoid thoughts. Would this person be able to step back and evaluate his own paranoid distortions? Would not the paranoia itself already disrupt the attempt to evaluate his own thoughts and skew them in that paranoid way?

One need not reject the notion that the mind can sometimes evaluate its own ideas and perceptions, especially with the benefit of rigorous philosophical analysis. The belief that one could merely step back out of one's own perceptions, biases, distortions, and fantasies, however, as though this stepping back and viewing wouldn't also be distorted, is itself a fantasy. No discourse or method can guarantee immunity from irrationality or enable one to recognize how distorted one's thinking may be. To adhere to that fantasy already demonstrates a defiant denial of human weakness and limitation, an innately unrealistic assertion that one can somehow *know with certainty* that one isn't irrational, and be able to recognize and surpass one's own cognitive distortions. Such an assertion would already by a symptom of irrationality, if not a grandiose figment bordering on delusion. For there can be no *justifiable* certainty that one *knows* one is rational, and can recognize one's own irrationality. Were one distorting things, one could distort one's evaluation of whether one was distorting. Thus any assertion that one knows with certainty that one is rational is evidence that the wish to be immune to irrationality has utterly befuddled one's perspective on oneself, as well as the ability to recognize the incoherence of one's own claim. As La Barre writes, "It is a fatuity to suppose that just because we are conscious we already know ourselves. . . . What we think we know is the enemy of our knowledge."[24]

This would seem to be an insoluble philosophical and psychological problem, since certainty is no guarantee of reality, while the capacity to genuinely question and relinquish one's own perceptions is inversely related to one's trenchant emotional attachments to them. In other words, the more a belief becomes existentially crucial and self-protective, the more vehemently one defends it, fervidly guarding the belief and using the most furtive and desperate ways of making it seem rational and objectively true. An accruing body of research in terror management theory suggests not only that death anxiety impels adherence to religious and cultural worldviews, but that a surfeit of our rational decisions and beliefs are nonrational, post-hoc rationalizations for prior emotional commitments.[25] To quote Schopenhauer, "the intellect is the mere medium of motives."[26] The more a belief is defended and rationalized, the more it becomes necessary to protect the self from annihilation, whether that means wounds to the ego or ideas that threaten to shatter one's faith. And beyond the myriad desperate ploys and ceaseless rationalizations invoked to sustain one's fantasies is the potential for spite, hatred, and blinding rage toward those who threaten those sacred ego-sheltering illusions. Thus Davis asserts how ideology is itself an attempt to prevent the fear of emotional collapse that so often leads to panic, and even apocalyptic destruction.[27]

THE WORM THAT WON'T DIE

Hence, the notion of logically thinking oneself out of death anxiety is unrealistic. As intimated, one may surely use logic to calm the mind, but the conception of death as a simple, abstract notion that one can philosophize into nonexistence is more akin to magical thinking than reason. Ironically it is the philosophers themselves who explain in such poignant detail how much this dread of death pervades our lives beyond the powers of reason. Indeed, Unamuno sees the person with composure before death not as a rational human being but an aberration, a monster.[28] Unamuno writes of the immense sorrow that comes with the human awareness of death, a recognition of our finitude and mortality that reach into the depths of being. He muses: "if it is true that my consciousness returns to the absolute unconsciousness whence it sprang, and if a like fate befalls all my brothers in humanity, then our elaborate human lineage is no more than a doomed procession of phantoms trooping from nothingness to nothingness. . . . It is the Wherefore, the Wherefore of the Sphinx, that corrodes the marrow of our soul."[29] The dread of death is a maddening tempest, not an illogical idea that can be reasoned away.

Kierkegaard is the philosopher whose insights into despair are even more relevant to us in the 21st century. With uncanny detail, he describes what could be our own contemporary obsessions and flights from awareness and terror. In *The Sickness Unto Death*, Kierkegaard implores us to recognize just how devastated we are by our own anguish.[30] Despair is so obliterating and overwhelming that we are blinded by our own madness, and bury ourselves desperately in oblivion to shut out intimations of our own panic and awareness. The mind blinds itself to its own thoughts and emotions in order to live. And hence ordinary life is itself a form of madness that involves blotting out our own awareness and submerging ourselves in forms of normal socially sanctioned communally esteemed idiocy to escape ravagement by our own despair. The appearance of normality, calmness, reason, rationality, morality, and sanity are perverse masks that only reveal just how abjectly terrified we are. Only a human being would lobotomize oneself to escape from fear, and yet this is what Kierkegaard is suggesting (metaphorically) when he insists that human beings bury themselves in forms of blissful inanity to un-know themselves. People flock together and squawk about the weather, gossip about each another, judge each other's valor on the basis of frills and fashion, and clamor for attention, success, and glory. They find innumerable ways to shut out awareness of their desolation, whether they struggle for fame, blunt their minds with liquor, or seek oblivion in sensuality. Kierkegaard gives us a picture of a society of cretins who gossip, shop, swig, pontificate, and opine inanely as symptoms of a mind unwilling to recognize the tragic horror of existence.

The conventional platitudes of religious faith, piety, and sanctimony are also soothing social lullabies and ways of embracing imbecility, for according to Kierkegaard, our ridiculous postures of devotion reflect an unwillingness to die, to open oneself to torment and despair, to acknowledge the suffering of a self that yearns to fuse with eternity. Beneath all the vacuous cozening pleasures and stupefying distractions is a terrifying nakedness, a horrific sense of isolation and insignificance.

Immersed in the emptiness of social norms and virtues, a person is oblivious to the wellsprings of his despair but instead yearns for things, for objects to possess, for admiration and sensual gratification, or for another human being to fill in an agonizing void in the self. One lusts for erotic gratification, love, and fame because of this inner emptiness and intuition of being alone, nothing, and temporary. Further, one foolishly imagines that the attainment of those objects, sexual conquests, or celebrity will actually fill in that cavernous void and enable a person to become substantial. These symptoms of despair may be even harsher and more compulsive in the 21st century, in our self-absorption and obsession with mind-numbing television and web-addiction; the frenetic desperation of our urges to evade fear, loneliness, and pain through copious forms of oblivion, hedonism, sensualism, competition, ambition, materialism, acquisition, or exhibitionism; all the vacuous modes of narcissistic posturing and ego-inflation that anxiously attempt to persuade others (and ourselves) that we aren't insignificant and meaningless creatures of no more importance than a hapless poodle smushed by a Winnebago.

And indeed, part of being human is the anguish that comes from knowing that one will die, and suffering an intense yearning for something that assuages the terror of aloneness, insignificance, finitude, and death. Whether one consciously yearns for religious consolation is not the issue, for the insight here is that regardless of conscious belief (and whether one shamefully admits it to oneself or not), one may still yearn desperately for something eternal beyond the self, whether that means immersing oneself in diverse conduits to symbolic immortality, or even as Freud suggested, thirsting for some manner of oceanic ecstatic bliss that soothes fear and pain like a loving parent sheltering one in her caring arms.[31]

Perhaps Kierkegaard's insights are more sinister. For the intuition of inner void, nothingness, and insignificance before the ravages of time may affect us in profoundly different ways. Where some would meditate on death and loss, another might express his sadness in poetry, and another savor the beauty of love or nature while one can. Others, as suggested, might lash out against themselves or even innocents. Some might become sexually or financially predatory in defense against their own dread of weakness and finitude.

Others might flee frenetically into religious dogma and enforce it sanctimoniously, like an inquisitor, witch-hunter, or cleric who seeks to regulate the morality, speech, and sexuality of his society and believes that slaughter is justifiable in the name of God. Still others might seek solace by submersing themselves in a group and its comforting ideology, relinquishing their own capacity for analytical thought and individual conscience as they yield to the blissful pleasures and coercions of communal fantasy. Having surrendered their own moral judgment to the will of another, they may also lapse into hurtful behaviors sanctioned by the group and its ideology, indeed *using* anonymity in the group and its social sanctimony to expel their terrors of death onto others and maraud wantonly without guilt or culpability. This deliberate dependence also renders them susceptible to manipulation by those predatory inquisitors masquerading as prophets or saviors promising deliverance and prosperity while enslaving the group and massacring blasphemers, infidels, or various other harbingers of menacing evil.[32] And there might be those who, like the Kierkegaardian person aware of his nothingness, may seek to burn themselves away in order to merge with God and the eternal. Where Kierkegaard may extol such despair, there are also those whose feelings of inner nothingness and void impel such impassioned hunger that they would literally incinerate their own bodies in a holy conflagration of death while searing their enemies to ash. They too would burn away the boundaries between self and God; only here, the incineration literally destroys the physical body, amid the fantasy that purifying the self (and world) of evil catalyzes merger with God in death.[33]

Kierkegaard's insights on the dread of death, nothingness, and finitude offer a bleak vision of the ways in which we struggle to attain oblivion and flee our own despair *today*. We are provided with a nuanced image of humanity as suffering from its own intuitions of impermanence and the profoundly divergent ways we strive to endure our trepidation and despair. Human beings are not uniformly beset by terror, driven toward oblivion, suffering from an inner void, compelled to gossip, pray to God, or murder to transcend our feelings of nothingness. We are, however, vastly unconscious of ourselves, how terror may lurk beneath our conscious calm, how our ordinary and noble endeavors may be frenetic compulsions that conceal deeper wounds, and how our dark abysses of dread may result in callous, merciless, sadistic, and sacred forms of massacre, pretend though we may that the causes are rational, and righteous. Kierkegaard's answer to a philosophy that advocates rational thought as an antidote to death anxiety is to give us a starkly existential, psychological perspective on self-obscurity, the mortified self in wretched flight from awareness of its own nothingness, hurling itself into inanity, ambition, and religion to delude itself.

There are further facets of his obscurity. For we need to understand just why the dread of death is so ubiquitous, but crystallizes in so many divergent behaviors. To fathom death is to go even further beyond a philosophy that conceives of death as a static thing that could be dissolved by rational arguments, and to recognize the surreal, fractured, *symbolic* aura of death. This is where the research and insights of thinkers over the last few generations has begun to breach the depths of our fears.

THE SYMBOLISM AND METASTASIZATION OF DEATH

As Ernest Becker observes, death is a complex symbol.[34] This means that the ostensibly simple and concrete idea of death can have countless, obscure, confusing meanings. It also means that any seemingly insignificant or random thing can be unconsciously connected with death and annihilation, inspiring any number of powerfully emotional, defensive, compulsive, and compensatory responses. Any chance experience can be associated with some manifestation of death, though the connection may be obscured by a psyche struggling to ward off overwhelming dread and pain. And thus seemingly innocuous things like a butterfly, a pasture, or one's reflection on a bottle can reach back into the soul and arouse apprehension, nausea, panic, terror, loathing, or rage, and even stir intense philosophic, artistic, materialistic, erotic, tender, or religious yearnings.

A symbol is not merely an obvious metaphor whereby one thing is directly represented by something else (as in, e.g., the color black signifying death, or a rose signifying love). As Ricoeur suggests, the symbolization process involves a process of mystification, where waking logic gives way to a dreamlike surrealism of bewildering meanings.[35]

It is rarely clear what something means symbolically, and hence when we begin tracing the significance of death we are beyond concrete definitions or concepts, but in a realm of associations and intense emotions that vary according to the culture and individual. Where one person might continue to see death as a specific biological event, another may associate death with a worm severed by a plow, or a worm that goes a' progress through the guts of a beggar. Such images from Blake and Shakespeare may have profound emotional intensities for those persons alone, though others may well resonate with such allusions. Someone like the novelist Yukio Mishima might imagine death as a maternal wave that drowns one in disease, helplessness, suffocation, and feminine sexuality, whereas the fictive imagination of Batman associates death with a swarm of cave bats that come to symbolize the murder of his parents, his own weakness, emasculation, failure, loss, shame, ejaculation, sperm, and rebirth. Here literary images are evoked just to point out that the abstract concept of death is saturated with meanings that may be entirely elusive and irrational, and far beyond the naïve notion of merely philosophizing until they flee into the night like scared bats.

Any discourse that confines death to one-dimensional and rational meanings neglects the surreal, symbolic complexities of death, missing all but the most wooden, *misleading*, surface meanings. Symbolic diffusion rather spans the confusing logic of metaphor and hallucination, not rationality. When in some religious traditions, for example, hemorrhaged feminine birth blood is a contaminating death spatter that can only be ritually cleansed with male circumcision blood, we are in the symbolic sphere, not rational assessment of actual danger.[36] When women are seen (and loathed) as defiled, contaminated, poisonous, and evil, we have entered a realm where chaotic fears of death, decay, and sexuality coalesce into a fantasy, projected onto the outer world as if the misogynistic mirage were a rational assessment of real feminine wickedness. This doesn't merely reflect the most reasonable attitude of people in a given cultural and historical time period, but panic and fantasy erupting in the face of something so terrifying that it cannot grasped, and must therefore be ritually purified, exorcised, or slaughtered.[37] Hence Beit-Hallahmi could appropriately criticize scholars who attribute the fear of death to the contagion posed by corpses, when indeed the dread is unrelated to actual disease.[38] As Ricoeur illustrates, in the symbolic realm impurity is never literally a stain, and neither is death merely literal death but a *fantasy*, an ocean of swirling meanings.[39]

The sundry symbolizations of death form through experience and emotion. Death doesn't merely pop into existence as detached abstraction like Athena springing forth fully formed from Zeus' forehead. While there may certainly be a scientific definition of death, this has nothing to do with the way the developing psyche comes to process and comprehend death, and nor with the various associations, images, encounters, shocks, confusions, or trauma that come to be associated with death as a child begins to explore the world.

A child's concept of death bears little resemblance to the desiccated concept of a philosopher, as the growing child may be perplexed, horrified, and run screaming to its mother when it sees a splattered squirrel in the road, loses a beloved pet, or witnesses the wasting sickness of an elderly relative. The growing child may come to associate death with sudden destruction of flesh and bone, with age, sickness, and rotting, with the malicious rage of an explosive parent, or with falling leaves, serenity, sleep, and comfort. The images flow and merge, gradually become associations and concepts, and are processed by a psyche that may wish to dissociate, isolate, deny, project, or inflict its horrors on others. It is the diversity of these experiences and symbolizations of death—the immense variability of the terrors and traumas, the encounters with love, nurturance, loss, coldness, suffocation, or malice—that crucially affect whether the dread of death shrinks or grows into a grotesque monstrosity within the psyche.

The maturing concept of death is so complex and layered that the adult *abstract* concept is barely a shadow of its unconscious, lurking, emotional intensity. In the realms of death and the symbolic, things are rarely what they seem to the conscious mind. Hence one needs to fathom just how elusive and meaning-laden death can be, and for that matter, how death may lurk beneath serenity, beauty, and love. For some the soothing repose of nature may be the peaceful environment of their youth, while for others, nature may represent savagery, muck, swarms, offal, and writhing chaos that need to be purified and sculpted into tame beauty. Only then can nature be beautiful. Shakespeare and Joyce show us how beauty can be an antidote to the ugliness of nature as spawning and rotting, the bilious treacle of bodies in graves, dogs melting into the sand, bones becoming coral, and eyes replaced by pearls in a skull after suffering a sea-change five fathoms below. For some, love and erotic intimacy are the merging of human beings who can be fully open to one another without shame or constraint, while for others intimacy is annihilation of the ego, and sexual satisfaction cannot be attained without domination, emotional closedness, and humiliation (of self or other). Hence echoing Kierkegaard, psychoanalyst Joyce McDougall could write of the sundry erotic and perverse behaviors that are desperate attempts to obliterate the dread of death.[40]

The visible is manifest content, the façade that hides the complex workings of death within the psyche. One just cannot assume from the placid exterior whether the appearance of love, altruism, piety, or philosophic rationality don't conceal rage, despair, disgust, or terror. Conscious calm in the face of death, a scientific detachment, or courageous stoicism may mask deeper chaos and panic. As La Barre declares, what one thinks he sees in the outer world is ultimately a statement about one's unknown self.[41] All manner of inner wound, terror, and conflict may be confused for threats and evils in the outer world, and then inflicted on others as puritanical morality, faith, or philosophy. Death is a fractured, surreal, nonrational multiplicity symbolized and displaced into the outer world, confusing our perceptions, and deceiving ourselves about what is real, menacing, and evil.

Hence the fear of death (whatever its origins) can be displaced into subtle and gross forms of violence, where people find ways of inflicting their own dread onto others in so many acts of personal, professional, and political acts of cruelty, predation, and brutality. The spiteful and scornful cynic, the surgeon who lacerates bodies, the health fanatic who nourishes her physique, and the lover who delights in smooth skin, may all be horrified of the decaying body, the notion of wasting into worm food, the idea that beneath youth and strength are fetid bowels.[42] Some may deny death by overtly claiming that death is not the end of life, preaching instead of the glories of eternal bliss in paradise. This may still be one of the more common consolations, and even today polls indicate that some 80 percent of Americans believe in Heaven.[43] Yet even with the decline of traditional religions in the 21st century, countless others flee from their own horror and disgust, banishing torment from consciousness, while inflicting that terror in so many acts of *banal* aggression. And this is what needs exploring, for our contemporary fear of death has not declined. Without the comforts of faith, we may even be more vulnerable and threatened, and hence resort to other desperate modes of oblivion, callousness, or destructiveness, even if we don't recognize our pleasures and habits as flights from death.

Thus the conscious belief about how one thinks or feels about death is a paltry fragment of the obscure death work within the deeper registers of the psyche.[44] And here in the 21st century there is just a massive amount of evidence supporting the idea that beyond our awareness or control, the dread of death is utterly intertwined with our beliefs, ideologies, politics, compulsions, prejudices, sexual desires (and aversions), and the potential for violence.[45] This is why philosophy is utterly unequipped to fathom, much less begin to ameliorate the intricate, disjointed, violent chaos of the psyche, or the bewilderingly surreal ways in which it suffers, symbolizes, and flees the dread of annihilation. For here, as just described, the psyche defends itself against the irruption of horrific, obliterating perceptions through means unknown to itself. One's perceptual reality is distorted to dissolve conscious dread and awareness of those loathsome apprehensions. And thus the notion of rationally disempowering the conscious fear of death is like wiping the tears from someone's eye and declaring her vision clear when the anguish was actually caused by a ravaging swarm of cancerous tendrils invisibly worming their way through her dying organs.

The notion of dispelling fear by confronting it with rational discourse may well be a reasoned approach to anxieties lingering at the threshold of consciousness, which are founded on errors in logic, misinformation, or ignorance. The notion of using reason to abolish fears that operate beneath the threshold of consciousness, however, is utterly senseless. Here one would be appealing to the reason of a consciousness that is itself already a collage of fantasies and deliria, an *un*consciousness unaware that its perceptions of reality (and oneself) are already a patchwork of absences, erasures, wishes, fictions, and deceptions. There is no mantra or chime that can just stop us from fearing the reaper. Again, the belief that reason could fathom and dispel the dark intricacies of the dread of death would *itself* be a death-denying fantasy that pretends that the ego has complete mastery of its thought process, is completely aware of itself, and controls all its emotions.

CONCLUSIONS: NOT RATIONALISM BUT DERACINATION

It would seem that the psyche is helplessly deluded, irrational, invulnerable to reason, and beyond any attempts to comprehend or transcend its complex dread of death. There are no profound insights, radical scientific formulae, or stunning revelations that will suddenly enable us to illumine and resolve our fears. The urge to impart rare and edifying wisdom or rescue those who are suffering reveals only one's own distress and fantasies of magical power over helplessness and death. Grandiose fantasies of soothing dread and pulling people from the brink of despair may momentarily salve that trepidation but may impede the possibility of actually fathoming or resolving another's agony. Nor can any sage advice, guru guidance, or Zen meditation reach down into the recesses of the psyche to sever every tendril of death.

This is why Zen master Dogen's advice (quoted earlier) not to embrace or flee from death is so empty. We don't even understand the complicated fears within us, perceive how they impel us to behave, or distort our understanding. For there *may* be ways of grasping the elusive wisps of death, but they aren't uprooted by mere will alone, or by rational arguments, or by enlightenment, or by meditation that eventually allows the terror of death evanesce into nothingness.

If there is any possibility of working through our fear of death, it is through an excruciating process of dissection and uprooting. As Nietzsche writes, "one must wrestle for truth every step of the way, one must abandon almost everything which otherwise our heart, which our love, our faith in life hangs on."[46] It is an agonizing, protracted, ugly, relentless process of deracination, of uprooting the vilest horrors, traumas, and truths that we fear and despise with every fiber of our being and mask with figments and fantasies so precious and sacred that we might detest or slaughter those who threaten those illusions.[47] Davis describes the uprooting, deracinating process as "that dialectical and psychological process in which 'spirit is the life that cuts back into life' . . . the process of actively reversing one's psyche from within by eradicating every belief, value, and need that stands in the way of taking up one's responsibility to history."[48] If this is dimly possible, it is a laborious process, an agonizing process, and if there are those who can facilitate this uprooting, they offer no cures, soothing consolations, or paternalistic knowledge. They cannot save us, give us clichéd homilies, or mollify us with inane and vacuous drivel about the connectedness and serenity of all life; they can buoy us, but only while we struggle to uproot excruciating and detestable realities. This is why Davis calls for *existential engagement,* not rational arguments, metaphysical consolations, or frivolous platitudes—the manic avoidance of tragic suffering in a contemporary self-lobotomizing culture that seeks easy, uplifting, self-esteem-boosting baloney. Anything less than deracination and existential engagement becomes pacification of the ego that craves bliss, strains to avoid pain and tragic memory, and yearns for the warming soporific arms of a parent, so that one can fall back into oblivious sleep. None of this means that there is only one specific method of deracination, existential engagement, or confrontation with death. Indeed I've explicitly avoided prescribing any method or formula because pretending to have knowledge of a guaranteed procedure would be absurd, and it would inappropriately satisfy the reader's yearning to have someone else quell his or her anxiety by providing such a method. The possibilities may be diverse, however, whether that means the psychotherapeutic processes developed by Firestone and Catlett, or Yalom, or the analytical psychological approaches of Franz and Hillman, or others.[49]

Deracination and existential engagement need not be masochistic, joyless, or constant, nor is this advocating an ascetic and miserable life until one uproots every painful conflict. One engages in this process because oblivion blots out the world, because our self-absorption and avoidance allow brutality and unfairness to thrive in the world around us, and because obliviousness toward our own terror, angst, and trauma ineluctably wreaks havoc on others. The price of our own selfishness and fear of knowing ourselves is someone else's suffering. Whether we are merely selfish or callous, whether we act out on others in socially banal but predatory ways, whether we inflict our own inner horrors on our children, whether we turn a blind eye to rape, torture, or massacre across the planet, or whether we displace and project our cancerous dread and misery onto nature or other cultures, unconsciousness of our own metastasizing horror and dread will bleed into the world somehow.

The dread of death afflicts us differently, and we need no facile assertion that we are all rabidly deluded or consumed by vile evil. Rather, we are just frail enough that most of us suffer intermittently while loving and working amid ordinary lives, and only an unhappier few rape, torture, and slaughter others. The problem is, however, that we have trouble perceiving how distorted and deluded our perceptions are, how much we may inflict ourselves on others, and how much misery we allow across the globe when we pretend that we are good and sane beings who simply understand ourselves.

Hence the philosophical project of rationally dispelling the fear of death is not only ineffectual, it is also opens the floodgates to ethical irresponsibility and devastation. For when philosophers speak of eradicating fear in order to attain comfort and happiness, they are not seeking to fathom and uproot one's trenchant terrors, but merely attempting to prove them irrational. Instead of existential engagement with the ghastly torments lurking in one's inner crypt, one would explain philosophically why such fears are incorrect, as if explaining faulty reasoning would magically make terrors disappear. There will be no painful existential engagement with the distressed core of one's being, but rather disengagement, dispassionate distancing, intellectualizing and avoiding. Instead of grappling with inner torment, one seeks solace and would soothe away unwanted suffering. The striving for comfort is a form of flight, an escape from self-understanding, the antithesis of the bellicose encounter with those dark abysses of angst and anguish that spur people to unleash their inner hells upon others. As Davis writes, evil is the consequence of banishing psychological self-understanding.[50]

The ethical imperative here is to reject the seductions of comfort. For ennobling comfort as enlightenment becomes an easy excuse to avoid that agonizing process of opening the wounds and convulsions that give rise to our defenses, compulsions, aggression, and all manner of pathological, insidious stratagems of acting out and displacing those inner horrors onto others. We've barely breached the surface of death, not in our understanding of its labyrinthine complexities, nor of our own haunted derangement. If that surface has been breached at all, it has come with the recognition that the psyche is beguilingly complex, swarming with emotions beyond one's immediate understanding or control, and that we need to give up the pretence of such rational control to begin to fathom ourselves. Opening up to that bewildering chaos is already felt as the threat of death and annihilation, and so we continue to console ourselves with assertions of our rationality and self-awareness. Of comfort let no one speak, not at least when it comes to soothing oneself to avoid recognizing how we insouciantly disgorge our suffering onto others.

NOTES

1. Simon Critchley, *The Book of Dead Philosophers* (New York: Vintage, 2009), xv, xxvi.

2. Charles E. Winquist, *Desiring Theology* (Chicago: University of Chicago Press, 1995): 138

3. Arthur Schopenhauer, *The World As Will and Representation, Volume II,* trans. E. F. J. Payne (New York: Dover, 1958), 463.

4. Friedrich Nietzsche, *The Gay Science,* trans. J. Nauckhoff (New York: Cambridge University Press, 2001), sec. 108–25.

5. Winquist, *Desiring Theology,* 6–7; cf.: 65.

6. Ernest Becker, *The Denial of Death* (New York: The Free Press, 1973), 190, ix, 15.

7. Mohammed A. Bamyeh, *Of Death and Dominion: The Existential Foundations of Governance* (Evanston, IL: Northwestern University Press), 6.

8. Marcus Tullius Cicero, *Tusculan Disputations,* trans. J. E. King (Cambridge, MA: Loeb Classical Library, 1927).

9. Titus Lucretius Carus, *On the Nature of the Universe,* trans. R. E. Latham (New York: Penguin, 1994), 68.

10. Ibid., 12.

11. Ibid., 87.

12. Ibid., 13.

13. Michel de Montaigne, "That to Think as a Philosopher is to Learn to Die," *Essays I,* trans. G. B. Ives (New York: Heritage, 1946), 105–22.

14. Dogen, "Shoji," *Shobogenzo,* trans. T. Cleary (Honolulu: University of Hawaii Press, 1986), 122.

15. Michel de Montaigne, "On Physiognomy," *Essays III,* trans. G. B. Ives (New York: Heritage, 1946), 1434. It should be noted that the mature Montaigne evolves from a philosophy of constant rumination on death to one of pleasure in life. He admires the elegance of Socrates' approach to death, and disdains the wasteful angst aroused by philosophical rumination on mortality.

16. Baruch Spinoza, *Ethics,* trans. W. H. White and A. H. Stirling (Hertfordshire: Wordsworth, 2001), 212.

17. Thomas Nagel, *Mortal Questions* (New York: Cambridge, 1979); *What Does It All Mean?* (New York: Oxford, 1987). Jeffrie G. Murphy, "Rationality and the Fear of

Death," in *The Metaphysics of Death,* ed. John Martin Fischer (Stanford, CA: Stanford University Press, 1993), 41–58. Simon Critchley, *Very Little . . . Almost Nothing: Death, Philosophy and Literature* (New York: Routledge, 2004); *Book of Dead Philosophers.*

18. Critchley, *Book of Dead Philosophers,* xvii.

19. Ibid., 248–49.

20. Critchley, *Very Little,* 38.

21. Paul Ricoeur, *The Symbolism of Evil* (Boston: Beacon, 1967), 44. Such psychologizing the motives of a philosophical project has the potential to slip into *ad hominem* arguments. In this case, however, Critchley and Ricoeur are dissecting the *explicit* philosophical ambition of eliminating pain and fear with rationality, not rejecting the argument itself with derogatory psychological dismissals.

22. Murphy, *The Metaphysics of Death,* 53.

23. Walter A. Davis, *Death's Dream Kingdom: The American Psyche Since 9-11* (Ann Arbor, MI: Pluto, 2006): 231.

24. Weston La Barre, *The Ghost Dance* (New York: Dell, 1970), 50.

25. http://www.tmt.missouri.edu/. See also Benjamin Beit-Hallahmi, *Psychoanalysis and Theism* (New York: Jason Aronson, 2010). Jaak Panksepp. *Affective Neuroscience: The Foundations of Human and Animal Emotions* (New York: Oxford, 1998), 301.

26. Schopenhauer, *The World As Will and Representation,* 176. In a similar vein Davis writes, "Hamlet knows the truth that most people and most philosophers strive to deny. That we never escape the psyche. We always act from it and not from reason." Davis, *Death's Dream Kingdom,* 232.

27. Davis, *Death's Dream Kingdom,* xviii. Cf. also 16ff.

28. Miguel de Unamuno, *The Tragic Sense of Life,* trans. A. Kerrigan (Princeton, NJ: Princeton University Press, 1990), 46.

29. Ibid., 48.

30. Soren Kierkegaard, *The Sickness Unto Death: A Christian Psychological Exposition for Upbuilding and Awakening,* trans. H. V. Hong and E. H. Hong (Princeton: Princeton University Press, 1983).

31. The term "symbolic immortality" derives from Robert Jay Lifton, who described several modes of experiencing a sense of immortality through art works, progeny, nature, and so on. Robert Jay Lifton, *The Broken Connection* (Washington, DC: American Psychiatric Press, 1979). Sigmund Freud, *Civilization and Its Discontents* (London: Hogarth, 1953).

32. Cf. Becker, *The Denial of Death*; Freud, *Civilization and Its Discontents*; Lifton, *The Broken Connection.*

33. J. S. Piven, "Narcissism, Sexuality, and Psyche in Terrorist Theology," *The Psychoanalytic Review* 93, 2 (2006): 231–65; "Psychological, Theological, and Thanatological Aspects of Suicidal Terrorism," in *Top Ten Global Justice Law Review Articles 2008,* ed. Amos Guiora (New York: Oxford University Press, 2009), 285–310. Ruth Stein, *For Love of the Father* (Stanford, CA: Stanford University Press, 2010).

34. Becker, *The Denial of Death,* 18ff.

35. Ricoeur, *The Symbolism of Evil.*

36. Howard Eilberg-Schwartz, *The Savage in Judaism* (Bloomington, IN: Indiana University Press, 1990), 174ff.

37. For profuse examples Buddhistic associations of women with defilement, excrement, and death, see Bernard Faure, *Visions of Power* (Princeton, NJ: Princeton University Press, 1996). J. S. Piven, "Buddhism, Death, and the Feminine" in *The Psychology of Death in Fantasy and History,* ed. J. S. Piven (Westport, CT: Praeger, 2004), 37–70. See also Jean-Claude Schmitt, *Ghosts in the Middle Ages,* trans. T. L. Fagan (Chicago, IL: University of Illinois Press, 1999), 199–200. Schmitt writes of the way medieval Christians would dig up the bodies of women who died in childbirth and drive stakes through the cadavers to prevent the women from returning as ghosts. Schmitt also contrasts the dread and contempt of cadavers with the "imputrescible" Christian saints. Schmitt, *Ghosts in the Middle Ages.*

38. Benjamin Beit-Hallahmi, "Fear of the Dead, Fear of Death: Is It Biological or Psychological?" *Mortality: Promoting the Interdisciplinary Study of Death and Dying* 17, 4 (2012): 322–37.

39. Ricoeur, *The Symbolism of Evil,* 35ff.

40. McDougall prefers the term "neosexual" because it avoids the stigma of describing certain sexualities as sick and deplorable, whereas she believes that sexuality ("normal" and "perverse") span a spectrum of psychopathology that reflects emotional injuries, attempts to master situations of trauma, and defenses against fragmentation and death. Joyce McDougall, *The Many Faces of Eros* (New York: Norton, 1995).

41. La Barre, *The Ghost Dance,* 24.

42. Simone de Beauvoir, *The Second Sex* (New York: Vintage, 1989). Wolfgang Lederer, *The Fear of Women* (New York: Harcourt, 1968). J. S. Piven, *Death and Delusion: A Freudian Analysis of Mortal Terror* (Greenwich, CT: Information Age Publishing, 2004); *The Madness and Perversion of Yukio Mishima* (Westport, CT: Praeger, 2004).

43. http://www.gallup.com/poll/11770/eternal-destinations-americans-believe-heaven-hell.aspx

44. Andre Green, *Life Narcissism Death Narcissism* (London: Free Association, 2001).

45. Cf. the Terror Management Studies of Arndt, Greenberg, Pyszczynski, Solomon, and others, cited earlier in note 41. See also Robert Firestone and Joyce Catlett, *Beyond Death Anxiety: Achieving Life-Affirming Death-Awareness* (New York: Springer, 2009). J. S. Piven, *Death and Delusion.* Irvin Yalom, *Existential Psychotherapy* (New York: Basic Books, 1980).

46. Friedrich Nietzsche, *Der Antichrist* (Berlin: Walter de Gruyter, 1988), sec. 50.

47. Walter A. Davis, *Inwardness and Existence* (Madison, WI: University of Wisconsin Press, 1989); Walter A. Davis, *Deracination: Historicity, Hiroshima, and the Tragic Imperative* (Albany: State University of Albany Press, 2001).

48. Davis, *Deracination: Historicity, Hiroshima, and the Tragic Imperative Death's Dream Kingdom,* xx.

49. Cf. Firestone and Catlett, *Beyond Death Anxiety*; Yalom, *Existential Psychotherapy*; and also James Hillman, *The Dream and the Underworld* (New York: Harper & Row, 1979); M.-L. von Franz, *Shadow and Evil in Fairytales* (Dallas: Spring, 1987).

50. Davis, *Deracination: Historicity, Hiroshima, and the Tragic Imperative Death's Dream Kingdom*), 173. Hence this chapter echoes Davis, as he "situates ethical responsibility at a deeper register of our being than one finds in other ethical theories," 176, also cf. 220–2.

Chapter 8

Grim Discoveries: Agnès *Varda's* Vagabond (1985) and Karen Moncrieff's *The Dead Girl* (2006)

Marcelline Block

*T*his chapter examines the 2006 film *The Dead Girl*, directed by Karen Moncrieff, as a 21st-century counterpart to Agnès Varda's Sans toit ni loi/Vagabond, the winner of the Golden Lion at the Venice Film Festival and the César for Best Actress in 1985. Although made 20 years apart and on different continents, these two films—both written and directed by women filmmakers—bear significant similarities as each foregrounds how the untimely death of a young woman impacts the community around her in order to raise larger questions about male violence against women in patriarchal cultures and societies as well as reassert the continued need for a feminist filmmaking practice privileging female subjectivity, voices, and experiences. I place these films in dialogue by drawing parallels between their subject matters, narrative devices, and other points of convergence such as how death is mediated through female characters as well as considering their feminist potential. In particular, I situate The Dead Girl within the context of 21st-century American cinematic and popular cultures in light of the death of actress Brittany Murphy (1977–2009), who unexpectedly died three years after incarnating the film's titular role, thus becoming a "dead girl" on and off screen, complicating spectatorial engagement with and critical approaches to this film.

IN MEMORIAM: BRITTANY MURPHY (1977–2009)

If I don't tell their [women's] stories, who is going to?
                    —*Karen Moncrieff, writer/*
                    director of The Dead Girl

Que peu de temps suffit pour changer toutes choses!
                    —*Victor Hugo,* Tristesse d'Olympio/
                    The Sadness of Olympio *(1837)*

In the opening sequence of the film *The Dead Girl* (Karen Moncrieff, 2006), a female character named Arden (Toni Collette) discovers, in an orchard near her home, the mutilated and bloody nude corpse of an unknown and unnamed young woman whose open eyes stare, vacantly, into the distance—the stare of death. Who was she, and under what circumstances did she meet her brutal demise as a murder victim whose body was left in this rural setting? *The Dead Girl's* diegesis unfolds through the film's five sections that eventually yield answers to these questions: her name was Krista Kutcher (Brittany Murphy). She was a prostitute and a single mother, meeting her tragic fate at the hands of a male serial killer, Carl (Nick Searcy), targeting women living in a nondescript region located outside of Los Angeles. This dark, haunting film explores the aftereffects of the young woman's murder as filtered through the perspectives of various female characters linked to her on some level, whether they encountered her before or after her death—in other words, the "powerful ripple effect of a single act of violence"[1] upon a wider community, which, in the case of *The Dead Girl,* is primarily composed of women. To cite Jean-Michel Rabaté in his discussion of how murdered women are depicted in 20th-century mass culture, from crime scene photography to multimedia art installations, "facing murder, especially a young woman's murder—the most poetic theme, according to Poe—we all become orphans, widows, or widowers. We don't really know what we are mourning, or if it is really mourning or an expiation of guilt that we are after. We are not sure what we have lost, hence we huddle together all the more closely and try to extract some warmth from the terror and pity that these stories inspire."[2] The interlocking stories of *The Dead Girl* inspire such "terror and pity" as each narrates the victimization of women characters, starting and ending with the young woman's murder.

With a narrative that works backward, through flashbacks, and by foregrounding the perspectives and testimonials of characters linked to the dead figure, *The Dead Girl's* cinematic antecedents include a range of iconic films such as *Citizen Kane* (Orson Welles, 1941), *Rashomon* (Akira Kurosawa, 1950), *Sunset Boulevard* (Billy Wilder, 1950), *Une femme douce/A Gentle Woman* (Robert Bresson, 1968), and, most significantly for this discussion, *Sans toit ni loi/Vagabond* (1985), a film also written and directed by a woman, Agnès

Varda (b. 1928), one of the most important cinéastes of the 20th century. Varda is often referred to as the "mother" or "grandmother" of the French New Wave because her first feature, *La Pointe Courte* (1954), which introduced her signature aesthetic blending documentary and fiction, "was very well received by the group [*Cahiers du Cinéma*], especially by [André] Bazin . . . [it] has been cited as one of the most important precursors of the Nouvelle Vague"[3]and there is moreover a "continual interchange between historical context and issues of the female self in society at every stage of [Varda's] work."[4]

Preceding *The Dead Girl* by 20 years, like it, *Vagabond* centers around the death of a young woman, a vagrant named Mona Bergeron (played by 17-year-old Sandrine Bonnaire in her César-winning turn), whose corpse is discovered in the film's opening sequence in a bucolic setting similar to that in which Krista is found in *The Dead Girl*—but in the South of France, not Southern California. In both *Vagabond* and *The Dead Girl,* it is in an isolated and desolate no-(wo)man's-land that the titular woman's corpse is discovered in the film's opening sequence: In the former, Mona is fully clothed and initially could be thought to be sleeping, while in the latter, Krista is nude, covered in blood, with insects crawling on her.

The harsh winter climate of the French countryside caught up with Mona: malnourished and shivering from cold—her only protection against it a thin blanket—she tripped and fell into a ditch in a vineyard, her head hitting the ground. She does not seem to have the physical strength to stand up, and overnight, freezes on the very spot where she remained after her fall. On the

Figure 8.1
In *Vagabond,* Mona (Sandrine Bonnaire) freezes to death in the bitter cold of the winter in the French countryside (© 1985 ciné-tamaris. Used by permission)

Figure 8.2
In *Vagabond*, Mona (Sandrine Bonnaire) freezes to death in the bitter cold of the winter in the French countryside (detail) (© 1985 ciné-tamaris. Used by permission)

Figure 8.3
Arden (Toni Collette) discovers the bloody and mutilated corpse of Krista (Brittany Murphy) in the opening moments of *The Dead Girl* (© Lakeshore Entertainment)

other hand, 21st-century Krista unknowingly hitched a car ride from a male serial killer. What has most changed from the 1980s of *Vagabond* to the early-21st-century setting of *The Dead Girl* is the means by which the central female character dies. At stake in *The Dead Girl*'s updating of *Vagabond*'s thematic

Figure 8.4
Arden (Toni Collette) discovers the bloody and mutilated corpse of Krista
(Brittany Murphy) in the opening moments of *The Dead Girl* (detail)
(© Lakeshore Entertainment)

and formal concerns is an increase in violence against women. In *Vagabond*, Mona dies of natural causes largely brought about by her own decision to live outside of society's parameters. Yet, as we shall see, Mona's rejection of the roles imposed upon women in patriarchy is what arguably leads to her death. Whereas Mona is a victim of circumstance—simultaneously rejecting and rejected from a patriarchal system that expels her—leaving her exposed to the elements to die of cold, Krista is murdered by a male who is obsessed with killing women, and who, it is presumed, will continue doing so: it appears that the only person who becomes aware of his crimes is his wife Ruth (Mary Beth Hurt), who is unable to bring herself to turn him in to the police.

The narratives of the two films develop through several chapters: In *The Dead Girl*, there are only five, each of which is clearly labeled with a title based upon one of the film's women characters—"The Stranger," "The Sister," "The Wife," "The Mother," and "The Dead Girl"—while *Vagabond* is divided into 47–66 segments (as these sections are not clearly delineated nor labeled the way they are in *The Dead Girl*, the number of chapters in *Vagabond* has been debated by film scholars).[5] In *Vagabond*, as in *TheDead Girl*, "what emerges from the seemingly random encounters is both a carefully orchestrated story and an integrated vision . . . the chain of coincidence binds all of these disparate characters"[6] and stories. *The Dead Girl*, like *Vagabond*, progresses in a circular pattern from the opening scene when the female cadaver is "discovered . . . until the final moments"[7] of the film, which takes the viewer back to the dead woman found in the film's opening sequence.[8]

Vagabond explores how Mona's life and death had impacted those whom she encountered as she drifted over the course of her final winter throughout small towns and villages in the Hérault department, a well-known winemaking region in Southern France. In *Vagabond,* as in the later *Dead Girl,* "numerous persons attempt to transfix a meaning"[9]upon the female cadaver discovered at the start of the film. In examining the impact made by Mona and Krista upon those with whom they intersected during their final days, *Vagabond* and *The Dead Girl* converge on numerous points, including a genesis anchored in their directors' real-life encounters with memorable female figures who inspired the films: "Varda's first idea—to make a film about road people/vagrants (male and female) in the winter, who perish from the cold—became substantially modified when she encountered a hitchhiking vagabond, Settina. The starting point, then, is this young woman's experience."[10]For Moncrieff, it was "while serving as a juror on a murder trial of a prostitute" that "the seed for *The Dead Girl* was planted"[11]:

'Even though the murderer had been convicted, I just couldn't let go of this huge weight of sadness . . . I wanted to redeem her in some way. She was a series of contradictions: a passionate mother, an unmedicated bipolar, a drug addict, and a liar. But she was also a troubled human being who didn't deserve to die.' During the trial, Moncrieff encountered the people associated with the girl—customers, lovers, former convicts, pimps, dealers, family—and realized all formed a community. 'We didn't know each other, many of the witnesses had never met each other,' she sensed, 'and yet we were all affected by this act of violence, obviously some to a greater extent than others.'[12]

While both *Vagabond* and *The Dead Girl* posit feminist critiques of violence against women, that violence has increased exponentially in the two decades separating the two films, as demonstrated by Krista's brutal murder versus Mona's death mainly from exposure to the elements; although events occurring immediately before her death include an unexpected and traumatizing encounter with a quasi-pagan grape harvesting ritual led by aggressive male villagers, as we shall see. Both *Vagabond* and *The Dead Girl* foreground the death of a female protagonist in order to ask questions about not only female oppression in and by a male dominated society, but also, about the representation of female subjectivity in film and the constitution of a feminist filmmaking practice.

The Dead Girl is arguably the 21st-century counterpart of *Vagabond,* although there are two major differences between the films. First is the manner in which the female characters meet their deaths—exposure to the cold in *Vagabond* versus murder in *The Dead Girl*—and second, the fact that Brittany Murphy, the actress who played Krista in *TheDead Girl,* died at age 32 in 2009, three years after the film was made. This tragic turn of events lends the film a premonitory quality, as if it anticipated actress Murphy's death and her slippage from playing *The Dead Girl* to becoming one herself. The film now is imbued with commemorative capacity as if it were paying tribute to her, forming one of its major contributions to and legacy for 21st-century popular culture, as discussed in the final section of this chapter.

In placing these two films in dialogue, my discussion considers how each approaches and portrays male violence toward women, a violence which, during the two decades that separate them, escalates from one film to the other: from Mona's "natural" death due to the elements—the harsh winter—in *Vagabond* to the murder of Krista, and other women, by a male serial killer in *The Dead Girl*. In staging explorations of violence against women, both films demonstrate the continued need, in the 21st century, for a feminist filmmaking practice that foregrounds female subjectivity, voices, and narratives. Like *Vagabond, The Dead Girl* attempts to recuperate and construct women's subjectivity by narrating women's stories, but the latter film, more so than *Vagabond,* gives voice to the voiceless, as most of the film's characters are women, who, moreover, are victimized: they—or their female children—are abused, exploited, missing, and murdered, mired in a cycle of brutalization by men. Speaking about *The Dead Girl,* Karen Moncrieff states that, "I'm a woman, a female filmmaker, interested in telling women's stories. I feel like I could spend the rest of my life telling women's stories and I still wouldn't scratch the surface of all the stories to be told. If I don't tell them, who is going to?"[13] Moncrieff's question here underscores the fact that well into the 21st century, women's voices continue to be silenced—onscreen as well as off, reasserting the continued need for a feminist filmmaking practice privileging female subjects, voices, and experiences.

As a film that is "part social investigation and part feminist inquiry,"[14] *Vagabond* exemplifies such a practice: According to Susan Hayward, the film "is feminist in its conception and message," since it "subverts the traditional codes of classical narrative cinema which depict man as the gender on the move and woman as static."[15] Furthermore, as it is composed of "of 47 episodes," the film "takes to task the issue of image construction, or . . . 'the fetishizing action of the male perspective'" and thus challenges and resists "the established canons of western filmmaking practices,"[16] announcing what Annette Kuhn calls "a feminist politics of intervention at the levels of language and meaning, which may be regarded as equally applicable to the 'language' of cinema as it is to the written and spoken word."[17]

With *Vagabond,* Varda creates "a new discursive form that blends fictional construct with documentary research in a unique articulation which defies traditional categorization,"[18] including a cast that combines professional actors and regional residents of the filming locations in the South of France in the environs of the city of Montpelier and the departments of Gard and

Hérault. *Vagabond* "calls into question . . . the borders between . . . history and fiction":

> *Vagabond* presents the illusion of an oscillation between history and fiction; where each of these is located, however, becomes problematic. The documentary style is used when witnesses present their testimony to the camera. These moments appear as history, as the retelling of past events, while the events themselves are represented through the narrative fiction of the action sequences, more familiar to the audience.[19]

While *The Dead Girl,* unlike *Vagabond,* does not employ documentary aesthetics such as the breaking of the fourth wall, nor the "illusion of an oscillation between history and fiction," its nonlinear narrative foregrounds female subjects and examines themes such as mother-daughter relationships and the pervasiveness of male violence against women in order to "'get inside the woman's experience and tell the story from her own perspective.'"[20] The film's nearly all female ensemble cast is composed of renowned performers such as Rose Byrne, Toni Collette, Marcia Gay Harden, Mary Beth Hurt, Piper Laurie, Mary Steenburgen, Kerry Washington, and Brittany Murphy in the titular role. In these respects, *The Dead Girl* is a 21st century woman's movie in every sense of the term: written, directed, about, and primarily acted by women. Thus is revealed the feminist sensibility of *The Dead Girl,* although the film, along with *Vagabond,* focuses on female suffering rather than female empowerment, as nearly all the women in it are victims of male violence.

In foregrounding the female corpse at the start of each film, *Vagabond* and *The Dead Girl* manifest a politics of female death at the levels of content and form. The films closely associate women and death since death is mediated not only through Mona and Krista but also through other female characters and their proximity to death—whether as murder victims, having near-death experiences, or being on the brink of a natural death of old age such as Arden's mother (Piper Laurie) in *The Dead Girl* and Tante Lydie (Marthe Jarnias)[21] in *Vagabond.* In *Vagabond,* Madame Landier (Macha Méril) is nearly electrocuted when she touches faulty lamp wiring, while the imminent death of the octogenarian Tante Lydie is eagerly anticipated by her nephew and his wife so that they can inherit her home. Circulating throughout *The Dead Girl* are images of and references to Carl's other female victims as well as the missing person's flyer of the abducted teenager Jenny Louise Folger, which, posted in phone booths, is one of the film's *leitmotifs.* While both *Vagabond* and *The Dead Girl* investigate and articulate the systematic oppression of women within patriarchy, *The Dead Girl* depicts a far more dangerous environment for women: the images of Carl's previous victims are evidence not only of his past—and potential future—criminal deeds, but are also emblematic of the wide scale victimization of women, supporting the cliché that suffering is female destiny.

Mona and Krista circulate throughout the narrative economies of each film as marginalized women situated at the fringes of their societies, lacking traditional communal ties such as participation in legitimate forms of employment or adhering to heteronormative family configurations. Mona's "rejection of social and sexual productivity . . . erases the hegemonic image of women."[22] Moreover, "male discourses (whether uttered by men or women) cannot produce [Mona's] identity . . . her independence from a fixed identity is an assertion of her *altérité* (her otherness); her autonomy from male fetishization is an obligation to recognize her *différence*—woman as an authentic and not a second sex"[23] as in Simone de Beauvoir's formulation. While both female characters are subjected to gender-based violence, Mona and Krista continually strive against patriarchal dictates for women's roles: living by their wits and on their own terms, outside of the bounds of civilized society as in the case of Mona, who pitches her tent wherever she wishes, living, as reflected in the film's original French title, *Sans toit ni loi*: "Without Roof nor Law," which is derived from the French expression "sans foi ni loi" ("without faith nor law"). Krista inhabits a rundown motel room she shares with her female roommate, companion/lover, and fellow sex worker Rosetta (Kerry Washington), which therefore becomes an exclusively female space. Moreover, Krista's wish is to leave the city behind, moving to the countryside with her daughter and Rosetta, and thus create a gynotopia inaccessible to males. Krista, unable to raise her young daughter Ashley by herself, has left the child in the care of an unlicensed boarding center run by women, a site which also functions as a marginalized female space.

Moncrieff, when asked why she did not create a section of her film based on one of its (very few) male characters, stated, "I could have, but I feel like we've seen so many movies about serial killers, but nothing about a serial killer's wife."[24] Her comment here brings to mind an early action of the newly founded French women's liberation movement, the MLF (Mouvement de libération des femmes) when in Paris in August 1970, a group of feminist activists placed a wreath on the Tomb of the Unknown Soldier at the Arc de Triomphe. However, they did so not in order to commemorate the soldier—as was and still is customary—but rather, brought the flowers for his wife, who, they emphasized, was even "more unknown" than him. This action brought the first public media attention to the MLF. Thus a line of flight from the late 20th to the early 21st century—and across two continents—can be traced from the birth of the MLF more than 30 years before the making of *The Dead Girl* to Moncrieff's impetus for making this film, namely, the need to express often overlooked female voices and perspectives. In the 21st-century United States, as in the France of the 1970s, women are still relegated to a secondary subject position: whether the wife of the Unknown Soldier or the wife of a serial killer, their husbands' stories are privileged over theirs. Going against the grain of the traditional suppressing and silencing of women's voices are not only feminist activists such as members of the MLF, but also, filmmakers including Varda—"an avowed feminist"[25] whose "authorship presented a series of 'laboratories' in which she blended the dual concerns of film language and feminism in order to arrive at a concept of feminine cinematic writing (*filmer en femme*)"[26]—and Moncrieff who, through their works, provide a counter cinema that foregrounds women's voices, stories, and experiences, especially with male violence.

Krista's murder is not depicted onscreen (although her face, arms, and hand, covered with bloody gashes and crawling with insects, form one of the film's earliest images and the viewers' introduction to her). Moncrieff, in writing and directing *The Dead Girl,* chose not to present the woman's murder for visual consumption, but rather, only the moments leading up to and the aftermath of her death. Moncrieff "never wanted to see the moment" of Krista dying; despite the movie "dealing with issues of violence against women," Moncrieff does not want to portray "gratuitous images of women being bashed," nor "show this woman [Krista] being killed."[27] In this respect, the film's aesthetic follows Aristotelian theatrical conventions, which demand that violence not be shown to the spectator, but only be narrated, and take place offstage.

The Dead Girl's opening chapter shows, in a shot over Arden's shoulder, a small, blurry figure in the bottom right-hand corner of the frame, which is revealed to be the bludgeoned, bloody corpse of the titular female, who is lying in a field in a hilly orchard. Yet the focus is not upon her body, which is diminished in perspective and appears disproportionally small in comparison to Arden's foregrounded head and shoulders; Krista's face, however, will be shown in close-up, as will her hand, which is covered with defensive wounds.

The Dead Girl's opening scenes depicting Krista's body brings to mind another representation of the-nude-woman-lying-in-a-field, none other than one of the most iconic works of 20th-century modern art: Marcel Duchamp's multimedia installation *Etant donnés: 1° la chute d'eau, 2° le gaz d'éclairage . . . /Given: 1° The Waterfall / 2° the illuminating gas . . .* (1946–66)—considered the first mixed media art installation—whose permanent home is the Philadelphia Museum of Art. In *Etant donnés,* viewable through two peepholes in a nondescript wooden door is the effigy of a nude woman, lying in a field, her face obscured, yet her genitals on full display as her legs are spread apart. As Holland Cotter remarks,

> She reclines on a nest of dried branches, her legs spread wide to reveal oddly malformed genitals. Her face is obscured by her blond hair. Her lower legs and right arm are out of the range of vision. Her left arm is raised at the elbow, and in her hand she holds a small, glowing electric

lamp. . . . The sight, at once bucolic and freakish, provoked an uproar when the piece had its public debut 40 years ago. What are we looking at? The aftermath of rape, mutilation and attempted murder? A profane update of Bernini's 'Ecstasy of St. Teresa'?[28]

As Cotter's questions demonstrate, whether the woman in *Etant donnés* is a murder victim is a perennial question that arises among spectators and critics alike: while her peach-toned flesh—primarily made out of pigskin, among other materials—does not bear marks or signs of brutalization, as does Krista's in *The Dead Girl,* Jean-Michel Rabaté notes that "the front page of the *Philadelphia Inquirer* of July 8, 1969, titled its review of Duchamp's installation: 'Resembles Cadaver.'"[29]

As Rabaté observes, in *Etant donnés,* like a cadaver, "the total immobility of the woman's body contrasts starkly with the regular movements of the water and the flame,"[30] as in *The Dead Girl* in which "the total immobility" of Krista's body "contrasts starkly" with the hustle and bustle of nature at work, including busy insects scurrying over her and the birds circling high above, watching over a possible feast. Moreover, according to Rabaté, in *Etant Donnés,*

It looks as if Courbet's notorious *The Origin of the World* displaying a woman's legs and genitals had been reframed in a hallucinatory Victorian diorama while adding a macabre touch. Is this the scene of a crime? . . . what if the naked body of the woman who holds a lamp was just what it appears to be on first inspection—a dead body? The first visitors who discovered the installation in June 1969 had all the same impression: it looked like a woman's corpse . . . Another witness . . . felt that the reclining nude 'looked like a cadaver on which they would perform autopsies in a medical school.'[31]

Unlike viewers of Duchamp's *Etant donnés,* however, spectators of *The Dead Girl* are fully aware that the woman in the field is indeed a corpse who will be the cadaver on which a medical school autopsy will be performed in the film's second chapter. Whereas in *Etant donnés,* the woman's face is obscured and her malformed genitals are displayed to the viewer, the opposite holds true in *The Dead Girl,* in which the focus is placed on the woman's face rather than her body, which is obscured by its diminished positioning within the frame and which is, moreover, never fully displayed as is the nude woman of *Etant donnés.*

Although *Vagabond* shows how Mona dies as she struggles after falling in the ditch—her death throes reminiscent of those of Maciek (Zbigniew Cybulski) in *Ashes and Diamonds* (Andrzej Wajda, 1958), before he succumbs to his gunshot wounds while lying on a refuse heap[32]—Varda's film, like *The Dead Girl,* for the most part rejects onscreen depictions of violence against its female protagonist. For example, when Mona, earlier in the film, is raped in a forest, the camera cuts away and drifts upward, focusing on the leaves instead of the brutal assault taking place below the trees, away from the spectator's gaze, therefore disinviting voyeuristic pleasure in and fetishization of the on-screen spectacle of violence against women. Although the attack against Mona is not depicted onscreen, Mona's horrifying screams are heard by the spectator, an equally powerful depiction of her suffering and anguish.

Krista traverses the dark and tragic universe of *The Dead Girl,* a world in which "every girl is a potential victim" and in which the dominant moods are "grief, loss, longing, a need to connect, and darker emotions."[33] These dark emotions are underscored by the film's gloomy color scheme of blues, grays, and black, which create an aesthetic of despair. "A parent's worst nightmare: a missing child, a dead child, an abducted child, the murdered child, the child who you can't protect well enough from something terrible to happen"[34] are all palpably and explicitly displayed in *The Dead Girl.* Moreover, the child in these iterations explored by the film's scenario is a female: Krista's infant daughter Ashley, who becomes an orphan after her mother's death; the adolescent girl Jenny Folger, kidnapped in her teens, whose missing person's flyer is displayed on numerous occasions as a *leitmotif* throughout the entire film; or Melora (Marcia Gay Harden), called to identify her daughter Krista's body after she was murdered. Indeed, the film's narrative unfolding exemplifies a parent's worst nightmare.

As opposed to *The Dead Girl,* in *Vagabond,* women characters are victim-ized not only or necessarily by men, but also suffer from other causes such as the elements, faulty appliances, and old age, which do not seem to affect their male counterparts in the film. The bitter winter cold kills Mona; the much-anticipated death of elderly Tante Lydie is eagerly wished for by her nephew Jean-Pierre (Stéphane Freiss), heir to her large estate; tree specialist Madame Landier (Macha Méril) is almost electrocuted by the faulty wire of a lamp. Trembling from the waves of electricity coursing through her body, she is res-cued in extremis by her younger colleague Jean-Pierre, who, ironically, while desperately waiting for one woman (Tante Lydie) to die—and tired, of waiting, forces her into a nursing home, an antechamber of death, against her wishes—becomes a hero by rescuing another woman, his colleague Madame Landier, from imminent death by pulling her away from the lamp. Like Mona, Krista's corpse is found in a bucolic setting, but unlike Mona, the vagaries of the ele-ments did not lead to Krista's death: She was dumped there by her murderer. In fact, Krista had dreamt of moving to the countryside with her daughter; shortly before she is killed, she expressed her wish to leave the city for "some-place where there's trees and sky"—uncannily foreshadowing the location where her corpse is found, a location which is described, by Arden, after dis-covering Krista, as being "trees. And sky," which in other contexts would be an idyllic pastoral landscape.

Cutting to the heart of the American nightmarescape, *The Dead Girl* stages an exploration of female subjectivity as inextricably intertwined with death. Each of the film's female characters is associated with, and affected by, the death of the film's titular figure: whether biologically related to her as are her mother Melora and three-year old daughter, Ashley; whether having known her while she was alive, such as her roommate and lover Rosetta, a fellow drug addict and sex worker, or whether only having encountered her corpse such as Arden and forensics graduate student Leah (Rose Byrne), for whom Krista is the "Jane Doe" cadaver lying on her examination table. This film's female characters are linked to one another through an encounter with Krista, through whom they confront their own senses of mortality.

As previously mentioned, *The Dead Girl* follows a nonlinear course of five chapters with different yet overlapping stories and characters, each of which features a different female protagonist and is given a title: "The Stranger," "The Sister," "The Wife," "The Mother," and, finally, "The Dead Girl." This last chapter recounts and retraces Krista's final moments. Whether alive or dead, Krista's presence is felt and reflected in each segment. She is the point upon which the five chapters converge.

"The Stranger," the title of *The Dead Girl*'s first chapter, refers to Krista Kutcher's intrusion into the lives of those around her: she is a stranger to Arden, who finds her corpse and through this discovery, becomes important in her small town, going from obscurity to accidental fame, her life changes for the better: because of her newly acquired celebrity status, she meets a man, with whom she immediately leaves town, the two of them driving away in the sunset toward a better future—although her new boyfriend Rudy (Giovanni Ribisi) seems to be obsessed with recounting and detailing the deeds of male serial killers. In the film's second sequence, "The Sister," the corpse of Krista undergoes an autopsy by forensics graduate student Leah (Byrne), the sister of Jenny Folger—abducted 15 years earlier, and whose missing person's flyers are featured throughout the film. Leah believes Krista's corpse is that of Jenny, due to a tattoo that Jenny notices on the corpse's arm. The third chapter, "The Wife," is about Ruth (Mary Beth Hurt), whose husband Carl, she comes to discover, is a serial killer preying upon local women. The film's fourth segment, "The Mother," emphasizes Krista's estrangement from Melora, her mother, who has come to claim Krista's body. In this sequence, Krista's roommate Rosetta reveals to Melora the existence of Krista's three-year old daughter Ashley; Melora, who just learned that her daughter is dead, simultaneously learns that she has become a grandmother of a three-year-old that she will now inherit and raise. Ashley is the film's youngest female victim, as she is left an orphan: her mother is murdered on the morning of her third birthday at 12:13 A.M., the very time at which Ashley was born, thus recalling Mikhail Bakhtin's words that "the beginning and end of life [are] closely linked and interwoven."[35]

In the final scene of the film's last chapter, also entitled "The Dead Girl," Krista hitchhikes so that she can reach the birthday girl at her makeshift day-care. Krista's gift to Ashley—a large stuffed pink bunny rabbit—was never to be delivered. Krista, while sitting in Carl's passenger seat, chats about her daughter's birthday, bringing to mind a similar sequence in a film foreground-ing murderous male violence against women, Quentin Tarantino's slasher *Death Proof* (2007), in which a young woman is killed by the male stranger from whom she accepted a ride home. Whereas in *Death Proof,* Pam (Rose McGowan) begs the driver, Stuntman Mike (Kurt Russell), to spare her life, there is no such moment of recognition in *The Dead Girl,* as the film fades to black while Krista is chatting with the serial killer in the driver's seat: ironi-cally, the topics of her small talk are the joys of becoming a mother, of bringing forth new life—all while the killer is plotting to end hers, as understood by the spectators.

On her autopsy report, Krista is at first described as having "no known rela-tives," until her mother Melora is able to identify her and claim her body (in *Vagabond,* Mona's body is never claimed by anyone, and therefore, is buried in a potter's field, among other unidentified corpses). However, before Krista is identified, forensics graduate student Leah believed that the corpse was that of her abducted sister Jenny, a belief that originates after she notices the tat-too "12:13" on the cadaver's arm. The numerical sequence "12:13" leads Leah to the biblical verse "12,13" of Genesis in which Abram tells his wife Sarai to pretend she is his sister in order to prevent the men of Egypt from killing him. Abram believes that if the Egyptian men found out Sarai is his wife, they would kill him in order to possess her; the title of "sister," applied to Sarai, will spare Abram's life: "say you are my sister, so that . . . my life will be spared because of you." Also of significance in *The Dead Girl*'s second vignette, "The Sister," is the first name of its main character, Leah, a name of biblical origins. In the Old Testament narrative, two sisters, Leah and Rachel, known as the matriarchs, are linked in a complex sisterly relationship of love and competition. They both become wives of the same man, Jacob—one of the three patriarchs—who was tricked into marrying Leah although he was promised Rachel (and even-tually married both sisters).

Yet Krista's 12:13 tattoo commemorates the time of Ashley's birth at 12:13 A.M., as she tells Carl before climbing into his car; if this were a Greek tragedy, it would be fate that had decided that the time of her death would coincide with Ashley's birth, as this is the time displayed on serial killer Carl's car clock, soon after Krista steps inside his vehicle. These coincidences are made to ren-der the public aware of the small details around which Moncrieff constructs her narration. The fact that the time of the daughter's birth and the mother's death coincide is an uncanny element in a narrative already filled with other eerie coincidences linking the characters together.

As demonstrated by the opening chapter of *The Dead Girl,* women char-acters are cast as discoverers of death. Women bear witness to other women's deaths: Arden, Leah, and Melora encounter Krista's deceased body; Ruth, married to the serial killer Carl, finds the belongings of his female victims, such as their photos, clothes, and Krista's pink vest, hidden away in a secret storage unit—reminiscent of the tale of Bluebeard's wife, itself taken from the grim reality of Gilles de Rais, one of the most notorious serial killers in history—who entered his private, locked chamber in which he kept the mutilated and bloody bodies of his previous wives, whom he had murdered. In *The Dead Girl,* women encounter, discover, and confront death to a greater extent than in *Vagabond,* in which Mona's corpse is discovered by a male vineyard worker, and moreover, Mona's death is the only instance of a woman dying in the film—a death which is not directly related to a crime, as in *The Dead Girl.*

In her 2003 documentary, entitled *Remembrances,* about the making of *Vagabond* for the 18th anniversary of the film,[36] Varda asserts that no matter what happens to her, Mona is "not a victim." Such an assertion cannot apply to Krista or the other female characters in *The Dead Girl* who are emotionally and physically abused, victimized, and killed. Yet, although Mona has agency, Varda's statement is questionable, since Mona, like the women in *The Dead Girl,* is victimized by men on several occasions, such as when she is raped in the forest and later on when she is involved with a con artist at the train station who was hoping to pimp her and turn her into a porn star. The one time that Mona seems to have found—and accepted—a potentially stable living and working situation is with Assoun (Yahiaoui Assouna), a Tunisian migrant farm worker who takes her in, cooking and caring for her. However, when Assoun's fellow migrant workers return from Morocco, they insist that Mona leave as they refuse to share their cramped space with a woman. Mona denounces Assoun for cowering to their misogyny, throwing back at him the red scarf he had given her, reminiscent of the scene in *The Dead Girl* in which Krista curses and screams at Tarlow (Josh Brolin) when he reneges on his promise to drive her to see her daughter. Broken promises by male characters in both films seem to lead to the fatal undoing of these two women.

Hostile and violent acts toward Mona and Krista can be decoded within the broader context of an entrenched societal violence against women. Of the mistreatment of Mona by various male characters, Kelly Oliver has noted that

> These men see Mona there for the taking. . . . Like any other object, she is there for their exploitation. Either they do not concern themselves with her desires (objects do not have desires), or . . . they imagine that she 'wants it' because all female drifters chase men. What is more horrifying than the attitudes of these men is how normal it all seems. This sort of thing happens everyday. If upon reflection we find it offensive, even appalling, what is truly appalling is that it is also mundane and ordinary.[37]

Before the end of *Vagabond,* Mona tries to forage for food in the village closest to where she has most recently been camping. The village seems to be deserted; all stores are closed. Unbeknownst to her, this day is the traditional annual wine harvesting ritual, in which some men behave in a disorderly manner, as in a Dionysian carnival. They are dressed in burlap sacks, their faces covered with masks, leaves hanging in their hair. They brutally grab Mona, laughing and screaming in a scene that recalls the frightening charivari fertility ritual in Daniel Vigne's film *Le retour de Martin Guerre/The Return of Martin Guerre* (1982), which is set in rural medieval France. In that fertility ritual, masked men tyrannize village residents who have not yet produced offspring. Of the disturbing grape harvest rite in *Vagabond,* Oliver comments that, "this traditional French village festival celebrates the [grape] harvest by chasing away strangers. . . . Much like a religious purification ritual, the strangers are washed in blood-red wine. The village identity is maintained through this festival in which the abjected strangers are either purified or chased away."[38] Mona tries to run away from the inhospitable village, but the men catch her and throw her in a vat of wine. As the abjected stranger, who must be "either purified or chased away," Mona, unaware of their customs, is shocked and frightened by the costumed men's primitive ritual, reminiscent of a Dionysian bacchanal. In vain she attempts to hide from them in a phone booth in the village square, but the men chase her, banging their fists on the booth's glass pane, laughing at her screams, as they can see her through this transparent shelter. This further compounds Mona's estrangement from the prevailing social rites and customs and moreover, prefigures her death since because of the ritual, the village is completely closed down and she is thus unable to find bread. Mona, here the abjected stranger, foreshadows Krista, the titular "Stranger" of the first chapter of *The Dead Girl,* two decades later: the "strangeness" of these two women is endorsed, completed and repeated by their deaths, thus providing a provisional answer to Jacques Derrida's question, "what would a foreign woman be?"[39] According to *Vagabond* and *The Dead Girl,* the answer to this question is that this stranger, this strange woman, would be a victim, would be dead: these films represent the "strange"—or "foreign"—woman as deceased, her corpse left in a field for others to find, and from and about which they attempt to extract information and derive meaning.

Susan Hayward specifically situates this ritual within the realm of gender-based violence, calling it a "'rape' of Mona's identity."[40] For Hayward, this "patriarchal pagan rite (only the men can dress-up as the wine gods and daub the women)" is a "contributing factor" in Mona's death since "the male rite withdraws sustenance (as a result of their festivities she cannot obtain any bread)" and "the violence of her rejection of their ritual practices and of the implicit tyranny of the gaze (she blockades herself in a telephone booth and screams . . .) aggravates her already advanced stage of hypothermia."[41] The symbolic enclosed protective space of the telephone booth reinforces Mona's isolation. Once a technological advance, the phone booth is a now a historic relic as new cell phone technology has taken precedence over it and rendered it obsolete. Yet the phone booth in *Vagabond* functions as a hallmark of the film's setting in the 1980s, along with other cultural emblems that appear throughout the film, such as the diegetic music of one of the most popular French songs of the period, the hit 1985 single "Marcia Baïla" by the band Rita Mitsouko. This song, despite being a prime example of upbeat and lighthearted 80s music with a euphoric, danceable rhythm, actually functions as a eulogy that commemorates the female dancer Marcia Moretto who died in 1981 at age 32 from cancer. "Marcia Baïla" is thus another narrative of female death interwoven into the diegetic fabric of *Vagabond*, thereby reinforcing and overdetermining the film's central theme of the unexpected and tragic death of the young and beautiful woman. In this scene of *Vagabond*, the phone booth's function is subverted, as it becomes a nonfunctional space. It does not lead to any communication with the outside world that could have helped Mona and saved her life. As the refrain of the popular American song from the film *Ghostbusters* (Ivan Reitman, 1984)—preceding *Vagabond* by just one year—asks, "who you gonna call?"[42]: in *Vagabond*, the answer is no one, because Mona has severed her family ties, and, moreover, the phone booth becomes a faulty shelter in which she attempts to hide from the men chasing her, transforming the function of the phone booth as in it, she seeks to hide and not communicate with anyone as there is no one for Mona to reach out to by phone. Unlike E.T.—another iconic emblem of the 1980s context of *Vagabond*—who tries to phone home, Mona does not as she has no family ties, which is reinforced by her burial in a potter's field since no one claims her body. This phone booth is a dead zone that exposes Mona even more to the brutality of the villagers who view her as if she were an object on display in a window for their viewing pleasure, exacerbating their desire to harass her. The telephone booth is not a site of refuge, rescue, communication, or escape, as in other popular cinematic and televisual contexts such as *Superman* or *Dr. Who*, in which the telephone booth figures as an instrument for heroic deeds or time travel, respectively.

A parallel can be drawn from the phone booth in this scene of *Vagabond* to the phone booth as *leitmotif* in *The Dead Girl*, in which are posted the missing person's flyers of Jenny Folger. Whereas the phone booth in *Vagabond* is an example of contemporary 1985 technology at the time of the making of the film, in *The Dead Girl*, 20 years later, the phone booth has become an anachronism, a throwback to a previous era's form of communication that is rarely used, going backward in time from high speed 21st-century smartphones and information technology that renders phone booths obsolete relics of the past—much like Jenny Louise Folger, who has been missing approximately the same length as the phone booth's downward trajectory. Jenny's timeline is on par with that of the phone booth as both are on their way to disappearance. Much like a 21st-century reimagining of 19th-century poems "Tristesse d'Olympio" by Victor

Hugo and Alphonse de Lamartine's "Le Lac," time has continued on its march forward, leaving both the pay phone and Jenny behind, remnants of a not-too-distant past: Jenny's sister Leah has grown into adulthood and pay phones have been largely replaced by mobile phones. Yet in both *Vagabond* and *The Dead Girl,* phone booths appear and function in order to articulate the films' overdetermination of male violence against women: whether haunted by the abducted teenage girl Jenny or a site of entrapment for Mona as she attempts to escape the horde of men leering at, mocking, and threatening her.

Mona's death can be linked to her falling victim to male violence during this carnivalesque village grape harvesting ritual, even if she dies from natural causes, having frozen to death "with no marks on her" body as stated by the gendarmes who examine her corpse at the start of *Vagabond* in order to ascertain that there was no foul play.

After the initial discovery of Mona's corpse, *Vagabond*'s narrative moves backward to the time prior to her death when two men at the beginning of the film observe Mona emerging from the water where she was bathing, reminiscent of Botticelli's famous painting of Venus which is reinforced by Varda's voiceover stating that Mona "came from the sea," thus giving her a mythological dimension which is recuperated by the Dionysian grape harvest festival. One of the men looking at her remarks that "a girl all alone is easy," or in other words, that she can be preyed upon and consumed for the pleasure of others, not only for scopophilia.

Like Krista—whose murder is directly preceded by a man, Tarlow, breaking his promise to drive her, thrusting her into the arms of serial killer Carl, along similar lines as Assoun breaking his promise to Mona that he will "take care of her" but instead throws her out with nowhere to go, propelling her on the path toward her death—Mona *is* ultimately a victim of gender-based violence, even if it is the cold weather, rather than a man, that ends her life. In *Vagabond,* the deceased Mona becomes "the curious woman whose existence—framed and identified by her sexuality, her 'femaleness,' touches [the film's characters] (and us) deeply in some complicated way."[43]

Two decades later, Brittany Murphy, star of *The Dead Girl,* would herself become this woman who "touches [the film's characters] (and us) deeply in some complicated way," first onscreen when she played the titular role in *The Dead Girl* and, subsequently, in reality, since Murphy died in December 2009, three years after the film was released in December 2006. *The Dead Girl*'s legacy is, perhaps above all, its eerie foreshadowing of Murphy's own death, nearly three years to the day that *The Dead Girl* premiered on December 29, 2006. On December 20, 2009, Murphy, at age 32, died of pneumonia and a combination of multiple drug intoxication, setting off a media frenzy, which would be repeated, five months later, when her husband Simon Monjack (1970–2010) died on May 23, 2010, of the same cause and in the same home—and, found by Sharon Murphy, Brittany's mother, who had also found her daughter. Murphy and Monjack now "share a final resting place at Forest Lawn Memorial Park in Hollywood Hills."[44]

Murphy and Monjack's deaths occurred in 2009–2010, a period in the 21st century often referred to as "celebrity death season," due to the alarmist media- and new/social-media-fueled (mis)conception that, starting in the summer of 2009, after several high-profile performers and entertainers had passed away—including Michael Jackson on June 25, 2009—an epidemic of dying celebrities was sweeping the United States. By 2011, however, celebrity death season had given way to a "celebrity baby boom"—itself another perception driven by media coverage of celebrities who were expecting children that year: as one celebrity and popular culture blogger proclaimed, babies are "the must-have trend of 2011."[45] This second phenomenon parallels the first, as it shows that *what* sweeps the country is largely a media construction. Moreover, *how* the media-saturated public perceives death, and what aspects of death— or life, for that matter—are worthy of attention has become largely reduced to a matter of what drives television ratings up and/or inspires page views on new and social media outlets such as news websites, Twitter feeds, media/entertainment gossip blogs, Tumblrs, and Facebook pages. For example, "upon hearing of Jackson's departure, the media, public at large and fans worldwide stood still. A feverish rush of incredulous people, seeking to find out more about Jackson's death, caused websites including AOL Messenger, *The Los Angeles Times,* Twitter, TMZ, and Wikipedia to crash"[46]; "2.5 million tweets and retweets occurred within the first hour after the AP story broke" of Whitney Houston's death on February 11, 2012.[47]

In a chapter published in 2012, I examined the Murphy/Monjack deaths by situating them within the context of American popular culture in light of celebrity death season and Freud's essay "The Uncanny": "Monjack's death, following his wife's, reenacts a tragic scenario. This double inscription of the Murphy/Monjack passing—along with the shared initial "M" of their last names—brings to mind the Freudian concept of the uncanny, which is 'undoubtedly related to what is frightening, to what arouses dread and horror . . . with what excites fear in general' (1919, 219) . . . [according to Freud] *the 'double' has become a thing of terror . . . this inner 'compulsion to repeat' is perceived as uncanny* (Freud 1997, 212–214)."[48] As I have noted earlier regarding the uncanny, media-saturated death of Brittany Murphy:

> Was [her] death a case of life imitating art? In becoming-*Dead Girl*, Murphy's private and public personae coincided, demonstrating at this intersection that it is not only art that imitates life, nor life that imitates art, but moreover, that death imitates art: within *The Dead Girl* there are notable uncanny repetitions and doubles, such as a double "K," the initials of Krista Kutcher, the murder victim protagonist played by Murphy in the film. As if it were an example of the Freudian return of the

repressed, "Kutcher" is also coincidentally the last name of Murphy's previous love interest in real life, actor Ashton Kutcher (b. 1978), whose relationship with Murphy—all the way to their breakup—was fodder for gossip columns, as she became the butt of cynical comments when Kutcher partnered with a new love interest: Demi Moore. [Kutcher and Murphy's] romance and its unraveling—minutely detailed in the press— negatively impacted Murphy's career. Ironically, Murphy and Kutcher, who never married in "real life," did so in the film *Just Married* (Levy, 2003). Moreover, it is on the very set of *Just Married* that the two had met and became entangled, an item. Murphy's romances alternated between sequences onscreen and those in her Hollywood Hills cul-de-sac residence. Her truer life—truest in the Baudrillardian sense, as he believed that what is on TV is more real than what is outside of it—was what her onscreen image projected. Murphy's trajectory encompasses being *Just Married* in 2003 to being married to [producer Simon] Monjack on May 5th, 2007, and in between to becoming *Dead Girl* on December 29th, 2006 to dying for real on December 20th, 2009—not on the set of a movie, but in her own home—and finally, to being *Abandoned*[49]—the title of her penultimate film, posthumously released directly on video in 2010, which could be a reflection/description of the direction in which her life and/or career was heading. At that time, she was simultaneously abandoned by the Hollywood establishment and cruelly mocked, in an episode of *Saturday Night Live*, for being fired from the film *The Caller*.[50]

In *The Dead Girl* and in reality, Murphy was *Abandoned* to her tragic fate— like the abused, missing, and murdered women in *The Dead Girl*.

The Dead Girl inaugurates a complex politics of spectatorship as it commemorates Murphy, who, like Krista, her character in the film, died unexpectedly and too soon, affecting the wider mediatized community of her fans and spectators who immediately responded to her death by flooding the airwaves with images of, tributes to, and sound bites about her. *The Dead Girl* is transformed from a fictional narrative centering upon the perils of female existence in the 21st-century United States to a sober posthumous reflection upon Murphy's tragic demise, a media event filtered through the framework of 21st-century screen and celebrity cultures, an uncanny and uncomfortable blending of fiction and reality, mourning and underlying guilt for those who remain alive and for those who had not been kind to her during her lifetime, notably among them, the media which had mocked her in the weeks preceding her death for personal and professional tribulations such as being fired from a movie set.

Whereas *The Dead Girl* traces and explores the last days in the life of its fictional character Krista, extensive media coverage on a ceaselessly repeating news cycle posthumously examined the final moments of Murphy's life, bombarding the airwaves with stories about the star, piecing together and investigating the timeline of her own downward trajectory from the ingénue memorably playing new girl Tai, her breakthrough role in *Clueless* (Amy Heckerling, 1994) to unexpectedly becoming a nonfictional, real-life dead girl. If, as noted above, Varda's *Vagabond* innovates film form by creating "a new discursive form that blends fictional construct with documentary research," the boundaries between fiction and reality are once more disrupted by the narrative fiction film *The Dead Girl* as it intersects with Murphy's own demise and descent offscreen. Any viewing of the film after Murphy's death is filtered through and problematized by this prism, t(a)inted by the reality that the film's star, like the character she incarnated in this narrative, is a young, dead woman, thus complicating spectatorial and critical engagement with the film, as it becomes a work of mourning.

Krista Kutcher as interpreted by Brittany Murphy becomes the actress's uncanny double—and vice versa. Krista is the film's absent-omnipresent center onto which are collapsed Murphy's literal and metaphorical corpses, a double inscription of female death. *The Dead Girl* alludes to and prefigures the final days and tragic undoing of both its protagonist and its star, becoming a cinematic commemoration despite itself, lending a prophetic voice, a premonitory vision of an imminent future, a descent unto death. This film can be regarded as a memorial to a departed female onscreen and off, a young woman gone too soon, yet remembered here, forever haunting the screen—as is the deceased female figure in *The Dead Girl*—and ultimately, the viewers of the film, who become spectators of tragic tales set not only in rural Southern California but also within the mansions high in the Hollywood Hills, where Murphy succumbed: unlike Krista Kutcher, she was not discovered in a ditch, but rather, in the bathroom of her luxurious home, while her anguished mother called 911, unable to revive her. Despite being "an uncommercial, ensemble drama with all female leads . . . red marks against [it] in Hollywood,"[51] *The Dead Girl* nonetheless forms a lasting impact upon and legacy for 21st-century U.S. popular and cinematic culture in its function as a tribute and memorial to its own fallen star and dead girl, Brittany Murphy.

NOTES

    1. Shelley Gabert, "The Facts of Life: An Independent Karen Moncrieff Casts a Cold Eye on Death," *Written By: The Magazine of the Writer's Guild of America West,* January 2007, accessed March 1, 2013, http://wga.org/writtenby/writtenbysub.aspx?id=2281

    2. Jean-Michel Rabaté, *Given: 1° Crime, 2° Murder: Modernity, Murder, and Mass Culture* (Eastbourne: Sussex Academic Press, 2007), 2.

    3. Alison Smith, *Agnès Varda* (Manchester University Press, 1998), 7.

    4. Sandy Flitterman-Lewis, "Varda: *The Gleaner* and the Just," in *Situating the Feminist Gaze and Spectatorship in Postwar Cinema*, edited by Marcelline Block (Newcastle, England: Cambridge Scholars, 2010), 215.

5. For Susan Hayward, there are "47 episodes" (Susan Hayward, "Beyond the Gaze and Into *femme-filmécriture:* Agnès Varda's *Sans toit ni loi* (1985)," in *French Film: Texts and Contexts,* ed. Susan Hayward and Ginette Vincendeau (London and New York: Routledge, 1990), 286) in *Vagabond,* whereas Sandy Flitterman-Lewis makes a list of 66 "sequences" that forms a "graphic demonstration of *Vagabond's* fragmented, episodic structure and its extremely complicated form" (Sandy Flitterman-Lewis, *To Desire Differently: Feminism and the French Cinema* (New York: Columbia University Press, 1996), 295).

6. Flitterman-Lewis, *To Desire Differently,* 294.

7. Ibid., 286.

8. In this respect, both *Vagabond* and *The Dead Girl's* cinematic antecedents are films that begin with the discovery of a dead body and then work backwards to resolve the reasons for/circumstances surrounding the death—iconic examples include Billy Wilder's *Sunset Boulevard* (1950) and Robert Bresson's *Une femme douce/A Gentle Woman* (1968).

9. Hayward, "Beyond the Gaze," 286.

10. Ibid., 285.

11. Gabert, "The Facts of Life."

12. Ibid.

13. *The Dead Girl,* directed by Karen Moncrieff (2006; Bruin Grip Services, Lakeshore Entertainment, Pitbull Pictures), DVD commentary.

14. Flitterman-Lewis, *To Desire Differently,* 286.

15. Hayward, "Beyond the Gaze," 285, 288.

16. Ibid., 286.

17. Annette Kuhn, "Textual Politics," in *Issues in Feminist Film Criticism,* ed. Patricia Erens (Bloomington: Indiana University Press, 1990), 258.

18. Flitterman-Lewis, *To Desire Differently,* 286.

19. Kelly Oliver, *Subjectivity without Subjects: From Abject Fathers to Desiring Mothers* (Lanham, MD: Rowan and Littlefield, 1998), 177.

20. Moncrieff cited in Gabert, "The Facts of Life."

21. Jarnias is commemorated by Agnès Varda in her short film *Story of an Old Lady* (2003), included with the Criterion DVD of *Vagabond.*

22. Hayward, "Beyond the Gaze," 286.

23. Ibid.

24. *The Dead Girl,* DVD commentary.

25. Hayward, "Beyond the Gaze," 285.

26. Flitterman-Lewis, "Varda: *The Gleaner* and the Just," 214.

27. *The Dead Girl,* DVD commentary.

28. Holland Cotter, "Landscape of Eros: Through the Peephole," *The New York Times,* August 27, 2009, accessed March 7, 2013, http://www.nytimes.com/2009/08/28/arts/design/28duchamp.html?pagewanted=all_r=0

29. Rabaté, *Given,* 34.

30. Ibid.

31. Ibid., 34–6.

32. This scene pays homage to/is inspired by the death of Dix (Sterling Hayden) in *The Asphalt Jungle* (John Huston, 1950).

33. *The Dead Girl*, DVD commentary.

34. Ibid.

35. Mikhail Bakhtin, *Rabelais and his World,* trans. H. Iswolsky (Bloomington: Indiana University Press, 1984), 317.

36. Included with the Criterion Collection DVD of *Vagabond* (2007).

37. Oliver, *Subjectivity without Subjects,* 168.

38. Ibid., 170.

39. Jacques Derrida, *Of Hospitality: Anne Dufourmantelle Invites Jacques Derrida to Respond,* trans. Rachel Bowlby (Stanford, CA: Stanford University Press, 2000), 73.

40. Hayward, "Beyond the Gaze," 291.

41. Ibid.

42. The refrain of "Ghostbusters" (Ray Parker, Jr.) the theme song of the eponymous film is "Who you gonna call? Ghostbusters!"

43. Flitterman-Lewis, *To Desire Differently,* 287.

44. Marcelline Block, "Poor Little Rich Dead: Michael Jackson's Moonwalk through the Pharmaco-Narco Netherworld and Other Tales of Celebrity Death and Inequality," in *Unequal Before Death,*ed. Christina Staudt and Marcelline Block (Newcastle: Cambridge Scholars Publishing, 2012), 165.

45. Michael K., "MiserAlba's Scowlface Legacy Will Live on Again," *Dlisted,* February 16, 2011, http://www.dlisted.com/node/40851

46. Block, "Poor Little Rich Dead," 152.

47. Jacqueline Lee, "Whitney Houston's Death Reported on Twitter Before Official Associated Press Release," *TMC.net,* February 13, 2012, accessed February 19, 2012, http://www.tmcnet.com/topics/articles/2012/02/13/265908-whitney-houstons-death-reported-twitter-before-official-associated.htm

48. Block, "Poor Little Rich Dead," 165.

49. Directed by Michael Feifer and posthumously released only on DVD on August 24, 2010.

50. Block, "Poor Little Rich Dead," 166.

51. Gabert, "The Facts of Life."

Chapter 9

Unveiling the Corpse in the 21st Century

Kathryn Beattie

*T*wenty-first-century American culture finds itself in the midst of a paradigm shift regarding social attitudes toward death, and art presents us with an invaluable window onto this timeless theme. The works of contemporary artists explored in this chapter provide a measure of insight into this fragile relationship between visual culture and mortality.

Mass media consumption in the 20th century decoupled representation from reality, perhaps even the corpse from the body. This culminated in what Hans Belting has observed about the 21st century: "Though our image consumption today has increased to an unprecedented degree, our experience with images of the dead has lost its former importance altogether."[1] Working outside this image overload pathology are a number of contemporary artists exploring their own relationships between the corpse, mourning, loss, and denial, on the one hand, and art practice, aesthetics, and public presentation on the other. The photographs of corpses by Sally Mann, for example, offer personal approaches and insights into our changing journey to the end. The viewers exhume their own meanings from images discussed in the paper, recognizing an emerging twenty-first-century attitude toward death and confirming Julia Kristeva's words, "But what use is art if it can't help us look death in the face."[2]

INTRODUCTION

> *Art is a form of communication that is simultaneously privileged and outside the conventions of everyday language. This vexed relationship to discourse arguably allows it to articulate or, at least approach, death in a way that can't be sustained in everyday discourse.*
> —*Jennifer Webb and Lorraine Webb*[3]

Twenty-first-century American culture finds itself in the midst of a paradigm shift regarding social attitudes toward death. Art presents us with an invaluable window onto this timeless theme, providing a measure of insight into the fragile relationship between visual culture and mortality. Mass media consumption in the 20th century decoupled representation from reality, and perhaps, even, the corpse from the body. This culminated in what Hans Belting has observed about the 21st century: "Though our image consumption today has increased to an unprecedented degree, our experience with images of the dead has lost its former importance altogether."[4] Working outside this image overload pathology is a growing number of contemporary artists, both American and international, who are exploring their own relationships between the corpse, mourning, loss, and denial, on the one hand, and art practice, aesthetics, and public presentation on the other. Martha McWilliams suggests two categories in contemporary artwork dealing with death. Firstly, work that considers one's own impending death and secondly, work that deals with the body after death.[5] It is the latter, representations of the corpse, that will be addressed in this chapter, more specifically, the photographs of decomposing corpses by American photographer, Sally Mann. Her two exhibitions and accompanying books, *What Remains* (2004) and *The Flesh and the Spirit* (2010), offer a personal approach and insight into our changing journey to the end. Mann invites viewers to exhume their own meanings from these unsettling images, recognizing a slowly emerging 21st-century attitude toward death. Her photographic approach and the resulting images of corpses confirm, without a doubt, Julia Kristeva's words, "But what use is art if it can't help us look death in the face."[6]

THE LAST TABOO

Twenty-first-century American society continues, on the whole, to suppress discussion of death and generally considers it to be one of the last taboos. An observer unfamiliar with American culture might question the truth about this denial of death when they note how inundated we are with images of real and fictional death: corpses and war-torn bodies in the news, in movies, and in the never-ending parade of television shows addressing death and graphic autopsies. Georges Bataille claims that "taboos founded on terror are not only there to be obeyed. There is always another side to the matter. It is always a temptation to knock down a barrier; the forbidden action takes on a significance it lacks before fear widens the gap between us and it and invests it with an aura of excitement."[7] But is the barrier really destroyed or is it actually made even more impenetrable by the unceasing barrage of anesthetizing images of death that seem, in fact, to remove us even further from the reality of actual death—especially our own.

Real death, on the other hand, generally remains distanced from the consciousness and sight of the general public. The aged and dying are relegated to nursing homes, hospitals, palliative care units, and hospices where they die—out of sight, out of mind. Their bodies are then removed directly to the funeral home where embalming and/or cremation save the mourners from the uncomfortable and disturbing realities of the corpse and all it connotes: that the person no longer exists as well as the constant reminder of the eventual death of the still living. Just as Belting claims we have lost touch with images of death so, too, have we lost touch with the reality of the corpse.

THE CORPSE: "ABJECT OBJECT *PAR EXCELLENCE*"[8]

For centuries, the corpse represented contagion and infectivity, and was removed, buried, cremated as quickly as possible to protect the living from its impurities. In spite of the fact that it has been scientifically proven that corpses are not contagious, we continue in the 21st century to see them as "polluting factors that must be handed over to the funeral directors to dispose of them,"[9] to embalm or cremate, to place in coffins or urns and to inter in graves at which time they begin their decomposition hidden under six feet of earth. Today, the *idea* of the corpse brings forward the unthinkable: decomposition, impurity, decay. But for most contemporary Americans, the only dead bodies they actually see are very unnatural embalmed corpses located in funeral homes. As Jenny Hallam suggests, we "differentiate between the unprepared corpse as a disordered and dangerous object and the prepared dead body as an extension of self."[10] No longer do we accept the centuries-old belief that the corpse represents part of the natural order or life cycle. Rather, we see it, in Julia Kristeva's words, as "death infecting life. Abject."[11] Is it any wonder, then, that Ingrid Fernandez reports that in spite of there being a plethora of books and articles written on the culture of death in 21st-century America and that our entire history is "literally 'grounded' on the dead," "scholarship on the representation and meaning of the corpse is a relatively new, and still marginal, field of study."[12]

Let me be clear at this point that I am not suggesting that we make it a practice of leaving bodies out in the open in order to witness natural decomposition, but rather that the reality of the final transformation of the corpse after burial needs to be disinterred and at least acknowledged—a difficult undertaking, indeed. "We no longer believe in contagious magic, but which of us could be sure of not quailing at the sight of a dead body crawling with maggots?"[13] Photographer Sally Mann can. Her photographs of corpses in varying states of decay encourage the viewer to question why we quail at the sight of a decomposing corpse and hopefully direct us to a recognition and perhaps an eventual acceptance of the inevitable fate of us all.

POSTMORTEM PHOTOGRAPHY—A BRIEF HISTORY

Photographs of the corpse, in the form of postmortem memorial photography, appeared almost simultaneously with the invention of the photographic process in 1839. Interestingly, the first photograph of a corpse was not taken for memorial purposes but rather technical ones. On October 14, 1839, just one month after the first daguerreotypes were invented, Dr. Alfred Donné reported to Les Comptes rendus de l'Académie des Sciences (Proceedings of the Academy of Sciences) in Paris that he had obtained a very good result by taking the image of a dead person.[14] It did not take long for memorial photography to achieve popularity and quickly become an important part of every photography studio's business. Indeed, the superb clarity of postmortem daguerreotypes, as opposed to the often fuzzy portraits of the living, is a direct result of the medium's technical requirement for absolute stillness, a need easily met by the corpse. Interestingly, although the first postmortem daguerreotypes were taken in France, today the largest numbers of such images are archived in the United States.

Nineteenth-century postmortem photographs in the form of daguerreotypes, *cartes-de-visite,* and the larger cabinet cards, generally showed tidy representations of burial-ready corpses, washed and dressed in burial clothes, and appearing as "odorless and enduring substances[s] like marble or wax."[15] The fact that the majority of these memorial images were of dead children reflect several things. The infant mortality rates of the time were very high. Because so many died so young, the postmortem photograph was often the only lasting image the parents had of their dead children. For many Victorians "death did not really occur. People did not die. They went to sleep."[16] Certainly, sleep was a crucial metaphor in helping the Victorians come to terms with death. Therefore, it is no surprise that the majority of the postmortem photographs of babies and children depict them as asleep (see Figure 9.1). Photography studios such as Southworth & Hawes in Boston reassured bereaved families of this fact: "We take great pains to have Miniatures of Deceased Persons agreeable and satisfactory, and they are often so natural as to seem, even to Artists, in a deep sleep."[17]

As the 19th century came to a close, postmortem photographs gradually became a less popular and accepted means for remembering the dead. Although the tradition continued into and throughout the 20th century, the

Figure 9.1
Wm. Notman & Son, Mrs. Morrice's dead child, Montreal, QC, 1886, Silver salts on paper mounted on paper—Albumen process, 17.8 × 12.7 cm., McCord Museum, Montreal, II-79705.1

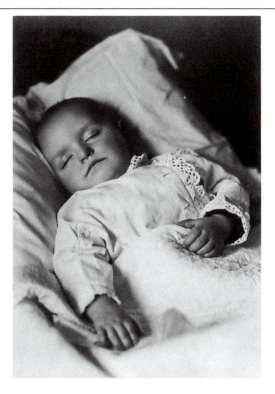

practice became increasingly associated with a ghoulish morbidity and consequently, lost its social acceptability. Boxes, drawers, albums, and archives became the tombs and final resting places for the photographic visual remembrances of the dead, to be disinterred for viewing only by immediate family, close friends, and in the case of archives, researchers. The exceptions, of course, were the postmortem photographs of friends and loved ones made by artists and photographers who felt compelled to share them with the viewing public. Richard Avedon's 1973 exhibition of photographic portraits of his dying and dead father, Nan Goldin's postmortem photographs, *Cookie at Vittorio's Coffin NYC, September 16, 1989,* and *Cookie in her Casket, November 15, 1989,* David Wojnarowicz's *Untitled (Peter Hujar),*1989, and A.A. Bronson's *Felix, June 5, 1994,* are but a few.

Although we appreciate these artists for pushing the boundaries by making very private images public, it appears that the way in which the corpses are photographed has not generally changed over the past century and a half. The corpses are either very recently dead leaving no time for decomposition to commence, or they have been prepared for burial. A. A. Bronson photographed Felix just hours after his death and although he "suffered from extreme wasting" he is "arranged to receive visitors and favorite objects are gathered about him: his television remote, his tape-recorder, and his cigarettes."[18] Goldin's image of Cookie shows her body prepared for burial and lying in her coffin. The subjects/objects in these photographs are obviously dead but there seems to be a continuing, innate wish to preserve the memory of the deceased as they were in life, whether it is accomplished by photographing the body moments after death, by including familiar objects in the photograph, or by viewing the embalmed body. In André Bazin's words, the postmortem photographs are, in fact, an attempt to "embalm time."[19] Similarly, Ingrid Fernandez suggests that like embalming, "memorial photography wishes to counteract death by providing the corpse with a visible life-like presence that allows it to unthreateningly inhabit the space of the living for a prolonged time."[20] But these attempts do not bring back the dead as Nan Goldin states in her interview with Steven Westfall: "I'd always believed that if I photographed anything or anyone enough I would never lose them. With the death of seven or eight of my closest friends . . . , I realize that there is so much the photograph doesn't preserve. It doesn't replace the person and it doesn't stave off mortality like I thought it did. It doesn't preserve a life."[21]

Artists continue to take postmortem and memorial photographs in the 21st century and although they remain very private tools of memory and mourning, we, the public, continue to be allowed limited access to them. However, they often come attached with specific parameters and guidelines. Annie Leibovitz's *Susan Sontag at the Time of her Death, Dec. 28, 2004,* was part of her 2007 exhibition *Annie Leibovitz: A Photographer's Life, 1990–2005.* Sophie Calle's 2006 postmortem photograph of her mother was exhibited in *Rachel, Monique* in Paris (2010) and in Avignon (2012). For Leibovitz and Calle, their images remain extremely personal and private remembrances and both artists continue to adamantly refuse any reproduction requests for publication. Elizabeth Heyert's *The Travelers* (2003–2004) is a series of color photographs of embalmed and beautifully dressed bodies from a Harlem funeral home. Although she knew none of them personally, Heyert remains very protective of the memory of the dead and their survivors. These postmortem photographs continue to represent embalmed, burial-ready corpses, with no acknowledgment of the reality of what they are: decomposing shells of people no longer there.

Scattered throughout the last 40 years is a handful of American photographers who moved beyond traditional memorial photography to explore new territory when they photographed unclaimed and anonymous bodies in morgues. These explorations include Jeffrey Silverthorne's *Morgue Work* (1972–1991), Gwen Akin's and Allan Ludwig's *Sliced Face in Jar, No. 1* (1985), Andres Serrano's *Morgue Series* (1994), and Joel-Peter Witkin's photographs of corpses and body parts harvested often from Mexican hospital morgues dating from the 1980s onward. All of these works have raised controversy and continue to do so, not so much because they are images of dead bodies but because of the anonymity of the corpses and the perceived lack of respect and privacy for them. But even with the very visible bruises, the dissected face in formaldehyde, the glaring postmortem Y-sutures, the sliced skulls, severed limbs, and headless bodies, the remains are still recognizably those that were once living people. At the same time plenty of scientific quantitative photographic records of decomposing human bodies have been recorded in the name of forensic research, but the images are buried in databases and entombed in filing cabinets, far from the eyes of the general public. When Sally Mann introduced her photographs of decomposing corpses in 2004, the viewing community was finally, through art, faced with what forensic scientists had been studying and recording for years. Unlike traditional postmortem memorial photographs, Mann's photographic images of dead bodies transport the viewer past the confines of embalmed time, where we would prefer to remember the dead, into another more difficult dimension where real time continues in the form of decomposing corpses lying in nature exposed to the elements. Mann, in a manner of speaking, resurrects the corpse as a symbol of the natural order or life cycle.

THE ART OF SALLY MANN

> *corpses do not generally meet the conventions of beauty, nor are they sublime subjects . . . as subjects they are hardly enlightening, since they demand that artists and audiences pay attention to that which most of us prefer to disavow: decline, decay, and death.*
> —*Jennifer Webb and Lorraine Webb* [22]

American photographer Sally Mann was born, raised, and has lived all of her adult life in Virginia. She rose to prominence in the early 1990s with the publication of her exhibition and book, *Immediate Family,* in which she raised eyebrows and controversy by documenting, through photographs, the very personal lives of her three children over a seven-year period. During her 40-year career, Mann has become adept at pushing the boundaries and bringing us, through her photographs, face to face with difficult, forbidden and often unmentionable subjects. Here, I look at one particular taboo, the corpse. Mann claims her pragmatic view on, and unending curiosity about, death stems from growing up in a family where her father, a medical doctor, was fascinated with the iconography of death. She recalls her father's attitude toward death and dying: "Not for him the euphemisms of death—it was a dead body, not "remains," nobody "passed," there was no "eternal rest." People died and that was that."[23]

Why, indeed then, would anyone be surprised when Mann unflinchingly approached the forbidden topic of death and decomposition by photographing corpses in various states of decay at the University of Tennessee's Forensic Anthropology Center? This unique place of scientific study was nicknamed the body farm and will be referred to as such throughout this chapter. Here, corpses, some donated to science, others anonymous and unclaimed, are left out in an enclosed space in nature in various states: clothed, naked, wrapped in plastic, submerged in water. The results of decomposition are observed and recorded in the name of scientific research. Mann compels us with her body farm images, to consider the decomposing corpse and what it represents to us all: our own eventual death. Kristeva writes: "corpses show me what I permanently thrust aside in order to live. . . . There, I am at the border of my condition as a living being."[24] Mann attempts to ease the viewer ever closer to that border with her photographs of corpses in varying stages of decay.

Mann has often focused on the topic of death throughout her photographic career but, except for the body farm series, always through a metaphorical lens. Her still life Polaroids from the mid-1980s of decomposing seeds and pods, dying flowers, and a snake skin, all floating in the murky water in her children's wading pool, suggest that she had been considering aspects of death even then. In 2000 she documented, in photographs, the place on her property where an escaped convict shot himself, wondering if or how the earth is transformed when someone dies there. Shortly after photographing the body farm corpses, she made a series of black and white photographic prints of some of the most famous battlefields of the American Civil War: Appomattox, Manassas, Fredericksburg, Chancellorsville, and Antietam, the site of the bloodiest battle in the history of the United States military where 23,000 soldiers were killed, wounded, or missing. In photographing these sites, Mann attempts to portray through her photography the feeling that remains in the death-, memory-, and loss-filled landscape even after over a century has passed. She describes it as: "Walking among the accretion of millions of remains—the bones, lives, souls, hopes, joys and fears that devolved into the earth—walking, in effect, on the shifting remains of humanity."[25]

When her greyhound, Eva, died, Mann was devastated but at the same time curious to know what the earth does to a corpse after death. She had the dog's body interred in a metal cage, waited 14 months, and then exhumed and photographed the bones, a claw, and tiny bone fragments, amazed at what remained of her much-loved pet. Upon observing the changes in Eva's corpse, Mann was drawn to the obvious next step, addressing through her photographic lens the journey that the human corpse continues on from the point of death. She obviously could not exhume human remains and instead looked to the body farm at the University of Tennessee.

Mann initially photographed the bodies at the body farm in the fall of 2000 while on a photo shoot for *the New York Times* and consequently obtained permission to return a second time a few months later. Mann's photographs for the initial 2004 exhibition at the Corcoran Gallery in Washington D.C. were photographed with a 100-year-old 8 × 10 bellows view camera. She preferred antique and often damaged or scratched antique lenses, valuing the imperfections they provided in the finished photographs. She used the 19th-century collodion wet-plate process to produce her black and white gelatin silver enlargement prints. At the same time she also made digital color prints, which were not exhibited publicly until their introduction in *The Flesh and the Spirit* exhibition in 2010.

To some extent, Mann continues photographing death through her metaphorical lens in the body farm prints, by placing a veil of sorts between the image and the viewer. Although she has photographed actual corpses in various stages of decomposition, the fact that the images are black and white protects the viewer from the hard reality of color. The bodies appear to meld with a dark and sometimes shadowy, almost ghostly, background. The viewer can step back slightly from the subject matter to marvel at the sheer beauty of the photographs.

Photography historian and curator Geoffrey Batchen writes: "In order to see what the photograph is of, we must first repress our consciousness of what the photograph is. As a consequence, in even the most sophisticated discussions, the photograph itself—the actual object being examined—is usually left out of the discussion." Batchen claims, however, that when looking at photography's earliest processes "the physicality of the photograph is an unavoidable feature."[26] Nineteenth-century daguerreotypes are prime examples in that their object-ness goes beyond the subject in the photograph. The often intricately decorated handheld case must be opened in order to see the image. The beautiful lining and often ornate frame become part of the experience of looking at the person represented in the photograph. In the case of Sally Mann's body farm photographs, we are certainly confronted with the sight of decomposing bodies. However, she makes it almost impossible to repress our "consciousness of what the actual photograph is" by combining the physical reality of corpses and the results of the 19th-century collodion wet-plate process.

The collodion wet-plate process was invented in 1851 by Frederic Scott Archer and became the photographic process of choice for the next 30 years. The method consists of coating a well-cleaned and polished glass plate with collodion, a solution of pyroxylin in alcohol and ether. In a dark room the coated plate is then covered with a solution containing light-sensitive silver nitrate. The plate, still wet, is inserted into a light-proof box which is placed in the camera and a slide cover is removed from the box to expose the collodion and silver nitrate–coated plate. The camera's lens cap is removed, allowing light onto the light-sensitive plate. Exposure time can last from 20 seconds to 5 minutes, at which time the lens cap is replaced, the cover is returned to the plate holder, and the box is removed from the camera and taken to the dark room. All of the preceding steps must be completed before the plate dries, about 10–15 minutes. The developer, a solution of iron sulfate and acetic acid, is poured over the plate, rinsed with water, and placed in a tray of sodium thiosulfate, which acts as a fixing agent to stop the developing process. The plate is washed again with water, dried, and finally coated with varnish. The result is a negative image ready to be developed.[27]

Although the original very finicky process produced amazingly perfect photographs, Mann welcomes any imperfections that occur, claiming they are as much part of the final photographs as are her photographing and developing processes. The viewer is always aware of the marks and scars and sometimes peeling collodion that lend the appearance of a state of decay and decomposition to the photographs themselves. The reality of the bodies in their various stages of sometimes gory decomposition is thus, in part, safely hidden under the collodion wet-plate process and masked by the dark allusive backgrounds. There is almost a 19th-century feel to the photographs resulting in the viewer perhaps not fully accepting them as contemporary corpses. The sheer elegiac beauty of the gelatin silver enlargement prints takes our mind off the magnitude of what we are looking at: decomposing bodies. But only for a moment.

Even though Mann seems to soften the impact of the photographs with the 19th-century collodion process, the use of black and white and the enigmatic backgrounds, she makes no attempt to embalm time. Just the opposite, she demonstrates with her photographs the passing of time and the actual process of decomposition, displaying the changes that the corpse goes through on its journey back into the earth. Figure 9.2, a close-up of head and shoulders, shows every minute detail from the white hair to the individual pores in the skin on the shoulder, and the face and neck seem to be covered or draped with a cloth or veil. The remains seem to be gradually melding with the ground and leaves around it, gently becoming one with the earth. Another image shows a dark, barely visible background with a naked alabaster-white corpse lying face down in the foreground, reminiscent of a fallen marble statue (Figure 9.3). The corpse is there, and yet it is not. The dark shadowing of the head and parts of the lower legs suggest, as in Figure 9.2, the process of being quietly swallowed back into the earth. Figure 9.4 requires the viewer to strain her eyes in order to find the last evidence of three decomposed corpses. The earth and leaves, combined with the peeling collodion and the scarring of the negative, have nearly completely consumed the remains, leaving only hints of barely visible skeletal matter. Mann with her unwavering eye and her camera's flawed and imperfect antique lenses begins to bring these corpses to the surface of the photograph for us where we are able to comprehend the continuing cycle of our bodies after death. Nevertheless, they remain at a shadowy distance caught between the peeling veil of collodion and an otherworldly background.

Mann waited six years before removing the last shroud from the black and white images in order to draw the viewer even closer to the reality of

Figure 9.2
Untitled, 2000. Gelatin silver enlargement print from 8 × 10 in. (20.3 × 25.4 cm) collodion wet-plate negatives, with Soluvar matte varnish mixed with diatomaceous earth ca. 30 × 40 in. (76.2 ×101.6 cm) (Courtesy Gagosian Gallery © Sally Mann)

decomposing corpses by exhibiting her digital color print versions of the body farm series. Here she has dissolved any last hint or suggestion of the symbolic and has replaced her metaphorical lens with one of veracity and truth. She reclaims the authenticity of landscape and moldering bodies and does not crop out the stark reality of where they are situated. One partially decomposed corpse, in all its raw putrefaction, appears to be just another detail in a normal yard scene, lying between discarded cement blocks, a power box, a fence and a garbage can. Another surreal landscape finds a corpse, dressed in a glaring red track suit, lying supine in the middle of a brown, almost monotone, autumn scene of fallen dead leaves and lifeless bare trees.

Unlike the viewing experience of the veiled black and white photographs, there is no avoiding these rotting corpses in the digital images, with their full palettes of color. They are just a little too authentic. Most viewers find them disturbingly real and difficult to look at. It's almost as if Mann has attempted to ease us, initially, with the help of the black and white prints, into feeling that we can look at rotting corpses without cringing or being afraid. But the

Figure 9.3
Untitled, 2001. Gelatin silver enlargement print from 8 × 10 in. (20.3 × 25.4 cm) collodion wet-plate negatives, with Soluvar matte varnish mixed with diatomaceous earth ca. 30 × 40 in. (76.2 × 101.6 cm) (Courtesy Gagosian Gallery © Sally Mann)

brilliance of the color prints seems almost too real and is reminiscent of the intense incandescent-like, cinematic colors that we suppose to be visual effects in movies. Do we subconsciously convince ourselves that in fact Mann's photographs are no different than the fictional ones?

In viewing Mann's color digital prints of the corpses, as Geoffrey Batchen claims, the observer is no longer concerned with or even aware of the photograph itself but is mesmerized by the content. We discover that the gray veil obscuring the face and neck in Figure 9.4 is actually a layer of crawling yellow maggots, a fact disguised in the black and white image by the slow exposure time of the antique camera. Mann uncovers the reality of decomposing flesh in the color digital prints and pushes the viewer through any last remaining boundaries into the reality of the luminous multicolored, maggot-ridden bodies, slowly transforming into the next cycle of life. Here she invites us to appreciate the true colors of rotting flesh and to understand her fascination with them. In the documentary film *What Remains,* she wanders through the body farm, examining the corpses without hesitation or trepidation, telling the camera: "I love mummified skin. It feels so amazing. It's so beautiful. It looks like fabric. It has such an organic vital feeling to it. It undulates and moves. It seems alive." And as she looks at a decomposing foot she exclaims: "Look at the brilliance of that orange. It's gorgeous!"[28] These words are not surprising for one who refers to H. L. Mencken's words as one of her working principles: "nothing attains maximum beauty until touched by decay."[29]

For most people, Mann's comments might seem chilling and macabre but as stated at the beginning of this chapter, artists often communicate "outside the conventions of everyday language . . . and approach death in a way that can't be sustained in everyday discourse." They see past the object and focus on color, shape, form, texture. Claude Monet, after painting his dead wife Camille in 1879, wrote: "even before I had the idea of setting down the features to which I was so deeply attached, my organism automatically reacted to the colour stimuli, and my reflexes caught me up in spite of myself."[30] Immediately after the death of Peter Hujar, David Wojnarowicz writes: "I closed the door and pulled the super-8 camera out of my bag and did a sweep of his bed: his open eye, this open mouth, that beautiful hand with the hint of gauze at the wrist that

Figure 9.4
Untitled, 2000. Gelatin silver enlargement print from 8 × 10 in. (20.3 × 25.4 cm) collodion wet-plate negatives, with Soluvar matte varnish mixed with diatomaceous earth ca. 30 × 40 in. (76.2 × 101.6 cm) (Courtesy Gagosian Gallery © Sally Mann)

held the IV needle, the color of his hand like marble, the full sense of the flesh of it."[31] Likewise British portraitist Daphne Todd, when painting a very naturalistic posthumous portrait of her mother in 2009, claims: "She was riveting to look at and I was concentrating too hard to feel much emotion."[32] During the painting process Todd also noted that "people do change and move after death. They sink into themselves; they continue on their way."[33] With comments such as these, artists encourage us, the viewers, to attempt crossing Bataille's barrier and to at least consider the realities of death, not with the phantasmagorical images of fictional and media death but rather with photographs of actual dead bodies.

The representation of corpses in 21st-century art has not been restricted to photography or to American artists. Sally Mann's photographs join the depictions of decomposing and anonymous dead bodies that are emerging into public view from around the world. Thai video artist Araya Rasdjarmrearnsook used the corpse as her subject in a series of videos (2000–2005) in which she reads to, talks to, and dresses unclaimed female bodies in a Thai morgue. South African painter Marlene Dumas included several paintings of corpses in her 2009 exhibition, *Measuring Your Own Grave*. The 2010 BP Portrait Prize in the United Kingdom was awarded to British portraitist Daphne Todd, who painted a disturbingly naturalistic posthumous portrait of her 100-year-old mother. The fact that the portrait of a dead body won this prestigious prize is evidence that perhaps we are beginning, slowly, to at least catch a glimpse of the face of death.

CONCLUSION

There is definitely a paradigm shift occurring with regard to attitudes toward the corpse in early-21st-century America. But which way is it shifting? In our changing journey to the end, which fork in the road will we finally take? Will it be the one of continued denial right to the end or the one to acknowledgment of our mortality and the reality of the corpse? It appears that perhaps it is time to take a closer more realistic look at the corpse and what it has to offer, possibly even to give it an agency that we have not allowed it to this point. Boris Groys suggests that gradually throughout modernity we have lost our faith in the immortality of the soul. He gives us hope, however, that perhaps we can still speak of life after death, but through the physical body instead of the soul. "Even though the vestiges of the corpse can no longer be identified it doesn't mean the body has disappeared, but simply that its elements—molecules, atoms, etc.—have dispersed throughout the world to such an extent that the body has practically become one with the entire world."[34]

Mann's body farm photographs support the idea of Groys' transformative process of the dead body with an unwavering, but at the same time poetic, directness. She states: "When the land subsumes the dead, they become the rich body of earth, the dark matter of creation. As I walk the fields of this farm, beneath my feet shift the bones of incalculable bodies; death is the sculptor of the ravishing landscape, the terrible mother, the damp creator of life, by whom we are one day devoured."[35] Mann adamantly believes that her body will carry on even after her death: "I don't care what they do with me, leave me for the buzzards, let the little foxes eat me, put me out there and let me nourish those creatures. There's not a lot of me but enough to support some earth process."[36]

Jean Baudrillard claims that every other culture but the Western one believes that "death begins before death, that life goes on after life and that it is impossible to distinguish life from death."[37] Mann, with her sometimes hauntingly beautiful, often disturbingly graphic photographs of corpses, attempts to bridge this cultural gap by exhuming the idea of the corpse imprisoned within cultural taboos, camouflaged by embalming and cremation, and concealed in a coffin below the earth's surface. She sets out to convince us that, in spite of beliefs to the contrary, corpses can be beautiful and sublime subjects and are definitely enlightening. In guiding us from her monotone elegiac silver prints to the stark jarring reality of the digital color prints, she encourages us to put away our disavowal of decline, decay, and death, remove the veil of avoidance, and look the corpse full in the face.

NOTES

1. Hans Belting, "Image, Medium, Body: A New Approach to Iconology," *Critical Inquiry* 31, 2 (2005): 307.

2. Julia Kristeva, *Possessions,* trans. Barbara Bray (New York: Columbia University Press, 1998), 9.

3. Jennifer Webb and Lorraine Webb, "Dead or Alive," in *Images of the Corpse: From the Renaissance to Cyberspace,* ed. Elizabeth Klaver (Madison, WI: University of Wisconsin Press, 2004), 212.

4. Belting, "Image, Medium, Body," 307.

5. Martha McWilliams, "Death Watch: Visions of Mortality in Contemporary Art," *New Art Examiner* 26, 4 (December 1998/January 1999): 41.

6. Kristeva, *Possessions*, 9.

7. Georges Bataille, *Death and Sensuality: A Study of Eroticism and the Taboo* (New York: Walker and Company, 1962), 48.

8. Randall van Schepen, "The Quick and the Dead: Jeffrey Silverthorne's Morgue Photographs," in *Constructing Death, Mourning and Memory Conference October 27–29, 2006 Proceedings,* ed. Lilian H. Zirpato (Woodcliff Lake, NJ: The WAPACC Organization, 2006), 159.

9. Sheila Harper, "The Social Agency of Dead Bodies," *Mortality: Promoting the Interdisciplinary Study of Death and Dying* 15, 4 (November 2010): 310.

10. Jenny Hallam quoted in Harper, 310.

11. Julia Kristeva, *Powers of Horror: An Essay on Abjection* (New York: Columbia University Press, 1982), 4.

12. Ingrid Fernandez, "The Lives of Corpses: Narratives of the Image in American Memorial Photography," *Mortality: Promoting the Interdisciplinary Study of Death and Dying* 16, 4 (November 2011): 343, accessed September 4, 2012, http://dx.doi.org/10.1 080/13576275.2011.613270

13. Bataille, 46.

14. Joelle Bolloch, "Photographie après décès : pratique, usages et functions," in *Le Dernier Portrait,* ed. Emmanuel Héran (Paris: Musée d'Orsay, 2002), 112.

15. Luc Santé, "Evidence," in *The Corpse: A History,* ed. Christine Quigley (Jefferson, NC: McFarland & Company, Inc., 1996), 22.

16. Kenneth Ames, "Ideologies in Stone: Meanings in Victorian Gravestones," *Journal of Popular Culture* 14 (1981): 654 quoted in Jay Ruby, *Secure the Shadow: Death and Photography in America* (Cambridge, MA and London: The MIT Press, 1995), 63.

17. Ruby, *Secure the Shadow,* 30–1.

18. A. A. Bronson, accessed February 22, 2010, http://www.aabronson.com/artmir rormirror/lookingglassfelix2.htm.

19. André Bazin, "The Ontology of the Photographic Image," in *Classic Essays on Photography,* ed. Alan Trachtenberg, notes: Amy Weinstein (New Haven, CT: Leete's Island Books, 1980), 242.

20. Fernandez, 346.

21. Stephen Westfall and Nan Goldin, "The Ballad of Nan Goldin," *BOMB* no. 37 (Fall, 1991): 31, accessed November 24, 2012, http://www.jstor.org/stable/40424261.

22. Webb and Webb, 217.

23. Sally Mann, *What Remains* (New York: Bullfinch Press, 2003), 5.

24. Kristeva, *Powers of Horror,* 3.

25. John B. Ravenal, ed., *Sally Mann: The Flesh and the Spirit* (New York: aperture, 2010), 54.

26. Geoffrey Batchen, *Each Wild Idea: Writing, Photography, History* (Cambridge, MA: The MIT Press, 2001), 60.

27. "The Wizard of Photography: Wet-Plate Photography," accessed February 1, 2013, www.pbs.org/wgbh/amex/eastman/sfeature/wetplate.html.

28. Steven Cantor, *What Remains: The Life and Work of Sally Mann* (2006, DVD 80 min, Color, USA).

29. Ravenal, 90.

30. Linda Nochlin, *Realism* (London: Penguin Books, 1990), 63.

31. David Wojnarowicz, *Close to the Knives: A Memoir of Disintegration.* (New York: Vintage Books, 1991), 102, quoted in Emily Colucci, "Peter Hujar & David Wojnarowicz "Some Sort of Grace," *American Suburbx,* accessed November 24, 2012, www .americansuburbx.com/2011/02/peter-hujar-david-wojnarowicz-some-sort-of-html

32. "Duty Calls," *London Evening Standard,* 19 November 2010, accessed May 16, 2011, http://www.thisislondon.co.uk/lifestyle/article-23835658-daphne-todd-its-my-job-to-find-beauty-in-whatever-im-looking-at.do

33. Charlotte Higgins, "Artist Daphne Todd's portrait of mother after death makes BP prize shortlist," *The Guardian,* 29 April 2010, accessed May 14, 2011, http://www .guardian.co.uk/artanddesign/2010/apr/29/artist-daphne-todd-portrait-mother-death-bp-prize-shortlist

34. Boris Groys, *The Immortal Bodies* (video lecture, color, sound, 29 min, loop) 2007. Text accessed April 3, 2011, http://cubittartists.org.uk/index.php?module=reso urcesmoduleaction=viewid=13

35. Mann, 6.

36. Cantor.

37. Jean Baudrillard, *Symbolic Exchange and Death,* trans. Iain Hamilton Grant (Los Angeles: Sage, 1993), 158–159.

Until This Return

The valley is altogether quiet. Noises, though, are some birds buzzing and tweeting. A saw in the distance. Voices speaking another language. A dive buzzing bee every 5 minutes or so. And the soft hum of Martin speaking to Frank in that husband and wife way of those who have been working side by side for decades.

In the mirror I see how the breeze, the sun, the sounds, the sea, and the work mold old lady faces with strong jaws and intent but soft-focused eyes, noses pointed with purpose, those faces I see carrying groceries down the gravel roads, minding shops full of embroidered pillow covers.

Here are the rocky hills, the ivory-striped tufts of green hair, the trees and shrubs. Oh those rocks are my heart, left as if by accident on the back shelf, yes here it is, my heart. Baking under the island sun. Baking until now. Until this return. Almost tears. And beating faster. My heart, again, still here.

Jumping ahead, I hope, forty years or so, I feel my bones attach to the sea blue, attach and in attaching give me the message: here here, I lie, will lie, wish to lie when the breath and beating are done, when the rest time comes, here, floating in the mineral blue. This is an ancient and a future home.

Catherine Rogers

Section III

Transforming the Aftermath

Chapter 10

Expansion of New Rituals
for the Dying and Bereaved

Sherry R. Schachter and Kristen M. Finneran

*F*rom ancient Egyptian sarcophagi, crypts, and pyramids to American naval
*ships, from ancient Native American burial grounds to bronze grave markers and
cemeteries, we, as individuals and as a society, find ways to honor our dead. The
rituals we create, maintain, and continue to develop help sustain us and in some
ways provide a roadmap for us to follow in our journey of grief. Even though death
is universal, the response to death varies and so too the rituals surrounding families. The focus of this chapter will be on describing new and creative rituals that
have been created both for those who are dying and for the bereaved survivors following the death. The chapter begins with a brief overview of the importance of rituals and their potential to provide support for dying patients and those who survive
them. The authors discuss two major events that they believe have affected the way
individuals conceptualize and utilize rituals in their healing. Abundant examples
of innovative and creative rituals are offered from the authors' over thirty years of
clinical experience working with the dying and their bereaved family members.
(The coauthors' case stories are identified by "SRS" or "KMF" to denote the source.)*

THE PURPOSE OF GRIEF RITUALS

Kenneth Doka defines rituals as acts invested with meaning and the power
to engage both the conscious and the unconscious.[1] Although there may be

some confusion differentiating rituals from routines, habits or tasks, rituals can be differentiated, in that rituals take prior thought and planning—they are intentional actions with a specific purpose and aim.[2] Routines are generally perfunctory and momentary with little conscious thought or planning.[3] While rituals rely on symbols and symbolic actions, tasks and routines are more concrete with little emphasis on symbols.[4] Barbara Fiese et al. note that "[a]ny routine has the potential to become a ritual once it moves from an instrument to a symbolic act."[5]

Rituals have many facets and can be expressed in many ways including, but not limited to, ceremonial practices, patterns, and gestures; art forms and artifacts; special food, clothing, or places; and prayers and meditations.[6] Defining rituals into separate categories is not an easy task to accomplish. Rituals can take many different formats and can include spontaneous or planned ritual, permanent or ongoing ritual, therapeutic ritual, and even moving rituals, that is, the AIDS quilt which is moved from city to city. Rituals of any kind can have various effects on an individual as people experience their own unique response. In certain circumstances, the ritual, if not prescriptive, might hold little or no meaning, perhaps even causing more harm than good. Different meanings are derived from rituals as they are intimately personal. Although many people may participate in the same ritual, each individual may derive substantial and unique benefits from the ritual. This chapter will focus not on the theories of ritual, but rather on the powerful examples of ritual and what those rituals accomplish.

Different theorists have classified rituals into categorical references. Doka and Pamela Vale-Taylor are just two of those who have written about rituals and their uses.[7] Each author uses his or her own language to refer to a ritual's purpose. Doka writes about rituals of continuity, rituals of transition, rituals of reconciliation, and rituals of affirmation. Vale-Taylor writes of rituals carried out for the deceased linking the bereaved to the deceased and community rituals of remembrance. In many rituals it may be challenging to separate out just one therapeutic advantage. Often times, a single ritual can have many different uses. The rituals presented in this chapter are from the authors' clinical case experiences and any one example accomplishes many of the therapeutic benefits listed above.

Rituals are generally influenced by the culture in which they are used and therapists must be sensitive to the needs of the individual, recognizing that a ritual that may be helpful to some may be unhelpful, or even offensive, to others. Clinicians should be mindful that the rituals we initiate in an attempt to be supportive have to be sensitive to the religious and/or cultural beliefs of the bereaved family members with whom we are working. A Swedish study describes neonatal clinicians who routinely made footprints and took photographs of a deceased child, with the aim to use these objects in therapeutic interventions to support the bereaved parents. Although helpful to many families, not all parents found this ritual to be therapeutic. For some bereaved Arab mothers, these rituals added an additional level of stress.[8]

Stan Goldberg questions the significance of ancient rituals and their relevancy in our contemporary lives, curious if medieval rituals are pertinent to today's world.[9] Goldberg concludes that indeed rituals continue to help define who we are and thereby distinguish us from others. For example, the secret handshakes of fraternal organizations or the wearing of team uniforms serve to separate us from others. Although rituals connect us to the past, at the same time they can help navigate us toward the future.

Maurice Eisenbruch notes: "When it is impossible to carry out traditional rituals that have great meaning and serve to comfort the bereaved, the stress of bereavement is amplified."[10] While there may be validity in this statement, there are times when traditional rituals are either not appropriate or may be viewed by the bereaved to be unhelpful. Frequently, rituals can also create family conflicts within generations when younger members rebel against traditional rituals and attempt to create new ones. Doka notes that when "the needs of family members differ and compromises fail, counselors may suggest that individuals create their own rituals to meet their needs."[11]

A BRIEF RECENT HISTORY OF GRIEF RITUALS

For thousands of years humans have used rituals to create bonds and establish interpersonal relationships with one another. The very earliest evidence of rituals related to burial customs dates from the Upper Paleolithic Period. Prior to that, older skeletons showed no signs of deliberate burial or any rituals surrounding the burial.[12] This is not the place for a full history of grief rituals, a rich territory to mine for an understanding of human culture. However, in order to understand the changing dynamics of rituals in the 21st century, we must first look back to the process of dying in recent times. In most Western cultures, there has been a significant shift in the way people die and in the way we grieve. Cas Wouters refers to this shift as the emancipation of the dying, or rather the emancipation of emotions, and explains the shift in how medical staff dealt with dying patients and their families.[13] During the 1800s and easily carried into the 1950s, there was a trend that Philippe Ariès referred to as the regime of silence.[14] During this time it was customary for doctors not to inform dying patients of their deteriorating condition. Patients were not told that they were dying or that their medical condition was terminal. Silence and denial became part of the norm and there was a need to suppress pain and fear. This regime of silence was carried over to the dying patient's family and into the grieving process. Wouters further explains this era or regime of silence:

> Even among intimates, showing grief, anxiety or anger was soon interpreted as weakness. To share these feelings, as is normal and expected

today, was hardly accepted; it soon counted as 'letting oneself go' or 'exposing oneself'. One had to bear ones grief in a dignified way, which boiled down to showing as little of it as possible. Although in some communities this old code is preserved to some extent, many people today consider it to be almost barbaric and certainly unhealthy.[15]

Following this silence was the shift Wouters called the emancipation of emotions or the emancipation of the dying.[16] Patients began demanding the right to make decisions in their treatment and in end-of-life care. As this transition began to emerge, there was a redefinition of the meaning of courage at the end of life. Previously, courage while dying was strictly defined as silence and denial. With this change, courage was viewed as the ability to face end of life and to empathize with those who were dying rather than deny their deaths and in turn to truly be denying their life. Keith Watkins also notes that the perceived attitudinal changes in the role and functions of funeral directors and clergypersons have contributed significantly to changes in rituals.[17] No longer are these individuals the sole necessary providers of rituals at the time of death for the bereaved.

Our world is continually changing and growing and so too are our rituals we perform. We—the authors of this chapter (designated SRS and KFM in the text)—believe that there were two major current events that have impacted the way we deal with our grief, almost insisting and crying out that we design new rituals to meet our overwhelming grief. The first was the onslaught of HIV/AIDS in the mid- to late-1980s when people had to deal with the multiple deaths and losses of loved ones, and the second event was the terrorist attacks on September 11, 2011.

The AIDS quilt was born out of grief. Since the beginning of the AIDS epidemic over 30 years ago, it is estimated that nearly 30 million people have died from AIDS-related causes. UNAIDS describes that many of these AIDS-related deaths happened in major cities worldwide, but it was not until the 1980s that Cleve Jones brainstormed the now famous AIDS Memorial Quilt.[18] Following a memorial candlelight march after the assassinations of gay rights activists Harvey Milk and Mayor George Moscone in San Francisco, California, on November 27, 1978, Jones discovered that within that city, over 1,000 persons had died due to AIDS. It was after this demonstration that Jones enlisted the help of his friends. Together they began writing on index cards the names of friends and loved ones who had died of AIDS. These index cards were then taped to the walls of the San Francisco Federal Building. When completed, it resembled a large patchwork quilt.

Nearly a year later, Jones created the first panel of the AIDS Memorial Quilt. Today the quilt is ever growing and contains roughly over 50,000 panels. "The quilt has redefined the tradition of quilt-making in response to contemporary circumstances. A memorial, a tool for education, and a work of art, the quilt is a unique creation, an uncommon and uplifting response to the tragic loss of human life."[19] In a community where death was often disenfranchised, people needed to move outside the norms of traditional memorial services. Overwhelming numbers of young people were dying from AIDS at alarming rates. People needed to be able to express their pain and acknowledge their losses in a way that meaningfully reflected these numerous tragedies. The AIDS Memorial Quilt and NAMES project offered individuals a way to share their pain and remember those who died. Wouters wrote:

> Only one new ritual has succeeded in becoming established in many countries: International AIDS Memorial Day. The first one was held in San Francisco, USA, in 1983, when the cause of AIDS was still unknown. By then end of the 1980s, this Memorial Day and the AIDS Memorial Quilt had come to create a sense of global solidarity, partly because it attracts world-wide attention. The shock caused by the death of young people was strong and widespread; it triggered many other attempts at creating new ritual.[20]

Today, the AIDS quilt is still growing and can be viewed on display throughout the country and indeed, the world.

The second event that dramatically influenced and changed our mourning rituals was the terrorist attack on September 11, 2011. As a community, there were almost no prescribed rituals to meet our needs. On September 11, the population of New York City was filled with such overwhelming sorrow that personal rituals of grief spilled out of private lives and homes into public spaces. Feelings of loss were inscribed on the city itself as people used every available medium to express themselves. Some even scrawled messages in the dust from the explosions that coated vehicles and windows. Public surfaces were almost immediately plastered with photographs of missing people and posters seeking to find loved ones. Parks, firehouses, subway stations, traffic islands, and even curbsides became sites of continually evolving shrines of flowers, candles, poems and artwork. There were no prescribed rituals for mourning thousands of people so we invented new rituals as we went along. With a couple of candles and a bunch of flowers we transformed ordinary sidewalks and street corners into sacred spaces. Here friends, family, or people passing by could pause to pray, reflect on the tragedy, and leave whatever offerings they deemed appropriate. Visitors left messages addressed to the dead with the shared belief that words, in this newly consecrated space, would somehow find their way.[21] These memorials on the streets of Pennsylvania, Washington D.C., New York, as well as all across the United States, and indeed the world, were an attempt to make sense of all the deaths and destruction.

Perhaps because both of these events, that is, the AIDS epidemic and the terrorist attacks, were newsworthy and in the public eye, rituals surrounding the deaths of celebrities have also become increasingly public in the 21st century. But popular, street spectacles surrounding celebrity deaths are not a new phenomenon. Certainly, Rudolph Valentino's death (August 23, 1926) at the age of 31 created long lines in his funeral procession as an estimated 100,000 people lined the streets of New York City to pay their respects.[22] Al Jolson's death on October 23, 1950, was also deemed one of the biggest funerals in show business with an estimated 20,000 people in San Francisco witnessing the funeral procession.[23] Today the funerals of movie stars and other celebrities can be viewed on television or instantly via the Internet. Many more rituals have evolved as these deaths ignited an outpouring of grief. The death of Diana, Princess of Wales, on August 31, 1997, created an avalanche of flowers and wreaths at the tunnel in Paris, the site of her death, and at Kensington Palace, her home in London.[24] Over a million people lined the four-mile route from Kensington Palace to Westminster Abbey bearing witness to the funeral service for Princess Diana.[25]

Doka notes that the role of mass media allows for collective participation.[26] Bull et al. looked at the impact of Princes Diana's death and found an increased utilization of grief support and counseling services.[27] A team of researchers surveyed 65 community organizations ultimately revealing a pattern of increased service requests in the three weeks following Diana's death. The study indicated that people coped with Princes Diana's death in different ways including talking, crying, using help lines; making extra appointments with their counselors, therapists, and doctors and increasing use of medications. While some individuals purposely avoided the intense media coverage, many others relied on Internet sites, using message forums, and signed condolence books to directly express personal messages to Diana and the Royal Family. This was also true for many grievers living outside of England since the nature of media coverage today allows instantaneous access to others around the world.

On October 5, 2011, the death of Steve Jobs moved millions of people to express their sadness publicly. Makeshift memorials sprung up all over the world and on the Internet. Metronews captured one of these memorials, set up outside a 24-hour Apple store in Manhattan on Fifth Avenue.[28] Millions of Twitter users memorialized Jobs in their own online obituaries and one teenager from Hong Kong, Jonathan Mak, redesigned the Apple logo in order to memorialize the man who made it all possible. Mak simply replaced the graphic logo of Apple by removing the bite mark and replacing it with a silhouette of Steve Jobs's face. When speaking about his design, Mak said: "It's just a quiet realization that apple is now missing a piece. It's just kind of implying his absence."[29]

THE EMERGENCE OF SECULAR RITUALS

In most cultures grief rituals have traditionally been religious in nature, and religious rituals and ceremonies are also dominant in the United States in the

21st century. They have proven particularly helpful in traumatic deaths. Most religions have rituals associated with the dying process as well as important rituals to commemorate and worship deceased ancestors. Although not always the case, religious or sacred rituals are generally associated with services occurring in churches and other religious houses of worship. These rituals, handed down from generation to generation, kept us connected with our ancestors and helped us "to recognize, understand, and process our beliefs about dying and death."[30] Additionally, in the past, religious funeral rituals centered on communal loss and were events where members of a community came together to share their grief and sadness. The clergyperson was clearly the actor on stage while family and friends sat passively in the audience. It is currently thought that with the decline in religiosity, the rituals of the past are becoming less common and perhaps are no longer meeting our needs. One of the results of this change is that we no longer see clergy as the necessary providers of rituals at the end of life; grieving individuals are developing new rituals.

As we shift into the 21st century, there has become an increased need to incorporate nonbelievers, that is, individuals who have doubts about religion, into newly created secular rituals. Wouters states that "non-religious people as well as those with doubts about religion had to be taken into account with the increase both in their numbers and in the intensity of these doubts."[31] Nonreligious or secular rituals tend to be individualized and encourage our expressions of grief or joy as they mark the transitions in our life.

THE IMPORTANCE OF RITUALS

Possibly, a certain ritual is helpful to us for the simple reason that we *believe* that it will be helpful.[32] Rituals and the ceremonies we develop can help us embrace the changes in our lives in positive ways. Regardless of who we are or our status in life, through meaningful ceremonies we are able to connect with one another and strengthen our social relationships. Rituals, which are rich in symbolism, can help us identify who we are as individuals, and as a society, and show us how we can connect and build bridges with our deceased loved ones. After a death there is often a division between what our head knows and our heart feels. Rituals allow us to reexperience the reality of our loved one's death in meaningful ways.[33] Rituals are important because they imply and create a sense of order, and order implies safety—we know what is expected of us and we know what to expect. It can represent a model of behavior during times of crisis.[34] Death rituals indicate a clear path for us to follow, as there are prescribed ways for the community, and particularly for the mourners to relate to one another providing an ordered way to say good-bye.[35] Our experience with bereaved group members includes listening to their descriptions of feeling out of control and not knowing how to behave; they often question their emotions and feelings, describing themselves as "probably inappropriate or abnormal."

Rituals, whether religious or not, are vital to family life. Having dinner to-gether every night—without any television and the cell phones turned off—is crucial. So too are rituals related to the end of life of critical importance for a family's emotional well-being. Rituals are healing in that they can be transfor-mational: emotionally, physically, and spiritually. Rituals help to create order by offering an experience of sameness. However, they also confront ambiva-lence. Rituals can create a safe place to express conflicting emotions or anger.[36]

Repeatedly in our bereavement groups we (SRS and KFM) have been struck by the ways people increasingly express their grief by telling stories and cre-ating personal rituals. Such creative projects counter the destructiveness of death and give mourners a focus that allows them to work through their grief. The versatility of rituals is widespread as rituals can be performed consistently or only once or twice. They may be performed by a single individual, by a group, or by the entire community; in arbitrary or random places, or in places specifically reserved for the ritual; either in public, in private, or before spe-cific people.[37] Clinical examples of rituals will be conceptualized and described into four subcategories: (1) rituals for the dying, (2) rituals for the dying child, (3) rituals for the bereaved, and (4) community rituals.

RITUALS FOR THE DYING

Researchers have identified the potential benefits of creating rituals when someone is dying and at the time of death that can later also be helpful coping tools for the bereaved.[38] A phenomenological research study of dying cancer patients and their family caregivers was conducted looking at their experi-ences of dying at home.[39] A total of 241 interactions occurred including 102 home visits, which were tape recorded, 107 telephone calls, numerous e-mails, and reviews of journal entries submitted by the patient or the family caregiver. Two major themes that are pertinent to this chapter include the importance of creating rituals and participating in an ongoing life review, and the need for patients to make sense of and find meaning, in their lives as well as their deaths. The process of continually reviewing one's life, looking at the meaning of existing rituals and the exploration of new rituals, was significant to the participants in the study. This allowed people to review and determine the helpfulness of past rituals and worked to help them resolve contradictions and support the changes and transitions they were experiencing. People focused on traditional and spiritual rituals as well as created and designed new family rituals that the dying patient hoped would be passed down to future genera-tions. One month after her husband's death from pancreatic cancer at the age of 58, his wife Barbara noted:

My husband was never much for rituals. I was the one to whom anni-versaries and holidays were important. Our last Thanksgiving, when my husband felt good, we were on a macrobiotic diet. It was important to me to have a . . . celebration with people we cared about. We had a macrobiotic Thanksgiving with a tofu turkey . . . I was always aware that this may be our last and it was.[40]

Another woman, Carol, was a patient who at 50 years of age had never achieved her "perfect" idealized family that she always dreamed of creating. She had a difficult, abusive childhood, past marital experiences, and a long psychiatric history including major depression, panic attacks, and two suicide attempts. She lived alone in a third-floor walk-up apartment. Carol continually focused on the importance of creating future rituals for her sons, daughters-in-law, and granddaughter:

The family is coming over to make ice cream. I got a machine and my oldest son has a machine so we can do two ice creams at once. My youngest son was saying he's not going to get an ice cream machine 'cause how many times do you do it—once a year? But I said some things you do and you do because you have wonderful memories. . . . It doesn't matter if it's once a year or more than once a year. You remember licking the dasher from childhood and it gives you pleasure now. What difference does it make how often you did it? [41]

One month later, Carol said:

The kids are coming over for the annual Christmas cookie bake off. . . . We make cookies and decorate them. It gets very competitive. Rituals are important. They [are] always were. But now it's even more so. It's amazing how fast something becomes a ritual. I started sewing my granddaughter's Halloween costume. Every year she expects me to make one. When I asked her what she wants to be next year, she said, "a sidewalk" . . . You know, all you leave behind when you die is an imprint in people's minds that they can recall when something evokes it. I would like for my granddaughter to have memories of grandma making dolls for her, making homemade ice cream, and of course, the making of the Christmas cookies. I have lots of rituals. . . . If you don't have a belief in religion then rituals become an important substitute. They're things to look forward to; you know the ground rules. You know how to behave and what is expected. I find them very supportive. It started before the cancer and they've gotten me through the rough patches.[42]

One advantage of creating a unique ritual is that it offers the dying person or surviving bereaved individuals opportunities to design, plan, and implement something that will be a unique remembrance to them. In a way, this freedom encourages individuals to self-soothe and comfort themselves as they create the ritual which will be the most meaningful to them. One 49- year-old woman I (SRS) worked with was dying of lung cancer and had young children at home. We had been talking about making videotapes or tape recordings for her children. After much thought she told me:

> I've been thinking about the tapes. I want to make them for my daughter. I started my journal again. I don't want to write in it when I'm feeling down. I only want positive things. I've come a long way. Before I thought that journaling or making tapes is like a death sentence. Now I see it differently. It's like the clothes I gave away. Before I thought cleaning out the closets and getting rid of stuff was like cleaning the dead woman's things before she died. But after I did it I felt such a sense of freedom . . . writing in the journal feels good. It's freeing.[43]

In my early years as a registered nurse, I (SRS) witnessed a young lawyer who would visit his grandfather every day after work. His grandfather was dying of cancer and they obviously had a close relationship. The young man had recently married and purchased an old fixer-upper house. Every evening he would sit at his grandfather's bedside and ask questions: "How do I rewire the circuit breaker? How do I put in a vegetable garden? What should we do about adding on an extension?" His grandfather, a retired contractor, would answer his questions with a sense of pride of being able to help his grandson. The young attorney really wasn't planning to undertake any of these projects immediately; however, he shared with me (SRS) that the sharing of this wisdom was meaningful for his grandfather and that he would always remember the time they spent discussing these mundane projects. The nightly ritual continued for weeks until his grandfather's death.

Capturing a memory can be done without words. Maybe it is done with a look, a sound, a touch, a smell, or a taste. In the Brown's family, memories and good times were often captured through the creation and taste of food. In November 2011, I (KMF) was given the pleasure of working with a family from Southern Italy. Walking in the halls of the hospital one could smell the delicious aroma of fresh baked banana bread or homemade polenta. Any or all who entered the room were offered a place to sit and a bite to eat. Walter, the dying patient, no longer had an appetite for food, but his wish was that all who came to his room would sit and eat, and share a drink. In his mind Walter had secured a safe home for his family. One evening, after everyone had eaten and had a drink in hand, Walter made a toast saying: "The heat bill has been paid, the house is warm. This is a great party, I will sleep well tonight." Walter died at three o'clock that morning. After Walter's death his large family shared in the comfort of Walter's last words. For them food and drink were always a ritual of family and love. Many of the memories they shared about

Walter began with the description of a lamb roast or the smell of butter and sage sautéing on the stove.

Another patient, Beth, a 43-year-old single woman was dying at home of lung cancer. She was fiercely independent and did not want around-the-clock caretakers in her small apartment. She was adamant about what she was willing to accept although her medical condition continued to deteriorate. She would initially bemoan the fact that she could no longer take long showers because she feared falling. During one home visit she described to me (SRS) the following: Two of her friends braved a winter snowstorm and showed up at her doorstep. When they came inside the apartment and took off their coats, they were dressed in bathing suits. They all climbed in the shower and shampooed Beth's hair, later giving her a manicure. This improvised beauty session became a weekly ritual that was helpful to Beth and also to her girlfriends as they shared these special moments together.

I (SRS) worked with a woman who was dying of kidney cancer. She wanted to die at home and although she had a large and spacious house, she did not want to be alone in her bedroom. We set up her hospital bed in the living room so she could still be at the center of her family's activities. Living at home were her husband, her nine-year-old daughter (who was an only child), and her father, a retired physician from Europe. The patient's brother had come from Poland to say good-bye to his dying sister. The entire family sat around the hospital bed, as the brother told stories about his sister from a time when the two of them were young. He related stories about the "trouble" the two of them got into. The patient's daughter was wide-eyed as she listened to her uncle, whom she had never met before, tell these stories about her mother. A family friend videotaped this conversation filled with laughter and sadness. Years later, I received a heart-felt letter from the patient's daughter telling me how grateful she was for this video and for the memories she has of her family reminiscing around her mother's bed. The showing of this video had become a yearly ritual as she and her father would watch and listen to the stories on the anniversary of her mother's death. The video has also become a link to her uncle, now her only living relative on her mother's side of the family.

Receiving eulogies and memorial services while still alive have sparked interest in some who are dying. On occasions, eulogies are given to those who are severely ill or elderly in order to express words of love and gratitude before they pass away.[44] These services, referred to as living funerals, life celebrations, living wake, life tribute, and friendship services, are on the rise and include individuals who are diagnosed as terminally ill, or have diagnoses of dementia or Alzheimer's. Patients, family members and friends recognize the impact of both the telling and the hearing of the tributes to the dying person.[45] Gail Rubin tells the story of Edward Sugars's living memorial service.[46] Diagnosed at age 66 with lung cancer, Sugars decided to have 200 family members and friends gather together for a pot-luck dinner with live music in order to eulogize him.

In his words, "It's been a great three months, to know that you are fading fast and still accepting the joy of life . . . nothing is ever so bad that you can see joy in a day. I will remember this as one of the high points of my life."[47] At the services, Sugars was eulogized by his daughter, his son, and his many friends. He also used the opportunity to tell all who were present that he loved them and that they should not be scared: death is a part of life. Two days later, Edward Sugars died. In his obituary, he asked for no further services and that anyone who wanted to could add pictures or memories to the book that was started at the memorial. Those memories were to be passed on to his grandchildren.[48]

After giving a lecture at a local church, I (SRS) met a lovely woman who shared two recent rituals with me, one for her dying father-in-law and the other for his children and 21 grandchildren:

> Being the head of a large family of faith we [sic] selected a Lenox ornament of the Holy Family [as a symbolic Christmas gift from the dying family patriarch to his offspring]—fortunately it arrived on Monday 12/19—we printed a note for each package on Tuesday 12/20 and on Wednesday the 21st met at my father-in-law's house and sat with him, playing Andrea Bocelli on the CD player—we had him touch each gift (which now totaled 35—[one for] each grandchild, great-grandchild and the 8 children) and then we wrapped. . . . We dimmed the lights and kept Andrea on the CD player and in the middle of the night he just went. Such a wonderful life, such an example of marriage and family and such a peaceful passage.[49]

After his death, his daughter, a quilter, made scarves using 2×2 squares of her father's ties. She explained, "He was a huge tie-wearer—every day, every place so this is a fitting remembrance and hug from him."[50]

Reflecting on the clinical examples above, it is easy to see how a ritual created for the dying often has implications and meaning for the bereaved. Blessing his Lenox ornaments was both a ritual for the dying patient and for the 35 family members that received those ornaments. Year after year these family members would be reminded of their father, grandfather or great-grandfather every time they encountered those blessed ornaments.

RITUALS FOR THE DYING CHILD

Although there continues to be worldwide incidence of stillbirths, miscarriages, and infant deaths, there exists a limited acceptance of the need to provide bereavement support for devastated families leaving bereaved parents and other family members feeling isolated and disenfranchised.[51] Advances in the hospice and palliative care movements have led to an increased awareness of the importance of death rituals and in particular funeral rites.[52] Kathie Kobler et al.

describes the dimensions of death rituals including meaning making (i.e., finding ways for parents to create meaning of their loss), the role of intention (i.e., what are the parents, or staff, hoping to accomplish with this ritual), and the role of participation since rituals take the form of active thoughtful participation (and not just passive observation).[53] Recognizing that "not all parents are open to the use of rituals in their grief work,"[54] Kobler and her nurse colleagues describe various rituals including emergency baptism; engaging siblings and other family members gathered in the hospital creating a ritual of good-bye; prayers offered by hospital chaplains, and, if possible, offerings of footprints or handprints or a lock of the child's hair. Parents of infants can also be offered the baby's blanket, identification bracelet, or a photograph. These tangible rituals can validate and recognize the depth of their loss and confirm their need to continue their bonds with their child. When hospital caregivers encourage parents to bathe and dress their child, they offer significant opportunities for creating unique rituals and bonding.

The Afghans for Angels Project began in 2001, when a six-year-old girl wanted to contribute to her school's fund raising effort for a third-grade boy, Angel, who had an inoperable brain cancer. This six-year-old and her mother created the "Afghans for Angel Project" initially asking for donations of scrap yarn or "granny squares" they could sew together to make a blanket for Angel's fundraiser. Within a short time, yarn and material started arriving from around the world (United States, Canada, England, Finland) including nearly 3,000 crocheted "granny squares." Several blankets were donated for the fundraiser and with the remaining material they decided to make blankets for other children diagnosed with cancer or other life-threatening illnesses. Over the years similar projects have begun, making booties and hats for neonatal intensive care units, and chemo caps for kids in addition to the blankets. These items are given to children, usually by the request of a friend or family member and at no cost to the child or the child's family.[55]

A similar project, Project Linus, [56] is also a nonprofit organization whose "mission is to provide love, a sense of security, warmth and comfort to children who are seriously ill, traumatized, or otherwise in need through the gifts of new, handmade blankets and afghans, lovingly created by volunteer blanketeers."[57] Blankets are donated and distributed to hospitals, shelters, and social service agencies. The agency was first started in 1995 after the founders read a heartwarming story about a child receiving intensive chemotherapy who said that her security blanket helped her get through her treatments.

RITUALS FOR THE BEREAVED

Music therapy can enable and provide a mechanism for both the dying patients and those who will survive them—a means to acknowledge and support impending death.[58] When 21-year-old Alex was undergoing a bone marrow transplant, he and his older brother Scott (25 years old) would spend hours writing songs together. After Alex's death, Scott attended a bereavement group for siblings with me (SRS). With the permission of other group members Scott brought in a recording of a song that he had written and recorded after Alex's death. He presented each group member with a laminated copy of the song's words and the group was able to sing the song. At the same time, the boys' mother attended a group for bereaved parents. She frequently described a new family ritual where the family would gather around Alex's photo, light a scented candle, and sing Scott's song. The music, the words, and the connection to memories—all—were therapeutic and helpful in this family's grief.

To enhance and publicize the need for cadavers to help medical students in Taiwan, an innovative program called Silent Mentors was instituted. After family members make the decision to donate their loved one's body to the medical school—or if the patient makes the decision that the body should be donated to science—they are asked to write a short biography about the deceased, which is later shared with the medical student who will be working with the deceased. The student meets with the family and encourages the family to reminisce about the loved one. A photo of the deceased and the prepared biography are framed in a large—3 × 12 feet—frame along with the name of the medical student and hung in the halls of the medical school (Figure 10.1). At the end of the academic year, all the medical students, again, meet with the family and give thanks for the teaching experience they have had. The deceased is cremated and family members are offered the option of having their loved one's cremains housed in exquisite cut glass urns in individual niches at the medical school.

The use of tattoos in recent years has become more popular with the bereaved. Barbara is a member of my (SRS) weekly bereavement group for parents who have lost adult children. When her son died of testicular cancer, she had a tattoo placed on her forearm reading: "Two Sons; One in Heaven."

While vacationing in the Amazon Jungle in Brazil, I (SRS) met a young woman who had her father's name tattooed on the back of her neck along with the words: "Tanto Amor Tanta Saudade Sua Filha" (Figure 10.2). In halting English she told me this meant: "So much love; I miss you so much; your daughter." This woman explained that her father had suddenly died when she was 18 years old. She had a difficult time coping with her loss: her two sisters were married and living on their own but she still lived at home with her mother. She told me that she "took her father's death very hard" and when she reached 36 years of age she realized she had lived half her life without her father. It was now time for her to "dream new dreams" and she then had this tattoo done in memory of her dad.

An Israeli study of pediatric clinicians making bereavement visits after the deaths of their patients highlight the importance of these visits and the role of rituals in healing.[59] These visits, made early in the bereavement process, allowed clinicians to observe bereaved parents and facilitate opportunities for

Figure 10.1
Silent Mentors. Buddhist Tzu Chi University, Taiwan (Photograph by Joel Schachter)

emotional support. Religious rituals surrounding the two major religions in Israel (Judaism and Islam) are generally practiced after the burial of loved ones. Although the rituals are not new or innovative, the details of these pre-scribed visits, including timing, conversations related to leave-taking behav-iors exhibited by the deceased child, visiting the deceased child's room, and sharing food with the family, are significant.

Figure 10.2
Woman with tattoo memorializing her father; Amazon Jungle, Brazil
(Photograph by Joel Schachter)

Tanto amor...	So much love...
Tantas saudades...	I miss you so much...
Sua filha.	Your daughter.

Every December, The Compassionate Friends, a not-for-profit support organization for families who have lost a child, sponsors a worldwide candle-lighting ritual, which literally consists of thousands of bereaved parents around the world. At a specified time, each bereaved family (or person) in its geographical location lights a candle in memory of its child. As the candle burns down, other bereaved parents in another time zone light their candles. In this way, candles are burned throughout the world in a 24-hour period.

Options to memorialize and create rituals are only limited by our creativity. Authors Nancy Gershman and Jenna Baddeley speak about a new way to merge creativity with memory.[60] A photomontage, or what the authors refer to as a healing dreamscape, is focused on creating continuing bonds with the deceased. In this relatively new technique, the bereaved individual works with both a grief therapist and an art therapist in order to create a new digital image that incorporates memory, fantasy, reality, past, present, and future in one visual object. The photomontage therapies take place in five stages. First is the intake phase that resembles narrative therapy whereby the client flips through old pictures while telling their story. Second is the brainstorming phase where the client and the artist decide what kind of future picture they will create either one of "preferred future or preferred legacy."[61] Phase three consists of a detailed photo search where the client looks for photos that show specific missing details such as a facial expression or missing body parts. After all the necessary pictures are collected, phase four starts the creation of the dreamscape picture. During this phase the artist and client work together to digitally and artfully create a new picture from the future that incorporates important symbols and meaning from the past. During the fifth phase the client shares the new dreamscape with family and friends. Through this prescriptive art the hope is that a higher level of understanding or meaning making is made. The Healing Dreamscape method is a very new technique and has not yet been subjected to empirical studies. However, we can see that every day new techniques and rituals are being created which often involve the usage of new technology.

Bereavement, as challenging as a process as it is, has the potential to offer the mourners new and distinctive ways to make meaning out of the death. We are able to construct personal, familial, cultural, and even political meanings that are highly individualized.[62] Joan Berzoff describes an activity at Bo's Place (Texas), which symbolically represents a break in one's family. Bereaved families are given pieces of a pot and instructed to put the pot together. However, when put together there are holes in the pot symbolizing the missing person. A similar project is conducted at Calvary Hospital (New York) around holiday time in December: bereaved family members are given clay pots and asked to think about their loved ones who have died. Instructions on what to do what the clay pots are given in sequence, and members are told what to do only phase by phase. As we talk about our loved ones and the upcoming holidays, members are instructed to draw or write on the clay pots with Sharpie markers. Some draw the memory itself, others write words with special meaning, some draw symbols, or even write song lyrics. Each clay pot is unique to the creator. Members are then asked to share their pots and then everyone places their pots into a plastic Ziploc bag. Facilitators instruct members that the next phase will ensue. Without any warning the facilitator takes out a hammer and breaks his or her own pot. Many group members are shocked, as often times we are in death. Every group member is passed the hammer: for some it is too painful to break it, others smash the pot into many pieces.

After the pot is broken, glue is handed out, and together we start to puzzle our clay pots back together piece by piece. In the end you are left with a clay pot that has cracks and holes, Discussion is held on how the pot can be a metaphor for our grief. It is a powerful ritual that brings up all sorts of feelings, emotions, and thought processes. One group member remarked that putting the pot back together was exactly how he was feeling in his own grief. He said that right now he wanted to just give up and not finish the puzzle. However, he wanted the image on the pot to be seen again. He drew a tree on his pot in memory of his wife. Recently they had held a tree planting service in dedication of her life and that made him proud. Also attending the workshop were his adult son and daughter in law. At one point his son reached over and held a piece of the pot so that he could finish the puzzle.

A young mother in one of my (SRS) support groups whose only child died in an accidental drowning created a special ritual to help her cope with the loss of her 20-year-old daughter. Her daughter loved traveling, and yet never had the chance to really travel. This mother gives pictures of her daughter to friends who are traveling and asks them to take the photo with them. When they return, they share with the mother all the places her daughter "traveled and visited." The mom keeps a map of the world and marks all these special places that her daughter has seen.

One of Calvary Hospital's Brooklyn bereavement groups took an age-old love ritual and gave it a new twist. "Lovelocks" have been used since ancient times and can be found most notably on the Great Wall in China. Couples buy a lock with a key and attach the lock to the chains that line the inner walkways of the Great Wall. After securing their lock, the couple throws the key off the wall symbolizing that their love is forever. Eternal lovelocks can also be found in Florence, Italy, on the Ponte Vecchio, the bridge that joins two parts of the city. In Italy, the keys are thrown into the river to show that the couple's love is locked forever. Lovelocks are springing up all over the world and have recently made their way into New York where one can find sporadic lovelocks lining the Brooklyn Bridge (Figure 10.3). Many of these locks are decorated with initials, and some are even engraved with names and dates.; Most Internet sources trace the locks back to China; however, Venice Italy attributes their lovelocks to Moccia's book, *I Want You*.[63] In Moccia's book, young lovers lock their love on the Rialto Bridge and throw their key into the canal below. Although the lovelocks were originally designed for new couples marking the beginning of their lives together, one of my (KMF) groups for bereaved spouses became intrigued with the concept and meanings of the locks. The group decided to create a new ritual that they perceived would be helpful to them. Nicholas, one of the group members, had his lock engraved with the name of his deceased wife and a message of love. Two women in the spouse/partner bereavement group were fascinated by this idea and Nicholas wrote down their loved ones information and had two more locks engraved for the women. Watching the women receive their locks was extremely moving. Three weeks before these members were strangers to one another and now they had come together to help one another heal. On our last night of the group, members painted their locks: some put initials encased in a heart; others used red, white, and blue to represent the military services from which their loved ones retired. Each lock told a story and as we shared our creations, it became clear that lovelocks were not just for those who are beginning a relationship. Each lock represented the lives that were lost and the love that was and is shared. The group organized a trip and together they walked across the Brooklyn Bridge, each finding their own special spot on the bridge. One young spouse placed her lock on the

Manhattan side of the Bridge because that is where she and her husband lived during their 10 years of marriage. She described feeling comforted knowing that the lock is on the bridge and that a piece of her husband will remain in the city that he loved so much. For the time being she can walk by his lock whenever she wants or just envision the physical space it inhabits. Rituals are constantly morphing and changing to meet the needs of those who perform them. Not every group ritual will resonate with everyone, but each ritual the group performs helps the members recall their loved ones.

Medical institutions offering bereavement memorial services have become more prevalent in recent years. A review of the literature between 1984 and 2004 revealed numerous examples including 64.5percent of hospice programs and a small number of other medical institutions offering memorial services.[64] However, the review did not reveal any references of memorial services arising from any hospital's critical care units (CCU) in the United States. The CCU at the Royal Preston Hospital (England) decided to initiate a new ritual, that is, providing a yearly memorial service as part of their already existing bereavement services. Since its inception in 2003, the attendance has soared and the written evaluations and verbal feedback received overwhelmingly confirms the significance of the memorial service as an important ritual following death in the CCU.

Figure 10.3
Brooklyn Bridge Locks (Photograph by Kristen Finneran)

Calvary's Camp Compass®, a weeklong bereavement camp for children 6–18 years, often concludes with a "letting go" rock ceremony. The children and counselors gather at the lake with rocks that they have previously chosen. These stones may have appealed to them because of their shape, color, texture, or size. The campers paint, write messages, or draw (with marking pens) on the rocks. After they silently say a prayer or think about the deceased, the campers throw their rocks into the lake recognizing that their special rock will always remain in that lake.

Cemeteries are safe places to contemplate, pray, remember, envision, and cry. Family members sometimes have a stone bench placed in the cemetery so that they, and others, will have a place to sit and reflect on the one who has died. Memorial benches may be found in places other than a cemetery. They may be placed along hiking trails in memory of those who have enjoyed the trails or on the beaches in memory of those who have died at sea. They provide a place to rest and refresh, both physically and spiritually.

As times change new rituals are invented in order to meet the needs of the changing generations. With the world becoming more technological and the movement toward green living, it was only a matter of time before we saw those needs being met in mourning. Technological advances have given mourners the ability to stream live footage of funeral services to family or friends who were unable to attend. Webcasting funeral is becoming available to those who are overseas or cannot travel due to health or cost.[65] Evan Selinger, professor of philosophy at Rochester Institute of Technology, has written about the death of his biological paternal grandfather in Massachusetts. The funeral, which occurred during the aftermath of Hurricane Sandy, was streamed online so that mourners, who were unable to travel to attend the funeral, were able to be present. Selinger and his family watched the live webcast in their own home and noted: "It would be a mistake, though, to say that the webcast dehumanized or even sullied the experience. Convenience always comes with costs, and we didn't feel that the sacred had been sacrificed for the expedient. Our emotional attunement was limited, but we weren't desensitized. And it was certainly better than not being present at all."[66]

Facebook offers a place to create a living memorial to those who have died. A member of one of my (KMF) bereavement groups shared that she often writes private messages to her husband on Facebook as a way to stay connected. In her words she is not the type to keep a journal, but Facebook meets her needs and gives her a record of what she has written.

Smartphones are no exception. Family members are placing QR (Quick Response) and NFC (Near Field Communication) chips on the back of grave markers and urns. Friends and family who come to visit can simply scan the bar code or tag pictures and, instantly, videos of the deceased are streamed to their smartphones.[67] Individuals report keeping their deceased's cell phone numbers active so that they may call and hear the voice of their loved one on the voicemail. Patrick Swayze's wife of 34 years reports texting him "I love you" on the year anniversary of his death. Her feeling was "Either somewhere out there he received the message, or someone's going 'somebody loves me' and you know what? I figured it was a win-win situation."[68]

Burial services are no exception to these technological and green changes. Green burials have been reported in Britain. There is no embalming and no metal or concrete, only wood caskets and a planted tree that marks the grave.[69] South Carolina founded a similar preserve in 1998, which offers hand-dug graves, plain wood boxes, no grave liners, and natural stones to mark the grave.[70] Eco-friendly accelerated natural decomposition is being offered though alkaline hydrolysis.[71] This process speeds up the natural body decomposition in two to three hours and requires no harmful chemicals.[72] Human remains are given to families in a canister that holds the liquid ashes. These remains can then be safely poured onto the earth or into the water. Artificial implants such as knees or hips are left unhindered and donated to Doctors Without Borders for use in developing countries.[73] All these new processes/rituals boast cleaner air with less CO_2 emissions and less waste of metal and concrete materials. In a new age, the traditional needs are still being met.

COMMUNITY RITUALS

Deaths that are sudden and traumatic tend to shatter the assumptions we have as our world view may no longer provide us with a sense of safety.[74] Mourning rituals may serve to reaffirm the social networks of the survivors, strengthen group bonding, and enhance cultural identities.[75] Rituals are thought to be particularly beneficial after traumatic deaths as individuals seek to define the tragedy and do not necessarily have to be on-going or be repetitive in order to be effective.[76]

When a chartered America Army jetliner crashed shortly after takeoff from Gander, Newfoundland, in 1985, all 248 soldiers on board were killed. The group ritualized mourning activities conducted at Fort Campbell (the home base for these soldiers) facilitated healing and provided support to the survivors. Initially there was a Presidential Memorial Ceremony led by then-President Ronald Reagan, which consisted of a three hour nationally televised ceremony held at the base. This ceremony consisted of eulogies and speeches. At the conclusion, President Reagan and his wife Nancy spoke individually with, and physically touched, each surviving family member who was present. One week after the crash a Division Memorial Service was held. Three months later, there was a Community Minute of Silence. There were special battalion memorial services held four months after the crash. Ten months after the crash a newly planted grove of trees was formally dedicated to the memory of the soldiers whereby 248 trees represented the 248 deceased soldiers. Pearl Katz and Paul Bartone suggest that these ceremonies provided not only important confirmation and recognition that this horrific event indeed occurred but these rituals facilitated the acceptance of death and the reestablishing of boundaries between the living and the dead.[77] This was especially significant since there were no bodies or tangible evidence of the disaster. The ceremonies also reaffirmed the solidarity of the community. People were pulled together and were provided an opportunity to grieve openly, sharing their grief with others. The services further helped individuals and the community to reestablish a sense of control. Not only the memorial services themselves, but also the elaborate and detailed preparations also provided a sense of regularity and order that was reassuring for many.

The April 19, 1995, bombing of the Murrah Federal Office Building in Oklahoma City shocked, saddened, and angered Americans and people of good will around the world. The bombing resulted in the deaths of 168 adults and children. There were many rituals, from the placing of flowers at the bombsite to the memorial service attended by then-President Bill Clinton, to the nationwide minute of silence held on the first anniversary of the bombing. These rituals gave us a sense of participating in the mourning process, supporting the survivors, and sharing in communal grief.

Rituals can also help educate the public on dangers that exist in the world. For example, all one needs to do is walk the streets of any major city or large intersection across the country and the world to find ghost bikes (Figure 10.4). These bikes are more frequently found in cities or densely populated areas. The first ghost bikes were created in St. Louis, Missouri, in 2003 and currently there are over 500 ghost bikes in over 180 locations throughout the world.[78] Ghost bikes are bicycles that are painted all white and chained to a signpost at the scene of an accident. Small plaques, fixed to the bike, name the deceased and remind all of the tragedy that took place and the life that was lost. These ghost bikes warn us of dangers that exist, remind us to be more cautious as we recall those who were killed.

Food and drink is often incorporated into ritual. As humans we eat to survive, but we can and often do use food as a symbol. Fox describes food from an anthropological perspective stating: "food becomes not just a symbol of, but the reality of, love and security."[79] Drink, or more specifically alcohol, has become major part of a new ritual started by young Marines from the Second Battalion, Fourth Regiment. During a 2004 deployment in Iraq, this regiment returned home with 34 marines dead and 255 wounded.[80] Each year on Memorial Day, a group of these Marines travel throughout the county to visit the grave of one of their own. Each year they visit a different cemetery and stay a few days. Together they tell stories, some are funny and others are haunting. One seat remains empty in memory of the Marine that was killed. As the weekend progresses, this seat is filled with empty alcohol bottles. One year a knife was thrust into the side of a tree at the campsite. From the knife hung 34 dog tags, representing the 34 lives lost.[81]

Figure 10.4
Ghost Bike Brooklyn, New York (Photograph by Joel Schachter)

Rituals for hospital staff, as well as other medical institutions, can be initiated to provide emotional support for staff members caring for dying patients. Calvary Hospital, New York—our place of work—has approximately 5,000 deaths each year; a bell is softly rung when a patient dies. Our staff takes a moment or two to reflect on who has died and their relationship with that patient or family member. Memories can be shared as healing begins and we acknowledge that someone we cared for is no longer physically here.

Computers can be a source of connection allowing individuals to interact with one another despite geographical distance. Advances in technology have affected the dying person as well as bereaved family members. Sites such as caringbridge.org allow the patient and/or others to post up-to-date information on the patient's status. This not only decreases the amount of telephone calls a family makes, easing their burden of informing numerous people and repeating the information, but also increases the family support system as people leave notes of encouragement or prayers. Online memorial websites allow individuals to share memories, leave tributes in memory of the deceased with music of one's choice playing in the background. Bereaved family members have the option of opening the website or keeping it private. See Chapters 11 and 12 in this volume for further details regarding technological interventions.

An interesting community ritual, which began many years after World War II in the Netherlands, takes place in a lonely Jewish cemetery in the northern part of the country in the town of Groningen. Where once there was a flourishing Jewish community of 2,843 people in 1941, most were sent to concentration camps and the remaining Jews were deported; only 10 persons survived.[82] The Jewish cemetery had fallen into disuse and disrepair since World War II. Once a year since May 4, 1948, on the anniversary of Kristallnacht, also called the Night of Broken Glass, the people living in the town of Groningen spend time cleaning up the graves of long-forgotten residents. The cemetery is a source of pride and has enabled the residents of Groningen to come together as a community.

Although rituals can be generic or individualized, in order for them to be helpful and meaningful to the bereaved they must be relevant.[83] Research conducted by Vale-Taylor found that the majority of bereaved individuals in hospice programs reported that informal rituals were more significant to them than large planned events, for example, memorial services.[84] Although a small study, results indicated significant differences in which rituals were identified as being important: Men chose rituals that were all solitary whereas women identified community rituals as being the most helpful.

Rituals are needed for both the dying and the bereaved. Wouters speaks about the importance of rituals for both, noting that with more rituals human beings become more aware of our mortality: "Those who are mourning will receive more societal recognition and support, death and dying would to a somewhat larger degree, become integrated into everyday life, and the obvious need for modern and nonreligious *memento mori* would be accommodated."[85]

CONCLUSION

Ever since the existence of humans there has been a need for rituals. As discussed in this chapter, rituals help sustain our very survival. Specific examples of rituals for both the dying and the bereaved have been presented through many years of hands-on experience and through research. Together we (SRS and KMF) have seen a shift in the way people are choosing to die and in how we grieve. Those who are dying are demanding a say in their medical choices and in the care they receive. With this new voice comes the opportunity to plan rituals of significant symbolism.

September 11 and the AIDS epidemic demanded that new bereavement rituals be created. Overwhelming numbers of people were dying and all who witnessed were affected. Tragedy shook the world and our general assumptions of safety were challenged. Today one would be hard pressed to find an individual who has not been directly or indirectly affected by the AIDS epidemic or the 9/11 terrorist attacks. Born out of these tragedies were the creations of countless meaningful rituals. Each ritual gave power and voice to those suffering the tragedy of death(s). New rituals gave the world the right to grieve in new ways and to speak about the unspeakable. Most importantly, these new rituals allowed individuals a dual advantage: to gain support from one another and to create unique vessels in order to meet individual needs.

All four types of rituals—rituals of continuity, rituals of transition, rituals of reconciliation, and rituals of affirmation—serve the same purpose: preservation of legacy. In a generation of technology and individual identity, our contemporary rituals—green burials, Facebook memorials, customized, tattoos and photomontages—reflect the needs of the people who utilize them. It is not important which ritual is utilized or created, but it is important to make sure the ritual is prescriptive in meeting the needs of participants. As helping professionals we never want to cause undue harm. It is always important to be aware of both culture and individual needs. As long as there is death and dying, there will be a need for ritual.

NOTES

1. Kenneth J. Doka, "Memorialization, Ritual, and Public Tragedy," in *Living with Grief: Coping with Public Tragedy,* ed. Marcia Lattanzi-Licht and Kenneth J. Doka (New York: Brunner-Routledge, 2003), 179–89.

2. Maryam Henein, "The Importance of Ritual," *California Psychics,* January 19, 2009, http://blog.californiapsychics.com/blog/2009/01/the-importance-of-ritual .html/

3. Barbara H. Fiese, Thomas J. Tomcho, Michael Douglas, Kimberly Josephs, Scott Poltrock, and Tim Baker, "A Review of 50 Years of Research on Natuarlly Occurring Family Routines and Rituals: Cause for Celebration?" *Journal of Family Psychology* 16, 4 (2002): 381–90.

4. Evan Imber-Black, J. Roberts and R. Whiting, *Rituals in Families and Family Therapy* (New York: W. W. Norton & Company, 1988).

5. Fiese et al., "A Review," 383.

6. International Work Group on Death Dying and Bereavement (IWG), "Rituals for the Dying and Bereaved." Tucson, Arizona, 2004.

7. Doka, "Memorialization." Pamela Vale-Taylor, "We will Remember Them," *Journal of Palliative Medicine* 23, 6 (2009): 537–44.

8. Kamyar Hedayat, "When the Spirit Leaves: Childhood Death, Grieving, and Bereavement in Islam," *Journal of Palliative Medicine* 9, 6 (2006): 1282–91.

9. Goldberg, "The Power of Ritual." www.basearticles.com/Art/789723/111/ The-Power-of-Ritual.html.

10. Maurice Eisenbruch, "Cross-Cultural Aspects of Bereavement, II: Ethnic and Cultural Variations in the Development of Bereavement Practices," *Culture, Medicine and Psychiatry* 8, 4 (December 1984): 330.

11. Doka, "Memorialization," 182.

12. "Paleolithic," last modified November 2, 2012, http://en.wikipedia.org/wiki/ Paleolithic.

13. Cas Wouters, "The Quest for New Rituals in Dying and Mourning: Changes in the Well Balance," *Body & Society* 8, 1 (March 2002): 1–27.

14. Philippe Ariès, *The Hour of Our Death: The Classic History of Western Attitudes Toward Death Over the Last One Thousand Years,* trans. Helen Weaver (London: Allen Lane, 1982).

15. Wouters, "The Quest for New Rituals," 5.

16. Wouters, "The Quest for New Rituals."

17. Keith Watkins, "Searching for New Rituals for Death and Dying," *Keith Watkins Historian,* March 4, 2012, accessed April 27, 2012, http://keithwatkinshistorian .wordpress.com/2012/03/04/searching-for-new-ritualsfor-death-and-dying/

18. UNAIDS, *Unite for Universal Access: Overview Brochure on 2011 High Level Meeting on AIDS.* http://www.unaids.org/en/media/unaids/contentassets/documents/ document/2011/20110204_HLM_Brochure_en.pdf

19. "The AIDS Memorial Quilt, The Names Project Foundation," http://www .AIDSquilt.org

20. Wouters, "The Quest for New Rituals," 13.

21. Sherry R. Schachter, "9/11: A Grief Therapist's Journal," in *Living with Grief: Coping with Public Tragedy,* ed. Marcia Lattanzi-Licht and Kenneth J. Doka (New York: Brunner-Routledge, 2003), 15–25.

22. "Rudolph Valentino," last modified November 2, 2012, http://en/wikipedia.org/ wiki/Rudolph_Valentino.

23. "Al Jolson," last modified November 1, 2012, http://en.wikipedia.org/wiki/ Al_Jolson.

24. "Roadside Memorial," last modified November 1, 2012, http://en.wikipedia .org/wiki/Roadside_memorial.

25. Ibid.

26. Doka, "Memorialization," 179–89.

27. Michael A. Bull, Sheila Clark, and Katherine M Duszynski, "Lessons From a Community's Response to the Death of Diana, Princess of Wales," *Omega* 46, 1 (2002–2003): 35–49.

28. James Pomfret and Sisi Tang, "Hong Kong Teen's Design for Jobs a Cyber Hit," *Reuters,* October 6, 2011, accessed November 4, 2012, http://uk.reuters.com/article/ 2011/10/06/us-apple-hongkong-icon idUKTRE7952E620111006.

29. Ibid.

30. Gerry R. Cos, "Relgion, Spirituality, and Traumatic Death," in *Handbook of Thanatology,* ed. David Balk, Carol Wogrin, Gordon Thornton, and David Meagher (New York: Routledge, 2007), 263–68.

31. Wouters, "The Quest for New Rituals," 11.

32. D. Kearny Saprano, "The Importance of Rituals to Daily Life," *Helium,* January 20, 2010, accessed November 4, 2012, http://www.helium.com/items/1717 443-myth-religion-ritual-joseph-campbell-catholicism

33. Stephanie Frogge, "The Role of Ritual Following a Major Loss," *Open to Hope,* December 29, 2009, accessed November 4, 2012, http://www.opentohope.com/ 2009/12/29/the-role-of-ritual-following-a-major-loss/

34. Joan Castle and William L. Phillips, "Grief Rituals: Aspects that Facilitate Adjustment to Bereavement," *Journal of Loss and Trauma* 8, 1 (2003): 41–71.

35. Kathie Kobler, Rana Limbo, and Karen Kavanaugh, "Moments: The Use of Ritual in Perinatal and Pediatric Death," *MCN* 32, 5 (September/October 2007): 288–95.

36. Marie Putter, *The Memorial Rituals Book for Healing and Hope* (New York: Baywood Publishing Co, 1997).

37. "Roadside Memorial," last modified November 1, 2012, http://en.wikipedia.org/wiki/Roadside_memorial

38. K. A. Moneymaker and J. Traeger, "Creating Space and Ritual for the Time of Death," *Journal of Palliative Medicine* 10, 1 (2007): 270–1. Castle and Phillips, "Grief Rituals."

39. Sherry R. Schacter, "The Experience of Living with a Life-Threatening Illness: A Phenomenological Study of Dying Cancer Patients and their Family Caregivers" (Ph.D. diss., Union Institute Graduate School, 1999), 290. To maintain confidentiality and protect privacy, all names used in this chapter are pseudonyms.

40. Ibid., 166.

41. Ibid.,169.

42. Ibid., 170.

43. Ibid.,168.

44. "Eulogy," last updated October 23, 2012. http://en.wikipedia.org/wiki/Eulogy

45. Denise Carson, "A Living Tribute Honors a Life," *OC Register,* August 16, 2010, accessed November 5, 2012, http://www.ocregister.com/articles/bill-262297-senior-family.html

46. Gail Rubin, *A Good Goodbye: Funeral Planning for Those Who Don't Plan to Die* (Albuquerque: Light Tree Press, 2010).

47. Ibid., 60.

48. Ibid.

49. E-mail to author, March 22, 2012.

50. E-mail to author, March 22, 2012.

51. Kobler et al. "Moments." Doka "Memorialization."

52. Irion, "Changing Pattern of Ritual Response to Death," *OMEGA* 22, 3 (1990): 159-72.

53. Kobler et al., "Moments."

54. Ibid., 292.

55. Kate Johnson Burroughs, "The AFA Project: Beginnings," http://afaproject.org/beginnings1.html

56. Project Linus, http://projectlinus.org/about.html

57. C. O'Callaghan, M. Mus, and B. Mus, "Lullament: Lullaby and Lament Therapeutic Qualities Actualized Throuugh Music Therapy," *American Journal of Hospice & Palliative Medicine* 25, 2 (April/May 2008): 93–9.

58. Jerry Stein, Anat Peles-Borz, Ilana Buchval, Anat Klein, and Isaac Yaniv, "The Bereavement Visit in Pediatric Oncology," *Journal of Clilnical Oncology* 24, 22 (August 2006): 3705–7.

59. Nancy Gershman and Jenna Baddeley, "Prescriptive Photomontage: A Process and Product for Meaning-Seekers with Complicated Grief," *Americanpsychotherapy. com* (Fall 2010): 28–34.

60. Ibid., 32–3.

61. Joan Berzoff, "Narratives of Grief and their Potential for Transformation," *Palliative and Supportive Care* 4, 2 (June 2006): 121–7.

62. Tom Kington, "Italy's Bridges Weighed Down by Locks of Love," *The Guardian,* August 23, 2011, accessed November 5, 2012, http://www.guardian.co.uk/world/2011/aug/23/italy-bridges-locks-of-love.

63. Jane Platt, "The Planning, Organising and Delivery of a Memorial Service in Critical Care," *Nursing in Critical Care* 9, 5 (2004): 222–9.

64. Rubin, *A Good Goodbye.*

65. "The Online Funeral," www.huffingtonpost.com/evan-selinger/technology-funeral-ceremon_b_2100917. Retrieved November 11, 2012.

66. Laura Petrecca, "Mourning Becomes Electric: Tech Changes the Way we Grieve," *USAtoday.com,* May 7, 2012, accessed May 30, 2012. http://www.usatoday.com/tech/news/story/2012-05-07/digitial-mourning

67. Laura Petrecca, "The Way We Grieve Now," *Hello Grief,* September 20, 2012, accessed May 17, 2012, http://www.hellogrief.org/the-way-we-grieve-now/print/

68. Rubin, *A Good Goodbye,* 44.

69. Ibid., 45.

70. Ibid.

71. "Alkaline Hydrolysis for Human Remains," June 29, 2012, accessed June 29, 2012. http://alkalinehydrolysis.com

72. Rubin, *A Good Goodbye,* 46.

73. Ronnie Janoff-Bulman, *Shattered Assumptions: Towards a New Psychology of Trauma* (New York: Free Press, 1992).

74. Pearl Katz and Paul Bartone, "Mourning, Ritual, and Recovery after an Airline Tragedy," *Omega* 36, 3 (1997–1998): 193–201.

75. Gerry R. Cox, "Religion, Spirituality, and Traumatic Death," in *Handbook of Thanatology,* ed. David Balk, Carol Wogrin, Gordon Thornton, and David Meagher (Routledge, 2007), 263–8.

76. Katz and Bartone, "Mourning, Ritual, and Recovery."

77. Ibid.

78. www.ghostbike.org

79. Robin Fox, "Food and Eating: An Anthropoological Perspective," *SIRC: Social Issues Research Centre,* http://www.sirc.org/publik/foxfood.pdf, 1.

80. James Dao, "Learning to Heal, One Memorial Day at a Time," *New York Times,* May 29, 2012, accessed November 4, 2012, http://www.nytimes.com/2012/05/29/us/2-4-marine-regiment-marks-ramadi-losses.html?pagewanted = all_r = 0

81. Ibid.

82. "Jewish Groningen," last modified September 23, 2012, http://www.wikipedia.org/wiki/Jewish_Groningen.

83. Vale-Taylor, "We Will Remember Them."

84. Ibid.

85. Wouters, "The Quest for New Rituals," 23.

Chapter 11

Virtual Memorials: Bereavement and the Internet

Candi K. Cann

*T**his chapter examines different types of virtual memorials—funeral industry virtual memorials offered as part of burial packages, community-driven bereavement sites, and spontaneous social network memorial sites—and how they are being used to mourn and interact with the dead. Particular attention is paid to how the language utilized by the bereaved in these memorial sites contributes to the shifting of mourning from a fixed physical location to a virtual and public sphere.*

VIRTUAL MEMORIALS AND THE FUNERAL INDUSTRY

Memorialization on the world wide web remains a rather new area of both activity and study, with relatively little research available on the origins of virtual memorials and the impact of the Internet on bereavement and mourning. Even with their comparative newness, however, there are many types of Internet memorials. Commercial Internet memorials are sold with funeral packages in addition to the embalmment, entombment of the body and/or cremation, and visitation. Such a site is sold as part of the memorialization package and the bereaved community is encouraged to post to the site as part of the memorialization process. These virtual memorials are touted as a way to *be* at the actual funeral service, if one cannot attend the service, simultaneously allowing the mourner to memorialize, for posterity, their feelings and thoughts about the deceased. Internet memorials in the funeral industry also serve to direct the mourning community to make monetary contributions in the deceased person's memory, with links to the charity/fund of the deceased person's choice; some funeral homes even link flower delivery services on these memorial web pages so that clients can purchase flowers for the actual funeral service itself. The virtual memorial, often titled on funeral websites Visitations or Guestbook, generally consists of the published obituary and personal reflections or remembrances, and is open to anyone who visits the site. Friends and family can post photos and depending on the level of sophistication of the funeral home website, even post audio reflections of the deceased.[1] It will undoubtedly be not long before people will start uploading videos as well. Many funeral home memorial web pages offer an additional service of presenting virtual free gifts to the deceased, such as social network sites where one can give a *hug* or a virtual present. The gifts run the gamut from candles and teddy bears to virtual lilies and even a cup of coffee. In this way, Internet memorials can operate as an *additional* mourning space along with the actual funeral home, and like real-life spaces, they allow the bereaved to preserve their memories and pass them down to future generations. Funeral home virtual memorials also allow for transactional ease in the monetary accouterments of a funeral, such as flowers for the actual funeral service or visitation, and/or donations made in the deceased person's name, while simultaneously allowing participation by mourners that may not traditionally be considered part of the inner circle of grievers. In the funeral ceremony, a hierarchy of those surrounding the deceased is often replicated with the immediate family sitting nearest the deceased, and those more distantly related, or friends, sitting in the outer aisles. In the virtual memorial, however, everyone has equal access to remembering the dead, and the real-life hierarchy is forgotten. The only limitation is one's own technological ability. In this way, the virtual memorial is not merely a replication of the material memorial, but an addition to it, as mourners on virtual memorials are often those who are geographically and/or relationally marginalized in their relations to the deceased. Those who cannot come to the funeral can still be present in their memorializing, and others who might not typically be given a voice to speak at a funeral, such as friends of the deceased, are able to express their grief in a public forum. This does not mean, however, that giving greater access to the previously and currently marginalized among the bereaved is necessarily a good thing; in fact, one widow expressed to me her frustration that the social network memorial of her husband seemed to be a platform for grieving and remembering her husband in a way that made her feel excluded from the process. However, Internet memorialization does allow those who have traditionally been forgotten in the hierarchy of grieving, such as friends, to have a greater role in self-identifying themselves as bereaved. Even more importantly, virtual memorials can highlight the many different aspects and roles a person can play in his life; the frustration of the widow may have been partly in response to the fact that she no longer controlled the narrative told about her deceased husband, and the memories traditionally held in private are now released in a public forum, which can be disconcerting, if not jarring. It is an important function of the virtual memorial that it democratizes bereavement and allows equal access to the dead in a way that society does not. Similarly, where an obituary can function as a tightly controlled narrative, the virtual memorial does not; each remembrance written on the virtual memorial website is given the same priority and weight as others, which can be disturbing to the traditional hierarchy of grieving, for example, the widow who wanted to be at the center of the grieving process, while liberating to others who in the past may not have been recognized or given a voice.

This hierarchical distinction among grievers is mirrored in contemporary society, with corporate policies that only allow time off from work for those who are immediate family. Grandparents, for example, are *not* considered immediate family in many bereavement leave policies. In contrast, the virtual memorial gives everyone an equal opportunity to claim social capital as bereaved and voice one's grief for the dead.[2] That being said, however, while Internet memorialization allows for a greater democratization of bereavement, the danger is that this same access leaves room for marginal actors in someone's life to step forward and claim a greater role in postmortem grieving, asserting a central role in the memorialization of a person. As Christina Staudt puts it, "Why is it a good thing that a distant cousin could dominate the site with a major story/donation and can appear central in the deceased's life?"[3] In this way, Internet memorials are not unlike obituaries, in that the narratives can sometimes function as a way to rewrite one's life so that the life reflected upon can appear very different than the life actually lived.

INTERACTIVE MEMORIALS

More recent developments in the funeral industry offer interactive tombstones that allow the embedding of a barcode that is read by a smartphone and allows the bereaved to interact with the deceased through prerecorded video or audio clips, as well as favorite quotes or narratives predetermined by the deceased themselves or selected by the family for those visiting the gravesite.[4] Additionally, gravestone smart chips can embed the geographical location of the tombstone with a GPS marker, allowing the deceased to be remembered virtually *and* physically with a grave marker that is easily found. Once this marker is scanned by a smartphone, the barcode allows a re-creation of the funeral ceremony itself, so that visitors to the gravesites are able to access many of the stories and memories of the deceased within a virtual community of the bereaved, while simultaneously mirroring the real-life physical space of the headstone. Extending the idea of tombstone barcodes, the concept of virtual avatars in the afterlife captures the likenesses and gestures of the deceased person whom one can visit online at any time. These avatars are touted as a way to build an online legacy, or even to bring deceased ones back to life through socially constructed memory projects. The most popular websites currently building Internet avatars are called Lifenaut and Virtual Eternity, and are geared expressly toward the purpose of creating life after death on the world wide web. The success of the avatars remains to be seen, but the tombstone barcodes are already a reality and becoming more and more popular, particularly since smartphones already have the microchip technology built into them. Visits to the cemetery are shifting now into both a physical and virtual experience, and it should not be long before social media captures this as well. Funeral homes in the future will likely be able to tie the gravestone's site to a social network memorial, allowing for an interactive memorial that simultaneously allows grievers to virtually visit the site, while also promoting the funeral home's business. Other countries, such as China, are already utilizing this technology to promote the notion of virtual visitation as a way to cut down on foot traffic to cemeteries during the festivals for the ancestors; in the United States where visiting the actual physical site of the body is relatively rare,[5] the virtual memorial may not merely supplement the physical visitation, but supplant it.

In addition to the embedded barcodes and Internet avatars located in the tombstone itself, there are also new smartphone applications that allow grievers to create and carry with them their own virtual cemeteries. One new such program, titled Pocket Cemetery, allows users to create personalized tombstones on their smartphones, send prayers, messages, light candles, and even leave flowers on a virtual grave at any time. On iTunes, Pocket Cemetery downloads to one's phone for a onetime fee of $2.99. Like a funeral company's memorialization services, Pocket Cemetery offers opportunities for charitable donations and even audio sermons in memory of the deceased.[6] Gary Laderman, author of several books on death in America, notes the do-it-yourself mentality of memorials, stating: "It's part of the post-60's consumer empowerment, where everything can get caught up in commercialization. Before, it was left to the funeral home. Now you take the production into your own hands and have it your way."[7] Today's grievers are no longer grieving according to societal mores; car decal memorials, t-shirt memorials, and makeshift spontaneous memorials, such as the one that emerged in Aurora, Colorado, following the cinema shootout in the summer of 2012, are all indicative of the popular trend towards remembering the dead at the grassroots level. As technology continues to expand, memorialization endures, and the repertoire of services for Internet and smartphone memorialization is growing exponentially to keep up with the growing demand of creating virtual life after death.

POPULAR MEMORIALS IN VIRTUAL SPACE: COMMUNITIES FOR THE BEREAVED

In addition to the commercial endeavors of virtual memorials directly associated with funeral companies, the construction of popular virtual memorials, both entrepreneurial and nonprofit, is created intentionally for grieving communities. These online memorials serve similar purposes of offering online support and community for the bereaved, while constructing meaning out of death through public memory and life narratives. Online memorials for mourning serve parents of babies who have died from SIDS and families of suicide victims as well as survivors of individuals who have died of more common causes. They are seen as alternate spaces and additional avenues of grieving. Most studies of these virtual memorials note their general therapeutic value.[8] It is in response to these memorial sites that the funeral industry began its own commercial version of virtual memorials, and their popularity and functionality as grieving support groups reveal a continuing need for alternate grieving spaces online. These sites often highlight deaths that are either not discussed, such as the deaths of children or babies, or deaths that are not always taken seriously by others, like the deaths of pets.[9] With increasingly low infant mortality rates in the United States, for example, infant and baby deaths have become occurrences at once both rare and taboo. Grieving parents have few places to turn to express and discuss their loss, and the Internet provides that space. The Internet allows marginalized grievers to come together in a public forum that is at once exclusive, yet safe, giving support and demonstrating to the community members that although infant death may not be widely discussed, it still occurs.

Another example of marginalized grievers includes those grieving the death of their pets. One website, www.petmemorial.com, allows bereaved owners to create memorials for their various dead pets complete with pictures, testimonies, obituaries, and even audio and video clips. Like other virtual memorials, these bereavement communities have related smartphone applications so that the chat room is instantly accessible from any location, such as the Petloss Chatroom, a forum for those who have experienced the death of a pet.[10] Though some funeral homes have caught on to the desire and need to create public grieving spaces for pets, many individuals still have no public outlet for mourning the death of a pet, and often feel silly or awkward expressing their great sadness over an animal's death. Both the Internet memorial websites and the chat rooms allow the grievers a space to mourn openly and comfortably, while memorializing their pet in a way that may grant the deceased animal, and the bereaved owner, more recognition than the typical backyard disposal might provide.

SOCIAL NETWORK MEMORIALS AND
UNCENSORED GRIEVING

In addition to the more intentionally constructed funeral memorial and community grieving websites, spontaneous Internet memorials have emerged. These are generally social network sites of a person who has died, which, following death, has become the locus of memorialization with a continued following of the community remembering the particular life and death of the deceased person. Spontaneous memorials reveal an organic, popular, and uncensored form of grieving that is not as easily discerned in other forms of online memorials that are intentionally or commercially constructed. Spontaneous memorials have no recognizable power discourse, no web page moderator, nor any tie to monetary gain, except perhaps in preprogrammed social network pop-ups. When spontaneous memorials first materialized on the web, social networking sites had no formal policies regarding what to do with pages of the deceased, but the overwhelming popularity of spontaneous memorialization has created the need for official company and legal policies for web pages of the dead. Initially, when this phenomenon first occurred, family members and friends wanted to continue to have access to social network pages so they could continue to visit the dead and share memories of the deceased, as well as grieve together in a public, yet intimate, forum. Soon, however, glitches in these social network programs became evident, as Internet ghosts began to emerge. These ghosts were essentially program-generated prompts that functioned as part of the social network application, such as the suggestion to *like* something or become friends with somebody, because one's friend is a friend of someone else. The problem, however, emerged when these prompts occurred when a person was deceased, creating the notion of a virtual ghost that lingered around the Internet, acting on behalf of the deceased.[11] After my grandfather's death, for example, I was repeatedly invited to play a virtual game with him, and to answer questions that he supposedly asked about me on Facebook, although he was not the one who actually initiated this contact. To respond to the proliferation of ghosts in the system, social networks now memorialize individual web pages—essentially deactivating a page from active status to a dead site that can be visited and perused, but no longer operates with computer generated prompts and links to other user pages. In some ways, memorializing web pages replicate the terminal endpoint of real lives, marking an endpoint in a timeline for a social network site, which ironically, has run counter to the original usage of social network sites, where a person's page kept living after their real life had ended. Officially memorializing social network sites, however, creates issues of legality: who retains the right to access, view, and shut down information once someone has died? The sites also cause difficulties for the organic grieving communities that have come to view these social network sites as safe places to conduct their mourning. For this reason, Facebook and MySpace created official policies regarding what happens to social network information once someone has died.[12] The legal issues have also spawned a whole new generation of companies geared to the management of virtual information after one's death, one of the faster growing industries on the Internet in regards to death today.[13] Because of the proliferation of spontaneous memorials, and the growing practice of mourning online on someone's defunct site, social networks have also generated extended memorial services that have begun to grow in popularity as sites for the bereaved. One such example, MySpace, spawned a postmortem version known as MyDeadSpace, www.mydeadspace.com. It released its first smartphone application on January 29, 2012. Sites such as MyDeadSpace allow users to post obituaries, construct memorials, and post thoughts for grieving communities surrounding a deceased person. MyDeadSpace seems to reach beyond the immediate grieving community, however, in that it also receives visitors interested in the macabre; nevertheless, it is deigned to be a virtual cemetery that reminds those perusing the site that they are not alone in their experience of grief.[14]

MEMORIAL DISCOURSE: THE LANGUAGE OF GRIEF

In all of these virtual memorials—both commercial and spontaneous—one feature is saliently similar: the mourning discourse used by the bereaved to express their grief online. This language is predominantly informal, in the present tense, and addresses the deceased in the second person singular voice. This mourning discourse is strikingly different from the formal ritualized language and public speeches used in traditional funeral and memorial services. The terms funeral service and memorial service are often used interchangeably; technically a funeral service implies that the remains of the deceased are present. Religious funerals have aims linked to the dogma of the faith; for example, the Christian funeral marking the transition from one's earthly life to one's afterlife in heaven with God or the Buddhist funeral marking one's transition from a life of suffering to the release from that suffering. These services often use ritual texts and highly stylized language. While the language at traditionally conducted funerals tends to be more formal than at the contemporary, commonly individualized, memorial services, both present markedly more structured speech than is found in the virtual space of the Internet. The very public nature of these services is reflected in the formality of the discourse they contain. One of the functions of the service is to mark a shift in the dead person's status from alive to dead, from community participant to historical person. This is achieved largely by a retelling of the person's biography.

Depending on the faith tradition, the commemorative tributes—eulogies or remembrances—can be offered by friends and family or by a clergy person, who may or may not have had contact with the deceased but is responsible for conducting the final ceremony. In some Jewish traditions and among the Quakers, most of the service consists of such remembrances delivered by different people who interacted with and/or knew the deceased. Occasionally, someone directs their words partially or wholly to the deceased, speaking in second person and present tense. However, the speakers are located in an open public forum and are communicating with an audience in front of them, and their reminiscences are created accordingly. An analysis of funerary language, Christian or Jewish, English or Spanish, finds the formula generally the same: the life is constructed in a neatly packaged way, and death is the end of the story. The third person is used in telling the story of the deceased, for example, "She was a good person, interested in . . . whose life touched those around her . . . " and the past tense is utilized, placing the person both publicly and firmly in the past. Her life is over, and the community comes together to acknowledge that fact. In conjunction with traditional liturgical texts, the speeches produce a service that simultaneously makes sense and offers meaning.

Obituaries operate similarly. As the hallmark of the biographic retelling of life and the narrative reconstruction of life after death, they offer a range of content, depending on the context and the author. A professional journalist will write the obituary for a famous person, while others may be written by survivors close to the deceased. A person may even be remembered in several obituaries, placed by different groups of people who wish to pay tribute, such as former colleagues and organizations the deceased has served. These obituaries provide complementary narrative voices to those at the funeral or memorial service.[15] Lucy Bregman writes in her book *Preaching Death: The Transformation of Christian Funeral Sermons* about the importance of packaging lives into obituary discourse and the traditional funerary formula that ensues

> 'Someone was here,' and it is very important that it was not just an anonymous Anyone, but a unique individual with a life, loves, vocation, hobbies, and so on that can be lovingly recalled. 'To do right by' this person requires evoking all of these in a spirit of gratitude for the life he or she lived. Therefore the key phrases for opening the ritual become, 'We give thanks for the life of *x*' or 'We celebrate the life of *x* as we gather here together.' Note that neither 'the body' nor 'the soul' is really the subject of this event, it is 'the person' and his or life that matters.[16]

Eulogies and obituaries are concerned with constructing a biography, a narrative, and an understanding of a life through biographic retelling. Bereavement language in social network memorialization, on the other hand, often seems to circumvent this general biographic formula with language that seems as though it is in conversation with the deceased, though the audience includes the grieving community's responses, thoughts, and ideas. Though there is no real-time response from the deceased, the bereaved write to the deceased as though he is still an active participant in the conversation. This is in nearly complete opposition to the language utilized in funerary discourse in which the person is quite firmly placed in the past. The bereaved explain to the deceased how his death has affected them, and they often talk to the dead in intimate details, revealing dreams, visions, and other more private experiences, such as what life feels like without the deceased. This is strikingly different from the discourse commonly used in funerals and public mourning rituals, in which formal language is employed and the deceased is generally referred to in the third person past tense, emphasizing the distance of the mourners from the dead. Mourners on memorial websites tend to speak in the second person present tense to the dead, as though the deceased is still alive, and they are in conversation with them. The timeline aspect of social network sites facilitates this use of the present continuous tense, and because one can literally and figuratively access the past on one's website, both in images and things said and thought, it may not strike the bereaved as strange when writing in the present tense to the deceased.[17] The deceased person's social network site is still functioning as a visible reminder of his previous existence, and in a way, offers a virtual repository of his life, making him virtually present if not necessarily responsive.

Memorialization language on social network sites is also much more informal than that used in funerary and obituary discourse, and reflects the spoken and written language generally used in texts or brief e-mail messages in everyday discourse. For example, there is often the written substitution of letters and words that are so prevalent in everyday smartphone and text communication— r for are, u for you—particularly when the deceased is young. This in itself reflects the often spontaneous nature of the communication initiated by the bereaved towards the deceased, but also indicates the different function of a social network memorial from the more formal obituary. Obituary discourse places the dead in the past, and rewrites their lives into digestible narratives, while memorial discourse is bereavement language, and reflects the previously private language of grief made public through virtual space. Examples from two different memorialization sites of two people who died recently reflect this trend:

Happy Hanukkah____! Just watched old *SNL* with Adam Sandler singing his Hanukkah Song and thought again of you and all the many fun?times we had with you! I'm laughing and crying at the same time! Miss you!![18]

R.i.p daddy always loved and never forgotten your memories will be forever cherished for many many generations to come :*([19]

In both quotes, the bereaved write directly to the deceased, as though the deceased is listening. There is an acknowledgment of the death, so the language is not denying the reality of death, but rather, the language is informal and intimate, in much the same way as a private conversation one might overhear at a cemetery between the bereaved to the deceased. When I first began examining this phenomenon, I wondered if the conversations of the bereaved to the deceased might reflect an unwillingness to accept death, but over time, I have come to see this as the private discourse between the bereaved and the deceased that has probably always occurred, but has rarely been documented. The private discourse differs greatly from the public funerary language in which the deceased is presented in a packaged narrative. The medium of the Internet, both informal and intimate, public yet private, presents us with a way of documenting these private conversations that people have with the deceased. In the second message, which accompanies pictures of the griever with the deceased uploaded by a mobile phone, in addition to the informal style, an emoticon is used in order to convey the griever's feelings of sadness, and virtual crying. Thus, the griever's sentiments, in addition to her words, are expressed through this medium that is at once accessible, instantaneous, private, yet public. The social network memorial guarantees an instant audience, providing spectacle for emotions from the mundane to the profound, acknowledging and granting both social status and social capital to the bereaved in a way that the real-life world no longer offers.

The utilization of informal language seems to run true for both those familiar with the deceased, and those for whom the deceased remained unknown, such as the in the case of a famous person who has died. Two entries on the page of Whitney Houston's In Living Memory Facebook[20] page reflect this tendency:

> ICON, MOTHER, DAUGHTER, SISTER AND SO MUCH MORE WHITNEY THERE IS NOT A DAY THAT GOES BY THAT I DON'T THINK ABOUT YOU. YOU ARE TRUELY MISSED I STILL CRY WHEN I HEAR YOUR VOICE OR SEE YOU ON TV OR ANYWHERE ELSE EVEN THOUGH WE ARE NOT BLOOD RELATED YOU JUST FELT LIKE FAMILY I LOVE YOU WHITNEY AND I WILL ALWAYS KEEP YOU CLOSE IN MY HEART!!!! R.I.P WHITNEY AND NO WHITNEY WE WILL ALWAYS LOVE YOU
>
> Tears still falling. One day i will come to accept you are no longer here but not just yet x

Though the Internet is a public forum, the language utilized in memorials is more reflective of private conversation or thought, which is then publically shared or sanctioned. Like the personal comments by mourners to those they know, these entries also are informal, personal, and use more casual language, including such minutiae as particular fonts, all capital letters in the first entry, and symbols like the kiss in the second entry to convey this informality. Internet mourning language is thus simultaneously private and public. The dually private/public nature of the Internet allows the bereaved to claim social status as grievers. In other words, creating and maintaining spontaneous memorials not only allow grievers the social space to grieve, but also allow them to self-identify as one who is grieving. The urge and desire of the bereaved not only to remember the dead, but also to be *recognized* as remembering the dead is important and cannot be overlooked. Only 50 years ago, grievers were readily identifiable with social markers such as black armbands or black clothing. Today, when there are no readily identifiable markers of one's status as bereaved, it is little wonder that Internet memorials provide an alternate reality where one's status as griever is immediate and recognizable. Internet traditions regarding death are fast becoming established, and today, when one's friend or relative dies, it is common practice to post a profile picture of oneself with the deceased person as one's primary picture. This instantly claims one's status as mourner, providing a visual marker of one's status as bereaved, and lets one's friends recognize that status. Recognition is important for both the griever and community alike, and proclaiming one's status as bereaved through status updates, pictures with the deceased, and conversations with the deceased allow both the bereaved and the community surrounding the bereaved the ability to support and move through the stages of grief, while providing a public platform through which to continue to shape the narrative of and about the dead.

Additionally, in virtual memorials it is not only public discourse that intersects with private thought or expression, but past events seem to intersect with present and future in such a way that time itself seems blurred. The dually private/public nature of virtual discourse allows traditional constructions of time to be distorted, so that past/present/future are no longer rigid divisions, but socially malleable and publicly sanctioned distinctions.[21] Certain social network sites, such as Facebook, have intersecting timelines between users, so that one person's status appears in another person's news feed, further blurring the notions of past, present, and future, as status updates are not necessarily chronologically ordered in real time, and users comment on events that may or may not have recently occurred.[22] The constant references in the various Internet memorial services ranging from virtual avatars to information protection agencies also reinforce this idea of a virtual afterlife through language. Even the names of Internet memorial services reflect this language of Internet memorialization as a memory that serves to extend life, rather than understand or prepare for death. It is an important distinction—Internet afterlife as an extension of life—that reflects a particular trend of the shifting function of memorialization. Spontaneous memorials may reflect the limits of funerary and religious discourse in the bereavement process, and may offer publicly sanctioned forms of interacting with the dead when the real-life world no longer condones such expressions of grief. In a world where mourning clothing is no longer worn, time off from work is limited to the time it takes to prepare for and attend a funeral, and mourners are expected to return to normalcy in a short amount of time, perhaps spontaneous memorials provide a public form where mourners can continue to maintain their identity as grievers, and feel as though it is accepted to mourn.[23]

CONCLUSION

The language of bereavement on the Internet continues to evolve and change, reflecting several trends that diverge from traditional funerary discourse. Simultaneously, however, there is an emergence of both spontaneous mourning sites for communities with particular concerns—survivors of suicide, for example—and social network sites that once belonged to the living, but have shifted to become centers of bereavement for the deceased. These offer a glimpse into the private/public world of grieving on the Internet. Language in these spontaneous memorials is dramatically different from traditional funerary and obituary discourse, dismissing the third person past narrative voice, and embracing instead a second person present tone that is at once intimate and informal, and reflects a relationship with the dead that is almost completely at odds with the publicly sanctioned language in funerals and memorials. This spontaneous memorial language evokes as many questions as it answers, many of which are beyond the scope of this short chapter: Are spontaneous memorials indicative of a problem in our culture regarding the bereavement process? Do we make such sharp distinctions between private and public mourning that people must create their own private mourning discourses because they are not readily available in public forums? Why do people feel the need to create their own mourning rituals when there are standard ritual observances already in place? Does this mean that the current bereavement practices in our society are neither answering nor responding to the needs of grieving communities? And, finally, is it even healthy to extend real lives in virtual ways? The language of all virtual memorials, though, reflects a deep personal and communal need to mourn, and be recognized as mourner, in a world that no longer has readily identifiable markers for those that are grieving. Virtual bereavement is not just an alternate reality, but allows for an alternate identity in a world where other expressions of grief have all but disappeared.

NOTES

1. Examples of funeral websites include www.flannerbuchanan.com and www.dignitymemorial.com.

2. Beyond the scope of this chapter, but worth noting nonetheless, are studies of the relationship between social networks and social capital that are just emerging. For one of the more interesting and detailed studies, see Alain Cucchi and Chantal

Fuhrer, "Relations between Social Capital and Use of ICT: A Social Network Analysis Approach," *International Journal of Technology and Human Interaction* 8, 2 (April–June 2012): 15.

3. E-mail communication with Christina Staudt, November 23, 2012.

4. Quiring Headstones provides "living headstones" with microchip technology that allows people to communicate "regardless of where they reside."

5. See Robert A. Neimeyer, Darcy L. Harris, Howard R. Winokuer, and Gordon F. Thornton, *Grief and Bereavement in Contemporary Society* (New York: Routledge, 2011).

6. "New iPhone App Memorializes Dead Loved Ones in the Palm of Your Hand," *PRWeb,* last modified July 6, 2009. http://www.prweb.com/releases/2009/07/prweb2609424.htm

7. Gary Laderman, quoted in Allison Engle. "In the Rear Window, Tributes to the Dead." *New York Times*, December 11, 2005.

8. See Christopher J. Finlay and Guenther Krueger, "A Space for Mothers: Grief as Identity Construction on Memorial Websites Created by SIDS Parents," *Omega: Journal of Death and Dying* 63 (2011): 21–44. Alison Chapple and Sue Ziebland, "How the Internet is Changing the Experience of Bereavement by Suicide: A Qualitative Study in the UK," *Health: An Interdisciplinary Journal for the Social Study of Health, Illness and Medicine* 15 (March 2011): 173–87.

9. I am grateful to George Dickinson for this idea of pet grief as another category of marginalized grieving.

10. "Petloss Chatroom," http://www.petloss.com/newchat.htm. Accessed September 18, 2012.

11. Jenna Wortham, "As Facebook Users Dies, Ghosts Reach Out," *New York Times,* July 17, 2010.

12. Caleb Johnson, "How to 'Memorialize' the Facebook Pages of the Recently Deceased," *Huffington Post,* October 27, 2009.

13. Beyond the scope of this paper, these industries are growing exponentially, and a brief, but incomplete list can be found at and includes various organizations concerned with access to digital information following one's demise. Some of these organizations are AfterSteps, AssetLock, Dead Man's Switch, Death Switch, E-Z Safe, Entrusted, Estate, EstateLogic, Eternity Message, GreatGoodbye, If I die.org, Legacy Locker, Legacy Organiser, Life Ensured, Lifestrand, Mento Mori, My Last Email, My Web Will, My Internet Data, Parting Wishes, SecureSafe, and VitalLock.

14. Mikita Brottman addresses this at length in her chapter, "Death in Cyberspace: Psychoanalysis and the Internet," in *The Many Ways We Talk about Death in Contemporary Society,* ed. Margaret Souza and Christina Staudt (New York: Mellen, 2009), 121–34.

15. I am in debt to Christina Staudt for some of the distinctions here regarding the differences in these three types of narrative re/constructions.

16. Lucy Bregman, *Preaching Death; The Transformation of Christian Funeral Sermons* (Waco, TX: Baylor University Press, 2011), 169.

17. I am grateful here to Donald Joralemon, and his e-mail discussion with me on these ideas.

18. "RIP Jamshid Rastegar," http://www.facebook.com/jamshid.rastegar?sk=wall. Accessed September 14, 2012.

19. "Personal Facebook," http://www.facebook.com/photo.php?fbid=25223787581
79&set=a.1242128352719.28239.1814652542&type=1&theater. Accessed September 26,
2012.

20. "Whitney Houston in Loving Memory," http://www.facebook.com/whitney
houston.inlovingmemory. Accessed September 18, 2012.

21. For more on the importance of time and the heavy emphasis on the present in
status updates, and social networks in general, see Alexandra Georgakopoulou, *Small
Stories, Interaction and Identity* (Philadelphia: John Benjamins Publishing Company,
2007).

22. See Ruth Page's "Re-examining Narrativity: Small Stories in Status Updates,"
*Text & Talk: An Interdisciplinary Journal of Language, Discourse & Communication
Studies* 30, 4 (July–August 2010): 423.

23. Cathy Lynn Grossman discusses a similar trend of memorializing through posting one's picture with the deceased as one's Facebook photo. This trend then identifies grievers as a community, not unlike the Victorian mourning practice of wearing a
black armband. Cathy Lynn Grossman, " 'Today we are all Hokies' on Facebook," *USA
Today,* April 18, 2007.

Chapter 12

Strange Eternity: Virtual Memorials, Grief, and Entertainment

Angela Riechers

*T*his chapter explores the relationship between traditional personal memorial objects and digital memorials, considering how Internet RIP pages, avatars, and other multimedia forms of commemoration have changed the process of remembrance once triggered by a relic or physical object such as mourning jewelry or a photograph of the deceased. Of particular interest are ways in which issues of authenticity, editorial control, and the creation of personal mythology present in all memorials are interpreted and played out in the digital realm—including the potential subversion of grief into a form of idle diversion.

The reasons why we continue to need personal memorials—to pay tribute to the dead while displaying both grief and fond remembrance, to soothe the bereaved and generate sympathy, to sublimate the fear of one day being forgotten ourselves—remain constant, even as formats evolve in response to advances in manufacturing capability, digital imaging, information technologies, and social networking. Reassuringly solid memorial objects, items grounded in the real world as well as memorials stored in the depths of the Internet, lacking corporeal substance, spring from a common origin even though they diverge widely in their functionality as part of the bereavement process. As a component of modern grieving, digital memorials represent a complex mix of the genuine and deeply felt impulse to pay tribute to the dead, an extension of social media culture that

considers every subject fodder for entertainment, and an example of the continu-
ing suppression of real-life dialogue and engagement with death in contemporary
Western society.

INTRODUCTION

Personal memorial objects, such as mourning jewelry containing a lock of hair
or a small portion of cremated ashes, maintain a strong grip on the human
imagination because a viewer can sense the wealth of narrative contained in
these small-scale creations made to honor and remember the dead, even in
the absence of key details such as who the object is meant to commemorate.
These intimate memorials function as compasses to guide individuals through
private landscapes of grief, rather than establishing myths of grandeur and
heroism meant for public consumption as traditional monuments do. Mourning objects created by the bereaved reflect a single point of view and present a
specific exit image of the lost loved one to be drawn upon for future recall and
comfort. Physical relics, defined as objects both esteemed and venerated because of their association with a saint or martyr, date as far back as the Middle
Ages. Similarly, remnants left after decay, disintegration, or disappearance of a
loved family member or friend can be thought of as modern relics. Such items
were common in the 19th century. For example, a lock of hair woven into a
brooch or bracelet served as a direct link to the absent body of the dead person.[1] The use of such personal relics in memorial objects persists to this day.
The presence of the departed lingers in that last leftover fragment, transforming ordinary things into artifacts of solace.

Residing in the sterile and intangible environment of the Internet, digital
memorials are by necessity relic-free, far removed from the unpleasant reality
of a dead body. Artificial intelligence pioneer Marvin Minsky predicted that
future technology would free us from "the bloody mess of organic matter"
entirely.[2] The absence of a relic, or indeed of any physical object at all, as a
focus for mourning can make a digital memorial feel almost like a show to be
watched, something created for entertainment and visual pleasure. Immense
amounts of personal material and content including audio clips, slide shows,
video, and interactive avatars evoke the departed in a heretofore unimaginable level of detail, summoning up an almost living image that strengthens the
magical thinking that the dead might somehow return, or might not really be
dead after all. Our expectations for a memorial object do not generally include
its having an entertainment value, a different set of preconceptions from those
brought to bear each time we access a memorial on a device screen. An object's
haptic qualities as well as its uniqueness as a singular object gives that item an
inherent gravitas that encourages, even demands, serious personal contemplation. In contrast, a digital file can be copied and distributed endlessly; while
the content of the file may elicit strong emotions in the viewer, who may or

may not have known the deceased, the viewer's engagement is likely less personal and intimate.

Facebook and MySpace RIP pages and other online tributes provide a comprehensive portrait of the dead person in a common space where many different circles of acquaintance can come together to grieve and reminisce. But the very nature of mourning as practiced online has begun to blur the boundary between public and private, shifting from an individual act for friends, family members, and the local community to a public forum with the potential of an unlimited number of unwelcome participants. To limit intrusions by outsiders, some sites require passwords or payment but broad accessibility and participation are still the norm. This coauthoring process is a hallmark of the postmodern memorial: presenting a host of potential interpretations that change as content is added instead of a didactic, fixed narrative.[3] Easily accessed by any and all unless password-protected, such memorials grow over time into compilations reflecting several often-conflicting viewpoints. Although these multiauthored tales fulfill all memorial objects' primary function of honoring the dead and soothing the bereaved, they can become trivialized into mere diversion for those who had no real life connection to the deceased. Grief tourists, strangers who eagerly participate in the online dialog and tragedy of loss, and trolls, who for their own amusement browse the Internet with the purpose of launching vicious attacks targeting the emotions of family and friends, will be discussed later in this chapter. Both groups become part of a once-private mourning process now played out in public, contributing to the legacy of the deceased in previously unimaginable ways.

RELICS

Relics in memorials establish ownership and specificity by narrowing down the provenance of the item—the trace—to a single individual. Before discussing the 21st-century digitally accessed relic and its usage, the role of relics, in their traditional physical form and context for remembering the dead, must be considered. Incorporating relics into mourning or funerary objects is a cultural practice stretching back to the beginnings of recorded human history. The Catholic Church still presents drops of dried blood, chips of bone, limbs or digits, and sometimes the entire body of a dead saint for veneration. During the Renaissance, men of science and letters were similarly honored, as evidenced in the History of Science Museum in Florence, where Galileo's middle finger is prominently displayed in an ornate reliquary.

The undeniably powerful presence of a relic in a memorial object often can summon up a visceral fear and dread response in a viewer, invoking Freud's theory of the uncanny: "that species of the frightening that goes back to what was once well known and had long been familiar."[4] Relics provide cold, hard proof not only that someone once lived, but also that they died. An observer may feel confusion and anxiety when confronted with a relic-containing memorial object, such as "look, here's a piece of a dead body!" In an uneasy both/and situation, the inert scrap is *person* and *not-person* at the same time. Physical relics add a tangible veracity lacking in the digital realm. Nevertheless, a parallel can be found in the use of the recorded voice of the deceased in 21st-century memorials. Listening to the recording closely mimics the tension between present and absent that we experience when confronted with traditional physical relics. While classifying voice as a category of relic may step outside the usual definition, memorials making use of audio create that same uneasy bridge between the world of the departed and the present in which a trace points uncannily to someone who is gone. Like physical relics, the voices, while intangible, nevertheless are precise and specific to one person in the same way as are fragments of the body. The development of recording technology in the 19th century made it possible to preserve someone's voice for posterity, and today merging recorded voice with video images represents a further evolution of the memorial form.

From the 16th to the 19th centuries in Europe and North America, locks of hair exchanged between close friends and lovers during life or gathered after death were worked into various forms of jewelry, small boxes, and framed displays for wall or tabletop to symbolize friendship and fond remembrance.[5] These items were exchanged as gifts or tributes, rather than offered for sale. By the mid- to late 1800s, mourning attire and memorial rings, lockets, and bracelets were only part of the symbolic representation of grief; a wealth of newly available consumer goods added to the ways to publicly display bereavement at the time of the Industrial Revolution.

> Mass production multiplied souvenirs till every public occasion was aflutter with paper and ribbons, cheap ephemera sold in the streets. . . . Funerals had portrait buttons set in black rosettes, flags with black bows, black streamers for children to wave, and memorial cards. . . . China was popular; there were mugs, plates and little dishes with portraits enclosed in black wreaths, and, for the death of Victoria, Goss issued china in the shape of her first shoe. Handkerchiefs with black borders and portraits were made in every material from silk to calico, and there were portraits in every kind of frame, silver through tin and stamped paper.[6]

Today, overnight printing technology and low cost overseas manufacturing provide mourners with inexpensive personalized memorial goods such as printed T-shirts and coffee mugs, souvenirs bearing a likeness of the deceased that do not usually contain any physical part of him or her, although the capacity to do so exists.

Ashes are a relatively clean form of relic, not subject to further decomposition and decay, and are a component of several memorial products available

from merchants pursuing a brisk commercial trade in the name of remembrance. The makers of customized Memory Bears, teddy bears that are created from a loved one's bathrobe or favorite shirt and emblazoned with a heat
transferred photograph of the deceased, merge the categories of souvenir and
relic by offering the option to have cremated ashes sewn into the bear's stuff-
ing. LifeGems are made in a laboratory from carbon extracted from crematory
ash, then compressed into a sparkling jewel. In 2009, a Connecticut autograph
dealer purchased a lock of Michael Jackson's hair (singed off during the filming of the now-infamous 1984 Pepsi commercial) for $100,000, and collabo-
rated with LifeGem to produce a limited edition of Michael Jackson memorial
diamonds. Three LifeGems created in 2007 from Beethoven's hair sold for
$240,000 each.[7]

Funeral urns fashioned from bronze, marble, or other valuable materials
have been used for the dignified storage and display of human ashes since
times of antiquity. Dignity no longer appears to be a primary objective, however, of contemporary items such as Cremation Solution's $2,600 personalized
portrait urn, which allows a family to keep a lifelike head of the deceased,
filled with the irrefutable proof of death, on the mantel. Other options for incorporating ashes into personal memorials are available from And Vinyly, a
company that will press cremated ashes into up to 30 vinyl records along with
customer-supplied audio, which can be music, a soundtrack of a spoken farewell message to the world, or just silence, so the bereaved can listen to the pops
and crackles generated as the turntable's tone arm skips over the gritty ashes.
For an extra fee, artist James Hague will paint a portrait album cover using pig-
ments mixed with ashes. Holy Smoke of Stockton, Alabama, packs ashes into
ammunition cartridges. The bereaved need only specify the caliber or gauge,
ship them the ashes, and Holy Smoke will load up cartridges that can be used
for anything from duck hunting to a 21-gun salute. The level of creativity in
these efforts to keep human remains around, disguised in an unrecognizable
form, is intriguing, but it is worth contemplating how close in spirit these objects are to formerly deeply venerated relics of saints.

Apart from these specialized commercial products, artists also use relics in
their works to explore issues of mortality, persistence, and decay, and to comment upon consumer society's bewildering array of death-related merchan-
dise. Even the practice of weaving and plaiting hair into memorials is not quite
extinct: Anna Schwamborn, a student at Central St. Martins College of Art in
London, used the hair of a terminally ill friend and black bone china incorporating the friend's ashes to create her series, Mourning Objects. Her collection
includes a rosary, necklace, and watch chain finished with a tiny urn-shaped
vial to catch falling tears. Artist Darin Montgomery's Urn-a-matic products
include a gumball machine that dispenses ashes sealed in individual plastic
bubbles and a vacuum canister urn that plays home video of the deceased, accompanied by the Terry Jacks song "Seasons in the Sun."

Dutch industrial designer and artist Wieki Somers used a 3-D printer to transform human ashes into somewhat ironic memorial objects including a toaster, a bathroom scale, and a DustBuster. A more meditative approach to memorial containers for ashes can be found in the work of product designer Nadine Jarvis. Her project entitled Carbon Copies consists of a box containing a set of 240 pencils whose lead is made from compressed human ashes. A built-in sharpener deposits the shavings into the box, slowly transforming it into an urn, and a small window atop the box shows the amount of pencils left as the days and years go by. Jarvis also designed a bird feeder molded from seeds, beeswax, and human ashes. As the birds peck at the food, the urn disintegrates. Over time the object disappears entirely, like the lost body of the deceased, leaving behind only the small wooden perch inscribed with his or her personal information as a memory object.

DIGITAL MEMORIALS

Removing physical objects from the memorial equation entirely, leaving only unstable images behind like the grin of the Cheshire Cat, as is done in digital memorials, raises the question of how well the intangible can take the place of a cherished object held close to the heart. After my grandmother's death, I inherited her heavy gold charm bracelet. Not created as a mourning object, and containing no relic of her physical self, it nevertheless serves as a repository of memories, and I think of her each time I wear it. I know the story behind each charm, the reason it was added to this chronicle of my grandmother's life. When I'm no longer around to tell these tales, the bracelet will maintain its value as an object of intrinsic and aesthetic worth but its narrative will be silenced, a dead language with no native speakers left. Memory separated from an object loses powerful triggers for recall, such as the smooth warm heft of the bracelet, or the cheerful jingling sound made by its charms.

As we use objects, we change them. They acquire a patina of history, recording traces of our living selves. Consider the wooden handle of an axe worn smooth over decades of use, bearing a record of all the hands that have held and used it. We crave the imperfection of an object's small flaws—its nicks, dents, and scratches—seeing them as proof of the past made apparent. This sense of imperfection and visible history is what digital objects lack.[8] Walter Benjamin noted in 1936 that "The authenticity of a thing is the quintessence of all that is transmissible in it from its origin on, ranging from its physical duration to the historical testimony relating to it."[9] A digital photo, something seemingly close to its earlier physical manifestations, lacks any haptic quality or sense of unique authenticity—a front with the image and a back where perhaps someone jotted the name and date of the subject or an inside joke in his or her own unique handwriting, the ink faded or blurred with age. Perhaps this accounts for the popularity of the applications Instagram and Hipstamatic which distress pristine digital images in an attempt to suggest a visual history by applying creases, scratches, dust marks, worn spots, and other marks that accrue naturally in analog photos. The Harinezumi digital camera available in Japan shoots images that are deliberately grimy and overexposed, in a random and unpredictable way, obliterating the digital perfection we expect.[10] At the 2011 AOL 7 on 7 conference held at New York's New Museum, team researchers Camille Utterback and Erica Sadun developed an experimental iPad application that would show traces of each activity performed on the screen, building up ghost images, wear patterns, and permanent trails where objects were dragged and moved, much in the same way a school's wooden desktops build up layers of student graffiti, scratches, carvings, and the like. Their project was meant to give digital objects the patina of age that a real object acquires naturally, in an environment that wouldn't otherwise show any visible signs of decay.

Digital objects carry their history around in a more accessible manner than their real world predecessors ever could. Their embedded metadata, as granular as the geotagged location data and camera information, permanently attaches their stories, allowing them to travel intact to indefinitely wider audiences. Memories preserved in digital photos, videos, and audio are readily traceable back to their source no matter how far they roam, and will always have their tales at hand, ready to be told independently of a human narrator. But detaching a memory from a solid object does not, in the long run, make it any more durable, but rather, only emphasizes memory's ephemeral quality.

Physical objects are subject to the ravages of time, but data is susceptible to its own death too, as anyone who has ever mourned a lost hard drive knows. Digital memorials, much like our own human memories, are simultaneously fragile and persistent. They depend on technologies and online services that rapidly advance and grow obsolete. Online memorial files may become corrupted, and future technological developments all but guarantee that someday, the format of a memorial will be unreadable, representing a potential loss to future remembrance. Additionally, we are fickle with digital structures of all types; when something newer and better comes along, we rapidly abandon our previous loyalty to a digital product or service with barely a backward glance.[11]

Recognizing this challenge, designers have tried to bridge the gap between the virtual and the real by creating physical objects in which to store collections of digital memories. An example is Vanitas, an application for iPhone and iPad meant to invite contemplation on mortality, according to its designers Auriea Harvey and Michael Samyn.[12] A customized memorial stored on a smartphone—a small, personal object kept close to the body, similar to mourning jewelry—could represent a near perfect fusion of modern format with traditional function. Vanitas is a contemporary *wunderkammer,* a general collection of symbolic images, not a specific memorial honoring an individual. Describing it as "a memento mori for your digital hands," Harvey and Samyn's website elaborates on the application:

> Referring to still life paintings from the 16th and 17th century, Vanitas presents you with a gorgeously rendered 3D box filled with intriguing objects. Close the box and open it again to see new objects. You can move the objects by tilting your iPhone or pushing and dragging the objects with your fingers. To create pleasant arrangements that inspire and enchant. Some objects decay. A flower blooms. A bubble pops. Life like an empty dream flits by. [13]

Despite its solemn intent as keeper of the memento mori tradition, Vanitas operates at a disadvantage: a user can easily switch to lighter fare when the topic of mortality gets too depressing. The level playing field of the smartphone operating system environment offers up the choice to contemplate death or just play a few rounds of Angry Birds instead, giving equal weight to either option and removing some of the solemnity from considering one's future demise. It's true that traditional memorial objects can also be put away when a viewer has had enough remembering for the time being—the photo album replaced on a shelf, the mourning brooch tucked back into its velvet-lined box—but being able to select Vanitas from among all the bright shiny apps arranged in neat rows on a smartphone screen removes some of the gravity from the decision to think about death and mortality. The context of the action has changed in such a way as to lighten its grimness considerably.

A collection called Technology Heirlooms, by Richard Banks, a designer at Microsoft Research in the United Kingdom, is more targeted toward the individual, addressing both the need to preserve personal memories in a digital format and our desire for a physical object. Banks's TimeCard looks like a digital photo frame that displays images in a timeline, demonstrating the passing of the days, months, and years as the subject ages. The Digital Slide Viewer is designed to replace the photo album as a way of thinking about and honoring a person who has passed away. It allows families to back up and keep a deceased relative's Flickr account at home instead of maintaining it online. The slide viewer encourages family members to share the photos and reminisce in a more elegant and socially intimate shared ritual than awkwardly crowding around a computer monitor and going through folder hierarchies. The Backup Box is a wooden box containing a hard drive connected to the Internet that constantly backs up a person's tweets.[14] Over the years, its accrued history of activity creates a sociological record that becomes a valuable memory resource. In 2010, the Library of Congress announced its plan to permanently archive the entire Twitter feed since its inception in 2006, and is still working out the user interface and other details of how to store, tag, and manage 50 million daily tweets. The archive will be a rich repository of preserved memories for future research, spanning the gamut from what people ate for lunch to groundbreaking historic events to RIP tweets, all covered in real time.[15] The hardware and file servers will become the only objects involved in creating this minutely detailed record, yet the physical spaces needed to house them will not likely be considered memorial locations, in much the same way as a newspaper archive or library containing personal diaries are not in themselves memorials.

SPACES FOR DEATH

Just as personal memorial objects now coexist somewhat uneasily with digital counterparts, physical spaces for memory such as cemeteries do, too. Researchers Jed Brubaker and Gillian Hayes analyzed the comments on dead people's MySpace pages, finding that visits to digital memorials follow the pattern and timing of visits to actual graveyards. For instance, a family might traditionally visit a grave on a holiday to place flowers or a wreath and reinforce their connection to the dead person. And the number of posted comments on dead people's memorial pages spikes on their birthdays, the day after their death was announced, and on holidays, suggesting that people visit the virtual memorial in much the same way they do a real world memorial.[16]

Websites such as iTomb and Virtual Cemetery allow mourners to create an online grave, a death space that by necessity contains no physical trace of the deceased. Such services enable far-flung family and friends to gather at a central location to pay respects and reminisce via comments, posted images, and texts. Real graves need maintenance—weeds pulled, wilted flowers replaced with fresh blooms, headstones kept upright should they begin to tilt to prevent them from looking forlorn and forgotten. Virtual graves need upkeep, too. Unless visitors regularly check in, post a thought or a photo, maybe add a candle or bouquet from the selection of the site's add-ons, the grave will begin to look neglected. And just as real cemeteries charge grounds keeping and maintenance fees, a subscription to iTomb costs $120 per year while a one-time fee for inclusion in the World Wide Cemetery has a price of $20. At present iTomb is mostly populated with filler content—long-dead kings, Thomas Jefferson, various departed celebrities—making it a lonely place to consider adding a memorial to a beloved relative, and suggesting that people still hold reservations about the value of such services.

QR tags (Quick Response Codes with high storage capability) are now being added to the granite monuments at cemeteries, bringing digital capacity directly to the gravesite. Snapping a picture of the tag with a smartphone brings the mourner to a web page dedicated to the deceased buried directly underfoot. The family of musician Chris Ethridge, a member of the country-rock band the Flying Burrito Brothers who died in 2012, is planning to use a QR coded tag at his burial site to enable visitors to see concert clips, hear songs, and learn more about his life.[17] Such websites can also be easily accessed from a desktop computer without incurring travel time or expense, raising the question of whether viewing them at the actual graves adds anything beyond distraction to the experience of visiting a location as an act of remembrance. As the distance to real world sites increases and mourning is experienced through computer screens, a different set of rules and expectations for behaviors and customs evolves. The graveyard—once a quiet space of remembrance, where the bereaved could gather for focused mourning—is now on its way to becoming a dynamic, interactive device-based experience, directed less at personal reflection and more toward passive observation.

ONLY SLEEPING

Beginning in the 19th century and continuing to the present day, postmortem photos portray the subject as only sleeping, creating a permanent visual record that appears to deny the reality of death. Now I Lay Me Down to Sleep (NILM-DTS) is a contemporary volunteer organization of photographers who make their services available at no charge to families who have suffered an early infant loss, traveling to the hospital at the time of delivery and documenting the experience as completely or as minimally as the parents wish. Just as in Victorian times, family portraits may be taken with parents and siblings holding the baby wrapped and swaddled as if peacefully asleep.

This only-sleeping fantasy persists in online memorials and becomes enhanced, to some degree. On the Internet, time and space become unreal estates, a magical spirit world where we can almost believe that the dead can still communicate with us.[18] The notion that it's possible to contact the dead has a long and rich history across many cultures; at lunar New Year, the Chinese burn paper replicas of everything from cash to the latest audio/video equipment as gifts offered up to departed family members, according to the tradition that ancestors have a continued existence in the afterlife and are still able to influence the world they have left behind. Death Switch and Legacy Locker operate in reverse, initiating contact with the living from beyond the grave. After a subscriber dies, these services send emails or video messages composed in advance to designated individuals, bequeathing them the details and passwords for the subscriber's digital assets and accounts. People tuck cell phones into coffins so the deceased can continue to receive text messages, emails, and voicemails, even though the phones will quickly run out of battery power and end up just as dead as their onetime owners. According to Frank Perman, a Pittsburgh funeral director,

> We had a young man die this past summer and they put his cell phone in the casket for the viewing and it rang constantly . . . it was turned to

silent, but you could see the phone light up so you knew people were calling. And they were leaving messages. They knew he was dead, but they were still calling.[19]

As long as the account is active and able to receive messages, the fantasy is secure. The mourner's relationship with the deceased persists for the foreseeable future as long as technology allows, keeping the dead available for contact if not interaction.

Avatars created through socially constructed memory projects like Lifenaut and Virtual Eternity magnify this aspect of fantasy or fictionalization, installing the deceased as robotic resurrections in a twilight zone of artificial existence. These services attempt to continue the well-established practice of conveying future messages to the dead that once took the form of written letters and later, videotapes and audio files. Lifenaut's tagline is "Eternalize!" while Virtual Eternity's website beckons, "Permanently preserve your legacy and heritage with an intellitar that looks, sounds, and acts just like you."[20] Well, not exactly. The technology is still primitive enough that the avatars are not overly convincing as surrogate versions of lost loved ones. These walking, talking simulacra may be more unnerving to the bereaved, in an uncanny way, than they are soothing. Built from still photos and choppy audio snippets strung together, most avatars have a lifeless quality, with animation limited to blinking their eyes and wagging their chins up and down as they speak prerecorded answers to questions typed into a chat box. Seemingly basic inquiries like, "Are you dead?" or anything else that requires an answer outside of the avatar's library of responses will be met with, "I may need some more training to answer that." "How long will my intellitar live/last?" yields the answer "As long as your custodian maintains your family tree, your intellitar will 'live' indefinitely." To the question "What happens to an intellitar when the person pass [sic]?" the avatar responds:

"You may choose to train an intellitar to say when it would like to become inactive, possibly reflecting personal thoughts towards the matter. Otherwise, the family's Custodian will assume control of the intellitar."[21]

Can the bereaved draw real solace from an avatar, or are avatars nothing more than online animated chatbots, a more humanized version of customer service?[22] A father with a terminal illness could record a message to be delivered by an avatar to his baby daughter years later on the eve of her prom, for instance. But the girl might feel uneasy about watching her dead father's avatar and hearing it speak his words to her, as well as feeling conflicted or guilty about having these reservations in the first place. The experience differs from watching a prerecorded video or listening to an audio recording, because rather than seeing and hearing a true image of the father and his voice, that voice is emanating from an animated, and not necessarily accurate, version of his body. Perhaps as technology advances and the avatars become more believably human-looking the boundary will blur enough to allow a better interactive reunion with the dead.

In the world of entertainment, we have become accustomed to the spectacle of posthumous performance, which reared its head in the past two decades. Writer Jack Hamilton describes such appearances as "a mutually-agreed upon sham between performer and audience, the high-tech version of the Elvis impersonator."[23] Fans can watch and listen to a hologram of Tupac Shakur rapping at the 2012 Coachella Festival 16 years after his death, or enjoy "Still Unforgettable," combining audio and video of Nat King Cole's 1961 recording of "Unforgettable" with vocals sung by his daughter Natalie Cole in 1992. You can't tell from the audio alone, but parent and child were both 42 years old at the time their individual recordings were made, an absurd detail that becomes apparent only on video where the father appears younger-looking than the daughter. Frank Sinatra has been a popular posthumous duet partner, chosen by Celine Dion, who recorded a virtual duet of "All the Way" with the late singer in 1999, and by Alicia Keys in 2008, joining in on "Learnin' the Blues" with a video clip of Sinatra from the first Grammy ceremony in 1958. Permission to use the vocals and filmed images was granted by the estates of these dead performers, obviously, but the practice raises the question of whether the singers would have agreed to the arrangement, had it been possible to consult them. In other words, would Frank Sinatra have wanted to pair up with Alicia Keys? His input on the matter was not available. Viewing such performances inevitably becomes a bittersweet experience, amplifying the audience's nostalgic longing for the dead singer, to *really* see and hear him in concert again. At some point, we are forced to surrender our belief that he might return, no matter how much we wish he could. At the same time, while the recording emphasizes the entertainer's permanent unavailability in the flesh, it confirms that his legacy—his art and our memory of it—remains alive and that he continues to shape and influence his art form.

TROLLS AND GRIEF TOURISTS

Mourning as practiced online can become its own strange category of entertainment for grief tourists—people lacking any real-life connection to the deceased—and ever-present trolls, individuals who deliberately use Internet forums as springboards for mischief and outright malice. Online memorials draw upon the well-established convention of creating a social space for mourning, although it takes different form than dictating the length of the mourning period, proper attire, and restrictions upon behavior that were in place in the United States from colonial times until well into the 20th century. To neglect these codes would have cast a shadow upon the dead person's reputation, as they were meant to reconfirm the social standing of the deceased as well as to announce to the world that the bereaved had suffered a loss and were

in need of sympathy. Social media tributes to the dead offer an instant community for support and sympathy and a forum to express grief, as well as maintain
a media presence for the dead, just as traditional monuments maintained the
deceased's social presence, keeping them visible in today's culture that increasingly defines community as virtual rather than physical proximity.

With digital memorial sites, relics or tangible objects are not the only things
missing: just as the body of the deceased is not present, neither is that of the
mourner.[24] Very few people drive around in their cars searching for the wakes
and funerals of complete strangers to attend as a form of entertainment. But
Facebook RIP pages and other social-media-based memorials, like interactive newspaper obituaries or virtual funeral parlors, make it possible to do
just that. Visiting a memorial page can be a passive sort of mourning: death
viewed from a safe distance, an easy opportunity to type a sentence or two into
the comments box and then log off. Participation also casts the commenter as
a sensitive, caring individual unafraid to share in other people's emotionally
difficult situations. This self-appointed role is a good deal simpler to assume
as an anonymous poster on the Internet than it is in real life, where grief is
immediate and visceral rather than kept at a distance mediated by technology

Digital memorials provide forums for commenters to address the larger
topic of mortality, along with their own emotions and personal experiences
of death, from a distant and removed vantage point. The audience for online
grief sites splits into three main groups: the genuinely bereaved seeking comfort and solace; grief tourists eager to participate in an anonymous dialog of
sorrow and loss; and trolls who prey on them by posting provocative responses
meant to shock and outrage. In addition, we can assume a fourth group made
up of web lurkers who peruse RIP pages but remain invisible by declining to
engage with other users.

When strangers feel free to jump into the grief process and view a death as
an opportunity for either their own diversion or mischief, we find ourselves in
seemingly new cultural territory. However, this type of behavior has precedent
among the sensation seekers who enjoyed the 19th-century penny press, with
one important difference: an immediate and ongoing dialog in the media was
not possible during the 1800s. Readers gossiped about sensational murders
and crimes they read about in the scandal sheets, and possibly wrote letters to
the editor, but that was the end of their personal involvement. By the turn of
the 20th century, photomechanical reproduction of images allowed ordinary
people to appear in the pages of newspapers for the first time alongside actors,
politicians, and kings. Everyone could be a star, and all lives could now be visually documented. The masses assumed a place in the firmament.[25] In a similar vein, a century later, the Internet bestows a moment in the spotlight upon
everyone—both the memorialized and the grieving—with greater freedom
than ever before. Our easy access to tragedy through social platforms allows
us to retweet, comment, and rehash the details of a death endlessly, keeping

the tragedy in public view but also desensitizing us to the emotional impact of loss—turning "horror into humdrum."[26]

Once someone has died, friends and family can choose to terminate or memorialize a person's existing Facebook account. Memorial pages are closed to new subscribers and only people who were previously friends of the deceased can view the page or write on the person's wall. RIP pages on Facebook or MySpace are a bit different. The majority of them are created for deaths widely reported in the media—mainly those of children and teenagers, young women, and celebrities—and are not generally set up by the deceased's family (who are presumably mourning in private).

Comments like the following, on MySpace page RIP Anna, are fairly representative:

> Hey there Anna, i know we havent met yet but i would like to let you know that i still havent broken the promise i made you, i havent seen anything happen yet but im letting you know that im still willing to sacrifice my life to save someone in need thank you for the courage.
>
> No, we have never met, but your story has touched me. I came across your story about 2 years ago, I still think about it constantly.
>
> I know i didnt know you but still, thanks to you and me alot more people will be able to live without fear.[27]

Though users have to join the RIP group or "like" the page to post condolence messages or interact with other members, the pages are often accessible to all, making them private social spaces in theory but public ones in reality.[28] Adding one's voice to the comments on a memorial page is akin to signing the guest book at a wake—except that online, people can, and do react, often in surprising ways, to what was written by previous visitors. Allowing people across the entire Internet to participate in creating a memorial leads to a loss of editorial control, resulting in RIP pages crowded with unrelated, inappropriate, and mean-spirited items. The memorial becomes less about a specific person and more about the dialog itself, something to be followed, "liked," and eventually forgotten. Loss of centralized control means that some people's contributions will inevitably upset some others. The combined comments create a fable stitched together from fragments that can ultimately add up to a portrait of the deceased that bears little resemblance to whom that person was in life. The opportunity to publish comments and upload photos, videos, and other links can also become problematic for memorials by taking away a single mourner's privilege to establish the definitive exit image of the deceased.

RIP trolling, meant to call grief tourists out on their strange hobby, reflects perhaps the darkest aspect of memorials posted on the Internet. The trolls' gleefully cruel comments don't commemorate the dead person; instead, they refocus attention onto the trolls and away from the genuine grief expressed by others. The bad behavior on display at online memorials has a real world parallel, too. Thanatourism or dark tourism, an activity where people travel to public sites where death or suffering occurred, resembles visiting virtual memorial sites in that both are ways to consume or experience death, that is, the death of others whom they will not mourn specifically on a personal level, in a safe and socially sanctioned environment. It requires little emotional investment and at the end of the day, can be left behind.[29] When people who did not directly experience an event visit its memorial site and find little to engage them, appropriate behavior can be difficult to enforce. Consider the New York City teenagers disciplined for throwing trash into the reflecting pool during a class trip to the 9/11 memorial site in June of 2012:

> One student explained that they just didn't find the field trip very entertaining. 'No one was disrespecting. It wasn't nothing like that,' said the student. 'No one was being serious. Everyone was kind of bored and it was just something to do.'[30]

Like these teenagers, bored trolls in need of an activity find a solution to their ennui at memorial sites. An important difference, of course, is that the teenagers were perhaps unwilling visitors to the memorial and therefore likely to be bored or unengaged, whereas trolls appear on memorial sites of their own volition. Trolls string along a false dialog as long as they can, exposing what they consider to be the cheap, easy sentimentality of grief expressed online by treating it as fodder for entertainment. They pick over the cultural landscape for the most upsetting material they can find, like the sad death of Amanda Cummings, a 15-year-old girl from Staten Island, NY, who threw herself under a bus because she was being bullied in person and on Facebook. In addition to legitimate RIP pages for Amanda generated by friends and family, trolls set up several of their own. One featured an image of a city bus bearing down on a girl as its profile picture, and the first posted comment read: "Yes, hell is quite hot and she is good company lol." Trolls use such tragic stories as jumping-off points for provocative posts and inappropriate comments that predictably draw furious reactions from unsuspecting readers and often garner a fair amount of media coverage along the way:

> They laugh at the body, they laugh at its destruction. They force their victims to confront precisely those things that motivate the popularity of memorial pages—fear of helplessness, fear of losing a loved one, fear of human parts. Thus RIP trolls post pictures of car crashes onto car crash victims' pages. They post pictures of dead kids onto dead kids' pages. They post movie stills from films like *Dumb and Dumber* captioned with the phrase 'LOL YOUR DEAD,' PhotoShopped pictures of babies in meat grinders, and images of anally impaled corpses.[31]

The mayhem created when trolls show up creates a spectacle, but of a very different sort from that associated with prior traditions of public mourning intended to honor the deceased and call attention to the person's virtues. Instead, trolls create a diversion by attacking social norms and expectations. Their activities disrupt idealized and false visions of an Internet memorial site as an emotionally safe place where people can come together as a community to grieve. It should be noted that the media is complicit in the harnessing of grief for personal gain. By publicizing trolls' antics, often in tones of shock and moral outrage, the media gains audience and advertising revenue, just as the trolls gain by succeeding in their objective of causing offense in the first place.[32]

Many trolls decline to go after real RIP posters, family and friends of the deceased who are presumed to be legitimately grieving, directing their venom at the grief tourists instead. Trolls tend to view the latter as charlatans, who could not conceivably be in genuine mourning for someone they didn't know. "This isn't grief," troll Paulie Socash once argued, "This is boredom and a pathological need for attention masquerading as grief."[33] Wilson Mouzone, another troll, agreed that family members should be considered off-limits,[34] reinforcing a commonly held position that the troll-able deserve their fate by posting something dumb or self-serving or objectionable enough to merit a place in the troll's crosshairs.

By calling out the contradictions inherent in anonymous online grieving, trolls are performing an odd form of cultural criticism that, while painful and distasteful, illuminates a necessary truth. We may not like what we see, but nevertheless we recognize that sensational deaths have always fed the public's insatiable appetite for scandal, a need the media leaps to fulfill. Half-truths, distortions, misrepresentations, and outright lies are just part of the equation. Grief tourists and trolls form a microsystemic food chain, where the tourists feed upon the genuine sorrow expressed online and the trolls feed upon the tourists. Because the Internet bestows upon all the cloak of anonymity, it's possible for grief tourists to publicly express feelings they might otherwise have left unexplored, and for trolls to deliver doses of hideousness they might not have had the inclination to publish with attribution.

CONCLUSION

Modern memorial objects perform essentially the same functions in the complex process of human remembrance that their predecessors did, fulfilling the same need to confer permanent form upon ephemeral memories. As a trigger for specific recall, an artificial gemstone made from crematory ashes differs little from a bracelet woven from locks of a dead person's hair. Our systems of remembering have expanded beyond the world of solid objects to include and even depend upon digital formats, a change more of form than of function. Digital memorials represent an evolution of the process of authorship and intent, in a world that is increasingly dependent on social media and the notion that everything should be shared, liked, or commented upon. They continue the tradition of visually recalling a dead person through a memorial image—an updated, more technologically sophisticated rendering of the 19th century's portrayal of the dead as "only sleeping." Digital memorials also introduce darker issues for mourners such as an ever-increasing loss of editorial control and even the potential for emotional damage caused by unkind commenters or trolls. Yet for many, sharing an online memorial with friends and family in far-flung locations despite these risks outweighs the value of an object that can be held close but has a limited ability to be widely viewed by others. The analog version of anything is slower, more cumbersome, and has inferior storage capacity compared to its digital incarnation; in a society that demands speed, portability, and endless quantities of information on demand, the trade-off that sacrifices physicality seems worth it.

Practices that may seem odd to some, such as burying a cell phone to continue leaving messages for the deceased, or chatting with an online avatar, can provide as much solace to the bereft as any other activity performed in remembrance, such as laying flowers on a grave or handling a personal memorial object. In any format—a reassuringly solid relic to be held in the hand or something lacking corporeal substance that can be accessed from a computer at any time—memorial objects exist and operate in a strange liminal space between past and present, and demonstrate the persistence of human yearning to keep those we loved vivid and close, safe from oblivion. For the bereaved, a memorial's format ultimately matters less than how well it aids in the reparative process of grieving.

NOTES

1. Lauren F. Winner, "From Black Crepe to Blue Ink: Mourning Tattoos and the Practice of Embodied Bereavement," in *The Many Ways We Talk About Death in Contemporary Society*, ed. Margaret Souza and Christina Staudt, foreword by Lesley A. Sharp (Lewiston: The Edwin Mellen Press, 2009), 139.

2. Rob Walker, "Cyberspace When You're Dead," *The New York Times Magazine*, January 5, 2011, accessed January 14, 2013, http://www.nytimes.com/2011/01/09/mag azine/09Immortality-t.html

3. Sayantani DasGupta and Marsha Hurst, "Death in Cyberspace: Bodies, Boundaries, and Postmodern Memorializing," in Souza and Staudt, *The Many Ways We Talk about Death,* 107.

4. Sigmund Freud, *The Uncanny,* trans. David McClintock (New York: The Penguin Group, 2003). Originally published as "Das Unheimliche," *Imago* 5 (1919): 123–44.

5. Elizabeth Hallam and Jenny Hockey, *Death, Memory, and Material Culture* (Oxford: Berg Publishers, 2001), 136.

6. Barbara Jones, *Design for Death* (Indianapolis: The Bobbs-Merrill Company, 1969), 250.

7. Samuel Goldsmith, "Diamond Company LifeGem Turning Lock of Michael Jackson's Hair into Jewels," *New York Daily News,* July 27, 2009, accessed January 14, 2013, http://www.nydailynews.com/entertainment/michael_jackson/2009/07/27/2009–07–27_jewelry_company_lifegem_turning_michael_jacksons_hair_into_diamondsby_.html

8. Richard Banks, *The Future of Looking Back,* foreword by Bill Buxton (Redmond: Microsoft Press, 2011), 100.

9. Benjamin, Walter, *The Work of Art in the Age of its Technological Reproducibility and Other Writings on Media,* ed. Michael W. Jennings, Brigid Dohery, and Thomas Y. Levin (Cambridge: The Belknap Press of Harvard University Press, 2008), 22.

10. Banks, *The Future of Looking Back*, 101.

11. Ibid., 82.

12. "Tale of Tales: Vanitas," accessed January 14, 2013, http://tale-of-tales.com/Vanitas/

13. Ibid.

14. Banks, *The Future,* 77.

15. Ibid., 132.

16. Jed Brubaker and Gillian R. Hayes, "'We will never forget you [online]': An Empirical Investigation of Post-mortem MySpace Comments" (proceedings of CSCW 2011, Hangzhou, China, March 19–23, 2011).

17. The Associated Press, "Interactive Chris Ethridge Memorial Coming," *The Meridien Star,* September 5, 2012, accessed January 14, 2013, http://meridianstar.com/newstory/x620794041/Interactive-Chris-Ethridge-memorial-coming

18. Mikita Brottman, "Death in Cyberspace: Psychoanalysis and the Internet," in Souza and Staudt, *The Many Ways We Talk About Death,* 125–6.

19. Diane Mapes, "Bury Me with My Cellphone," *Msnbc.com,* December 16, 2008, accessed January 14, 2013, http://www.msnbc.msn.com/id/28182292/ns/technology_and_science-tech_and_gadgets/t/bury-me-my-cell-phone/#.UF-r5qTLxQZ

20. "Virtual Eternity," accessed January 14, 2013, http://www.virtualeternity.com.

21. Ibid.

22. Walker, "Cyberspace When You're Dead."

23. Jack Hamilton, "Hologram Tupac Was Inevitable," *The Atlantic,* April 17, 2012, accessed January 13, 2013, http://www.theatlantic.com/entertainment/archive/2012/04/hologram-tupac-was-inevitable/255990/

24. DasGupta and Hurst, *The Many Ways We Talk About Death,* 115.

25. Gerry Beegan, *The Mass Image: A Social History of Photomechanical Reproduction in Victorian London* (Hampshire: Palgrave Macmillan, 2008), 2–3.

26. Kate Miltner, "How the Aurora Shootings became Fodder for Lulz," *The Atlantic,* July 27, 2012, accessed January 14, 2013, http://www.theatlantic.com/technology/archive/2012/07/how-the-aurora-shootings-became-fodder-for-lulz/260444/

27. "RIP Anna," accessed January 14, 2013, http://www.myspace.com/loving_memory_anna

28. Whitney Phillips, "LOLing at Tragedy: Facebook Trolls, Memorial Pages and Resistance to Grief Online," *First Monday* 6, 12/5 (December 2011), accessed January 14, 2013, http://www.uic.edu/htbin/cgiwrap/bin/ojs/index.php/fm/article/viewArticle/3168/3115

29. Katia Hetter, "Memorial Tourism Bears Witness to Tragedy," *CNN Travel.com,* May 28, 2012, accessed January 14, 2013, http://www.cnn.com/2012/04/24/travel/memorial-tourism/index.html

30. Margaret Hartmann, "Terrible Teens Defile 9/11 Memorial," *NYMag.com,* June 25, 2012, accessed January 14, 2013, http://nymag.com/daily/intelligencer/2012/06/terrible-teens-defile-911-memorial.html

31. Phillips, "LOLing at Tragedy."

32. Whitney Phillips, "When Research Attacks, Part One Million," July 11, 2012, accessed January 13, 2013, http://billions-and-billions.com/?s=when+research+attacks

33. Phillips, "LOLing at Tragedy."

34. Ibid.

Chapter 13

Roadside Memorials: A 21st-Century Development[1]

George E. Dickinson and Heath C. Hoffmann

*G*rief *in the 21st century tends to be moving out of the private sphere and into public places, as evidenced by Facebook, automobile memorials, such as a sticker or writing on a back window of a vehicle typically with the name, birth-death dates, and perhaps a phrase in reference to the decedent, and roadside memorials. Grief shared is grief relieved. Roadside memorials, in particular, epitomize the place of death in the open for all to share in contrast to gravesites in the cemetery, mostly out of sight of human activity. As one drives on the highways of the United States, roadside memorials are ubiquitous, yet varied in appearance. Thus, our objective was to determine the roadside memorial policies of the 50 states through a survey of the Departments of Transportation (DOTs) in each state. We received a response rate of 98 percent.*

Our findings revealed that 23 states have adopted a roadside memorial policy, yet all states act on issues related to memorials whether they have a policy or do not. The most common memorial symbol is a cross. For some individuals, the place where death occurred is where the soul left the body, thus a sacred spot. If viewed as a religious symbol, rather than a cultural tradition, the cross displayed on public property may be a violation of the separation of church and state doctrine. With roadside memorials increasing across the United States, it appears that this way of sharing grief will continue in the 21st century.

BACKGROUND

Across Europe, North and South America, and Australia in the 21st century, it is not unusual to see along our highways a cross or a secular reminder of a death that occurred on or near that spot.[2] Such memorials in the United States have been popular for the past 25 years or more.[3] They make grief visible and can be of significant importance to bereaved families and friends.

Roadside memorialization in the United States likely originated in the Southwest, reflecting Hispanic customs and the influence of Roman Catholic practices, going back to the Spanish in the 16th century.[4] The crosses marked rest areas for participants of funeral processions from the church to the cemetery; undertones of the religious origin remain embedded in today's markings.[5] The cross marks the sites as sacred.[6]

Roadside memorials occupy a unique place among memorial markers: they are created to remember ordinary people in a public venue, while, traditionally, memorials in public spaces honor the famous and heroic.[7] Most commonly, roadside memorials are erected after a sudden and violent death of a young person. They may be decorated with flowers, a teddy bear, a football sweatshirt, a toy, a photograph, or some other personal item of the deceased individual. Decorations often change with anniversaries and holidays. The marker typically has a plaque with names, dates, and sometimes messages.

Roadside memorials serve several intertwined purposes. Minnesota Department of Transportation's official definition simply describes the memorial marker as: "a physical object that is placed on a highway right-of-way, marking the site of a fatal crash."[8] Folklorist George Monger suggests two primary reasons for them: memorialization and warning. They enable a connection between the personal lives of the deceased and the impersonal sites, reinforcing their role as memorial spaces.[9] By extension, they engage passersby in issues of death and the afterlife. They can become part of a devotional practice; Monger describes the action of maintaining the site of the fatality as a "private and individual pilgrimage."[10] Roadside memorials participate in the survivors' ongoing grief work.[11] When a relative or friend passes the memorial, there is the reminder of the life, and death, of that person. Cultural geographers Kate Hartig and Kevin Dunn have proposed that roadside memorials may be filling a gap caused by the trend toward gardens of remembrance and plaque-gardens, which leave the survivors with no personalized space to visit.[12] On a practical and purely secular level a roadside memorial cautions drivers that a particular part of a road is potentially dangerous and that it may be wise to slow down.

Roadside memorials support the 21st-century idea that the dead should live on in our memories. As has been proposed elsewhere, in America, the Living Death (1600–1830) and the Dying of Death (1830–1945) epochs have been followed by the Resurrection of Death period (1945–present).[13] In post-1945 times, we do not accept death as integral to life, as in the Living Death period, but rather we strive to keep the deceased person alive by constructing his or her symbolic immortality. The dead are resurrected in symbolic gestures and tangible objects that remind us of the previously living individual, for example the placement of a photo, typically oval-shaped, on the memorial marker. To make the photo seem alive, a motion-sensor device can trigger the recorded voice of the deceased person and welcome the visitor to the site. Other elaborate attempts to bring back the dead include preserving voice recordings and recording stories told of the departed. Ways of remembering the dead through material items include keeping the cremains of the deceased person in a jar on the mantelpiece, fabricating a diamond from the carbon of the corpse and placing it inside a locket or bracelet, and adding cremains to pigment to paint a portrait of the deceased. The embellishment of roadside memorials is part and parcel of the same impulse to incarnate the spirit of the departed and make them tactual and visible.

Yet the resurrection that occurs at the roadside memorial has a unique character. Within the borders of a cemetery, the dead are kept within a structured order that is unrelated to how they lived and died. Roadside memorials can express the social and personal identity of the deceased in creative ways that are not possible in most cemetery graves.[14] At the roadside memorial, the visitor meets the resurrected dead in the midst of the world of the living, without the protective framing accorded by a space designated solely for commemorating the dead. These memorials are close, and often unexpected, encounters with those who were, not long ago, among us. They are also, inescapably, constant reminders of how they died.

Traveling from state to state, we observe no uniformity among the various roadside memorials. They may vary in size and shape, be located on or near the public road (the right-of-way), or in overall appearance. Federal laws prohibit placement of anything along roads except highway-related signs and devices, thus an inconsistent patchwork of state policies controls these memorial sites.

The purpose of this research endeavor is to ascertain the status of roadside memorial policies in the 50 states in the 21st century. For example, do they have policies to regulate roadside memorials? What are the states' rules regarding placement of a structure beside the road to memorialize a deceased individual? Is there a limited amount of time they are allowed to stay up? Is there any effort to have green memorials?

METHOD

We obtained the mailing addresses of the Director of the Department of Transportation (DOT) in each of the 50 states via the Internet. The initial survey was mailed on June 23, 2008. Two follow-up mailings were then sent to the states that were nonresponsive. Each of the mailings offered the possibility of electronic submission, if so requested.

The states which had adopted a roadside memorial policy were asked a range of questions relating to the content of the policy, such as if the memorials must be uniform and if certain size dimensions and a specific material were required, how individuals applied for the erection of a memorial, and whether permission was necessary. We asked what percentage of memorials were religious in nature, the action taken if the memorial falls into disrepair, if an annual budget exists for erection and maintenance, and whether counties, cities, or precincts have their own regulations. We also wanted to know whether roadside memorials are considered to present a safety problem, if a tree can be planted near the site of the highway fatality, whether vandalism is a problem, and what action is taken if roadside memorials are erected in defiance of state law. See the survey in Appendix 1 for all questions contained in our survey.

RESULTS

We received responses from 49 states. The only state not responding was Alaska. Of the 49 states, 23 noted that they "have adopted a policy regarding the placement of roadside memorials along state highways." Some states have a Driving Under the Influence Memorial Sign program. Others have an Adopt-A-Highway program for volunteer participation in roadside litter removal along designated roads. These groups are recognized with a sign, which in some cases acknowledges the deceased person for whom they have adopted a stretch of road.

The state of Montana does not have a policy regarding roadside memorials but goes along with the Montana American Legion White Cross Highway Fatality Marker Program. Begun in 1953, the Montana practice is to place a white cross at the site of a fatal traffic accident. Ten states' policies have the memorials erected by the state, with an average cost per memorial of $414.

In 11 states roadside memorials must be applied for by submitting a paper application, while 2 states allow either a paper or an online electronic form. The policies of 12 states require that if friends wish to erect a memorial, they must first obtain permission from the family. Particular dimensions must be adhered to in 15 states, with variations ranging from a 15-inch round form to rectangular sizes from 24 × 24 inches to 60 × 48 inches. Eleven states have the memorial "facing oncoming highway traffic." Other states, such as Texas, specifically place the markers so that they cannot be read from the highway main lanes; they are usually placed in rest or picnic areas or turnouts designed to be read by pedestrians.

In 17 states the memorial is placed "on the right-of-way," whereas 3 states place the memorial on the "edge of the right-of-way but not on it." Fifteen

Table 13.1

Characteristics of policies for states (*n* = 22) that have adopted a policy regarding the placement of roadside memorials along state highways

	Markers Erected by DOT	Cost of Erecting Memorial (in US$)	Cost to Victims' Family (in US$)	Requests via Online (O), Paper (P), by Phone (Ph), Letter (L), or E-mail (E)	Friends Need Permission from Family	All Fatalities or Drinking and Driving (DUI) Only	Memorial Size Specs (in inches)	Face Oncoming Traffic or Parallel to Highway	Must Be on Right-of-Way	Must Be on Edge of Right-of-Way	Requires Memorials to Be Made of Specific Materials	Keeps Record of Victims' Names Who Have a Memorial	Time Limit Memorial Can Remain (in years)
Alabama	Has No Policy												
Alaska[1]	No	N/R	0	O, P	No	All	30 × 60	N/R	Yes	–	Yes[2]	Yes[3]	10
Arizona	Has No Policy												
Arkansas	Has No Policy												
California	Yes	1,000	1,000	Letter	Yes	DUI	30 × 36	Oncoming	Yes	No	Yes	Yes	7
Colorado	Yes	1,000	100	Paper	Yes	All	42 × 36	Oncoming	Yes	Yes[4]	Yes	Yes	6
Connecticut[5]	Has No Policy												
Delaware	No	N/A	N/A	N/A	No	N/A	No	No[6]	No[6]	No[6]	No	No	No
Florida	Yes	25	0	L, P, E	Yes	All	15 (round)	Either	Yes	–	Yes	No	1

(Continued)

231

Table 13.1 (Continued)

	Markers Erected by DOT	Cost of Erecting Memorial (in US$)	Cost to Victims' Family (in US$)	Requests via Online (O), Paper (P), by Phone (Ph), Letter (L), or E-mail (E)	Friends Need Permission from Family	All Fatalities or Drinking and Driving (DUI) Only	Memorial Size Specs (in inches)	Face Oncoming Traffic or Parallel to Highway	Must Be on Right-of-Way	Must Be on Edge of Right-of-Way	Requires Memorials to Be Made of Specific Materials	Keeps Record of Victims' Names Who Have a Memorial	Time Limit Memorial Can Remain (in years)
Georgia	Yes	N/R	0	O, P	N/R	DUI	36 × 24	Oncoming	Yes	–	Yes	Yes	5
Hawaii	No	N/A	N/A	Paper	No	All	No	Either[7]	Yes	–	No	No	1/12
Idaho	No	N/A	N/A	Paper	Yes	All	36×16	Other[8]	Yes	–	No	Yes	No
Illinois	Yes	150+[9]	150+[9]	Paper	Yes	DUI	36 × 24	Oncoming	Yes	–	Yes	Yes	2
Indiana	Has No Policy												
Iowa	Has No Policy[10]												
Kansas	No	N/A	N/A	N/A	No	All	No	Either	–	Yes	No	No	No
Kentucky	Has No Policy												
Louisiana	Has No Policy												
Maine	Has No Policy												
Maryland	No	N/A	N/A	N/A	N/A	N/A	N/A	N/A	N/A	N/A	N/A	N/R	N/R

Massachusetts	Policy is being developed												
Michigan	Has No Policy												
Minnesota	Has No Policy[11]												
Mississippi	Has No Policy												
Missouri	Has No Policy												
Montana	No[12]	N/R	N/R	N/R	N/R	All	12 × 16	Oncoming	Yes	–	Yes	N/R	N/R
Nebraska	Has No Policy												
Nevada	Has No Policy												
New Hampshire	Has No Policy												
New Jersey	No	N/A	N/A	N/A	No	All	No	No Specifications or Placement Requirements					
New Mexico[13]	Has No Policy												
New York[14]	Has No Policy												
North Carolina	Yes	250	250	Paper	Yes	All	No	Other[15]	Yes	–	Yes	Yes	No
North Dakota	Has No Policy												
Ohio[16]	Has No Policy												
Oklahoma	Has No Policy												
Oregon	Yes	N/R	600	Paper	Yes	DUI	48 × 36	Oncoming	Yes	–	Yes	Yes	7–10
Pennsylvania[16]	Has No Policy												
Rhode Island	Has No Policy												
Rhode Island	Has No Policy												
South Dakota	Yes	200[17]	0	Other[18]	N/R	All	24 × 24	Oncoming	–	Yes	Yes	Yes	Yes[19]
Tennessee	Has No Policy												
Texas	Yes[20]	N/R	300	Paper	N/R	DUI	N/R	N/R	Yes	–	Yes	N/R	1

(Continued)

233

Table 13.1 (Continued)

	Markers Erected by DOT	Cost of Erecting Memorial (in US$)	Cost to Victims' Family (in US$)	Requests via Online (O), Paper (P), by Phone (Ph), Letter (L), or E-mail (E)	Friends Need Permission from Family	All Fatalities or Drinking and Driving (DUI) Only	Memorial Size Specs (in inches)	Face Oncoming Traffic or Parallel to Highway	Must Be on Right-of-Way	Must Be on Edge of Right-of-Way	Requires Memorials to Be Made of Specific Materials	Keeps Record of Victims' Names Who Have a Memorial	Time Limit Memorial Can Remain (in years)
Utah	Yes	150	0	Paper	Yes	All	30 × 24	Oncoming	Yes	–	Yes	Yes	1
Vermont	Has No Policy												
Virginia	Yes	450	450	Paper	Yes	All	54 × 30	Oncoming	Yes	–	Yes	Yes	2
Washington	Yes	300–700	300–700	P, E, PH	Yes	DUI	60 × 48	Oncoming	Yes	–	Yes	Yes	~10
West Virginia	No	N/A	N/A	Paper	No	All	48 × 48	Either	Yes	–	No	Yes	No
Wisconsin	No	N/A	N/A	N/A	N/A	N/A	N/A	N/A	N/A	N/A	N/A	N/A	N/A
Wyoming	Yes	180	0	Paper	Yes	All	36 × 15	Oncoming	Yes	–	Yes	Yes	5

(D/K = Don't Know; N/A = Not Applicable; N/R = No Response).

1. We did not receive a completed survey from Alaska. The data reported here for Alaska comes from the Alaska DOT (2003a, 2003b, 2004).

2. In Alaska, private memorials cannot contain reflective material.

3. If it is a state-erected memorial, the submitted application allows for easy record-keeping. When private memorials are permitted, the DOT may request that the person erecting the memorial register it with the local DOT office (as is the case in Alaska).

4. In Colorado, private memorials must be placed outside the right-of-way; only state-erected memorials can be in the right-of-way.

5. At the time the survey was completed, the Connecticut DOT respondent said that a formal draft policy regarding private memorials had been created and would only be enacted if roadside memorials became more problematic.

6. In Delaware, private memorials must be placed on private property.

7. In Hawaii, memorials can face traffic or sit parallel to the roadway as long as the memorials are placed as far away from the highway as is possible and do not obstruct pedestrian traffic in the emergency lanes.

8. In Idaho, memorials are not allowed in highway medians or within city limits.

9. In Illinois, the cost is $150 plus $50 per name plaque.

10. The Iowa respondent reported that the state does not have a policy regarding the placement of roadside memorials but he did return a copy of the state's "Position Statement/Talking Points" on roadside memorials. This statement notes that memorials are not legal or illegal in Iowa but the "DOT has through practice adopted a somewhat standardized approach to handling roadside memorials that have been placed in the state-owned highway right-of-way."

11. The Minnesota respondent reported that the state does not have a policy regarding the placement of roadside memorials but he did return a DOT Maintenance Bulletin (No. 04-2) describing the state's "guidelines" for addressing roadside memorials.

12. The Montana respondent reported that the state does not have a policy regarding the placement of roadside memorials but she/he did return a description of the Montana American Legion Highway Fatality Marker Program which was approved by the Montana Highway Commission (now the DOT) in 1953. Thus, we have coded the attributes of Montana's policy based on the description of the American Legion program (Montana American Legion, n.d.).

13. New Mexico offers signs to commemorate fatalities for victims of drinking and driving accidents but reports that this is not part of an overall roadside memorial program.

14. While placing private/unofficial items in the highway right-of-way is illegal in New York, the respondent says they are trying to adopt a clear policy on how to manage roadside memorials.

15. North Carolina's respondent notes that the location will vary depending on roadside characteristics as memorials are "plantings" (e.g., tree).

16. Ohio and Pennsylvania encourage people to participate in the Adopt-A-Highway program "In Memory of" their deceased family member instead of erecting private memorials.

17. In South Dakota, the cost "varies greatly depending on location"; $200 was the reported amount, though.

18. Rather than completing an electronic or paper application, South Dakota indicates that "accident records/public safety notifies DOT of locations."

19. In South Dakota, state-sanctioned memorials remain in place until the highway is reconstructed or the sign fades. At that time, the sign is removed and not replaced.

20. Texas has several memorial marker programs including a Memorial Sign Program for Victims of Impaired Driving and a policy allowing family members to request permission to place a private memorial (in accordance with state specifications) in honor of a loved one who has died in a highway traffic accident. The information reported for Texas in Appendix I refers to the Program for Victims of Impaired Driving.

states' rules require that memorials be made of a specific material, whereas six states do not specify the material. Asked whether or not the states keep a record of the name(s) of the individual(s) honored by the memorial, 14 states said "yes" and 5 said "no." Thirteen states have a specific time limit as to how long a memorial can stay up: the average is 4.5 years, with a range of 30 days to 10 years or "until sign is faded," "deteriorated," or "life of sign." Six states have no such policy.

Thirty-seven states answered the question about whether roadside memorials consisted of religious symbols. The religious symbol displayed most often in all of these states was the cross. When broken down by state into the percentage of roadside memorials that were religious or nonreligious, the breakdown was 73 percent religious and 27 percent secular/nonreligious. When asked what action the state takes if the roadside memorial falls into disrepair, 29 said they remove it, while 5 states leave it in place. Individual answers included: "remove within 10–14 days regardless of condition," "remove with next work activity in the area," "depends on location," "attempt to contact the family," "remove within 30 days after notification of family," "depends on the district," and "handled on a case by case basis." None of the states has an annual budget for the erection, maintenance, and/or removal of memorials.

When asked if complaints are received about roadside memorials, the responses were: "yes frequently" (1), "yes occasionally" (18), "yes rarely" (20), "no" (4), and "no response" (6). In response to complaints about a roadside memorial(s), 39 states reported that they remove the memorial while 6 states leave the memorial; 4 states did not respond. Of those who responded "yes" regarding removal following a complaint, 3 said that they "destroy it," 28 "try to return it to the person who erected it," and others answered "other," specifying a variety of actions: "memorial is stored and returned if person requests it," "[remove] only after 10–14 days," "[remove] sometimes, but not often," "discretely remove," "work with person who erected it and try to get it relocated or removed," "store in maintenance yard," "remove within 30 days," and "depends on condition and construction." Regarding whether roadside memorials present a safety hazard, 28 states said "yes," 17 said "no," and 4 did not reply. Only 1 state felt that vandalism of roadside memorials is a problem, whereas 44 states did not feel that vandalism was a problem, and 4 states did not have an opinion.

A green movement for roadside memorials is developing in some states. Eleven states allow a tree to be planted near the location where a highway fatality occurred, 32 states do not allow this, and 6 did not respond to the question. Delaware was the first state to build a memorial garden dedicated to those who lost their lives in all types of traffic fatalities.

As noted, some states have roadside memorial policies and others do not, yet concern is shown in numerous states regarding the grief of survivors of

Table 13.2

Attributes of roadside memorials and how states respond to and manage roadside memorials, regardless of whether the state has a formal policy

	Memorials Containing Religious Symbols (%)	Memorials Containing Secular Symbols (%)	Cross Is Most Common Memorial Shape	Remove Private Memorials In Disrepair	Private Memorials In Disrepair Are Left Alone	All Private Memorials Removed	Budget To Manage Road Memorials (annual) ($)	Counties/Cities Have Own Regulations	Complaints Received about Memorials	Memorial Removed if Complaints Received	Removed Memorials Destroyed or Returned	DOT Feels Memorials Are Safety Hazard	DOT Allows Memorial Tree near Accident Site	Vandalism of Memorials Is a Problem
Alabama	99	1	Yes	Yes	–	–	0	DK	Rare	Yes	Return	No	No	No
Alaska	N/R	N/R	N/R	N/R	N/R	No	N/R	N/R	N/R	N/R	Return	N/R	N/R	N/R
Arizona	90	10	Yes	–	–	Yes	0	Yes	Occ	Yes	Return	Yes	No	No
Arkansas	25	75	No	–	–	Yes	0	No	N/R	Yes	N/R	Yes	No	No
California	D/K	D/K	D/K	–	–	Yes	0	Yes	Never	Yes	Return	Yes	No	No
Colorado	D/K	D/K	N/R	Replace[2]	–		0	Yes[3]	Occ	Yes	Return	Yes	No	No
Connecticut	75	25	Yes	Yes	–	–	0	No	Rare	Yes	N/R	Yes	No	No
Delaware	80	20	Yes	–	–	No	0	No	Occ	Yes	Return	No	No[4]	No
Florida	10	90	No	Yes	–	–	0	No	Rare	Yes	N/R	No	No	No
Georgia	50	50	No	–	–	Yes	0	No	Occ	Yes	Return	No	No	No

(Continued)

237

Table 13.2   (Continued)

	Memorials Containing Religious Symbols (%)	Memorials Containing Secular Symbols (%)	Cross Is Most Common Memorial Shape	Remove Private Memorials In Disrepair	Private Memorials In Disrepair Are Left Alone	All Private Memorials Removed	Budget To Manage Road Memorials (annual $)	Counties/Cities Have Own Regulations	Complaints Received about Memorials[1]	Memorial Removed If Complaints Received	Removed Memorials Destroyed or Returned	DOT Feels Memorials Are Safety Hazard	DOT Allows Memorial Tree near Accident Site	Vandalism of Memorials Is a Problem
Hawaii	D/K	D/K	No	Yes	–	–	0	D/K	Occ	Yes	Destroy	Yes	No	No
Idaho	80	20	Yes	Yes	–	–	0	Yes	Rare	Yes	Depends	Yes	No	No
Illinois	75	25	Yes	Yes	–	–	0	Yes	Rare	Yes	Return	Yes	No	No
Indiana	90	10	Yes	Yes	–	–	0	No	Rare	Yes	Return	No	No	No
Iowa	95	5	Yes	Yes[5]	–	–	0	No	Rare	Yes	Return	Yes	No	No
Kansas	D/K	D/K	Yes	Yes	–	–	0	No	Occ	Yes	Return	Yes	No	No
Kentucky	33	67	Yes	Yes	–	–	0	No	Occ	Yes	Return	Yes	No	No
Louisiana	100	0	No	–	Yes	–	0	No	Never	Yes	N/R	No	No	No
Maine	50	50	N/R	Yes[6]	–	–	0	No	Never	N/R	N/R	No	No	No
Maryland	80	20	Yes	Yes	–	–	0	No	Occ	Yes	Return	Yes	Yes[7]	Yes
Massachusetts	N/R	N/R	N/R	N/R	–	No	N/R	N/R	N/R	N/R	N/R	N/R	N/R	N/R
Michigan	90	10	Yes	Yes	–	–	0	No	Rare	Yes	Destroy	No	No	No

238

Minnesota	Most	D/K	Yes	In 6 Mo.	—	—	0	Yes	Rare	Yes	Return	Yes	No	No
Mississippi	D/K	D/K	Yes	—	Yes	—	0	D/K	N/R	Yes	N/R	Yes	No	N/R
Missouri	99	—	Yes	Yes	—	—	0	No	Occ	Yes	Other[8]	Yes	Yes	No
Montana[9]	N/R	N/R	N/R	N/R	N/R	N/R	N/R	N/R	N/R	N/R	N/R	N/R	N/R	N/R
Nebraska	N/R	N/R	Yes	Yes	—	—	0	N/R	Occ	Yes	Return	No	No	N/R
Nevada	99	—	Yes	Yes	—	—	0	No	Rare	Yes	Return	N/R	N/R	No
New Hampshire	100	0	Yes	Yes	—	—	0	No	Occ	Yes	Return	Yes	No	No
New Jersey	50	50	Yes	Yes	—	—	0	D/K	N/R	No	N/A	No	Yes	No
New Mexico	95	5	Yes	—	Yes	—	0	D/K	Rare	Yes[10]	Return	No	N/R[11]	No
New York	N/R	N/R	Yes	Yes	—	—	0	N/R	Occ	Yes	Return	Yes	Yes	No
N. Carolina	90	10	Yes	—	—	Yes	0	D/K	Occ	Yes	Return	Yes	Yes	No
N. Dakota	50	50	Yes	Yes	—	—	0	No	Never	Yes	Destroy	No	No	No
Ohio	90	10	Yes	Other[12]	—	—	0	Yes	Rare	Yes	Other[12]	Yes	Yes	No
Oklahoma	D/K	D/K	Yes	—	Yes	—	0	D/K	Rare	No	N/A	N/R	Yes	No
Oregon	60	40	Yes	Yes	—	—	0	No	Occ	Yes	Return	Yes	No	No
Pennsylvania	80	20	Yes	Yes	—	—	0	Yes	Rare	Yes	Return	Yes	Yes	No
Rhode Island	85	15	Yes	Case by Case	—	—	0	No	Occ	Yes	Return	Yes	No	No
S. Carolina	95	5	Yes	—	—	—	0	No	Rare	Yes	Return	No	No	No
S. Dakota	25	75	No	Depends on Memorial Location			0	No	Rare	Yes	Return	Yes	No	No
Tennessee	75	25	Yes	Yes	—	—	0	No	Freq	Yes	Depends	Yes	Yes	No

(Continued)

Table 13.2 (Continued)

	Memorials Containing Religious Symbols (%)	Memorials Containing Secular Symbols (%)	Cross Is Most Common Memorial Shape	Remove Private Memorials In Disrepair	Private Memorials In Disrepair Are Left Alone	All Private Memorials Removed	Budget To Manage Road Memorials (annual $)	Counties/Cities Have Own Regulations	Complaints Received about Memorials[1]	Memorial Removed If Complaints Received	Removed Memorials Destroyed or Returned	DOT Feels Memorials Are Safety Hazard	DOT Allows Memorial Tree near Accident Site	Vandalism of Memorials Is a Problem
Texas	D/K	D/K	Yes[13]	N/R	N/R	No	0	D/K	D/K	N/R	Return	N/R	No	D/K
Utah	50	50	Yes	Yes	–	Yes	0	No	Rare	Yes	Return	Yes	No	No
Vermont[14]	75	25	Yes	Yes	–	–	0	No	Rare	No	N/A	Yes	No	No
Virginia	50	50	Yes	Yes	–	–	0	No	Occ	Yes	Return	Yes	No	No
Washington	80	20	Yes	Yes	–	–	0	Yes	Occ	Yes	Return	Yes	Yes	No
W. Virginia	75	25	Yes	–	Yes	–	0	No	Rare	No	N/A	No	D/K[15]	No
Wisconsin	80	20	Yes	Yes[16]	–	–	0	D/K	Occ	Yes	Return	Yes[17]	Yes	No
Wyoming	D/K	D/K	Yes	–	–	Yes	0	No	Rare	Yes	Return	Yes	No	No

(D/K = Don't Know; N/A = Not Applicable; N/R = No Response)

[1]. The response categories for this question were "frequent complaints" (Freq), "occasional complaints" (Occ), receiving complaints "rarely" (Rare) or never (Never).

[2]. In Colorado, if official state memorials fall into disrepair, they are replaced.

[3]. In Colorado, the respondent noted that some large cities have their own policy but most do not.

[4]. Delaware does have a memorial garden dedicated to all people who have died in traffic fatalities. According to the Delaware DOT official, Delaware was the first state to build such a memorial garden.

240

5. In Iowa, whether a memorial in disrepair is removed depends on its location.

6. Maine removes memorials in disrepair only if they interfere with "state need."

7. Maryland was in the process of developing a Living Memorial Program where a grove of trees would be planted each year in honor of all people who died in roadway fatalities.

8. After receiving a complaint about a memorial, Missouri officials "work with the person that erected it and try to get it relocated or removed."

9. In New Mexico, complaints will result in the removal of memorials only if the memorial represents a safety hazard.

10. The respondent from New Mexico did not answer this question but did write, "we have not encountered this request."

11. In Ohio, whether memorials in disrepair are removed depends on the district in which the memorial is placed. Some personnel will remove them immediately, while others will leave them.

12. In Ohio, whether removed memorials are destroyed or returned depends on its condition and the materials from which it was constructed.

13. Texas has guidelines for the dimensions, content and materials to be used in private memorials, using a 30inch" ×× 18inch" cross as an example of the "typical marker" that would conform to the state's regulations.

14. Vermont's respondent indicated that roadside memorials would be discussed in the fall of 2008 to determine if legislation is appropriate to regulate them.

15. The respondent from West Virginia was not aware of requests to plant a tree as a memorial, suggesting a willingness to permit such a request.

16. All roadside memorials are eventually removed by Wisconsin DOT officials but memorials will generally be left alone unless they pose a safety hazard, interfere with routine road maintenance, fall into disrepair or are subject to complaints by others (Wisconsin DOT, 2006).

17. For Wisconsin, the primary safety concern revolves around pedestrian activity involved in setting up and/or visiting memorials, not that memorials will distract drivers.

deaths on the nation's highways. Overall a tolerance is displayed toward these memorials in the 21st century. For example, the respondent from the state of Oregon said:

> We try to take into consideration the sensitivity of this issue during a time when families are grieving. By contacting them directly, we can offer condolences and explain the safety issues for other drivers.

Arkansas reported:

> Roadside memorials are illegal but we try to be sympathetic during the initial grieving period. These are mostly funeral wreaths or flower baskets, occasionally a small cross. If the grieving person moves the memorial to the right-of-way line we will not bother it.

Yet, safety on the highways is also an issue. For example, Alabama noted:

> We recognize the need some people feel to express themselves in this way and have compassion for their loss. Yet, we do feel that the placement of memorials within the right-of-way is inappropriate. Mourners who stop to place or maintain a memorial not only place themselves in danger, but put other motorists at risk.

Likewise, Minnesota answered:

> Our DOT is understanding and compassionate about this sensitive issue. Our main concern is safety, so we will allow temporary memorial markers as long as it is not a safety hazard and does not affect traffic operations.

Mississippi's respondent said:

> Though we do not allow the permitting of these types of memorials, we are sympathetic to the families affected by these tragic accidents, and therefore, do not actively pursue removing these types of memorials when they first appear, unless they are potential safety hazards or affect our routine maintenance operations.

Regarding what the various states do if roadside memorials are not legal, one state answered that it leaves them alone, 27 states "take [memorials] down if they pose a safety hazard," 5 states "take them down only if they pose an eyesore," 5 states "always remove them," and others said "remove them after a 10–14 days grieving period," "remove them in two months or so," "remove only if a complaint is received," "remove only if severely damaged or in disrepair," and "take them down when mowing and vegetation control."

Table 13.3

The procedure for managing memorials in states where roadside memorials are illegal

	Leave Alone/Ignore	Remove Only If Safety Hazard	Remove If Considered an Eyesore	Always Remove Them	Remove after Specified Time for Grieving Period (days)	Removed If Obstructs Road Crews' Work
Alabama	–	Yes	–	–	–	Yes
Alaska	Private Roadside Memorials Are Not Illegal					
Arizona	–	–	–	Yes	–	–
Arkansas	–	–	–	–	10–14	–
California	–	–	–	Yes	–	–
Colorado	Private Roadside Memorials Are Not Illegal					
Connecticut	–	Yes	Yes	–	60	–
Delaware	–	Yes	–	–	–	–
Florida	Private Roadside Memorials Are Not Illegal					
Georgia	–	Yes	–	–	–	Yes
Hawaii	–	–	–	–	30[1]	–
Idaho	Private Roadside Memorials Are Not Illegal					
Illinois	–	Yes	–	–	–	Yes
Indiana	–	Yes	–	–	–	–
Iowa[2]	–	Yes	–	–	–	Yes
Kansas	Private Roadside Memorials Are Not Illegal					
Kentucky	–	Yes	Yes	–	–	–
Louisiana	–	Yes	–	–	–	Yes
Maine	Private Roadside Memorials Are Not Illegal					
Maryland	–	–	–	Yes	–	–
Massachusetts	Private Roadside Memorials Are Not Illegal					
Michigan	–	Yes	–	–	–	Yes
Minnesota	–	Yes	–	–	180	Yes
Mississippi[3]	–	Yes	–	–	–	Yes
Missouri	–	Yes	–	–	–	Yes
Montana[4]	N/R	N/R	N/R	N/R	N/R	N/R
Nebraska	Yes	Yes	–	–	–	–
Nevada	–	Yes	–	–	–	–

(Continued)

Table 13.3 (*Continued*)

	Leave Alone/Ignore	Remove Only If Safety Hazard	Remove If Considered an Eyesore	Always Remove Them	Remove after Specified Time for Grieving Period (days)	Removed If Obstructs Road Crews' Work
New Hampshire	–	Yes	–	–	180	–
New Jersey	Private Roadside Memorials Are Not Illegal					
New Mexico	–	Yes	–	–	–	–
New York	–	Yes	–	–	–	–
North Carolina	–	Yes	–	Yes	30	Yes
North Dakota	Private Roadside Memorials Are Not Illegal					
Ohio	–	Yes	Yes	–	–	–
Oklahoma	–	Yes	–	–	–	Yes
Oregon	–	Yes	–	–	–	Yes
Pennsylvania	Private Roadside Memorials Are Not Illegal					
Rhode Island	–	Yes	–	–	–	–
S. Carolina	–	Yes	–	–	–	Yes
South Dakota	–	Yes	–	–	–	–
Tennessee	–	Yes	–	–	–	–
Texas	Private Roadside Memorials Are Not Illegal					
Utah	–	–	–	Yes	–	–
Vermont	Private Roadside Memorials Are Not Illegal					
Virginia	–	–	–	Yes	–	–
Washington					180	Yes
West Virginia	–	Yes	–	–	–	Yes
Wisconsin	–	–	–	Yes	–	–
Wyoming	–	–	–	Yes	–	–

(D/K = Don't Know; N/A = Not Applicable; N/R = No Response).

[1] In Hawaii, families are asked to remove memorials after 30 days. If the family fails to do so, the DOT will remove the memorial.

[2] When memorials are placed in a problematic location, the Iowa DOT will move the memorial to the right-of-way fence-line and/or meet with the family to "establish a remedial solution amenable to both parties."

[3] Mississippi has no policy or law addressing roadside memorials. Memorials may be handled according to state laws regarding "right-of-way encroachments." Friends and family are encouraged to participate in the Adopt-A-Highway program to memorialize loved- ones.

[4] The Montana respondent reported that the state does not have a policy regarding the placement of roadside memorials but she/he did return a description of the Montana American Legion Highway Fatality Marker Program which was approved by the Montana Highway Commission (now the DOT) in 1953. Thus, we have coded the attributes of Montana's policy based on the description of the American Legion program (Montana American Legion, n.d.).

DISCUSSION

Fewer than half of the states in the 21st century have officially adopted a roadside memorial policy, yet the majority seems to take action on occasion. Memorials for fatalities related to drunk driving are found in a few states. A minority of states erect the roadside memorials. A few states require that an application be completed in order to put up a memorial. Such a lack of requirements and uniformity contribute to the hodgepodge of roadside memorials along U.S. highways.

The common element of roadside memorials is that of religious symbols, specifically the cross. Larson-Miller suggests that the establishment of roadside memorials is a type of popular religious activity.[15] The cross is typically itself *the* memorial when a religious symbol is displayed, perhaps a carryover of the Catholic influence in earlier days. Some individuals believe that the soul tends to linger after death and has the power to trouble the living if necessary steps are not taken.[16] Therefore, the construction of the cross could help persuade the dead soul not to haunt or harm passersby. The use of the cross in roadside memorials, likely, stems from the tradition among many Christians to carve a cross into grave markers or give the marker the shape of a cross.

The essence of religion is to divide the world into profane and sacred spheres or dimensions, according to French sociologist Emile Durkheim.[17] What a group notes as sacred, whether a totem animal or a roadside memorial, is to be approached and treated with respect and reverence. Thus, the spot where the roadside memorial is placed may be considered sacred, holy ground, yet not all members of the public recognize the location as sacred.[18] Those choosing the cross may not do so because the cross has a religious connotation but rather out of a cultural tradition going back many years. Collins and Rhine found that the expression of faith ranked low on the purposes of a memorial, suggesting that the use of a cross is in most cases not a religious expression, but a cross-cultural symbol rooted in the religious background of the deceased.[19]

Having a cross mark the spot, however, is controversial. Some individuals feel that the cross symbol as a marker of death is a violation of the constitutionally protected separation between church and state: a religious symbol in a secular space owned by the government. For example, in 2011, controversy emerged around a 43-foot-tall cross memorializing war veterans atop Mount Soledad near San Diego, California. The 9th U.S. Circuit Court of Appeals held that the cross is primarily a Christian symbol and its location on public land represents an official "endorsement of religion" by the government and is thus unconstitutional.[20] The U.S. Justice Department appealed the ruling to the U.S. Supreme Court arguing that the cross is not an endorsement of religion, but serves as a symbol of sacrifice and a memorial to honor the nation's fallen soldiers dating to World War I.[21] In June 2012, the Supreme Court declined to hear the appeal, allowing the 9th Circuit's decision to stand. At present, the cross still stands as congressional representatives and others continue to seek remaining legal avenues to preserve the memorial.[22]

The roadside memorial is a private expression of grief that turns a public place into sacred space, its sacredness directly constructed by individuals who would typically make no claim to such civil or religious authority.[23] It is a private expression of grief, yet hung out in public to be exposed to others to perhaps share in the grieving. Grief shared is grief relieved. Through sharing of grief, one's sense of isolation may be reduced, thus lessening the pain of grief. Shared grief seems in vogue in the 21st century. Through new technology, for example, the idea of shared grief is evident on Facebook where grief is shared with individuals not even necessarily known to the decedent.[24] Likewise, public grief is seen in automobile memorials: decals on cars with the birth and death dates of a friend or family member, sometimes accompanied by a saying. Certainly public grief was experienced after the terrorist attacks on 9/11 and with deaths of celebrities such as Whitney Houston, Michael Jackson, Princess Diana, John F. Kennedy, and Pope John Paul II. The expression of public grief is largely a consequence of the great attention paid to the death of public figures by today's mass media. Thus memorials are another way to share grief in the 21st century.

The Departments of Transportation (DOTs) in the United States are concerned about the appearance of their highways. Therefore, the removal of memorials in a state of disrepair complies with their mission of keeping roadsides well maintained. In addition, a shabby roadside memorial does not show respect for the deceased. Complaints about roadside memorials are not frequent, yet when they occur, action is taken for removal in the overwhelming majority of states.

Confrontations sometimes develop, however, over the removal of a memorial, as it is a private symbol located in a public place.[25] A recent situation in Massachusetts is a case in point: a cross, carved by the deceased man's father, was erected to commemorate the fatality of his 17-year-old son.[26] The parents of the deceased adolescent and the family living near the crash scene who wanted it removed went through mediation to determine the future of the cross. The nearby occupants argued that the cross reminds them of the horror of the accident the night they went to the aid of the accident victims. Mediation, unlike the court system, is not adversarial but a way for individuals to hear each other and perhaps become more flexible in their positions and perhaps reach a compromise that appeases all parties. In July 2008, the parents and residents living near the crash site resolved their dispute by agreeing on the construction of a new memorial.[27]

If roadside memorials present a safety hazard, most states take them down. Yet the states generally are sensitive to the grief of the survivors and are somewhat tolerant. Roadside memorials can provide solace to grieving families and be a reminder of the potential consequences of inattention at the wheel.[28] To others, however, these memorials are seen as distractions to motorists or as unsightly.

Roadside memorials are relatively new to the scene on U.S. highways, and they do not seem to be going away in the 21st century. Various states are adopting policies to address this influx. These memorials may serve as a reminder of the decedent each time a family member or friend passes by. To others, the memorial serves as an unpleasant reminder not wished on a regular basis. The construction of memorials may fit within a larger context of decreasing interest in church-based rituals and an increasing tendency to view spiritual authority as resting with the individual conscience.[29] Individuals may feel that they have the right to establish roadside memorials which function outside of official religion and burial grounds. In addition to serving as an enhancement to coping with grief for some individuals, roadside memorials are beginning to be viewed as a way of improving the landscape through cleaning up the right-of-way and planting trees and as a possible prevention to drunk driving. Indeed, Steinbeck's assertion that it is good to mark and to remember for a while the place where a man died is being adhered to in the United States in the 21st century with roadside memorials. The status of regulating the memorials, however, is as varied as is the appearance of the memorials themselves.

APPENDIX 13.1

Survey of State Departments of Transportation

1. Has your state adopted a policy regarding the placement of ☐ Yes ☐ No roadside memorials along state highways?

   IF YOU ANSWERED "NO" TO QUESTION #1, PLEASE SKIP DOWN TO QUESTION #12.

2. Does your policy require that memorials ☐ Yes ☐ No be erected by the DOT so that they are uniform?

   IF YES: What is the estimated cost of $ ——————— erecting each memorial?

   IF YES: How much do you charge the   ——————— ☐ The family is victims' friends/family to erect the memorial?   not charged

3. How do citizens apply for the erection of a roadside memorial?

   ☐ Complete an online   ☐ Submit a paper   ☐ The DOT does not erect
      electronic form   application   memorials for families

   ☐ Other, please specify: _____

4. Are friends of the victim(s) required to obtain the permission ☐ Yes ☐ No of the deceased's family prior to erecting a memorial?

5. Are roadside memorials allowed for all highway fatalities or only drunk driving fatalities?

   ☐ All highway fatalities   ☐ Drunk driving fatalities only

   ☐ Other, please explain: _____

6. Does your state's policy require that memorials conform ☐ Yes ☐ No to particular size dimensions?

   IF YES: What are these   Height: _____ Width: _____ Depth: _____ dimensions?

7. Are memorials required to: ☐ Face oncoming   ☐ Be placed parallel to
                                      highway traffic   the highway

   ☐ Other, please specify: _____

8. Do your guidelines require that the memorial be placed:

   ☐ On the right-of-way   ☐ On the edge of the right-of-way but not on it

   ☐ Other, please specify _____

9. Does your policy require that memorials be made of a ☐ Yes ☐ No specific material(s)?

   IF YES: What material(s) is required? _____

10. Does your policy require that memorials be made of a ☐ Yes ☐ No specific material(s)?

11. Do you have a specific time limit as to how long a ☐ Yes ☐ No
    memorial can stay up?

    IF YES: What is your time limit? _____

Though roadside memorials may not be legal in your state, people often do place memorials along state highways. The following questions apply to states with <u>and</u> without state authorized roadside memorials.

12. Approximately what percentage of the roadside memorials
    along your state's highways consist of:

    Religious Symbols: %   Secular/Non-Religious Content: %

13. If a roadside memorial falls   ☐ Remove the memorial   ☐ Leave the memorial
    into disrepair do you:

    ☐ Other, please specify: _____

14. Do you have an annual budget for the erection, maintenance ☐ Yes ☐ No
    and/or removal of

    IF YES: How much do you budget annually? $ _____

15. Do counties, cities or precincts in your state typically have ☐ Yes ☐ No
    <u>**their own regulations**</u> regarding roadside memorials?

16. Whether legal or not, do you receive complaints about roadside memorials?

    ☐ Yes, we receive frequent complaints

    ☐ Yes, we receive occasional complaints

    ☐ Yes, but very rarely

    ☐ No, we do not receive complaints

17. If somebody complains about a roadside memorial, ☐ Yes ☐ No
    will you remove it?

    If you remove a memorial,   ☐ Destroy it
    what do you do with it?
                                    ☐ Try to return it to the person who erected it

                                    ☐ Other, please specify:

18. Is the most frequent shape of a roadside memorial a cross? ☐ Yes ☐ No

19. Does your agency consider roadside memorials to present ☐ Yes ☐ No
    a safety problem, as motorists might be distracted by them?

20. Does your agency allow for a tree to be planted somewhere ☐ Yes ☐ No
    near where a highway fatality occurred to memorialize a
    deceased road victim?

21. Is vandalism of roadside memorials a problem in your state? ☐ Yes ☐ No

**ANSWER THE FOLLOWING QUESTION ONLY IF
ROADSIDE MEMORIALS ARE <u>ILLEGAL</u> IN YOUR STATE**

22. If roadside memorials are not legal on your state's highways, what procedure do you follow if memorials are erected in defiance of state law or your agency's policies?

☐ Leave them alone/ignore them

☐ Take them down only if they pose a safety hazard

☐ Take them down only if they are considered an eyesore

☐ Always remove them

☐ Other, please specify: _____

In the space below, please add additional comments that will help us to better understand your agency's approach to managing roadside memorials:

_____

Thank you for completing this survey! If you would like us to send you a copy of our published report, please provide your e-mail or mailing address in the following space:

_____

_____

NOTES

1. An earlier paper based on the same research was published in *Mortality* (George E. Dickinson and Heath C. Hoffmann, "Roadside Memorial Policies in the United States," *Mortality* 15, 2 (May, 2010): 154–67. Appreciation is expressed to *Mortality* for permission to use these data again.

2. Una MacConville, "Marking Death in Open Places," *Illness, Crisis & Loss* 19 (2011): 189–92.

3. Dickinson and Hoffmann, *Mortality,* 154–67.

4. Anna Petersson, "Swedish Offerkast and Recent Roadside Memorials," *Folklore* 120 (2009): 75–91.

5. Dave Nance, "Roadside Memorials on the American Highway," last modified May 2, 2012, http://photo.net/photodb/presentation?presentation_id=97863

6. Jennifer Weisser, "Micro Sacred Sites: The Spatial Pattern of Roadside Memorials in Warren County, Ohio" (MA thesis, University of Cincinnati, 2004).

7. Una MacConville, "Marking Death in Open Places," *Illness, Crisis & Loss* 19 (2011): 189–92.

8. Minnesota Department of Transportation, "Minnesota Department of Transportation Maintenance Bulletin, No. 04–2," last modified June 9, 2004, http://www.dot .state.mn.us/restareas/policies/pdf/memorial-marker-guidelines.pdf

9. Anna Petersson, "The Production of a Proper Place of Death" (paper presented at the Biennial Conference on Social Context of Death, Dying and Disposal, Bath, England, September 15–18, 2005).

10. George Monger, "Modern Wayside Shrines," *Folklore* 108 (1997): 114.

11. Holly Everett, *Roadside Crosses in Contemporary Memorial Culture* (Denton, TX: University of North Texas Press, 2002).

12. Kate V. Hartig and Kevin M. Dunn, "Roadside Memorials: Interpreting New Deathscapes in Newcastle, New South Wales," *Australian Geographical Studies* 36 (1998): 5–20.

13. Michael R. Leming and George E. Dickinson, *Understanding Dying, Death and Bereavement* (Belmont, CA: Wadsworth Cengage Learning, 2011), 54–7.

14. Anna Petersson, "The Production of a Proper Place of Death."

15. Lizette Larson-Miller, "Holy Ground: Roadside Shrines and Sacred Space," *America* 192 (2005): 11.

16. Anna Petersson, "Swedish Offerkast and Recent Roadside Memorials," *Folklore* 120 (2009): 75–91.

17. Emile Durkheim, *Elementary Forms of Religious Life* (New York: George Allen and Unwin, 1915).

18. Mirjam Klaassens, Peter Groote, and Paulus Huigen, "Roadside Memorials from a Geographical Perspective," *Mortality* 14 (2009): 187–201.

19. Charles O. Collins and Charles D. Rhine, "Roadside Memorials," *Omega* 47 (2003): 221–44.

20. *Jewish War Veterans v. City of San Diego.* 08–56415 (9th Cir. 2011).

21. David G. Savage, "Obama Administration Asks that Large Cross Remain as War Memorial," *Tribune Washington Bureau,* March 16, 2012.

22. Tony Perry, "Two Congressmen Continue Fight to Save Mt. Soledad Cross," *Los Angeles Times,* July 19, 2012, accessed September 29, 2012, http://latimesblogs.latimes

.com/lanow/2012/07/two-congressmen-continue-fight-to-save-mount-soledad-cross
.html

23. Jennifer Clark and Majella Franzmann, "Authority from Grief, Presence and Place in the Making of Roadside Memorials," *Death Studies* 30 (2006): 579–99.

24. Elizabeth Stone, "Grief in the Age of Facebook," *The Chronicle of Higher Education,* February 28, 2010, accessed March 5, 2011. http://chronicle.com/article/Grief-in-the-Age-of-Facebook/64345/

25. Lily Kong, "Cemeteries and Columbaria, Memorials, and Mausoleums: Narrative and Interpretation in the Study of Deathscapes in Geography," *Australian Geographical Studies* 37 (1999): 1–10.

26. Nick Grabbe, "Leverett Neighborhood Wrestles with Weight of a Cross," *Amherst Bulletin* (June 27, 2008), A1.

27. "In Leverett, Neighbors Agree on a New Memorial," *Daily Hampshire Gazette,* July 12, 2008, accessed on September 15, 2012, http://www.gazettenet.com/2008/07/12/leverett-neighbors-agree-new-memorial

28. Jennifer Clark and Majella Franzmann, "Born to Eternal Life: The Roadside as Sacred Space," accessed February 18, 2013, www.abc.net.au/religion/stories/s1000839.htm

29. Ibid.

Chapter 14

Reconfiguring Urban Spaces of Disposal, Sanctuary, and Remembrance

Karla Maria Rothstein

*E*nvironmental and social imperatives of 21st-century cities require fundamentally rethinking the infrastructures of death, including what we do with dead bodies and how progressive architecture may effectively support grief, memory, and the variant, individual and collective processes of letting go. Given rapidly depleting urban cemetery space, increasing annual American deaths, and the acute environmental toll of both burial and cremation, alternative funerary practices are inevitable, yet currently wholly unresolved. New methods of corpse disposal engage the natural chemical composition of the human body, accelerating biodegradation and absorption into the ecosystem. Design proposals described in this chapter include both theoretical work from my office, Latent Productions, and projects produced in the design studios I lead at Columbia University's Graduate School of Architecture, Planning and Preservation. The spaces and practices that may emerge between the essential indeterminacy of urban life and the inevitability of human death must engage new technologies and be integrated into the discussion of the future of our cities. Critical design aims to reinsert spaces of death and remembrance into the quotidian experience of the metropolis, introducing innovative models of civic and public space, and new modalities of memorial, while questioning the need for permanent repositories and markers of our dead.

URBAN HISTORY AND IMPERATIVE

The metropolis embodies a mortal palimpsest—accumulations and traces of humanity, death, and temporality. From sacred relics and charnel houses, to battlefields and potter's fields, humans have built around and above the remains of their dead. Through the 18th century, Western city cemeteries were collective yet hierarchical spaces embedded in the urban fabric. Mass graves, nested into and under churches and their yards, were encountered by congregants during the regular rhythms of daily life. The corpses of indigent strangers were similarly collectively gathered and, generally unremembered, deposited in lands not otherwise suitable for quotidian use. In our preindustrial cities, the destitute and detached, including victims of cholera and yellow fever epidemics buried rapidly en masse, filled these municipal spaces by the hundreds weekly.[1]

A city's cemeteries were also historically occupied as public spaces, extensions of the street and destinations in the era that preceded the creation of large urban public parks. In the century before New York City's Central Park was established by the 1811 Governor's Plan, cemeteries offered some relief to the congested Manhattan populace, and it was not uncommon to incidentally convene with the dead in cities that had few other public meeting places. The tradition of picnicking in cemeteries has origins in the ancient Roman festival of Feralia, an annual event of public mourning honoring the spirits of the ancestors by reinforcing mutual obligations between the living and the dead. Popular practices for propitiating the shapeless ghosts of the dead are described by the Roman poet Ovid, "the grave must be honoured. Appease your fathers' Spirits, and bring little gifts to the tombs you built. Their shades ask little, . . . a scattering of meal, and a few grains of salt, and bread soaked in wine, and loose violets . . . now ghostly spirits and the entombed dead wander, now the shadow feeds on the nourishment that's offered."[2]

By the 19th century burial rituals had become more individual and sanitized—each body tidily contained in its own box—and cemeteries were migrated to the urban periphery. Real and perceived public health crises necessitated the removal of corpses and their decay from immediate proximity with the living, and ex-urban oases of death emerged outside urban areas across America. Inspired by English gardens and Père Lachaise in Paris, Mount Auburn Cemetery was the first large, so-called garden cemetery in America. Situated on 174 acres including an arboretum, Mount Auburn straddles the towns of Cambridge and Watertown four miles northwest of Boston, and has offered a romantic refuge and sublime promenade remote from the city's density since 1831.

In 1825, the open space of a large potter's field in Manhattan was reprogrammed as a municipal military parade ground and eventually became Washington Square Park, a nearly 10-acre public open space in Greenwich

Village residing above the remains of an estimated 20,000 unnamed bodies.[3] New York's Rural Cemetery Act of 1847 triggered the transition from predominantly religious and private burial practices to massive cemeteries as commercial nonprofit business ventures, now regulated by the Federal Trade Commission. Through the mid-1800s both churches and land speculators purchased thousands of acres of farmland, staking out pastoral burial grounds in less densely populated outer boroughs. The associated proliferation of new, often nonsectarian, landscapes of death offered quiet refuge to tens of thousands of corpses—and their tombstones—that were disinterred in Manhattan to accommodate both increasing urban transportation infrastructure projects and more lucrative real estate development in the heart of the city. As metropolitan populations and transportation networks grew, these once-segregated, fringe locations were reabsorbed into the expanding urban territory.

Today, cemeteries exist largely isolated and remote from the lives of the bereft. The largest concentrations of the living have little contact with contemporary spaces of the dead. Roughly 57,000 people die every year in New York City. Yet for the past 160 years the creation of new cemeteries has been prohibited, and new earthen burials remain forbidden south of 86th Street in Manhattan.[4] An analogous enduring segregation of the dead occurred in Chicago with the 1859 Proposal and Ordinance to Stop Burials in City Cemetery, disinterring and relocating existing graves while terminating future urban burials in proximity to the public.[5] City Cemetery and Morgue was comprised of Catholic, Jewish, and municipal lots, and had been the only urban burial option within the city of Chicago. Its lakeside urban land became what is now known as Lincoln Park, and rural cemeteries, like Rosehill, Graceland, and Calvary, became Chicago's preferred destinations for both the living and their dead.

Recalibration of both zoning and land use policy is needed to enable new forms of urban corpse disposal and new opportunities for city residents to commune with the memory of the deceased. Akin to provisions related to public housing, trash disposal, and sewage treatment, public policy related to the death industry has been historically contentious and slow to evolve. The saturation of cemetery space has become so dire that the mayors of towns in Italy, France, Spain, and Brazil have passed laws prohibiting death in their districts until space to develop more cemeteries is allocated. Giulio Cesare Fava, the mayor of a small town north of Naples, Italy, has forbidden his residents to die, "because the cemetery is running out of room,"[6] and Mayor Gil Bernardi of Le Lavandou, France—where nearly one-third of the population is over 65— passed a similar law when designating land for a new cemetery was denied in court despite the reality that 19 corpses temporarily reside in friends' burial vaults due to lack of space in the existing town cemetery.[7]

We must wholly rethink how we design for the 154,000 deaths occurring worldwide each day.[8] In America, this is not uniquely a New York cemetery-story. Since the start of the 21st century, over 75 percent of the population of the United States is considered to live in urban areas,[9] rendering natural burials—involving no chemical additions that retard decomposition of the corpse nor robust casketing—in a proximate, picturesque rural environment impractical for the vast majority of environmentally aware and increasingly metropolitan populations. Intensifying urbanization, projected to be 85 percent worldwide in the next decade, amplifies the need to radically reconsider our corpse-disposal practices. Traditional funerary procedures and their associated structures are no longer commensurate with the environmental and social realities of our urban existence.

The imperative for retooling funerary protocols—while solidly grounded in palpable spatial constraints of the metropolis and increasing environmental burdens of both burial and cremation—is not solely pragmatic. Society is imprinted by context, and social dynamics are informed by the spaces we collectively inhabit. By reweaving the ubiquity of death into the fabric of our cities, we remind ourselves of the finitude of life, and the fragile responsibility the living share to fortify the future.

The broadening popularity of the garden cemetery type is said to have inspired the American park movement and the profession of landscape architecture. Emerging urban public parks with their tamed landscapes integrated into city planning superseded the appeal of meandering memorial paths and the cemetery-lawn as a social extension of the urban square. These new idealized forms of nature cast off any earlier association with death, and contemplative walks and picnics moved from the sanctuary and cultivated seclusion of the rural cemetery into secular, municipal parks, leaving the physical spaces of the dead increasingly unvisited and frequently untended. The expanse of American suburbs' homogenized sprawl further delineated these former spaces of liminal existence.

As terrains devised exclusively for leisure have been added to dense urban areas, and as death has become an increasingly medicalized event most commonly occurring in a hospital, the presence of the dead has diminished in public consciousness. Ostracized memorials are gated into necropoleis separated from where most of us live. This physical remoteness is amplified by the sphere of death being largely limited to the elderly, as child mortality in developed countries has dramatically declined through preventative measures and medical care advancements over the past century. Today, it is common for a family not to have faced a close occurrence of death in decades. Spatial environments shape our psyche, and the physical and emotional detachment of spaces of death and remembrance from everyday life—symptomatic of the increasing placeless-timeless-mediated reality of global existence—has atrophied our collective perception and appreciation of tangible human existence. This severing of experience facilitates death-denial and hinders cognitive and emotional acceptance of loss.

Together with the migrations of socio-spatial concentrations, our increasingly global cities produce intensely diverse cultural environments. This coexistence of customs both amplifies and flattens the evolution of belief. In 2012, the Pew Research Center's Forum on Religion and Public Life published a research paper subtitled, "One-in-Five Adults Have No Religious Affiliation." Survey data from 3,500 adults indicated that a full third of the U.S. population under age 30 consider themselves religiously unaffiliated, including 13 million self-described atheists and agnostics. Thirty-three million Americans (14% of the U.S. public) say they have no particular religious affiliation, and are not looking for one.[10] These numbers indicate a significant spectrum of nontraditional relationships to spirituality and ritual, and may presage increasing acceptance of new forms of corpse disposition and evolving associated funerary protocols. Although it remains largely unarticulated, I believe that a growing number of Americans desire sensible and sensitive alternatives to the limited and largely outmoded options currently practiced. Societal engagement of this issue should be a global imperative.

More people will die annually in America in 25 years than die today. While advances in health-awareness and medicine have led to a consistently declining death rate for the past 20 years in the United States, by 2020 annual deaths are certain to increase. By 2050, 20 percent of Americans will be over 65, resulting in a steady swelling of funerals as the dense post-World War II generation continues to age and dies. The U.S. National Center for Health Statistics and the U.S. Census Bureau project that 4,249,000 people will die in the United States in 2050—1.6 million more corpses to contend with than in 2010, and a return to percentages of deaths equivalent to the 1950s.

While our heritage of death practices may include some of humankind's oldest cultural patterns, the United States is a young country whose traditions are at most a few centuries deep, and persuasive circumstances inevitably shape evolution—even in seemingly ossified domains. The choices we make in honoring our dead should be influenced by individual and collective psychology, necessity, philosophy, and belief. Currently, options at death remain heavily prescribed by an archaic set of rituals that often dislocate the bereaved from how they choose to live, love, and honor the people in their lives. I will briefly sketch the context and impacts of prevailing mortuary activities and associated corpse decomposition, then introduce contemporary alternative technologies for corporeal metamorphosis that support new concepts of remembrance and provide potential replacements of, or at least additions to, extant earthen burial and cremation options.

CURRENT MORTUARY PRACTICES

Embalming

Embalming, linked to ancient Egyptian practices of mummification, began in the United States during the Civil War using arsenic to preserve dead soldiers on their journey home. Delaying natural decay became increasingly culturally anticipated after the intensive and repeated embalming that facilitated view-ings along President Lincoln's 19-day funeral-train following his assassination in 1865. American mortuary services have presented embalmed burial as the accepted norm since the late 1800s, with the option of cremation increasingly utilized during the second half of the 20th century. From the battlefield, the em-balming process moved into the home of an undertaker or embalming surgeon. The integrated services of corpse preparation and ceremony within the Ameri-can funeral parlor as we know it today first emerged less than 100 years ago. Until that time, the grief process was acutely connected to the intimate preparation of the corpse, allowing for a healthy and tactile connection to emotional loss.

Although considered a desecration of the body in some religions, embalm-ing remains common throughout the United States and Canada. To provide what is considered a desirable last image for the bereft, the corpse is disinfected, its eyes and mouth are set, stitched or sealed, after which two to three gallons of arterial chemicals are injected while blood from the corpse is drained into the municipal sewer. Remaining bodily gas and fluids are suctioned or des-iccated from internal organs which are then also injected and packed with embalming fluids, including formaldehyde, phenol, and other hazardous or carcinogenic chemicals, to disinfect and delay decomposition. Following the mechanics of preservation—which also include dyes to restore natural color-ation, and humectants to mimic living hydration—hair, clothing, and a resting position are styled to present the corpse as if in a benign yet enigmatic sleep.

Earthen Burial

Each year, cemeteries across the United States bury approximately 800,000 gallons of toxic embalming fluid, risking groundwater and soil leaching. Nearly two million caskets are purchased in the United States annually, with 45 percent sold through the Batesville Casket Company.[11] Most caskets are buried in ceme-teries three deep within concrete vaults. In aggregation, buried caskets consume over 90,000 tons of steel, 2,700 tons of copper and bronze, and over 30 million board feet of hardwoods annually. Burial vaults and vacuum sealed industrial casket bunkers which cause the body to putrefy in black isolation rather than actually return to the earth, are comprised of an additional 1.6 million tons of re-inforced concrete and 14,000 tons of steel annually.[12] No matter how fortified the bunker, eventually a fetid brew of embalmed tissue slowly leaches into the sur-rounding soil and groundwater. The perception that the corpse itself is somehow toxic is only made true by postmortem interventions that attempt to delay decay.

In addition to the issue of the intensive and noxious environmental impact of burials, cemeteries in many urban areas across America are at, or very near, capacity. Having already reduced plot sizes, co-opted pathways, and stacked multiple caskets underground, urban cemeteries are rapidly approaching full saturation in perpetuity. In the boroughs of New York City, many cemeteries have no further plots available and it is projected that most will be at full capacity as soon as 2015 and others no later than 2025.[13] We have less than a generation in which to acknowledge this crisis and implement a new infrastructural strategy requalifying the logistic of urban death at a vast metropolitan scale. The spatial imperative for options other than earthen burial in our cities is absolute.

Cremation

Cremation was gradually accepted in the United States after the first crematory was built in Pennsylvania in 1876. A small brick building containing two rooms, one for reception and one for the furnace, was built on a doctor's own land under his conviction that contagions borne from buried corpses were leaching into the soil and groundwater and spreading disease. But despite the reassurance offered by incinerating diseased flesh to put an end to phantom graveyard miasma, late-19th-century society was slow to embrace this new disposal option, and only 42 corpses were cremated there in the first 25 years of operation.[14] In 1965, shortly after the Catholic Church relaxed its ban on cremation, the cremation rate in the United States was still less than 4 percent. By 2010, however, the Cremation Association of North America reported over 40 percent of American corpses were cremated annually.

In contrast to the often slow pace of cultural evolution—with long-standing institutional and perceptual oppositions ossified in the built structures of our lives and the organization of our cities—the choice of cremation has increased radically over the past 50 years. This increase is not solely a response to logistic and economic constraints, but also a reflection of changing attitudes toward entrenched rituals surrounding death and memory. However, although the reduction of the corpse to less than 4 percent of its mass is spatially efficient, environmentally cremation is disfavored due to the required energy intensity, extensive use of nonrenewable fuels in combustion, and the sometimes-toxic hot gases released to the atmosphere during the burning, vaporization, and redistribution of the body. Through incineration, the chemical and biological potency of human biomass is subverted to relatively inert carbon ash, greenhouse gases, and other pollutants. Bodies are transformed into ephemeral smoke, and an environmental taint lingers as an imprint of the life that once was.

CULTURAL EVOLUTION AND
NEW METHODS OF CORPSE DISPOSAL

While promoting change in any established cultural tradition will meet resistance, there are precedents to alternative modes of corpse disposal. Organizing dead bodies vertically, rather than horizontally, is now practiced in London; and other global cities in Europe, Scandinavia, and South America have long employed a system of 25- to 30-year termed land leases in cemeteries rather than possession of a burial plot in perpetuity, which remains the norm in the United States. Further evolution in cultural perspective is evident in the accepted practical use of the corpse. Once scorned by most religious doctrine, organ donation to augment the life of another human and full body anatomical donation to support medical research have gained increasing public support, and are practices now sanctioned by most religions. Substantive changes in American practices around death, especially in our cities, are inevitable.

Education, myths, and worldview influence paradigms of behavior, and a Zeitgeist evolves. To accelerate the acceptance of alternatives to enduring cultural traditions, design has the capacity to help shape the evolution of informed imagination. Responding to contemporary social, scientific, and environmental realities, prohibition on the antiurban practice of burial is sensible, and the pragmatics of addressing urban-ecological challenges—which are human-crises, really—are an instigation for both our innovation and progressive perspective.

Juxtaposed to deep-rooted practices of embalmed burial are evolved beliefs which view our corporeal remains (after useful organs have been harvested and/or scientific research performed) as a form of biomass to be recycled in the most efficient and sustainable manner possible. Contemporary perspectives truly embracing resilient cycles of growth and decay catalyze a reconsideration of the already complex issues of identity and memory that are implicated at death. These enlightened positions require physical spaces that support both social and individual spirituality related to grief and remembrance, while advancing systems and processes that are environmentally sustainable.

Responsibly contending with human mortality and the physical remains of the dead in spaces designed to compliment contemporary society is an ethical and social obligation of any progressive civilization. More sensible technologies of corporeal metamorphosis have been developed, and existing scientific processes of accelerating biological decomposition are available to advance the funerary industry now. Each process engages the natural chemical composition of the human body, at least 60 percent of which is water. The remaining matter is comprised of degradable lipids and proteins (roughly 17% each), minerals (about 6%) and nonorganics (about 1%).

These technologies, together with new architectures of social space, enable a long overdue evolution in options to support the processes of grief while providing diverse forms and durations of memorial. Design can lead a sociocultural evolution embracing these alternative practices, instigating a serious reconsideration of whether the quintessential American individual autonomy must persist in our postmortem circumstances.

Promession

Promession is based on the principle that all organic matter should be recycled. The process engages cryomation, wherein a body is put in a bath of liquid nitrogen and subsequently vacuum-dried, making it brittle and easily reduced to fine particles. Other than the removal of water, human remains maintain their complete chemical composition—suitable for biodegradation and absorption in the ecosystem. The process requires 130 kilowatt-hour (kWh) of electricity, or about one-third the energy consumed by cremation.[15]

Susanne Wiigh-Mäsak, a Swedish marine biologist and environmental consultant, founded Promessa Organic Burial, which has developed and intends to offer an environmentally responsible method of freeze-drying human corpses, condensing an adult corpse to 20 to 30 kilograms (44–66 pounds) of fine, hygienic, odorless organic powder which serves as compost. The method was initially tested on pig and cow carcasses in Scandinavia and Europe, where the animal remains, when placed in a biodegradable container and buried in oxygenated soil, disintegrate within six months.[16]

The deceased is prefrozen to 0°F (−18°C) and then placed in a sealed Promator where the metamorphosis occurs. Immersed in about 22 gallons (83 liters) of liquid nitrogen (calibrated to body-size), the corpse is further frozen to −321° F (−196°C) and becomes crystallized. After two hours the liquid nitrogen evaporates into the atmosphere as harmless nitrogen gas, which naturally comprises 78 percent of Earth's atmosphere. Sixty seconds of ultrasonic vibration reduces the remains to powder. The promessed remains are then passed through a vacuum chamber where frozen water sublimates and is released as steam. A dry, odorless powder, about 30 percent of the original body weight, is left, and metals or any other foreign substances are easily selectively separated. Aerobic composting can further reduce the mass by an additional third. The organic promains may be placed in a container made from biodegradable corn or potato starch to be buried in shallow topsoil, or scattered for biodegradation and reabsorption into the ecosystem. The small particle size enables oxygen and microorganisms in the topsoil to accelerate organic decomposition, which for an adult corpse will be complete in six to eighteen months. Promession is most commonly envisioned as reducing a corpse to fertilizer to feed a living memorial tree or shrub, which may be planted privately or as part of a civic structure or memorial park.

The Church of Sweden has yet to fully embrace the practice, and after initial recognition of ecological burial, government officials and the Church Council have not moved forward with plans to build the first promatorium in Sweden.[17] Promessa is a nascent global business, with affiliates licensed to operate in the United Kingdom and South Korea, with legislation pending in Germany, Switzerland, and South Africa. It is represented on Facebook,[18] seeking a partner to enter into the U.S. market. As of January 2013, the company was in the process of choosing a licensee in California as the first American location for the process. The word Promessa is Italian for promise, as the technology, producing no water or air pollution, promises to deliver the body seamlessly back to nature.

Resomation/Alkaline Hydrolysis

Another contemporary alternative to traditional burial and cremation is re-somation, a term derived from a Greek word meaning rebirth of the body. It is essentially a chemical cremation, involving an accelerated process of alkaline hydrolysis, using lye under heat and pressure, to reduce a corpse to disposable liquid and a small amount of dry bone residue or mineral ash. The resomation process requires about 90 kWh of electricity, resulting in one-quarter the carbon emissions of cremation, consuming one-eighth the energy, while costing the consumer roughly the same amount as a cremation.[19]

In resomation, the body is placed in a silk bag and loaded into a resomator, which is filled with a solution of potassium hydroxide alkali, a strong base that breaks down the corpse into its underlying constituents. The solution is heated to a high temperature ($\pm160°C/350°F$) under high pressure, which prevents boiling. In less than three hours, the corpse is effectively dissolved into its chemical components and bone fragments. The outcome is a small quantity of DNA-free greenish-brown liquid containing amino acids, peptides, sugars, and salts, with no genetic tracers, and soft, porous white bone-remains comprised of calcium phosphate. The effluent liquid is treated and released. Magnets are used to extract any metals from the bone-ash, after which the remaining white-colored dust may be scattered or placed in a repository.

Amos Herbert Hobson patented alkaline hydrolysis in the United States in 1888, to produce fertilizer from animal carcasses. One hundred years later, two professors at Albany Medical College, Dr. Kaye and Dr. Weber, patented a modern tissue digester, which became the first commercial alkaline hydrolysis system to dispose of human cadavers. In 1993 in Scotland, Dr. David Taylor developed a hot alkali process to effectively destroy cow carcasses infected by bovine spongiform encephalopathy (mad cow disease). It continues to be the only process known to effectively remove all risk of further contamination. The process has been used to dispose of donated human research cadavers at the University of Florida in Gainesville since 1995 and at the Mayo Clinic in Rochester, Minnesota, since 2006.[20] Alkaline hydrolysis has more recently been approved for commercial use to decompose human cadavers in Colorado, Florida, Kansas, Illinois, Maine, Maryland, Minnesota, and Oregon.[21] The Anderson-McQueen funeral home in St. Petersburg, Florida, is the first location in the United States where the process, marketed as "flameless cremation," is available as a funerary option to the public. Sandy Sullivan, the founder of Resomation Limited, which produces high temperature alkaline hydrolysis vessels for single human disposition, has written, "cremation offered fundamental change in the way we approach human disposition and some serious convincing was required before it was fully accepted. . . . It is again time to reconsider, challenge, analyze and decide where we go next. The environment requires, and indeed demands it."[22]

Expanding on the water-based elemental alternative to fire or earth, in Australia, Aquamation Industries is led by a former funeral-home director, and has been offering a lower temperature and lower pressure version of alkaline hydrolysis as an option for corpse disposal since 2010. The original facility is located in Eco Memorial Park on Australia's Gold Coast, and its literature claims "every Funeral Director in Australia can arrange an Aquamation funeral." Edwards Funeral Service in Columbus, Ohio, offered the first Aquamation funeral services in America in 2011 using a 24-inch low-temperature commercial resomator produced by Bio-Response Solutions. After 19 dispositions utilizing bio-response alkaline hydrolysis, the Ohio Board of Embalmers and Funeral Directors questioned the legality of alkaline hydrolysis disposition under state law. Currently Edwards is not publically offering the service.[23]

Bio-Methanization

The production of biogas or methanogenesis is the natural end result of a three-stage process in the decay and decomposition of biomass, preceded by hydrolysis-liquefaction and acidogenesis.[24] The most common form of methanogenesis currently occurs on farms throughout the United States to transform animal waste into methane through anaerobic digestion, an oxygen-less process which breaks down organic matter and converts it to methane, carbon dioxide, and a nutrient-rich effluent. This process can be used as a means of disposing whole animal carcasses and is typically employed in cases of infected livestock, due to digester containment and controllability.[25]

Similar to the production of biogas from animal remains, human remains may also be rapidly decomposed by anaerobic digestion. The methane produced can be collected and utilized to produce electricity, or employed directly in a biogas heating system. Methanogenesis is the dominant method of breaking down organic matter in landfill disposal and is being studied in detail as a means to economically and ecologically reduce many forms of municipal solid waste. When coupled with an anaerobic membrane bioreactor (MBR) it can also be a low-energy alternative to municipal wastewater treatment, allowing the matter of the body to have remediative and generative impact.[26] Assuming increased technological efficiency of this energy transfer, ultimately the power produced from the corpse could offset some of the carbon footprint the person created during life.

* * *

Engaging the corpse on its biological basis, and enabling a more organic return to the earth, each of these relatively new disposition technologies is more spatially and environmentally sustainable than traditional mortuary practices. These processes also instigate us to challenge the notion of a memorial locus in perpetuity. The design proposals that follow here assume a growing moral consensus to responsibly depart from life with both dignity and minimal environmental burden.

NEW URBAN POTENTIAL

Sociocultural values, while rooted in historical contexts, are alive, resilient, and responsive to the contemporary realities in which they operate. As individual values evolve, communal rituals are reshaped and eventually political policy is informed by advancements in social context. Paradigm shifts in both spatial and cultural logics are vital to enable society to release ossified beliefs as to what is appropriate or desirable related to the disposition and honor of the deceased.

As architects, we enter the context of death through space—through the design of temporal memorials embedded in the public domain, and the reconception of spatial rituals associated with both mourning and respecting the dead. Our primary responsibility is to the living—to the intimate and collective experiences of individuals encountering and vitally engaging the places we design. These spaces and experiences carefully negotiate an intermingling of life and death. And we are committed to core values that recognize the immense responsibility and expenditure of resources implicated in any act of building—repercussions that will resonate for generations.

With my colleagues at Latent Productions and my students at Columbia University Graduate School of Architecture, Planning and Preservation, we are exploring how the certainty of death and practices of remembrance can be celebrated in extraordinary spaces sited within, rather than segregated from, urban vitality. We are inventing systems of transformation, imprinted by lives expired, to support public territories bridging remembrance and future possibility. These civic infrastructures allow the city to mourn while negotiating a seemingly incompatible confabulation between life and death. Although nondenominational in nature, our projects reassert spiritual concern and responsibility for honor, human civility, and a generational accountability to consider our collective environmental, spatial, and emotional resources, with precision and creativity.

Navigating the impermanence of biological life, memory, and building, these proposals are invested in the reconception and development of future urban environments, with the specific intention of expanding postmortem options. Each project explores unique sociocultural intersections of mortality and spatial experience, accepting the profound inevitability of death coupled with the potent alchemy of memory. Increased engagement with death and remembrance in public space affords society the opportunity to reconsider what we value, connecting individuals with others and to an aggregate past, to guide our intertwined future.

These proposals aim to renegotiate coexistence between urban collective-life and the intimacy of death. Our investigation goes beyond utilitarian improvements of corpse disposal practices by offering spaces to support new rituals honoring the dead, while coexisting with traditional funerary liturgy.

We envision a distributed network of memory-spaces incrementally transforming the urban landscape, enabling increased exposure and dialogue across generations and elevating the civic conditions of the living metropolis.

REMEMBRANCE AND SANCTUARY

Memento Mori (Latin for remember you must die) are reminders of our own mortality. They highlight the value of perspective, emphasizing our physical transience—both isolated and collective. Transcending representational imagery and symbolic narrative, our projects endeavor to productively augment cultural perspective while reclaiming public space, supporting human memory, and celebrating life.

The confidence of sanctuary is crucial to society, and should be understood as a part of civic infrastructure. Particularly amidst the cacophony and complexity of the metropolis, spaces of contemplation and reflection are paramount. In contrast to the sanctuaries that once offered the perpetually open doors of houses of worship, and perhaps most readily and symbolically were associated with religious cathedrals dominating their contexts, our contemporary projects are not overtly associated with any singular religion (or with religion at all for that matter), and are sometimes quite stealthy in their urban existence. Our intent is nonetheless, to provide spiritual spaces that challenge the American tendency to socially and physically isolate death and cemeteries. In our work, sanctuaries are receptive to a broad spectrum of ceremonial, practical, and contemplative occupations. Through built space and public landscapes, these projects negotiate realms of the sacred and profane, striving for concurrent states of quietude and profundity.

The increase in technology's capacity to digitally record, store, and search electronic memories is clearly a radical cultural transformation. The projects here included, however, vigorously support our imperfect cognitive and selective emotional memories—imprecise reflections which we collect and shed over time. The perceived permanence and comprehensive, minute detail of digital archives often displace the intimacy of a memory and the personal connection of individual experience to events. Remembrance is defined by what the living value and retain, regardless of factual accuracy or larger societal classification of significance. Remembrance has an utterly elegant and merciful capacity to gradually fade from the present.

Contemplating absence, memory, and identity, our ambition is to pull the present forward and inform the shape and substance of imminent urban society—reprioritizing what it means for a civilization to be civilized, and for mortals to be connected by mortality. In these proposals, architecture operates in dialog with the cycles of life and our unsettled relationship with memory. Prevailing funerary practices are unsustainable and on unsound foundation amidst 21st-century metropolitan environments populated by large groups of people who no longer subscribe to the practices of their religious heritage. The constructed permanence of traditional Western institutions memorializing the dead—most often inscribed as an eternal presence in stone—inadequately reflect a gradual release from the emotional hold of memory. This process of letting someone go echoes our natural relationship with time, our ability to filter the past—and even to choose to eventually forget. Moreover, contrary to the common understanding of death as the cessation of all biological activity, in the following three projects we offer examples of how we imagine urban cemetery spaces and death itself as a vital part of municipal ecology, remediative networks, and social grounding.

PROJECT ONE: RECONCEIVING CIVIC INFRASTRUCTURE

In 2009, Latent Productions responded to an international design competition calling for new ideas for American infrastructures—a contemporary version of Franklin Roosevelt's New Deal era WPA initiatives.[27] Cemeteries in New York City comprise an aggregate gated area more than five times the size of Manhattan's Central Park but are collectively nearing a state of complete saturation. Our proposed public infrastructure, illustrated in Figures 14.1 through 14.3, adds shared open space to the city and honors the deceased in short-term shrines, wherein the corpse is reconstituted to release energy, remediating the adjacent environment. This curative system allows urbanites a perpetual option to exit life locally, avoiding the environmental costs of airfreight, refrigeration, embalming, coffin vaults, or cremation. New urban infrastructures of remembrance allow the bereaved to recollect their dead in public spaces which help shape perspective and are integral to life.

Rather than continue to despoil the earth and consume additional isolated space with our extant funerary practices, convex temporal memorial chambers process organic human remains to catalyze the revitalization of contaminated water and soil—restoring health to existing urban brownfield sites and amplifying access to civic open space. The term brownfield site refers to "real property, the expansion, redevelopment, or reuse of which may be complicated by the presence or potential presence of a hazardous substance, pollutant, or contaminant."[28] As public works, these projects offer critical infrastructures to local urban neighborhoods and biospheres alike.

As opposed to forcing toxins into dead bodies in an effort to artificially counter decay, and then sealing them underground to putrefy, this new infrastructure utilizes controlled microbial methanogenesis to elevate and accelerate the natural processes of decomposition to cleanse previously contaminated bodies of water and land. Located above impure urban ground, microbial chemistries inside the digesters are specifically balanced to act in symbiosis with the earth to contend with local pollution types. Figure 14.1 demonstrates a horizontal organization of the system as it could extend laterally above and across an urban ground otherwise inaccessible to the public.

Figure 14.1
Perpetual field organized laterally; remediation diagram; ceremonial procession diagram; rendering of public park (Latent Productions, 2009)

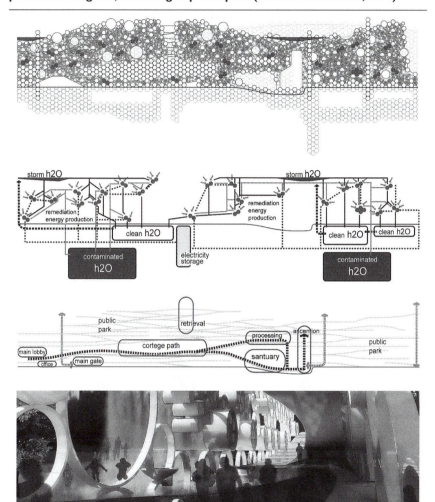

The deceased are commissioned into individual memorial chambers or pods. Autonomous, yet interwoven amidst a larger network, the belly of the pod cradles the corpse throughout its metamorphosis from inert mass to released energy. A flat elliptical surface above the vessel accommodates the bereaved throughout the stages of mourning. Oriented relative to sun and wind angles, the area immediately surrounding the chamber serves as a collective memorial site for both ceremony and solitary contemplation.

With the ability to be organized horizontally or vertically in response to site conditions and context, the armature contains vessels that collectively act as a

Figure 14.2
Vertical configuration offers both remote and intimate association
with remembrance; approximately 10,000 memorials annually facilitate
remediation of the Superfund site at the Gowanus Canal in Brooklyn, New
York (Latent Productions, 2009)

sponge to absorb precipitation and retard storm water. The aggregate network responds to individual ceremonial rituals and visits of the bereaved, the density of pedestrian flow, and climactic change. The infrastructure's temporal transformation, and its resilient conversion of individual deposits of biodegradable remains, generates a shimmering experiential effect, enlivening existing urban wastelands. The visitors' experience within these ephemeral territories of remembrance is activated by infiltrations of light, shadow, wind, rain and snow, creating a dynamic atmosphere of private encounters within this new, urban, public province. The porous spatial network is simultaneously a locus of private grief, a vertical public park, and a remediative machine whose interwoven territories facilitate confluences of diverse constituents, where events of loss and renewal converge.

Figure 14.3
Diagrammatic tower section and plan organization at three levels indicating diverse scales of sanctuary and civic space amidst temporal memorial chambers dedicated to the production of energy, remembrance, and remediation (Latent Productions, 2009)

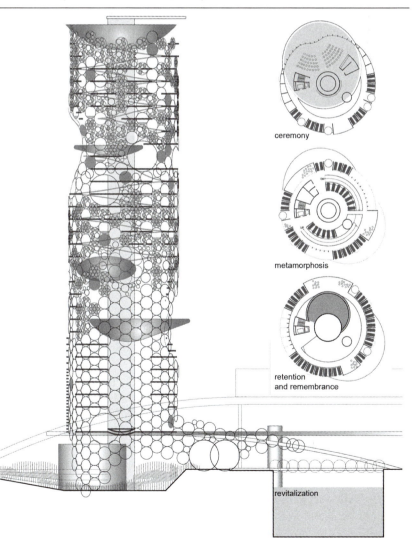

Bio-remediation is achieved through the use of microbial electrolysis cells (MEC), employing fuel cell technology to convert chemical energy into highly efficient hydrogen energy. The microbial digestion process absorbs contaminants and releases electrons, protons, and carbon dioxide as a by-product. Localized fuel cells charged with hydrogen gas–powered mourning lights are associated with the duration of an individual corpse's transformation, as well as serve to illuminate the public territories and remediation facility. Like remembrance itself, these lights have individual duration, and slowly fade. Bright for the first month, an individual mourning light will gradually dim over the course of the year following committal. When the chemical metamorphosis is complete, the glow extinguishes and the memorial chamber is ripe for renewed occupancy, becoming the site of another family's journey through grief. As an economically sustainable land-lease model, the project provides an enduring communal connection to place, while the physical presence of the body is allowed to dissipate.

This resilient infrastructure of short-term shrines dedicated to the production of energy, remembrance, and remediation rises amidst the city, offering loved ones and citizens a contemplative stroll, while the deceased are transformed into the vibrant energy they literally embody. Responding to occupancy, the structure's pores dilate and contract as biomass is converted, and the deceased, through decay, replenish some of the vast resources consumed during their lives.

Through a temporal memorial to the dead, a truly perpetual field is crafted for their remembrance—instrumentalizing natural cycles of growth, decay, and renewal. A vibrant, public sanctuary celebrates the fragility and poetry of life through a productive translation of the body after death.

PROJECT TWO: MEASURED RELEASE T HROUGH SPACE AND TIME

In an ever-more globalized and intertwined existence, the nostalgia of association to a physical homeland is fading and a capacity for new forms of affiliation has emerged. Incorporating the technology of alkaline hydrolysis, a proposal entitled "Synchronicity" engages the parameters of human memory, social conscience, and a temporal act of letting go. Transformed to pure white dust, individual human remains enter a 25- year protected lease within the envelope of an urban building. Discrete memories are reconstituted as a perpetual stranded network, envisioned in Figures 14.4 and 14.5. The choreographed coexistence of thousands of linear elements reflects the collective value and intersections of individual lives. Calibrated, large-scale indexical migrations echo the fading of memories and stages of grief, supporting both urban rituals and a personal and profound final displacement.

Representatives and remains hosted in a ten-inch by three-inch vessel ascend to one of the private sanctuary clearings within a field of memorial strands. The vessel is released into the constructed scaffold in a solemn and personal ritual, as the deceased's friends and family witness the inauguration of its journey as a micro-displacement within a forest of memory. The shifting spatial topography of the system operates as a measure of passing time.

Spaces are suspended within the parabolic volumes, allowing the ground plane to remain unobstructed and open to the city. The mourning and nonmourning publics traverse paths and respites throughout the building. Two worlds converge—the real and the ethereal—with sanctuary space mediating between.

Figure 14.4
Ground level public space beneath memorial trajectories (Tom McKeogh, 2010)

Specific spatial and temporal windows of overlap allow the bereaved to revisit the artifact as the remains traverse a mappable path. Opportunities for physical reconnection diminish throughout the lease term, encouraging a celebration of rare but potent, synchronic moments between a living person and a manifestation of memory. Offering expansive, protected public space amidst urban density, the proposal supports multivalent celebrations under an intertwined web of trajectories, each strand representing a life remembered.

Figure 14.5
Diagrammatic plan and sectional organization of 5,100 strands, 66,300 vessels, and 5 suspended sanctuary clearings of varying capacities (Tom McKeogh, 2010)

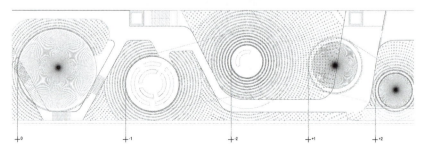

PROJECT THREE: TRANSIENT MEMORIAL GARDENS

Another project aspiring for social change through urban infrastructural evolution aims to de-stigmatize death by enfolding quotidian travel across a metropolitan bridge within a vibrant park of the dead. The project celebrates life and its normal activities, positioned in the most visible urban connections, to anchor the perception of death as an embedded part of living cycles. Transformation is the core of the project's philosophy, converting existing industrial transportation structures into cathedral-esque, continuous, public spaces. Engaging a monument of urban connection and growth with a mosaic of collective memory, corpses transformed into fertilizer, water, and calcium ash feed a public garden. The rigid metallic armature of the bridge becomes a nest for a scab of organic architecture that grows and deteriorates in continual evolution.

Three layers of material performance engage the interstitial spaces of a preexisting underutilized structure, generating a hanging skeleton, and offering a light porous calcium concrete substrate which is able to absorb the moist fertilizer effluent from alkaline hydrolysis to grow new forms of life such as mosses and ivy. The first and second layers are permanent, while the third sucks, feeds, and grows to reconfigure the spatial performance of the bridge.

Individual remains are unified into a breathing collective public network nourished by the organic by-products of disposition. The corpse's bone residue is cast and suspended in a matrix. This coral-like set of connections intensifies its growth until nature deteriorates the scab. Infiltration promotes disintegration, requiring the system to adapt and recalibrate. Exposure to climactic catalysts accelerates or slows the inevitable deterioration. Across time, these rhizoid networks are reshaped and ultimately dematerialize to a point of erasure. The duration of one's imprint within the emergent memorial field is projected to range from three to twenty years, although emotional connection to the evolving system is enduring. Slow to transform, the project behaves like an organism, living and dying, over and over again.

Accumulating memorial membranes recalibrate spatial and social boundaries tethering individual urban lives through iterative and reciprocal erosion and growth. A landscape of memory infused within the daily commute provides new territory for future recollection, responding to our biological finitude with the sanctity of providing an exquisite higher ground upon which to honor the dead. Here, land is replaced by air, permanence is minimized, and a system of spaces for both mourning and celebration memorialize a collective dead.

CONCLUSION

Death defines our mortality. Like every other bio-organism, human lives are finite. The Earth's resources are finite, and we cannot continue unsustainable practices indefinitely. Through the making of these new civic spaces of re-membrance, we aspire to translate the ocean's infinity and its capacity to erase into the density and dynamism of the city.

Trends toward reducing consumption have grown tremendously over the past several decades, and must now extend to more thoughtful options at the end of life. Americans started recycling household aluminum, glass, and plastics in 1972 with the passage of the first bottle bill. Since that time, the obligation to pay a recycling deposit on bottles and cans, together with increasing public education about climate change, has resulted in both awareness and changes in quotidian behavior. While not yet a moral consensus, it is time that we reinforce the responsible choices made while living, with progressive and conscientious options for what one can plan to do with one's corpse upon death.

Our imagination, informed by research and critical strategy, enables us to see possibility beyond entrenched social protocols and ingrained aesthetic expectations. We believe that human ritual matters enormously and deserves to be respected with critical and innovative vision, rather than remain entombed in obsolete socio-spatial convention.

Response to these proposals both within and outside of academia has been enthusiastic, signaling the American population's readiness for sensible yet elegant urban alternatives in how we honor our dead. As a culture, we have an ethical obligation to develop new options that support the grief and memories of the living while allowing the dead to depart with dignity. As a last imperative of life, we can resolve the body into its underlying biological elements, and foster a restorative period of sincere remembrance within an infrastructural sanctuary that honors the individual amidst the vitality of daily metropolitan life.

ACKNOWLEDGMENTS

I am indebted to my partner at Latent Productions, Salvatore Perry, for his un-flinching support of my multivalent aspirations, and to Jennifer Preston, who has grown from student, to assistant, to colleague on this quest. The Graduate School of Architecture, Planning and Preservation at Columbia University has served as the incubator of my ideas for 25 years, where the simultaneous liberty and rigor of Avery Hall enables the research and exploration of my interests related to urban spaces of death and memory, in dialog with brilliant colleagues and inspirational students. My gratitude extends especially to my graduate students and their unswerving willingness to believe in and explore the potential of architecture to change society. "Synchronicity" is the work Tom McKeogh produced in my Spring 2010 GSAPP studio. The transient moss garden is the work of Carolina Ihle from the Fall semester of 2012. Enthusiastic encouragement from the Columbia University Seminar on Death instigated the writing of this chapter.

NOTES

1. Thomas Bahde, "The Common Dust of Potter's Field: New York City and its Bodies Politic, 1800–1860," *Common Place* 6, 4 (July 2006). http://www.common-place.org/vol-06/no-04/bahde/

2. Publius Ovidius Naso, aka Ovid, *Fasti ("The Festivals" On the Roman Calendar)*, Book II: February 21: The Feralia. Likely first published posthumously ca. AD18.

3. Washington Square: Phase 1A Archaeological Assessment, NYC Department of Parks and Recreation. Joan H Geismar, PhD, LLC. August 2005, p. 30.

4. http://www.rootsweb.ancestry.com/~nynewyo2/cemeteries/

5. Pamela Bannos, "Hidden Truths: Chicago City Cemetery," Northwestern University, www.hiddentruths.northwestern.edu

6. Tess Vigeland, "Italian Mayor Bans Death. Marketplace for Thursday," March 15, 2012. American Public Media. http://www.marketplace.org/topics/life/final-note/italian-mayor-bans-death

7. Jon Henley, "Citizens Live Under Law's Dead Hand," *The Guardian*, World News, September 22, 2000.

8. http://www.prb.org/Publications/Datasheets/2012/world-population-data-sheet/data-sheet.aspx

9. World Resources Institute, http://www.wri.org/publication/content/8840

10. "'Nones' on the Rise: One-in-Five Adults Have No Religious Affiliation," The PEW Forum on Religion and Public Life; POLL October 9, 2012, http://www.pewforum.org/unaffiliated/nones-on-the-rise.aspx

11. "The Ten Companies that Control the Death Industry," *24/7 Wall Street,* January 13, 2011.

12. Statistics compiled from Casket and Funeral Association of America, Cremation Association of North America, Doric Inc., The Rainforest Action Network, Mary Woodsen, Pre-Posthumous Society, Hal Stevens, Cremation or Burial—Carbon Emissions and the Environment.

13. Marc Santora, "City Cemeteries Face Gridlock," *The New York Times,* Real Estate, August 13, 2010.

14. Montana State University, Cremation. MT200201HR, Revised 4/12 by Marsha Goetting, PhD, CFP®, CFCS, Professor and Extension Family Economics Specialist; Corinne Cramer, former Extension Family and Consumer Sciences Associate; Claire Del Guerra, MSU Cascade County Family and Consumer Sciences Agent (Retired); and Keri D. Hayes, MSU Extension Publications Assistant, and Washington County Historical Society, LeMoyne Crematory.

15. "Environmental Impact of Funerals: Life Cycle Assessments of Activities after Life," by Elisabeth Keijzer, EES 2011–112 M. University of Groningen, CIO, Center for Isotope Research and IVEM, Center for Energy and Environmental Studies.

16. "Science Now; Composting Dead Bodies," *bric.postech.ac.kr,* June 13, 2001 © American Association for the Advancement of Science.

17. Lisa Zyga, "Ecological Burial Involves Freeze-Drying, Composting the Corpse," March 8, 2011, http://phys.org/news/2011–03-ecological-burial-involves-freeze-drying-composting.html

18. http://www.facebook.com/pages/Promessa-Organic-Ecological-burial/110357752341120

19. "Dissolving Dead Bodies: Gross, but Green," http://dsc.discovery.com/news/2008/05/09/dead-bodies-lye.html. Alkaline hydrolysis has different names given by four different providers: BioSAFE Engineering calls it Water Resolution®, Eco-Green Cremation System calls it Natural Cremation, Matthews International, Inc. calls it Bio-cremation or Resomation®, and CycledLife calls it by its official name, alkaline hydrolysis.

20. "UK Firm: Don't Burn Bodies, Boil Them," *Physorg News,* August 6, 2007, October 2007 Newsletter of Worthing Crematorium, operated by Worthing Borough Council in West Sussex, England. Ruth Davis Konigsberg, "The Ninth Annual Year in Ideas: Resomation," *The New York Times Magazine,* December 13, 2009. Briggs, Bill, "When You're Dying for a Lower Carbon Footprint," *MSNBC.com,* January 18, 2011, retrieved January 19, 2011, http://abcnews.go.com/Technology/story?id=4828249&page1

21. Irene Klotz, "Green Cremation Offers Clean Departure," *Discovery News,* September 2011 and "Alkaline Hydrolysis: A 'Greener' Option?" Originally published in *The Cremationist of North America* 47, 3 (2011).

22. Resomation Ltd ® brochure, "Resomation: An Alternative to Cremation with Environmental Benefits," Company Information, Scotland 2007.

23. Kantele Franko, "States Consider: Is It Legal to Dissolve Bodies?" *The Seattle Times,* June 2, 2011.

24. Shefali Verma, Department of Earth and Environmental Engineering, Fu Foundation School of Engineering and Applied Science, Columbia University, 2002.

25. Larry E. Erickson, Eric Fayet, Bala Krishna Kaumanu. Laerence c. Davis, *Carcas Disposal: A Comprehensive Review, Chapter 7 Anaerobic Digestion*, National Agricultural Biosecurity Center Consortium, 2004.

26. P. M. Sutton, B. E. Rittmann, O. J. Schraa, J. E. Banaszak, and A. P. Togna, "Wastewater as a Resource: A Unique Approach to Achieving Energy Sustainability," *Water and Science Technology* 63, 9 (2011).

27. WPA 2.0: Working Public Architecture was organized by UCLA's cityLAB. The design competition was inspired by the Depression-era Works Projects Administration and the 2009 American Recovery and Reinvestment Act, and sought innovative, urban infrastructure proposals as a catalyst for urban recovery. Latent's WPA 2.0 team: Karla Maria Rothstein, Salvatore Perry, Jennifer Preston, Sean Dawson, Muchan Park, KooHo Jung. http://latentnyc.com/project/11/

28. http://www.epa.gov/swerosps/bf/overview/glossary.htm

From "Tales of Anatomy"

A tailbone doesn't last forever. No. It starts to bend around age 13 and bends more with every seat. Until middle age when it starts to crack and wear down. At 70 the tailbone reaches the chalk stage, every day scratching away little by little. And by 90 it's nearly gone. Scientists are searching for a cure to keep bones from turning to chalk. But most people just lose their tailbones after use.

Catherine Rogers

Conclusion: Additional Vistas

Christina Staudt

*A*t the end of this volume New Paths of Engagement, *it behooves us to note briefly a few areas in the geography of our death system that have not been discussed in the preceding chapters. They include vistas of promising, elegiac pastures, as well as of ominous morasses that may bring surprises on our journey. The intention here is not to delve into these areas in detail but merely to direct the reader's attention to them to give a more comprehensive survey of the territory.*

LOOMING THREATS AND UNCERTAINTIES

The possibility of war and acts of aggression are a constant on the horizon. The Iraqi and Afghan wars that dominated the media in the first decade of the 21st century are winding up in 2013 but bloody images from the Syrian civil war and other parts of the Middle East continue to make armed conflict first page news. Al Qaeda and other terrorist groups remain on the administration's watch list but the public frenzy and acute fear that followed the events of 9/11 have abated. Much of the nation is preoccupied with the need for jobs and sustained economic recovery after the financial crisis of 2008 and the subsequent major recession. Intermittent devastating acts, such as the Boston marathon bombings (April 15, 2013), intercede to remind us of the ever-present possibility of unpredictable, deadly actions and that we are never sure what form death will take.

Political and ethical debates determine laws of the land and shape public opinion. Ideological and political differences make us choose different paths to the end. Ethical and policy issues around killing and dying engage the public and prompt Congressional debate. That some of these issues can be conjured up by single appellations—"death panels," "Sandy Hook," "drone attack"—is evidence that they penetrate the public collective consciousness.

The notion of death panels was invoked by those opposing the original proposal for the Patient Protection and Affordable Care Act (PPAC), President Obama's health care reform bill. It included a provision requiring reimbursement of health care providers for counseling patients about their end-of-life treatment choices.[1] The reimbursement provision was eliminated from the final bill, when the PPAC was eventually passed and signed into law by the President in March 2010.[2] Many regretted that an opportunity was lost to change the discourse and better inform patients with serious illnesses about their treatment options and expanding the public's understanding of the need for conversations about the end of life.

Sandy Hook refers to the horrific massacre at the eponymous elementary school in Newtown, Connecticut, on December 14, 2012. A gunman armed with two handguns, a shotgun and a semiautomatic Bushmaster .223, a rifle with a high capacity magazine, designed for warfare, walked into the school and in a matter of minutes killed 20 first- and second-grade children along with five of their teachers and the school's principal, before taking his own life. Attempts at enacting more stringent federal gun control legislation immediately followed. Several months later no legislative outcome was evident on the federal level, despite a strong personal commitment and sustained public relations campaign by the President, much debate, and numerous statistics aimed at shaking up the status quo. This scenario does not take us down a new path. Other mass killings have prompted similar efforts with equally futile result. Diminishing powers of a well-financed lobby in Washington is not among the prevailing winds of change. More than heart wrenching media coverage and overwhelming public opinion are required to reframe this issue,

Deaths resulting from drone attacks have raised a different ethical quandary. According to newspaper reports,[3] thousands of people in Pakistan and Yemen have been killed by American drones, the attackers safely ensconced behind a computer thousands of miles away. That alone is a morally debatable action to some, but the issue engaged much of the media and Congress when an American citizen, Anwar al-Awlaki born in New Mexico in 1971, was deliberately targeted and killed by a drone strike in Yemen in 2011. With public opinion not yet coalesced around the issue in the summer of 2013, the debate was being shaped by constitutional rather than moral arguments.

Technological and scientific innovations will threaten our lives and will help defend us against attacks. Cyber warfare and pandemics are among major potential mass killers in the 21st century and potentially challenge our uninterrupted journey into old age. Given available technology in the early 21st century and the expectations of future advances, drones are quite primitive actors in cyber warfare. Much more complex and deadly cyber weapons are available and ready to be put into use, not just by developed countries but also by disgruntled, emerging nations, and rogue groups. A Central Intelligence Agency *Global Trends Report* has warned that future major terrorist offensives—state sponsored or independent—are likely to be cyberspace attacks targeting infrastructures and economic interests, rather than civilians.[4] Such attacks would have deadly consequences for the population even when no one is hurt in the actual moment of the strike. It has been estimated that New York City can endure about two weeks in case a blackout deprives the Northeast region of electricity; after that, major portions of the population will be starving.[5] If the power companies' defense systems have been compromised, an attack on critical nodes in the electric grid can be accomplished from any distance by a good hacker with a simple computer.

In 1996 President Clinton appointed the first commission to study the threat of cyber warfare. A number of reports and books followed in the first decade of the 21st century but the topic was not widely discussed among the public, beyond the hypothetical framing of a terrorist group detonating traditional bombs with remote controls. After the media reports of the Stuxnet attack on Iran's nuclear program in 2010, an attack many assume was engineered by the United States and Israel, the public became more aware and engaged. Subsequent cyber offensives against American businesses and banks, the South Korean defense system, and other sensitive targets were well publicized. The fear deepened with the realization that we were not only dealing with isolated terrorist groups and unstable individuals but also with state-sponsored cyber terrorism. The menacing uncertainty in the face of the unknown is not unlike the unease and watchful tension experienced in the 1960s when a nuclear attack by the Soviet Union loomed. Cyber warriors who hack computer systems and convey logic bombs to the enemy are flourishing in popular films and videos as signs of our 21st-century apocalyptic visions and imagination. Dozens of serious books on cyber warfare, published since 2010,[6] attest to the wave of concern, as do numerous study groups, convened by the government, not-for-profit advocacy groups, and regular hacking communities.

Discussions about other potential mass deaths are also part of the landscape. Biological and chemical warfare risks intermittently engage the public after discoveries of stashes of such weapons of mass destruction (WMDs). The topic surfaced in the media and bookstores after incidents such as the sarin gas attack on the Tokyo subway system in 1994, when WMDs became the pretext for invading Iraq in 2002, and after accusations about chemical weapons being used by the Assad regime in the civil war in Syria.

We have been on the watch for the peril presented by bacteria in daily life since the introduction of penicillin. We have learned that these organisms can be fended off with appropriate drugs, as evidenced in the successful battles against polio, small pox, pneumonia, and a variety of other bacterial infections that have either been eradicated or no longer have a high mortality rate. After outbreaks of severe acute respiratory syndrome (SARS) during 2002–2003 and the Asian avian influenza (beginning in 2003) were satisfactorily contained, a form of a triple-reassortant influenza A virus, composed of a combination of human, swine, and Eurasian avian strains, confounded the infectious disease community in 2009 and caused concerns among the public. Methicillin-resistant *Staphylococcus aureus* (MRSA) was a threatening bacterium in hospitals and nursing homes where patients already had compromised immune systems. In 2005, 19,000 people died from MRSA infection in the United States, most of them in hospitals and with other morbidities. According to a 2011 report by the CDC, the MRSA bacterium is waning[7] but highly resistant superbugs have replaced them.

Food poisoning on a mass scale such as the British outbreak of mad cow disease (Bovine spongiform encephalopathy) and E. coli infestations also garner the public's attention for brief periods. The ongoing challenge of the scientific and medical communities is to promptly identify new strains and develop antidotes. Increasingly, it is reported that we may not be winning the war against bacteria. More and more deadly strains are emerging from mutations. The best weapon against their onslaught is vaccine, but vaccine development often is not a profitable business for pharmaceutical companies and hence not necessarily a high priority. The course of a deadly bacterial threat may be shaped by the need to satisfy shareholders' desire for high profits.

The threat to our food sources is part of a larger environmental story about the long-term survival of humans on this planet, a matter that would engage the general public to a greater extent if it were possible to see the consequences of a certain behavior more immediately and if the cause and effect link was clear in everyday life. Stories about the mass death of honeybees and the slow contamination of the water supply by pesticides send temporary shivers through the population but only rarely sustain interest beyond the activist groups that address them. As a people we do not seem to worry about preparing for catastrophic events until days and hours before they happen: witness hurricanes Katrina (2005) and Sandy (2012) and the fact that people continue to build houses on fault lines in California, despite geologist projections of a major earthquake before mid-century. Looming threats and uncertainties are a fact of life and it seems that much of the population prefer to leave them unexamined.

LONG LIFE—AMBIGUOUS DEATH

A survey of mortality in the 21st century would be incomplete without a comment on the quest for perpetual life and what drives it. The dream of immortality goes back as far as the *Epic of Gilgamesh* and probably further. Twenty-first century immortality seekers, who label themselves transhumanists or futurists, differ from earlier dreamers in that they are pointing to science, rather than to miracles or the hands of gods, as the instrument that will achieve their goal. One of the most prominent persons in the movement in the United States is Ray Kurzweil, an engineer, inventor, and the author of several optimistic books about our future biology. His ideas have captured the imagination of large segments of the population, and his work and movement need to be included among the forces that are reshaping how we look at death and dying in this century. In a 2004 book, written with Terry Grossman, *Fantastic Voyage, Live Long Enough to Live Forever,* he amasses recent medical advances to show that we are constantly making new strides in medicine. With proper adoption of the new findings and inventions as they come along, he claims, we can live indefinitely.[8] He follows this up in 2009 with a handbook describing how our bodies break down and how to forestall aging by taking the following nine steps—talk with your doctor, relaxation, assessment, nutrition, supplements, calorie reduction, exercise, new technologies, and detoxification.[9]

In his 2006 book *The Singularity is Near: When Humans Transcend Biology,* Kurzweil looks further into the future, outlining the potential, benefits inherent in some of the technical devices we are already using today to enhance and treat the human body, such as artificial limbs and cochlear implants. The new being that emerges from this process, the Singularity, "will represent the culmination of the merger of our biological thinking and existence with our technology, resulting in a world that is still human but that transcends our biological roots. There will be no distinction, post-Singularity, between human and machine nor between physical and virtual reality."[10]

Singularities are perhaps better known as cyborgs—cybernetic organisms. They appear most commonly in science fiction but are also being referenced in the context of work done at major universities. A report of an interview with professor Charles M. Lieber, the Mark Hyman Jr. Professor of Chemistry at Harvard in August of 2012 begins "scientists have created a type of 'cyborg' tissue for the first time by embedding a three-dimensional network of functional, biocompatible, nanoscale wires into engineered human tissues" and Lieber notes that "[U]ltimately, this is about merging tissue with electronics in a way that it becomes difficult to determine where the tissue ends and the electronics begin."[11] This is a long way from creating singularity but the direction is set and even Kurzweil concedes that it will be decades before cyborgs will be developed to a point that they take over the function of our vital organs.

The Human Genome Project (announced in 1990) is another medical research development that plays a major role in transhumanists' optimistic scenario of effectively eradicating death. With the blurring of the lines between living and dying that has come about because of advances in medical treatments, which can prolong the life span even the illness cannot be cured, we now often speak about living with a certain disease rather than dying from it. The advantages to our health and longevity that the Human Genome Project promises have added new perspectives to the discourse on death and dying. Just as we might argue that if we gain immortality by becoming indistinguishable from machines we are no longer human beings, we might debate if a genetically reengineered body with infinitely renewable cells can be considered to house the same person as the one we were originally given. The transhumanist project is attracting a growing number of adherents and their presence in the public forum spur us to rephrase or speak differently about our journey to the end.

Studies of the boundaries between persistent vegetative state and a minimally conscious state, such as those conducted by Dr. Joseph J. Fins, already tamper with, and refine, the line between living and dying. One does not awake from a persistent vegetative state but can wake up after being in minimally conscious state, even after years in a coma.[12] Based on the President's Commission for the Study of Ethical Problems in Medicine and Biomedical and Behavioral Research, The Uniform Determination of Death Act (1980) stated as determination of death "irreversible cessation of all functions of the entire brain, including the brainstem." Informally referred to as "brain death," the definition is disputed among some orthodox Jews and many Muslims.

The "long death" that appears to occur when someone is in a persistent vegetative state may result in the need to redefine what it means to be dead. In addition, to the personal importance for the family involved, clearly delineating between a living human being and a corpse is necessary for organ harvesting. The processes of organ harvesting in 21st-century hospitals was presented in a readable, albeit often macabre, account to the general public in 2012 with the publication of Dick Teresi's *The Undead: Organ Harvesting, the Ice-Water Test, Beating Heart Cadavers—How Medicine is Blurring the Line Between Life and Death.*[13]

* * *

The level of engagement a particular trend engenders often depends on the media coverage the event receives. Horrifying or moving isolated events— school shootings, stoic deaths, miraculous returns from the dead, gruesome murders, and suicides of celebrities—have always made compelling stories. What is shaping these stories in new ways in the 21st century is not the events themselves so much as the growth of media outlets and devices that enable them instantly to go viral. In the 21st century, the public's level of engagement with deadly threats, as well as with hopeful signs that death can be held at bay, is more than ever, and increasingly, a matter of what is mediated in cyber space. That said, commitments to new trends and their embodiment in law and social practices are not merely the effect of getting the most publicity. What matters on a daily basis to ordinary people may eventually take form through grassroots actions. Change and progress are also a matter of policy decisions and political will, as well as a question of who has the resources to support the new trends and directions.

NOTES

1. "2012 Legislative Blueprint for Action," *Hospice Association of America,* 2012, http://www.nahc.org/facts/HAALeg2012.pdf

2. "The Patient Protection and Affordable Care Act," 111th Congress Public Law 111–48, 2010, March 23, 2010, http://www.gpo.gov/fdsys/pkg/PLAW-111publ148/pdf/PLAW-111publ148.pdf

3. See for example, "A Second Opinion on Drone Strikes," *Los Angeles Times,* February 18, 2013, accessed March 28, 2013, http://articles.latimes.com/2013/feb/18/opinion/la-ed-drones-court-targeted-assassinations-20130218

4. Central Intelligence Agency, "Terrorism-related Excerpts from Global Trends 2015: A Dialogue about the Future with Nongovernment Experts," accessed March 28, 2013, https://www.cia.gov/news-information/cia-the-war-on-terrorism/terrorism-related-excerpts-from-global-trends-2015-a-dialogue-about-the-future-with-non government-experts.html

5. Scott Borg, CEO, Director and Chief Economist, The United States, Cyber Consequence Unit, oral presentation at Little Forum, Bronxville, New York, April 2011.

6. Among the most popular is Richard A. Clarke and Robert Knake, *Cyber War: The Next Threat to National Security and What to Do About It* (New York: Harper Collins, 2010).

7. Centers for Disease Control and Prevention, "MRSA Surveillance," April 8, 2011, accessed March 27, 2013, http://www.cdc.gov/mrsa/statistics/MRSA-Surveillance-Summary.html

8. Ray Kurzweil and Terry Grossman, *Fantastic Voyage, Live Long Enough to Live Forever* (New York: Rodale Press, 2004).

9. Ray Kurzweil, *Transcend—Nine Steps to How to Live Forever* (New York: Rodale Press, 2009).

10. Ray Kurzweil, *The Singularity is Near: When Humans Transcend Biology* (New York: Viking Press, 2006), see also http://www.kurzweilai.net/the-singularity-is-near

11. Peter Reuell, "Merging the Biological, Electronic: Researchers Grow Cyborg Tissues with Embedded Nanoelectronics," *Harvard Gazette,* August 26, 2012, accessed March 30, 2013, http://news.harvard.edu/gazette/story/2012/08/merging-the-biological-electronic/

12. Joseph J. Fins, "Brain Injury: The Vegetative and Minimally Conscious States," in *From Birth to Death and Bench to Clinic: The Hastings Center Bioethics Briefing Book*

for Journalists, Policymakers, and Campaigns, ed. Mary Crowley (Garrison, NY: The Hastings Center, 2008), 15–20.

13. Dick Teresi, *The Undead—Organ Harvesting, the Ice-Water Test, Beating Heart Cadavers—How Medicine is Blurring the Line between Life and Death* (New York: Random House, 2012).

Bibliography

"2012 Legislative Blueprint for Action." *Hospice Association of America,* 2012. Accessed July 16, 2013. http://www.congressweb.com/nahc/docfiles/12-HAA-LegBP-Inside.pdf.

Adair, Robert K. *The Physics of Baseball.* San Francisco, CA: HarperCollins/Perennial, 2002.

"Alkaline Hydrolysis for Human Remains." June 29, 2012. Accessed June 29, 2012. http://alkalinehydrolysis.com.

Alvarez, Manny. "Doctors Should Not Rely on Computers for End-of-Life Decisions." *Fox News,* January 11, 2012.

Ariès, Philippe. *The Hour of Our Death: The Classic History of Western Attitudes Toward Death over the Last One Thousand Years.* Translated by Helen Weaver. London: Allen Lane, 1982.

Ariès, Phillippe. *Western Attitudes Towards Death: From the Middle Ages to the Present.* Translated by Patricia M. Ranum. Baltimore/London: The Johns Hopkins University Press, 1974.

Arndt, Jamie, and Jeff Greenberg, Sheldon Solomon, Tom Pyszczynski, and Linda Simon. "Suppression, Accessibility of Death-Related Thoughts, and Cultural Worldview Defense." *Journal of Personality and Social Psychology* 73 (1997): 5–18.

Ashbrook, James B., and Carol R. Albright. *The Humanizing Brain.* Cleveland, OH: Pilgrim Press, 2003.

Astley, Jeff, and Leslie Francis. *Psychological Perspectives on Prayer.* Leominster, UK: Gracewing Publishing, 2001.

Bahde, Thomas. "The Common Dust of Potter's Field: New York City and its Bodies Politic, 1800–1860." *Common-place: The Interactive Journal of*

Early American Life 6, 4 (July 2006). http://www.common-place.org/ vol-06/no-04/bahde/.

Bakhtin, Mikhail. *Rabelais and his World.* Translated by H. Iswolsky. Blooming ton: Indiana University Press, 1984.

Bamyeh, Mohammed A. *Of Death and Dominion: The Existential Foundations of Governance.* Evanston, IL: Northwestern University Press.

Banks, Richard. *The Future of Looking Back.* Foreword by Bill Buxton. Redmond: Microsoft Press, 2011.

Bannos, Pamela. *Hidden Truths: Chicago City Cemetery.* Northwestern University. Accessed November, 2012. http://www.hiddentruths.northwest ern.edu.

Barreca, Regina, ed. *Sex and Death in Victorian Literature.* Macmillan, 1990.

Barthes, Roland. *Camera Lucida: Reflections on Photography.* Translated by Richard Howard. New York: Hill and Wang, 1981.

Bataille, Georges. *Death and Sensuality: A Study of Eroticism and the Taboo.* New York: Walker and Company, 1962.

Batchen, Geoffrey. *Each Wild Idea: Writing, Photography, History.* Cambridge, MA/London: The MIT Press, 2001.

Baudrillard, Jean. *Symbolic Exchange and Death.* Translated by Iain Hamilton Grant. Los Angeles: Sage, 1993.

Bazin, André. "The Ontology of the Photographic Image." In *Classic Essays on Photography,* edited by Allen Trachtenburg with notes by Amy Weinstein Meyers, 237–44. New Haven, CT: Leete's Island Books, 1980.

Beauvoir, Simone de. *The Second Sex.* New York: Vintage, 1989.

Beck, Richard. "Defensive Versus Existential Religion: Is Religious Defensiveness Predictive of Worldview Defense?" *Journal of Psychology & Theology* 34 (2006): 143–53.

Becker, Ernest. *The Denial of Death.* New York: The Free Press, 1973.

Bedard, Michael, and Melissa Felteau. "Pilot Evaluation of a Mindfulness-Based Intervention to Improve Quality of Life Among Individuals Who Sustained Traumatic Brain Injuries." *Disability and Rehabilitation: An International, Multidisciplinary Journal* 25 (2003): 722–31.

Beegan, Gerry. *The Mass Image: A Social History of Photomechanical Reproduction in Victorian London.* Hampshire: Palgrave Macmillan, 2008.

Beit-Hallahmi, Benjamin. "Fear of the Dead, Fear of Death: Is It Biological or Psychological?" *Mortality: Promoting the Interdisciplinary Study of Death and Dying* 17, 4 (2012): 322–37.

Beit-Hallahmi, Benjamin. *Psychoanalysis and Theism.* New York: Jason Aronson, 2010.

Bendle, Mervyn B. "The Contemporary Episteme of Death." *Cultural Values* 5, 13 (July 2001): 349–67.

Besirevic, Violete. "End-of-Life Care in the 21st Century: Advance Directives in Universal Rights Discourse." *Bioethics* 24 (2010): 105–12.

Bellow, Saul. *Herzog*. New York: Viking, 1964.

Belting, Hans. "Image, Medium, Body: A New Approach to Iconology." *Critical Inquiry* 31, 2 (2005): 302–19.

Benjamin, Walter. *The Work of Art in the Age of its Technological Reproducibility and other Writings on Media,* Edited by Michael W. Jennings, Brigid Doherty, and Thomas Y. Levin. Cambridge: The Belknap Press of Harvard University Press, 2008.

Benson, Herbert, and Miriam Klipper. *The Relaxation Response.* New York: Wm. Morrow/HarperCollins, 2000; orig, 1975.

Berger, Peter L. *The Sacred Canopy: Elements of a Sociological Theory of Religion.* New York: Doubleday, 1967.

Berger, Peter L., and Thomas Luckmann. *The Social Construction of Reality: A Treatise in the Sociology of Knowledge.* New York: Doubleday, 1966.

Berzoff, Joan. "Narratives of Grief and their Potential for Transformation." *Palliative and Supportive Care* 4, 2 (June 2006): 121–7.

Besirevic, Violete. "End-of-Life Care in the 21st Century: Advance Directives in Universal Rights Discourse." *Bioethics* 24 (2010): 105–12.

Bioethics Forum (the Hastings Center Blog). http://www.thehastingscenter.org/ Bioethicsforum/

Blauner, Robert. "Review of Death, Grief, and Mourning. Geoffrey Gorer. London: The Cresset Press, 1965." *Psychoanalytical Review* 55 (1968): 521–2.

Bloch, Maurice, and Jonathan Parry. *Death and the Regeneration of Life.* Cambridge: Cambridge University Press, 1982.

Block, Marcelline. "Poor Little Rich Dead: Michael Jackson's Moonwalk through the Pharmaco-Narco Netherworld and Other Tales of Celebrity Death and Inequality." In *Unequal Before Death,* edited by Christina Staudt and Marcelline Block, 149–92. Newcastle: Cambridge Scholars Publishing, 2012.

Blood Ties: The Life and Work of Sally Mann. DVD. Directed by Steven Cantor and Peter Spirer. Los Angeles: Moving Target Productions, 1994.

Bochen, Christine M., ed. *Thomas Merton: Essential Writings.* Maryknoll, NY: Orbis Books, 2000.

Bognar, Steven, and Julia Reichert. *A Lion in the House.* Independent film. Premiered on PBS, June 21 and 22, 2006.

Bolloch, Joelle. "Photographie après décès: pratique, usages et functions." In *Le dernier portrait,* edited by Emmanuelle Héran, 112–45. Paris: Musée d'Orsay, 2002.

Borg, Scott. Oral presentation at Little Forum, Bronxville, New York, April 2011.

Borkenau, Franz. "The Concept of Death." In *Death and Identity,* edited by Robert Lester Fulton, 42–56. New York: John Wiley & Co, 1965.

Boyce, Barry. *The Mindfulness Revolution: Leading Scientists, Psychologists, Artists and Meditation Teachers On the Power of Mindfulness in Daily Life.* Boston, MA: Shambala, 2011.

Boyer, Pascal, and Pierre Lienard. "Why Ritualized Behavior? Precaution Systems and Action Parsing in Developmental, Pathological and Cultural Rituals." *Behavioral and Brain Sciences* 29 (2006): 595–650.

Bregman, Lucy. *Preaching Death; The Transformation of Christian Funeral Sermons.* Waco, TX: Baylor University Press, 2011.

Briggs, Bill. "When You're Dying for a Lower Carbon Footprint: Body-disposal Process Offers More Eco-Friendly Alternative to Cremation." *MSNBC News,* January 18, 2011. http://www.today.com/id/41003238/ns/business-oil_and_energy/.

Bronfen, Elisabeth. *Over Her Dead Body: Death, Femininity and the Aesthetic.* Routledge, 1992.

Brottman, Mikita. "Death in Cyberspace: Psychoanalysis and the Internet." In *The Many Ways We Talk About Death in Contemporary Society,* edited by Margaret Souza and Christina Staudt, 121–34. Lewiston, NY: Edwin Mellen Press, 2009.

Brubaker, Jed, and Gillian R. Hayes. "'We Will Never Forget You [Online]': An Empirical Investigation of Post-mortem MySpace Comments." *Proceedings of the CSCW 2011.* Hangzhou, China. March 19–23, 2011.

Brubaker, Jed R., and Gillian R. Hayes. "'We Will Never Forget You [Online]': An Empirical Investigation of Post-mortem Myspace Comments." *Proceedings of the ACM 2011 Conference on Computer Supported Cooperative Work (CSCW '11),* 123–32. doi 10.1145/1958824.1958843.

Bull, Michael A., Sheila Clark, and Katherine M Duszynski. "Lessons From a Community's Response to the Death of Diana, Princess of Wales." *Omega* 46, 1 (2002–2003): 35–49.

Burrowes, Jeff. "Interactive Chris Ethridge Memorial Coming." *WTOK.com,* August 31, 2012. Updated September 1, 2012. http://www.wtok.com/home/headlines/Interactive-Chris-Ethridge-Memorial-Coming-168190426.html.

Byock, Ira. *Dying Well—Peace and Possibility at the End of Life.* New York: Riverhead Books, 1997.

Byock, Ira. *The Four Things That Matter Most—A Book about Living.* New York: Free Press, 2004.

Caffrey, Thomas A. "When the Time is Ripe for Acceptance: Dying, with a Small 'd.'" In *Speaking of Death: America's New Sense of Mortality,* edited by Michael K. Bartalos, 227–36. Westport, CT: Praeger, 2009.

Callahan, Daniel. *The Tyranny of Survival and Other Pathologies of Civilized Life.* New York: MacMillan, 1973.

Camus, Albert. *The Plague.* Translated by Stuart Gilbert. New York: Vintage International, 1991.

Cantor, Steven. *What Remains: The Life and Work of Sally Mann.* DVD 80 mins. Color, USA, 2006.

Carson, Denise. "A Living Tribute Honors a Life." OC Register, August 16, 2010. Accessed November 5, 2012. http://www.ocregister.com/articles/bill-262297-senior-family.html.

Castle, Joan, and William L. Phillips. "Grief Rituals: Aspects that Facilitate Adjustment to Bereavement." *Journal of Loss and Trauma* 8, 1 (2003): 41–71.

Castleman, Michael, D. Gallagher-Thompson, and M. Naythons. *There's Still a Person in There: The Complete Guide to Treating and Coping with Alzheimer's.* New York: Penguin Putman, 1999.

Central Intelligence Agency. "Terrorism-related Excerpts from Global Trends 2015: A Dialogue About the Future With Nongovernment Experts." Accessed March 28, 2013. https://www.cia.gov/news-information/cia-the-war-on-terrorism/terrorism-related-excerpts-from-global-trends-2015-a-dialogue-about-the-future-with-nongovernment-experts.html.

Chapple, Alison, and Sue Ziebland. "How the Internet is Changing the Experience of Bereavement by Suicide: A Qualitative Study in the UK." *Health: An Interdisciplinary Journal for the Social Study of Health, Illness and Medicine* 15 (Mar 2011): 173–87.

Chapple, Helen Stanton. *No Place for Dying: Hospitals and the Ideology of Rescue.* Walnut Creek, CA: Left Coast Press, 2010.

Chen, Pauline W. *Final Exam: A Surgeon's Reflections on Mortality.* New York: Vintage, 2008.

Cicero. *Tusculan Disputations.* Translated by J. E. King. Cambridge, MA: Loeb Classical Library, 1927.

Clark, Jennifer, and Majella Franzmann. "Authority from Grief, Presence and Place in the Making of Roadside Memorials." *Death Studies* 30 (2006): 579–99.

Clark, Jennifer, and Majella Franzmann. "Born to Eternal Life: The Roadside as Sacred Space." Accessed February 18, 2013. www.abc.net.au/religion/stories/s1000839.htm.

Clarke, Richard A., and Robert Knake. *Cyber War: The Next Threat to National Security and What to Do About It.* New York: Harper Collins, 2010.

Cohen, Steven, and William Yu. *The Concentration and Persistence in the Level of Health Expenditures over Time: Estimates for the U.S. Population, 2008–2009.* Statistical Brief #354. January 2012. Agency for Health care Research and Quality, Rockville, MD. http://meps.ahrq.gov/mepsweb/data_files/publications/st354/stat354.shtml.

Collins, Charles O., and Charles D. Rhine. "Roadside Memorials." *Omega* 47 (2003): 221–44.

Cotter, Holland. "Landscape of Eros: Through the Peephole." *New York Times,* August 27, 2009. Accessed March 7, 2013. http://www.nytimes.com/2009/08/28/arts/design/28duchamp.html?pagewanted=all_r=0.

Cox, Gerry R. "Religion, Spirituality, and Traumatic Death." In *Handbook of Thanatology,* edited by David Balk, Carol Wogrin, Gordon Thornton, and David Meagher, 263–8. Routledge, 2007.

Cripe, Larry D. "The General." In *At the End of Life: True Stories about How We Die,* edited by Lee Gutkind, 37–50. Pittsburgh: Creative Nonfiction Brooks, 2012.

Critchley, Simon. *The Book of Dead Philosophers.* New York: Vintage, 2009.

Critchley, Simon. *Very Little . . . Almost Nothing: Death, Philosophy and Literature.* New York: Routledge, 2004.

Crouch, Mira. "Last Matters: The Latent Meanings of Contemporary Funeral Rites." In *Making Sense of Dying and Death,* edited by A. Fagan, 125–40. Amsterdam: Rodopi, 2004.

Damasio, Antonio. *Descartes' Error: Emotion, Reason and the Human Brain.* New York: Putnam, 1994.

Damasio, Antonio. *The Feeling of What Happens: Body and Emotion in the Making of Consciousness.* New York: Harcourt Brace, 1999.

Daniels, Stephen R. "The Consequences of Childhood Overweight and Obesity." *The Future of Children* 16, 1, Childhood Obesity (Spring 2006): 47–67.

Dao, James. "Learning to Heal, One Memorial Day at a Time." *New York Times,* May 29, 2012. Accessed July 16, 2013. http://www.nytimes.com/2012/05/29/us/2-4-marine-regiment-marks-ramadi-losses.html?pagewanted=all_r=0.

DasGupta, Sayantani, and Marsha Hurst. "Death in Cyberspace: Bodies, Boundaries, and Postmodern Memorializing." In *The Many Ways We Talk About Death in Contemporary Societ.,* edited by Margaret Souza and Christina Staudt. Lewiston, NY: Edwin Mellen Press, 2009,105–20.

Davis, Walter A. *Inwardness and Existence.* Madison, WI: University of Wisconsin Press, 1989.

Deignan, Kathleen. *A Book of Hours.* Notre Dame, IN: Sorin Books, 2007.

Deignan, Kathleen. *A Book of Hours: At Prayer with Thomas Merton.* Schola Ministries 2009, Audio CD set.

Departures. DVD. Directed by Yojiro Takita. Japan: Amuse Soft Entertainment, 2008.

Derrida, Jacques. *Aporias.* Translated by Thomas Dutoit. Stanford: Stanford University Press, 1993.

Derrida, Jacques. *Of Hospitality: Anne Dufourmantelle Invites Jacques Derrida to Respond.* Translated by Rachel Bowlby. Stanford, CA: Stanford University Press, 2000.

Derrida, Jacques. *The Work of Mourning,* edited by Pascale-Anne Brault and Michael Naas. Chicago: The University of Chicago Press, 2001.

Detsky, Alan S. "What Patients Really Want From Health Care." *Journal of The American Medical Association* 306, 22 (2011): 2500–1.

Dickinson, George E., and Heath C. Hoffmann. "Roadside Memorial Policies in the United States." *Mortality* 15 (2011): 154–67.

Dickman, Matthew. "Grief." *The New Yorker,* May 5, 2008.

Didion, Joan. *The Year of Magical Thinking.* New York: Vintage, 2007.

"Director's commentary." *The Dead Girl.* DVD. Directed by Karen Moncrieff. Los Angeles: Bruin Grip Services, Lakeshore Entertainment, 2006.

Dogen. *Shobogenzo.* Translated by T. Cleary. Honolulu: University of Hawaii Press, 1986.

Doka, Kenneth J. "Memorialization, Ritual, and Public Tragedy." In *Living with Grief: Coping with Public Tragedy,* edited by Marcia Lattanzi-Licht and Kenneth J. Doka, 179–89. New York: Brunner-Routledge, 2003.

Doss, Erika. "Death, Art and Memory in the Public Sphere: the Visual and Material Culture of Grief in Contemporary America." *Mortality: Promoting the Interdisciplinary Study of Death and Dying* 7, 1 (2002): 63–82.

Durkheim, Emile. *Elementary Forms of Religious Life.* New York: George Allen and Unwin, 1915.

Ehrenreich, Barbara. *Blood Rites: Origins and History of the Passions of War.* New York: Henry Holt, 2007.

Eilberg-Schwartz, Howard. *The Savage in Judaism.* Bloomington, IN: Indiana University Press, 1990.

Eisenbruch, Maurice. "Cross-Cultural Aspects of Bereavement, II: Ethnic and Cultural Variations in the Development of Bereavement Practices." *Culture, Medicine and Psychiatry* 8, 4 (December 1984): 315–47.

Erickson, Larry E., Eric Fayet, Bala Krishna Kaumanu, and Lawrence C. Davis. "Anaerobic Digestion." In *Carcass Disposal: A Comprehensive Review,* report prepared by the National Agricultural Biosecurity Center Consortium. Kansas State University, 2004. doi:2097/662.

Everett, Holly. *Roadside Crosses in Contemporary Memorial Culture.* Denton, TX: University of North Texas Press, 2002.

Faure, Bernard. *Visions of Power.* Princeton, NJ: Princeton University Press, 1996.

Faust, Drew Gilpin. *This Republic of Suffering—Death and the American Civil War* New York: Alfred A. Knopf, 2008.

Feifel, Herman. "Introduction." In *The Meaning of Death,* edited by Herman Feifel, xv–xvi. New York: McGraw-Hill, 1959.

Feifel, Herman, "Death in Contemporary America." In *New Meanings of Death,* edited by Herman Feifel, 3–12. New York: McGraw-Hill, 1977.

Fernandez, Ingrid. "The Lives of Corpses: Narratives of the Image in American Memorial Photography." *Mortality: Promoting the Interdisciplinary Study of Death and Dying* 16, 4 (2011): 343–64.

Fiese, Barbara H., Thomas J Tomcho, Michael Douglas, Kimberly Josephs, Scott Poltrock, and Tim Baker. "A Review of 50 Years of Research on Naturally Occurring Family Routines and Rituals: Cause for Celebration?" *Journal of Family Psychology* 16, 4 (2002): 381–90.

Finlay, Christopher J., and Guenther Krueger. "A Space for Mothers: Grief as Identity Construction on Memorial Websites Created by SIDS Parents." *Omega: Journal of Death and Dying* 63 (2011): 21–44.

Finney, John R., and H. Newton Maloney. "An Empirical Study of Contemplative Prayer as an Adjunct to Psychotherapy." *Journal of Psychology and Theology* 13 (1985): 284–90.

Firestone, Robert, and Joyce Catlett. *Beyond Death Anxiety: Achieving Life-Affirming Death-Awareness.* New York: Springer, 2009.

Flitterman-Lewis, Sandy. *To Desire Differently: Feminism and the French Cinema.* New York: Columbia University Press, 1996.

Fox, Robin. "Food and Eating: An Anthropoological Perspective." *SIRC: Social Issues Research Centre.* http://www.sirc.org/publik/foxfood.pdf.

Frank, Arthur. *The Wounded Storyteller: Body, Illness, and Ethics.* Chicago: University of Chicago Press, 1997.

Frank, Lone. "Composting Dead Bodies?" *Science Now Online,* June 13, 2001. http://news.sciencemag.org/sciencenow/2001/06/13–03.html.

Franko, Kantele. "States Consider: Is it Legal to Dissolve Bodies?" *The Seattle Times,* June 2, 2011. http://seattletimes.com/html/nationworld/2015214929_apusliquefyingbodies.html?syndication=rss.

Frazer, James George, and Erwin Panofsky. *Tomb Sculpture. Four Lectures on Its Changing Aspect from Ancient Egypt to Bernini.* New York: Harry N. Abrams, 1924.

Freud, Sigmund. *Civilization and Its Discontents.* London: Hogarth, 1953.

Freud, Sigmund. "Thoughts for the Times on War and Death" (1915). In *Collected Papers,* Vol. 4. Edited and translated by Joan Riviere. New York: Basic Books, 1959.

Freud, Sigmund. *The Uncanny.* Translated by David McClintock. New York: The Penguin Group, 2003. Originally published as "Das Unheimliche" in *Imago* 5, 1919.

Friedman, Michael. "Religious Fundamentalism and Responses to Mortality Salience: A Quantitative Text Analysis." *International Journal for the Psychology of Religion* 18 (2008): 216–37.

Frogge, Stephanie. "The Role of Ritual Following a Major Loss." *Open to Hope,* December 29, 2009. Accessed July 16, 2013. http://www.opentohope.com/the-role-of-ritual-following-a-major-loss/.

Fromm, Erich. *To Have or to Be?* New York: Harper & Row, 1976.

Fuchs, Lawrence H. *The American Kaleidoscope: Race, Ethnicity, and the Civic Culture.* Hanover NH: University Press of New England, c1990, 1995.

Fuhrer, Chantal, and Alain Cucchi. "Relations Between Social Capital and Use of ICT: A Social Network Analysis Approach." *International Journal of Technology and Human Interaction (IJTHI)* 8 (2012): 15–42.

Funk, Rainer, ed. *The Essential Fromm, Life between Having and Being.* New York: Continuum, 1995.

Gabert, Shelley. "The Facts of Life: An Independent Karen Moncrieff Casts a Cold Eye on Death." *Written By: The Magazine of the Writer's Guild of America West,* January 2007. Accessed March 1, 2013. http://wga.org/writtenby/writtenbysub.aspx?id=2281.

Gauberg, Elizabeth H., Maren Batalden, Rebecca Sands, and Sigall K. Bell. "The Hidden Curriculum: What Can We Learn from Third-Year Medical Student Narrative Reflections?" *Academic Medicine* 85 (2010): 1709–16.

Gawande, Atul. "Letting Go." *New Yorker,* August 2, 2010.

Gazzaniga, Michael. *Nature's Mind: Biological Roots of Thinking, Emotions, Sexuality, Language, and Intelligence.* New York: Basic Books, 1994.

Gazzaniga, Michael, Richard Ivry, and George Mangun. *Cognitive Neuroscience: The Biology of the Mind.* New York: W. W. Norton, 2009.

Geismar, Joan H. "Washington Square Park: Phase 1A Archaeological Assessment." New York City Department of Parks and Recreation, 2005.

Gennep, Arnold van. *The Rites of Passage.* Translated by M. B. Vizedom and G. L. Caffe. London: Routledge and Kegan Paul, 1960.

Georgakopoulou, Alexandra. *Small Stories, Interaction and Identity.* Philadelphia: John Benjamins Publishing Company, 2007.

Gershman, Nancy, and Jenna Baddeley. "Prescriptive Photomontage: A Process and Product for Meaning-Seekers with Complicated Grief." *Americanpsychotherapy.com,* Fall 2010, 28–34.

Gigerenzer, Gerd. "Moral Intuition=Fast and Frugal Heuristics?" In *Moral Psychology, Volume 2, The Cognitive Science of Morality: Intuition and Diversity,* edited by W. Sinnott-Armstrong, 1–15. Cambridge MA: MIT Press, 2008.

Goetting Marsha, Cramer, Claire Del Cuerra, and Keri D. Hayes *Cremation. MontGuide* (MT200201HR). Bozeman, MT: Montana State University Extension, 2012.

Goldsmith, Samuel. "Diamond Company LifeGem Turning Lock of Michael Jackson's Hair into Jewels." *New York Daily News,* July 27, 2009. Accessed July 16, 2013. http://www.nydailynews.com/entertainment/diamond-company-lifegem-turning-lock-michael-jackson-hair-jewels-article-1.429542.

Goodman, David C., et al. "Trends and Variations in End-of-Life Care For Medicare Beneficiaries With Severe Chronic Illness." The Dartmouth Institute For Health Policy and Clinical Practice, August 12, 2011.

Goodwin, Sarah Webster, and Elisabeth Bronfen, eds. *Death and Representation.* Johns Hopkins University Press, 1993.

Gorer, Geoffrey. "The Pornography of Death." *Death, Grief, and Mourning,* 192–9. Garden City, NY: Doubleday-Anchor, 1967.

Grabbe, Nick. "Leverett Neighborhood Wrestles with Weight of a Cross." *Amherst Bulletin,* June 27, 2008, A1.

Grandin, Temple. *Thinking in Pictures: And Other Reports From My Life With Autism.* New York: Doubleday/Vintage, 2010.

Grandin, Temple, and Catherine Johnson. *Animals In Translation: Using the Mysteries of Autism to Decode Animal Behavior.* New York: Scribner, 2005.

Green, Andre. *Life Narcissism Death Narcissism.* London: Free Association, 2001.

Green, James W. *Beyond the Good Death—The Anthropology of Modern Dying.* Philadelphia: University of Pennsylvania Press, 2008.

Greenberg, Jeff, Tom Pyszczynski, and Sheldon Solomon. "A Perilous Leap From Becker's Theorizing to Empirical Science." In *Death and Denial: Interdisciplinary Perspectives on the Legacy of Ernest Becker,* edited by Daniel Liechty, 3–16. Westport, CT: Praeger Publishing, 2002.

Greenberg, Jeff, Tom Pyszczynski, Sheldon Solomon, Linda Simon, and Michael Breus. "The Role of Consciousness and Accessibility of Death-Related Thoughts on Mortality Salience Effects." *Journal of Personality and Social Psychology* 67 (1994): 627–37.

Grossman, Cathy Lynn. "Today we are all 'Hokies' on Facebook." *USA Today,* April 18, 2007. Accessed July 16, 2013. http://usatoday30.usatoday.com/tech/webguide/internetlife/2007-04-17-facebook_N.htm.

Groys, Boris. *The Immortal Bodies.* Video lecture (color, sound), 29 min., loop. 2007. http://cubittartists.org.uk/index.php?module=resourcesmodule&action=view&id=13.

Gubi, Peter Madsden. *Prayer in Counseling and Psychotherapy: Exploring a Hidden Meaningful Dimension.* London and Philadelphia, PA: Jessica Kingsley Publishers, 2007.

Hall, Donald. *The Best Day The Worst Day: Life with Jane Kenyon.* Boston: Houghton Mifflin, 2005.

Hallam, Elizabeth, and Jenny Hockey. *Death, Memory, and Material Culture.* Oxford: Berg Publishers, 2001.

Hamilton, Jack. "Hologram Tupac Was Inevitable." *Atlantic.com/entertainment,* April 17, 2012. http://www.theatlantic.com/entertainment/archive/ 2012/ 04/hologram-tupac-was-inevitable/255990/.

Harper, Sheila. "The Social Agency of Dead Bodies." *Mortality: Promoting the Interdisciplinary Study of Death and Dying* 15, 4 (2010): 308–21.

Hartig, Kate V., and Kevin M. Dunn. "Roadside Memorials: Interpreting New Deathscapes in Newcastle, New South Wales." *Australian Geographical Studies* 36 (1998): 5–20.

Hartmann, Margaret. "Terrible Teens Defile 9/11 Memorial." *NYMag.com,* June 25, 2010. http://nymag.com/daily/intel/2012/06/terrible-teens-de file-911-memorial.html.

Hayward, Susan. "Beyond the Gaze and Into *femme-filmécriture:* Agnès Varda's *Sans toit niloi* (1985)." In *French Film: Texts and Contexts,* edited by Susan Hayward and Ginette Vincendeau, 285–96. London and New York: Routledge, 1990.

Hedayat, Kamyar. "When the Spirit Leaves: Childhood Death, Grieving, and Bereavement in Islam." *Journal of Palliative Medicine* 9, 6 (2006): 1282–91.

Henein, Maryam. "The Importance of Ritual." *California Psychics,* January 19, 2009.http://blog.californiapsychics.com/blog/2009/01/the-importance-of-ritual.html/.

Henley, Jon. "Citizens Live under Law's Dead Hand." *The Guardian,* September 22, 2000. http://www.guardian.co.uk/world/2000/sep/23/jonhenley.

Hetter, Katia. "Memorial Tourism Bears Witness to Tragedy." *CNN Travel. com,* May 28, 2012. http://www.cnn.com/2012/04/24/travel/memorial-tourism/index.html.

Higgins, Charlotte. "Artist Daphne Todd's Portrait of Mother after Death Makes BP prize Dhortlist." *The Guardian,* April 29 2010. Accessed May 14, 2011. http://www.guardian.co.uk/artanddesign/2010/apr/29/artist-daphne-todd-portrait-mother-death-bp-prize-shortlist.

Hillman, James. *The Dream and the Underworld.* New York: Harper & Row, 1979.

"History of Hospice Care." National Hospice and Palliative Care Organization. Accessed March 29, 2013. http://www.nhpco.org/history-hospice-care.

Hockey, Jenny. "Changing Death Rituals." In *Grief, Mourning and Death Ritual,* edited by J. Hockey, J. Katz and Neil Small, 185–11. Philadelphia: Open University Press, 2001.

Horney, Karen. *The Neurotic Personality of our Time.* New York: Norton, 1937.

Hoyert, Donna L., and Jiaquan Xu. "Deaths: Preliminary Data for 2011." *Division of Vital Statistics, National Vital Statistics Reports*, Volume 61, Number 6, October 10, 2012. http://www.cdc.gov/nchs/data/nvsr/nvsr 61/nvsr61_06.pdf.

Huntington, Richard, and Peter Metcalf, eds. *Celebrations of Death: The Anthropology of Mortuary Ritual.* Cambridge and New York: Cambridge University Press, 1979.

Ikiru. DVD. Directed by Akira Kurosawa. Tokyo, Japan: Toho Company, 1952.

Imber-Black, Evan, J. Roberts, and R. Whiting. *Rituals in Families and Family Therapy.* New York: W. W. Norton & Company, 1988.

International Work Group on Death Dying and Bereavement (IWG). "Rituals for the Dying and Bereaved." Tucson, Arizona, 2004.

Irvine, Craig. "The Ethics of Self-Care." In *Faculty Health in Academic Medicine: Physicians, Scientists, and the Pressures of Success,* edited by Thomas R. Cole and Thelma Jean Goodrich, 127–46. Totowa, NJ: Humana, 2009.

James, William. *The Varieties of Religious Experience: A Study in Human Nature.* New York: Longmans, Green & Co., 1902.

Janoff-Bulman, Ronnie. *Shattered Assumptions: Towards a New Psychology of Trauma.* New York: Free Press, 1992.

Jewish War Veterans v. City of San Diego, 08–56415 (9th Cir. 2011).

Johnson, Caleb. "How to 'Memorialize' the Facebook Pages of the Recently Deceased." *Huffington Post,* October 27, 2009. Accessed February 02, 2012. http://www.switched.com/2009/10/27/memorialize-the-facebook-pages-of-friends-who-pass-away.

Jones, Barbara. *Design for Death.* Indianapolis: the Bobbs-Merrill Company, 1969.

Kabat-Zinn, Jon. *Full Catastrophe Living: Using the Wisdom of Your Body and Mind to Face Stress, Pain and Illness.* New York: Bantam Dell, 2010.

Kabat-Zinn, Jon. *Wherever You Go, There You Are: Mindfulness Meditation.* New York: Hyperion, 1994.

Kahneman, Daniel. *Thinking, Fast and Slow.* New York: Farrar, Straus and Giroux, 2011.

Kastenbaum, Robert J. *Death, Society, and Human Experience.* Boston: Pearson, 2007.

Kastenbaum, Robert J. *Death, Society, and Human Experience.* New York: Pearson, 2011, 11th edition.

Katz, Pearl, and Paul Bartone. "Mourning, Ritual and Recovery after an Airline Tragedy." *Omega* 36, 3 (1997–1998): 193–201.

Kearl, Michael C. *Endings: A Sociology of Death and Dying.* New York/Oxford: Oxford University Press, 1989.

Keijzer, Elisabeth. "Environmental Impact of Funerals: Life Cycle Assessments of Activities After Life." MA thesis, University of Groningen, Center for Isotope Research and Center for Energy and Environmental Studies, 2011. EES 2011–112 M.

Kington, Tom. "Italy's Bridges Weighed Down by Locks of Love." *The Guardian,* August 23, 2011. Accessed November 5, 2012. http://www.guardian.co.uk/world/2011/aug/23/italy-bridges-locks-of-love.

Klaassens, Mirjam, Peter Groote, and Paulus Huigen. "Roadside Memorials from a Geographical Perspective." *Mortality* 14 (2009): 187–201.

Klotz, Irene. "Green Cremation Offers Clean Departure." *Discovery Channel News,* September 5, 2011. http://news.discovery.com/earth/green-cremation-110905.htm.

Kobler, Kathie, Rana Limbo, and Karen Kavanaugh. "Moments: The Use of Ritual in Perinatal and Pediatric Death." *MCN* 32, 5 (September/October 2007): 288–95.

Kong, Lily. "Cemeteries and Columbaria, Memorials, and Mausoleums: Narrative and Interpretation in the Study of Deathscapes in Geography." *Australian Geographical Studies* 37 (1999): 1–10.

Konigsberg, Ruth Davis. "The Ninth Annual Year in Ideas: Resomation." *New York Times Magazine,* December 13, 2009. http://query.nytimes.com/gst/fullpage.html?res=9504E1DD1E39F930A25751C1A96F9C8B63.

Kramer, Kenneth. *The Sacred Art of Dying: How the World Religions Understand Death.* Mahwah, NJ: Paulist Press, 1988.

Kristeva, Julia. *Possessions.* Translated by Barbara Bray. New York: Columbia University Press, 1998.

Kristeva, Julia. *Powers of Horror: An Essay on Abjection.* Translated by Leon S. Roudiez. New York: Columbia University Press, 1982.

Kuhn, Annette. "Textual Politics." In *Issues in Feminist Film Criticism,* edited by Patricia Erens, 250–67. Bloomington and Indianapolis: Indiana University Press, 1990.

Kurtzweil, Ray. *Fantastic Voyage, Live Long Enough to Live Forever.* New York: Rodale Press, 2004.

La Barre, Weston. *The Ghost Dance.* New York: Dell, 1970.

La peste. DVD. Directed by Luis Puenzo. France and Argentina: Compagnie Française Cinématographique, 1992.

Laderman, Gary. *Sacred Matters: Celebrity Worship, Sexual Ecstasies, the Living Dead, and Other Signs of Religious Life in the United States.* New York: The New Press, 2009.

Lahiri, Jumpa. *Interpreter of Maladies.* Boston: Houghton Mifflin, 2000.

Larson-Miller, Lizette. "Holy Ground: Roadside Shrines and Sacred Space." *America* 192 (2005): 11.

Lasch, Christopher. *The Culture of Narcissism: American Life in an Age of Diminishing Expectations.* New York: Norton, 1991, revised edition.

Latent Productions. *WPA 2.0: Re-conceiving Death.* 2009. http://latentnyc .com/project/11/2/.

Lederer, Wolfgang. *The Fear of Women.* New York: Harcourt, 1968.

Ledoux, Joseph. *The Emotional Brain: The Mysterious Underpinnings of Emotional Life.* New York: Simon and Schuster, 1996.

Lee, Jacqueline. "Whitney Houston's Death Reported on Twitter Before Official Associated Press Release." *TMC.net,* February 13, 2012. Accessed February 19, 2012. http://www.tmcnet.com/topics/articles/2012/02/13/265908-whitney-houstons-death-reported-twitter-before-official-associated.htm.

Leming, Michael R., and George E. Dickinson. *Understanding Dying, Death and Bereavement.* Belmont, CA: Wadsworth Cengage Learning, 2011.

Levinas, Emmanuel. *Totality and Infinity: An Essay in Exteriority.* Translated by Alphonso Lingis. Pittsburgh, PA: Duquesne University Press, 1969.

Levine, Carol. "Night Shift." In *Stories of Illness and Healing: Women Write Their Bodies,* edited by Sayantani DasGupta and Marsha Hurst, 241–46. Kent, OH: Kent State University Press, 2007.

Lide, David R., ed. *CRC Handbook of Chemistry and Physics.* Boca Raton, FL: CRC Press, 2005, 86th edition.

Lienard, Pierre, and E. Thomas Lawson. "Evoked Culture, Ritualization and Religious Rituals." *Religion* 38 (2008): 157–71.

Lifton, Robert Jay. *The Broken Connection.* Washington, DC: American Psychiatric Press, 1979.

Longfellow, Henry Wadsworth. "Morituri Salutamus." *Henry Wadsworth Longfellow: A Maine Historical Society Website.* http://www.hwlongfellow.org/poems_poem.php?pid=275.

Love, Norma. "New in Mortuary Science: Dissolving Bodies with Lye." *USA Today,* May 21, 2008. Accessed July 16, 2013. http://usatoday30.usatoday.com/tech/science/2008-05-08-mortuary-science-lye_N.htm?csp=tech.

MacConville, Una. "Marking Death in Open Places." *Illness, Crisis & Loss* 19 (2011): 189–92.

Manhattan AHGP (American History and Genealogy Project). "Manhattan, New York County, Cemetery and Burial Records." Accessed February 2012. http://www.rootsweb.ancestry.com/˜nynewyo2/cemeteries/.

Mann, Sally. *What Remains.* New York: Bullfinch Press, 2003.

Mapes, Diane. "Bury Me With My Cellphone." *Msnbc.com,* December 16, 2008. http://www.msnbc.msn.com/id/28182292/ns/technology_and_science-tech_and_gadgets/t/bury-me-my-cell-phone/#.UF-r5qTLxQZ.

Marquardt, Nick. "Implicit Mental Processes in Ethical Management Behavior." *Ethics & Behavior* 20 (2010): 128–48.

Marsden, Sara. "How Baby Boomers May Change the Notion of Death in Society." *US Funerals Online.* Accessed September 10, 2012. http://www.us-funerals.com/funeral-articles/how-baby-boomers-may-change-the-notion-of-death-in-society.html#.UUjiKzfS8ro.

May, Rollo. *The Cry for Myth.* New York: Norton, 1991.

May, Trevor. *The Victorian Undertaker.* Oxford: Shire Publications, 2007.

McDougall, Joyce. *The Many Faces of Eros.* New York: Norton, 1995.

McGraw, John J. *Brain and Belief: An Exploration of the Human Soul.* Del Mar, CA: Aegis Press, 2004.

McWilliams, Martha. "Death Watch: Visions of Mortality in Contemporary Art." *New Art Examiner* 26, 4 (Dec. 1998/Jan. 1999): 39–43.

The Meaning of Life. DVD. Directed by Terry Gilliam. United Kingdom: Celandine Films, 1983.

Miltner, Kate. "How the Aurora Shootings Became Fodder for Lulz." *Atlantic.com/technology,* July 27, 2012. http://www.theatlantic.com/technology/archive/2012/07/how-the-aurora-shootings-became-fodder-for-lulz/260444/.

Minnesota Department of Transportation. "Minnesota Department of Transportation Maintenance Bulletin, No. 04–2." Accessed February 18, 2013. http://www.dot.state.mn.us/restareas/pdf/memorial-marker-guidelines.pdf.

Moneymaker, K. A., and J. Traeger. "Creating Space and Ritual for the Time of Death." *Journal of Palliative Medicine* 10, 1 (2007): 270–71.

Monger, George. "Modern Wayside Shrines." *Folklore* 108 (1997): 113–4.

Montaigne, Michel de. "On Physiognomy." *Essays III.* Translated by G. B. Ives. New York: Heritage, 1946.

Montaigne, Michel de. "That to Think as a Philosopher is to Learn to Die." *Essays I.* Translated by G. B. Ives. New York: Heritage, 1946.

Montross, Christine. *Body of Work: Meditations on Mortality from the Human Anatomy Lab.* New York: Penguin, 2007.

Morgan, John. "Living Our Dying and Our Grieving: Historical and Cultural Attitudes." In *Readings in Thanatology,* edited by J. D. Morgan, 11–32. Amityville, NY: Baywood, 1997.

Morris, Joel. "Graves, Pits and Murderous Plots: Walter Benjamin, Alois Riegl, and the German Mourning Play's Dreary Tone of Intrigue." In *Walter Benjamin and the Architecture of Modernity,* edited by Andrew Benjamin and Charles Rice, 93–108. Melbourne: Re.press, 2009.

Moyers, Bill. "On Our Own Terms: Moyers on Dying." Produced by Public Affairs Television, Inc. and presented on PBS by Thirteen/WNET New York. Broadcast September 10–13, 2004.

"MRSA Surveillance." Centers for Disease Control and Prevention, April 8, 2011. Accessed March 27, 2013. http://www.cdc.gov/mrsa/statistics/MRSA-Surveillance-Summary.html.

Murphy, Jeffrie G. "Rationality and the Fear of Death." In *The Metaphysics of Death,* edited by John Martin Fischer, 41–58. Stanford, CA: Stanford University Press, 1993.

Murphy, Robert F. *The Body Silent: The Different World of the Disabled.* New York: W. W. Norton, 1990.

Nagel, Thomas. *Mortal Questions.* New York: Cambridge, 1979.

Nagel, Thomas. *What Does It All Mean?* New York: Oxford, 1987.

Nance, Dave. "Roadside Memorials on the American Highway." Accessed February 18, 2013. http://photo.net/photodb/presentation?presentation_id=97863.

Neimeyer, Robert A., et al. *Grief and Bereavement in Contemporary Society.* New York: Routledge, 2011.

Nelson, Charles, Michelle de Haan, and Kathleen Thomas. *Neuroscience of Cognitive Development: The Role of Experience and the Developing Brain.* New York: John Wiley and Sons, 2006.

New Old Age Blog, The. http://newoldage.blogs.nytimes.com.

Newberg, Andrew, and Eugene D'Aquila, eds. *Why God Won't Go Away.* New York: Ballantine Books, 2001.

Newberg, Andrew, and Mark Robert Waldman. *Born to Believe.* New York: Free Press, 2007.

Newberg, Andrew, and Mark Robert Waldman. *How God Changes Your Brain: Breakthrough Findings from a Leading Neuroscientist.* New York: Ballantine Books, 2010.

Nietzsche, Friedrich. *Der Antichrist.* Berlin: Walter de Gruyter, 1988.

Nietzsche, Friedrich. *The Gay Science.* Translated by J. Nauckhoff. New York: Cambridge University Press, 2001.

Nochlin, Linda. *Realism.* London: Penguin Books, 1990.

O'Callaghan, C., M. Mus, and B. Mus. "Lullament: Lullaby and Lament Thera-peutic Qualities Actualized Through Music Therapy." *American Journal of Hospice & Palliative Medicine* 25, 2 (April/May 2008): 93–9.

O'Neill, Mary. "Speaking to the Dead: Images of the Dead in Contemporary Art." *Health (London)* 15 (2011): 299–312. Accessed September 16, 2012. doi: 10.1177/136359310397978.

Oliver, Kelly. *Subjectivity without Subjects: From Abject Fathers to Desiring Mothers.* Lanham, MD: Rowan and Littlefield, 1996.

Olthius, Gert, and Wim Dekkers. "Medical Education, Palliative Care and Moral Attitude: Some Objectives and Future Perspectives." *Medical Education* 37 (2003): 928–33.

Ovid (Publius Ovidius Naso). "Book II: February 21: The Feralia." In *Fasti,* translated and edited by Anthony J. Boyle and Roger D. Woodard. London: Penguin Books, 2000.

Paddock, John R. "Guided Visualization and Suggestibility: The Effect of Perceived Authority on Recall of Autobiographical Memories." *Journal of Genetic Psychology* 162 (2001): 347–56.

Paddock, John R., and Mark Noel. "Imagination Inflation and the Perils of Guided Visualization." *Journal of Psychology* 133 (1999): 581–95.

Page, Ruth. "Re-examining Narrativity: Small Stories in Status Updates." *Text & Talk: An Interdisciplinary Journal of Language, Discourse & Communication Studies* 30, 4 (July–August 2010): 423–44.

Panksepp, Jaak. *Affective Neuroscience: The Foundations of Human and Animal Emotions.* New York: Oxford, 1998.

Passel, Jeffrey S., and D'Vera Cohn. "U.S. Population Projections: 2005–2050." Washington, DC: Pew Research Center, February 11, 2008.

"The Patient Protection and Affordable Care Act." 111th Congress Public Law 111–148, 2010, March 23, 2010. http://www.gpo.gov/fdsys/pkg/PLAW-111publ148/pdf/PLAW-111publ148.pdf.

PBS: Public Broadcasting Service. "The American Experience | The Wizard of Photography |Wet-Plate Photgraphy." Accessed February 1, 2013. http://www.pbs.org/wgbh/amex/eastman/sfeature/wetplate.html.

Perry, Tony. "Two Congressmen Continue Fight To Save Mt. Soledad Cross." *Los Angeles Times,* July 19, 2012. Accessed February 18, 2013. http://latimesblogs.latimes.com/lanow/2012/07/two-congressmen-continue-fight-to-save-mount-soledad-cross.html.

Petersson, Anna. "The Production of a Proper Place of Death." Paper presented at the biennial conference on Social Context of Death, Dying and Disposal, Bath, England, September 15–18, 2005.

Petersson, Anna. "Swedish Offerkast and Recent Roadside Memorials." *Folklore* 120 (2009): 75–91.

Petloss. "Petloss Chatroom." Accessed September 18, 2012. http://www.petloss
.com/newchat.htm.

Petrecca, Laura. "Mourning Becomes Electric: Tech Changes the Way we
Grieve." *USAtoday.com,* May 7, 2012. Accessed May 30, 2012. http://
www.usatoday.com/tech/news/story/2012-05-07/digitial-mourning.

The PEW Forum on Religion and Public Life. "'Nones' on the Rise: One-in-Five
Adults Have No Religious Affiliation. "October 9, 2012. http://www
.pewforum.org/unaffiliated/nones-on-the-rise.aspx.

Phillips, Whitney. "LOLing at Tragedy: Facebook Trolls, Memorial Pages and
Resistance to Grief Online." *First Monday Peer Reviewed Journal on the
Internet* 16 (December 2011): 12–15. http://www.uic.edu/htbin/cgiwrap/
bin/ojs/index.php/fm/article/viewArticle/3168/3115.

Phillips, Whitney. "When Research Attacks." *A Sandwich, with Words?* July 11,
2012. http://billions-and-billions.com/?s=when+research+attacks.

Piven, J. S. "Buddhism, Death, and the Feminine." In *The Psychology of Death
in Fantasy and History,* edited by J. S. Piven, 37–70. Westport, CT: Praeger, 2004.

Piven, J. S. *Death and Delusion: A Freudian Analysis of Mortal Terror.* Greenwich, CT: Information Age Publishing, 2004.

Piven, J. S. *The Madness and Perversion of Yukio Mishima.* Westport, CT: Praeger, 2004.

Piven, J. S. "Narcissism, Sexuality, and Psyche in Terrorist Theology." *The Psychoanalytic Review* 93, 2 (2006): 231–65.

Piven, J. S. "Psychological, Theological, and Thanatological Aspects of Suicidal
Terrorism." In *Top Ten Global Justice Law Review Articles 2008,* edited
by Amos Guiora, 285–10. New York: Oxford University Press, 2009.

Pizarro, David. "Nothing More Than Feelings? The Role of Emotions in Moral
Judgment." *Journal for the Theory of Social Behavior* 30 (2000): 355–75.

Plato. "Phaedo." *Five Dialogues,* 93–154. Translated by G.M.A. Grube. Indianapolis: Hackett Publishing Company, Inc., 2002.

Platt, Jane. "The Planning, Organising and Delivery of a Memorial Service in
Critical Care." *Nursing in Critical Care* 9, 5 (2004): 222–9.

Plante, Thomas G. *Contemplative Practices in Action: Spirituality, Meditation
and Health.* Santa Barbara, CA: ABC-CLIO/Praeger, 2010.

Pomfret, James, and Sisi Tang. "Hong Kong teen's somber design for Jobs a cyber
iit." *Reuters,* October 6, 2011. Accessed July 16, 2013. http://uk.reuters.com/
article/2011/10/06/us-apple-hongkong-icon-idUKTRE7952E620111006.

Population Reference Bureau. "2012 World Population Data Sheet." Washington,
DC: Population Reference Bureau, 2012. http://www.prb.org/Publications/
Datasheets/2012/world-population-data-sheet/data-sheet.aspx.

Promessa Organic AB. "Promession—Ecological Burial." Accessed January
2011. http://www.promessa.se/en/.

PRWeb. "New iPhone App Memorializes Dead Loved Ones In The Palm Of Your Hand." Last modified July 6, 2009. http://www.prweb.com/releases/2009/07/prweb2609424.htm.

Putter, Marie. *The Memorial Rituals Book for Healing and Hope.* New York: Baywood Publishing Co., 1997.

Pyszczynski, Tom, Jeff Greenberg, and Sheldon Solomon, S. "A Dual-Process Model of Defense Against Conscious and Unconscious Death-Related Thoughts: An Extension of Terror Management Theory." *Psychological Review* 106 (1999): 835–45.

Pyszczynski, Tom, Sheldon Solomon, and Jeff Greenberg. *In the Wake of 9/11: The Psychology of Terror.* Washington, DC: American Psychological Association, 2003.

Quigley, Christine. *The Corpse: A History.* Jefferson, NC: McFarland & Company, Inc., 1996.

Quiring Headstones. "Living Headstones: Internet connected Headstones." Accessed February 17, 2012. http://www.monuments.com/living-headstones.

Rabaté, Jean-Michel. *Given: 1 Crime, 2 Murder: Modernity, Murder, and Mass Culture.* Eastbourne: Sussex Academic Press, 2007.

Rabbit Hole. DVD. Directed by John Cameron Mitchell. Santa Monica, CA: Olympus Pictures, 2010.

Rank, Otto. *Will Therapy and Truth and Reality.* Translated by Jessie Taft. New York: Knopf, 1945.

Ravenal, John B. *Sally Mann: The Flesh and the Spirit.* New York: aperture, 2010.

Reichel-Dolmatoff, Gerado. "Funerary Customs and Religious Symbolism among the Kogi." In *Native South Americans,* edited by P. Lyon, 289–301. Long Grove, IL: Waveland Press, 1985.

Remembrances (2003). DVD. Directed by Agnes Varda. New York City: Criterion, 2007.

Resomation®, Ltd. "Resomation: An Alternative to Cremation with Environmental Benefits." Company brochure, 2007.

Ricoeur, Paul. *The Symbolism of Evil.* Boston: Beacon, 1967.

"RIP Jamshid Rastegar." Last accessed September 14, 2012. http://www.facebook.com/jamshid.rastegar?sk=wall.

Rothman, Sheila M. *Living in the Shadow of Death: Tuberculosis and the Social Experience of Illness in American History.* New York: Basic Books, 1994.

Rubin, Gail. *A Good Goodbye: Funeral Planning for Those Who Don't Plan to Die.* Albuquerque, Light Tree Press, 2010.

Ruby, Jay. *Secure the Shadow: Death and Photography in America.* Cambridge, MA/London: The MIT Press, 1995.

Salka, Sandra. "Enlisting the Unconscious as an Ally in Grief Therapy: The Creative Use of Affirmations, Metaphors, and Guided Visualization." *Hospice Journal* 12 (1997): 17–31.

Santé, Luc. "Evidence." In *The Corpse: A History,* edited by Christine Quigley, 157–62. Jefferson, NC: McFarland & Company, Inc., 1996.

Santora, Marc. "City Cemeteries Face Gridlock." *New York Times,* August 13, 2010.

Saprano, D. Kearny. "The Importance of Rituals to Daily Life." *Helium,* January 20, 2010. Accessed November 4, 2012. http://www.helium.com/items/1717443-myth-religion-ritual-joseph-campbell-catholicism.

Savage, David G. "Obama Administration Asks That Large Cross Remain as War Memorial." *Tribune Washington Bureau,* March 16, 2012.

"A Second Opinion on Drone Strikes." *Los Angeles Times,* February 18, 2013. Accessed March 28, 2013. http://articles.latimes.com/2013/feb/18/opinion/la-ed-drones-court-targeted-assassinations-20130218.

Schachter, Sherry R. "9/11: A Grief Therapist's Journal." In *Living with Grief: Coping with Public Tragedy,* edited by Marcia Lattanzi-Licht and Kenneth J. Doka, 15–25. New York: Brunner-Routledge, 2003.

Schachter, Sherry R. "The Experience of Living with a Life-Threatening Illness: A Phenomenological Study of Dying Cancer Patients and their Family Caregivers." PhD diss., Union Institute Graduate School, 1999.

Schleifer, Ronald. *Rhetoric of Death: The Language of Modernism and Postmodern Discourse Theory.* Urbana: University of Illinois Press, 1990.

Schmitt, Jean-Claude. *Ghosts in the Middle Ages.* Translated by T. L. Fagan. Chicago, IL: University of Illinois Press, 1999.

Schopenhauer, Arthur. *The World as Will and Representation, Volume II.* Translated by E.F.J. Payne. New York: Dover, 1958.

The Sea Inside. DVD. Directed by Alejandro Amenabar. Spain: Sogepaq, 2004.

Selinger, Evan. "The Online Funeral." *The Huffington Post,* November 10, 2012. Accessed November 11, 2012. http://www.huffingtonpost.com/evan-selinger/technology-funeral-ceremony_b_2100917.html.

Silverlake Life: The View from Here. DVD. Directed by Peter Friedman and Tom Joslin. New York: Zeitgeist Films, 1993.

Sinnott-Armstrong, Walter, ed. *Moral Psychology, 3 Volumes.* Cambridge MA: MIT Press, 2008.

Smith, Alexander K., et al. "Discussing Overall Prognosis with the Very Elderly." *The New England Journal of Medicine* 365 (2011): 2149–51.

Sobchak, Vivian. "Inscribing Ethical Space: Ten Propositions on Death, Representation and Documentary." *Quarterly Review of Film Studies* 9, 4 (1984): 283–300.

Solomon, Sheldon, Jeff Greenberg, and Tom Pyszczynski. "Tales From the Crypt: On the Role of Death in Life." *Zygon: The Journal of Religion & Science* 33 (1998): 9–44.

Sontag, Susan. *On Photography.* New York: Anchor Books Doubleday, c1977.

Sontag, Susan. *Regarding the Pain of Others.* New York: Farrar, Straus and Giroux, 2003.

Souza, Margaret, and Christina Staudt, eds. Foreword by Lesley Sharpe. *The Many Ways We Talk About Death in Contemporary Society.* Lewiston: The Edwin Mellen Press, 2009.

Spinoza, Baruch. *Ethics.* Translated by W. H. White & A. H. Stirling. Hertfordshire, ENG: Wordsworth, 2001.

St. John, Graham, ed. *Victor Turner and Contemporary Cultural Performance.* New York: Berghahn Books, 2008.

Stannard, David. *The Puritan Way of Death—A Study in Religion, Culture and Social Change.* New York: Oxford University Press, 1977.

Staudt, Christina. "Introduction." In *The Many Ways We Talk About Death in Contemporary Society: Interdisciplinary Studies in Portrayal and Classification,* edited by Margaret Souza and Christina Staudt, 1–42. Lewiston, NY: Edwin Mellen Press, 2009.

Stein, Jerry, Anat Peles-Borz, Ilana Buchval, Anat Klein, and Isaac Yaniv. "The Bereavement Visit in Pediatric Oncology." *Journal of Clinical Oncology* 24, 22 (August 2006): 3705–7.

Stein, Ruth. *For Love of the Father.* Stanford, CA: Stanford University Press, 2010.

Stewart, Garrett. *Death Sentences: Styles of Dying in British Fiction.* Cambridge, MA: Harvard University Press, 1984.

Stevens, Hal. "Cremation or Burial—Carbon Emissions and the Environment." *CemeterySpot.com,* March 15, 2008. http://searchwarp.com/swa310027.htm.

Stone, Elizabeth. "Grief in the age of Facebook." *The Chronicle of Higher Education* 56, 25 (2010): B20.

Sutton, P. M., B. E. Rittmann, O. J. Schraa, J. E. Banaszak, and A. P. Togna. "Wastewater as a Resource: A Unique Approach to Achieving Energy Sustainability." *Water Science & Technology* 63, 9 (2011): 2004–9.

Taylor, Susan. "Gerasim Model of Caregiving." *Death Studies* 21 (1997): 299–304.

"The Ten Companies that Control the Death Industry." *24/7 Wall Street,* January 13, 2011. http://247wallst.com/2011/01/13/the-ten-companies-that-control-the-death-industry/.

Terreri, Cara. "Alkaline Hydrolysis: A 'Greener' Option?" Accessed July 16, 2013. http://connectingdirectors.com/articles/38144-ask-the-expert-alkaline-hydrolysis-a-greener-option. Originally published in *The Cremationist of North America* 47, 3 (2011).

"The Way We Grieve Now." Hello Grief, September 20, 2012. Accessed May 17, 2012. http://www.hellogrief.org/the-way-we-grieve-now/print.

Titus Lucretius Carus. *On the Nature of the Universe.* Translated by R. E. Latham. New York: Penguin, 1994.

Todd, Daphne. "It's My Job To Find Beauty in Whatever I'm Looking At." *London Evening Standard,* November 19, 2010. Accessed May 16, 2011.

http://www.thisislondon.co.uk/lifestyle/article-23835658-daphne-todd-its-my-job-to-find-beauty-in-whatever-im-looking-at.do.

Tolstoy, Leo. *The Death of Ivan Ilyich.* Translated by Lynn Solotaroff. New York: Bantam Books, 1981.

Toynbee, J.M.C. *Death and Burial in the Roman World.* New York: Cornell University Press, 1971.

Turner, Victor W. *Dramas, Fields and Metaphors.* Ithaca: Cornell University Press, 1974.

Turner, Victor W. *The Forest of Symbols: Aspects of Ndembu Ritual,* 93–111. Ithaca: Cornell University Press, 1967.

Turner, Victor W. *The Ritual Process: Structure and Anti-Structure.* London: Routledge and Kegan Paul, 1969.

"UK firm: Don't Burn Bodies, Boil Them." *PhysOrg,* August 6, 2007. http://phys.org/news105641250.html.

UNAIDS. "Unite for Universal Access: Overview Brochure on 2011 High Level Meeting on AIDS." June 8–11, 2011. http://www.unaids.org/en/media/unaids/contentassets/documents/document/2011/2011 0204_HLM_Brochure_en.pdf.

Unamuno, Miguel de. *The Tragic Sense of Life.* Translated by A. Kerrigan. Princeton, NJ: Princeton University Press, 1990.

US Environmental Protection Agency. "Brownfields Definition." Accessed January 2013. http://www.epa.gov/swerosps/bf/overview/glossary.htm.

Vail, Kenneth, Zachary Rothschild, David Weise, Sheldon Solomon, Tom Pyszczynski, and Jeff Greenberg. "A Terror Management Analysis of the Psychological Functions of Religion." *Personality and Social Psychology Review* 14 (2010): 84–94.

Vale-Taylor, Pamela. "We will Remember Them." *Journal of Palliative Medicine* 23, 6 (2009): 537–44.

Vander Goot, Mary. *After Freedom: How Boomers Pursued Freedom, Questioned Virtue, and Still Search for Meaning.* Eugene, OR: Wipf and Stock—Cascade, 2012.

Vanmeenen, Karen. "Public vs. Private." *Afterimage* 39, 6 (2012): 3–4. Accessed November 25, 2012. http://search.proquest.com/docview/1023453443?accountid=14569.

Van Schepen, Randall. "Representation of the Infamous or Anonymous Dead: Gerhard Richter's Photopaintings and Jeffrey Silverthorne's Photographs." In *Constructions of Death, Mourning, and Memory Conference: October 27–29, 2006: Proceedings,* edited by Lilian J. Zirpolo, 157–59. Woodcliff Lake, NJ: The WAPACC Organization, 2006.

Vaucher, Andrea R. *Muses from Chaos and Ash: AIDS, Artists, and Art.* New York: Grove Press, 1993.

Verma, Shefali. "Anaerobic Digestion of Biodegradable Organics in Municipal Solid." MA thesis, Columbia University, Department of Earth and

Environmental Engineering, Fu Foundation School of Engineering and Applied Science, 2002.

Vigeland, Tess. "Italian Mayor Bans Death." *Marketplace*, American Public Media, March 15, 2012. http://www.marketplace.org/topics/life/final-note/italian-mayor-bans-death.

von Franz, M-L. *Shadow and Evil in Fairytales*. Dallas, TX: Spring, 1987.

Walter, Tony. *The Revival of Death*. London: Routledge, 1993.

Ward, John W., et al. "Recommendations for the Identification of Chronic Hepatitis C Virus Infection Among Persons Born During 1945–1965." *Centers for Disease Control and Prevention*, August 17, 2012. http://www.cdc.gov/mmwr/preview/mmwrhtml/rr6104a1.htm?s_cid=rr6104a1_w.

Webb, Jennifer, and Lorraine Webb. "Dead or Alive." In *Images of the Corpse: From the Renaissance to Cyberspace*, edited by Elizabeth Klaver, 206–27. Madison: University of Wisconsin Press, 2004.

Walker, Rob. "Cyberspace When You're Dead." *The New York Times Magazine*, January 5, 2011. http://www.nytimes.com/2011/01/09/magazine/09Immortality-t.html.

Watkins, Keith. "Searching for New Rituals for Death and Dying." *Keith Watkins Historian*, March 4, 2012. Accessed July 16, 2013. http://keithwatkinshistorian.wordpress.com/2012/03/04/searching-for-new-rituals-for-death-and-dying/.

Webster Goodwin, Sarah, and Elisabeth Bronfen, eds. *Death and Representation*. Baltimore/London: The Johns Hopkins University Press, 1993.

Weiner, Annette. *Women of Value, Men of Renown*. Austin TX: University of Texas Press, 1983.

Weisser, Jennifer. "Micro Sacred Sites: The Spatial Pattern of Roadside Memorials in Warren County, Ohio." MA thesis, University of Cincinnati, 2004.

Westfall, Stephen, and Nan Goldin. "The Ballad of Nan Goldin." *BOMB* 37 (Fall, 1991): 27–31. Accessed November 24, 2012. http://www.jstor.org/stable/40424261.

Whaley, Joachim, ed. *Mirrors of Mortality: Studies in the Social History of Death* (New York: St. Martin's Press, 1981.

White, Edmund. "Journals of the Plague Years." *The Nation*, May 12, 1997, 13–18.

"Whitney Houston In Loving Memory." Last accessed September 18, 2012. http://www.facebook.com/whitneyhouston.inlovingmemory.

Williams, William Carlos. "The Last Words of My English Grandmother." In *On Doctoring*, edited by Richard Reynolds and John Stone, 61–2. New York: Simon & Schuster, 2010.

Winakur, Jerald. "What Are We Going to Do with Dad?" *Health Affairs* 24 (2005): 1064–72.

Winner, Lauren F. "From Black Crepe to Blue Ink: Mourning Tattoos and the Practice of Embodied Bereavement." In *The Many Ways We Talk About Death in Contemporary Society*, edited by Margaret Souza and Christina Staudt, 135–48. Lewiston, NY: Edwin Mellen Press, 2009.

Winquist, Charles E. *Desiring Theology*. Chicago: University of Chicago Press, 1995.

Wojnarowicz, David. *Close to the Knives: A Memoir of Disintegration*. New York: Vintage Books, 1991. Page 102 quoted in Emily Colucci, "Some Sort of Grace—David Wojnarowicz's Archive of the Death of Peter Hujar." *American Suburbx*. Accessed December 1, 2012. http://www.americansuburbx .com/2011/02/peter-hujar-david-wojnarowicz-some-sort-of-html.

Workman, S. R. "Never Say Die? As Treatments Fail Doctors' Words Must Not." *The International Journal of Clinical Practice* 65, 2 (2011): 117–19.

World Resources Institute. "Facts about Urbanization in the U.S.A." Accessed March 2012. http://www.wri.org/publication/content/8840.

Wortham, Jenna. "As Facebook Users Dies, Ghosts Reach Out." *New York Times,* July 17, 2010. Accessed February 27, 2012. http://www.nytimes .com/2010/07/18/technology/18death.html.

Worthing Crematorium. *Newsletter, October 2007*. West Sussex, UK: Worthing Borough Council, 2007.

Wouters, Cas. "The Quest for New Rituals in Dying and Mourning: Changes in the We-l Balance." *Body & Society* 8, 1 (March 2002): 1–27.

Yalom, Irvin. *Existential Psychotherapy*. New York: Basic Books, 1980.

Yourman, Lindsey C., et al. "Prognostic Indices for Older Adults." *Journal of the American Medical Association* 307, 2 (2012): 182–92.

Zaleski, Philip, and Carol Zaleski. *Prayer: A History*. New York: Houghton Mifflin, 2005.

Zweig, Paul. *Departures: Memoirs*. New York: HarperCollins, 1986.

Zweig, Paul. "The River." In *Eternity's Woods,* 17–19. Middletown, CT: Wesleyan University Press, 1985.

Zyga, Lisa. "Ecological Burial Involves Freeze-drying, Composting the Corpse." *PhysOrg,* March 8, 2011. http://phys.org/news/2011–03-ecological-bu rial-involves-freeze-drying-composting.html.

About the Editors

CHRISTINA STAUDT (PhD art history, Columbia University) is the chair of the Columbia University Seminar on Death, presiding at monthly colloquia focused on timely inquiries of dying, death, and grief and organizing three interdisciplinary conferences sponsored by the Seminar. The cofounder and president of the Westchester End-of-Life Coalition, a board member of a local hospice, and cancer support team, she initiates and directs programs and speaks in the public and professional arena to foster education around mortality and mourning. She is the coeditor of and wrote the introduction to the anthologies *The Many Ways We Talk about Death in Contemporary Society* (Mellen 2009) and *Unequal Before Death* (Cambridge Scholars Publishing 2012); and contributed chapters on the literature of death and dying and on the imagery of death after 9/11 for *Speaking of Death—America's New Sense of Mortality* (Michael K. Bartalos, ed., Praeger 2009). An active hospice volunteer for 15 years, with a focus on assisting the actively dying and their families, she sits by the bedside of those at the end of life and is an advocate for improving the end-of-life experience for patients and their families.

J. HAROLD ELLENS (PhD in psychology of human communications, Wayne State University; PhD in Second Temple Judaism and Christian origins from the University of Michigan) is a retired university professor of philosophy and psychology, retired Presbyterian theologian and pastor, retired U.S. Army chaplain (colonel), executive director emeritus of the Christian Association for Psychological Studies, and founding editor and editor in chief of the *Journal of Psychology and Christianity.* He has published extensively on the interface of psychology and religion/spirituality. His recent publications include *The Destructive Power of Religion* (4 vols., 2004); *Psychology and the Bible* (4 vols., with Wayne Rollins, 2004); *God's Word for Our World, A Festschrift for Professor Simon John De Vries* (2 vols., 2004); *Sex in the Bible* (2006); *Text and Community, A Festschrift Commemorating Profess Bruce M. Metzger* (2 vols., 2007); *Radical Grace, How Belief in a Benevolent God Benefits Our Health* (2007); *Understanding Religious Experience, What the Bible Says about Spirituality* (2007); *Miracles: God, Science, and Psychology in the Paranormal* (3 vols., 2008); *The Spirituality of Sex* (2009); *Probing the Frontiers of Biblical Studies, A Festschrift in Honor of Professor David J. A. Clines* (2009); *The Son of Man in The Gospel of John* (2010); *The Healing Power of Spirituality, How Faith Helps Humans Thrive* (3 vols., 2010); *Honest Faith for Our Time: Truth Telling about the Bible, the Creed, and the Church* (2010); *Light from the Other Side, The Paranormal as Friend and Familiar* (2010); *Explaining Evil* (3 vols., 2011); *Psychological Hermeneutics of Biblical Themes and Texts, A Festschrift in Honor of Wayne G. Rollins* (2012); *A Dangerous Report, Challenging Sermons for Advent and Easter* (2012); *God's Radical Grace, Challenging Sermons for Ordinary Time(s)* (2012); *Heaven, Hell, and Afterlife: Eternity in Judaism, Christianity, and Islam* (3 vols., 2013); and *Winning Revolutions: The Psychology of Successful Revolts for Freedom, Fairness, and Rights* (3 vols., 2013). He has authored or coauthored 226 published volumes, 176 professional journal articles, and 282 review articles. He is a psychotherapist in private practice. He may be contacted at www.jharoldellens.com and at jharoldellens@juno.com.

About the Contributors

KATHRYN BEATTIE, MA, is an independent researcher and writer with a bachelor of fine arts degree and a master of arts degree in art history. Her MA thesis topic was "Aspects of Acceptance and Denial in Painted Posthumous Portraits and Postmortem Photographs of Nineteenth-Century Children" (2006). Her current interest and fascination with liminal moments of death and dying as experienced through art appreciation has expanded to manifest itself in a number of feminist negotiations with mourning and death in contemporary art. Her article, "From Private Places to Public Spaces: Mourning and Death in the Art of Four Contemporary Women Artists," is included in the book *Women and the Material Culture of Death* (2013) and was presented at The Art of Death and Dying Conference (October 2012, University of Houston) organized by the University of Houston Libraries, Houston, Texas. Presently, she is focusing more specifically on cultural attitudes toward, and representations of, the corpse in contemporary art. She is also coediting a hybrid curatorial and virtual art project and proposed electronic publication. Both projects track attitudes toward death and what appears to be an omnipresent concern with mortality and timelessness in global contemporary art.

MARCELLINE BLOCK, BA, Harvard; MA, Princeton, edited volumes including *World Film Locations: Marseilles* (Intellect/University of Chicago, 2013); *World Film Locations: Las Vegas* (Intellect/ University of Chicago, 2012); *World Film Locations: Paris* (Intellect/University of Chicago, 2011); and *Situating the Feminist Gaze and Spectatorship in Postwar Cinema* (Cambridge Scholars, 2008; 2010), which was named Book of the Month, January 2012, by its publisher. She coedited, with Christina Staudt, *Unequal before Death* (Cambridge Scholars, 2012, with a grant from Columbia University), named

Book of the Month, September 2012. Her other coedited works include *Gender Scripts in Medicine and Narrative* (Cambridge Scholars, 2010) and "Collaboration", volume 18 of *Critical Matrix: The Princeton Journal of Women, Gender, Culture* (2009). She contributed chapters to *The Many Ways We Talk about Death in Contemporary Society: Interdisciplinary Studies in Portrayal and Classification* (2009); *Vendetta: Essays on Honor and Revenge* (2010); and *Cherchez la femme: Women and Values in the Francophone World* (2011). Her articles appear in *Excavatio* (2007); *LINE* (2007; 2008); *The Harvard French Review* (2007), *Women in French Studies* (2009, 2010), and *Afterall* (2012). Her writing is translated into Chinese, French, Italian, Korean, and Russian. She is a PhD candidate at Princeton, where she has taught as a lecturer in history.

DANIEL CALLAHAN, PhD, philosophy, Harvard, codirector of the Yale-Hastings Program in Ethics and Health Policy, is a distinguished bioethicist who most recently has been focusing his attention to ethical issues in health policy. The recipient of numerous honors, including the Freedom and Scientific Responsibility Award from the American Association for the Advancement of Science (1996), Callahan is an elected member of the National Academy of Sciences. He cofounded the Hastings Center (Garrison, New York), a nonpartisan bioethics research institution, of which he was president (1969–1996) and where his current position is President Emeritus and Senior Research Scholar. Among his 41 books treating a vast range of health and health-care-related topics is *The Troubled Dream of Life: In Search of a Peaceful Death* (Simon & Schuster, 1993). Callahan's work frequently appears in academic and medical journals, and he was executive editor of *Commonweal,* the Catholic journal of culture, politics, and religion, from 1961 to 1968.

CANDI K. CANN, PhD, conducts research in death and dying and focuses on the impact of remembering (and forgetting) in shaping how lives are recalled, remembered, and celebrated. She examined this theme through the construction of martyr narratives in her early scholarship, and more recently has shifted to researching "virtual" memorials, specifically examining memorials found on the Internet, in tattoos, car decals, and other forms of bodiless memorials in honoring and remembering the dead. She is currently working on a manuscript, *Virtual Afterlives: Grieving the Dead in a World without Mourning,* to be published by the University of Kentucky Press in 2014.

GEORGE E. DICKINSON, PhD, professor of sociology at the College of Charleston, received his PhD in sociology from Louisiana State University. He authored/coauthored over 80 articles in peer-reviewed journals and 23 books/anthologies, primarily on end-of-life issues (*Understanding Dying, Death, and Bereavement* 7th ed., with M. R. Leming, Cengage/Wadsworth Publishers, 2011, and *Annual Editions: Dying, Death, and Bereavement* 14th ed., with

M. R. Leming, McGraw-Hill, 2013). His research and teaching about end-of-life issues goes back to 1974 when he taught his first course in death and dying. He has written about thanatology in medical, dental, nursing, child life, social work, pharmacy, and veterinary schools. He is on the editorial boards of *Mortality* (U.K.) and the *American Journal of Hospice & Palliative Medicine* (U.S.). Recent awards include the 2002 Distinguished Teacher/Scholar Award and the 2008 Distinguished Research Award at the College of Charleston, South Carolina, Governor's Distinguished Professor Awards in 2003 and 2008, the Association for Death Education and Counseling's Death Educator Award in 2009. In 1999 he was Visiting Research Fellow in palliative medicine at the University of Sheffield's School of Medicine, in 2006 at Lancaster University's Institute for Health Research in the International Observatory on End-of-Life Issues, and in 2013 at the University of Bristol's School of Veterinary Science.

KRISTEN M. FINNERAN, LMHC, is a bereavement counselor at Calvary Hospital/Hospice where she works with bereaved children, teens, and adults, coordinating both groups as well as individual therapy. Finneran is a graduate of Northeastern University where she received a bachelor of science. She received an MA from the College of New Rochelle and is a licensed mental health counselor. As an educator, Finneran provides educational services to mental health providers focusing on issues related to loss and death.

BRUCE HIEBERT, MDiv, Ph D, is a historical-theological ethicist and faculty member at University Canada West. He also teaches Mennonite studies at University of the Fraser Valley and is an adjunct faculty member in ethics at Vancouver School of Theology. His current research explores issues of brain functioning and decision-making processes. He is particularly interested in the impact of trauma on male decision making and the formation of masculinity as well as brain process–based models of decision making in religious communities.

HEATH C. HOFFMANN, PhD, associate professor of sociology and chair of the Department of Sociology and Anthropology at the College of Charleston (Charleston, South Carolina) received his PhD in sociology from the University of Georgia. Professor Hoffmann's teaching and research interests include criminal justice policy, prisons, prisoner reentry, and alcohol and other drug use. Professor Hoffmann has published scholarly articles relating to prison communication policies, prison programs for incarcerated parents and their underage children, and prison hospice programs. Professor Hoffmann has also taught two classes in prison, including a class in which traditional college students took a class in prison with incarcerated men. The latter class inspired a research project exploring the influence that interpersonal contact with those who are incarcerated has on college students' attitudes toward people in prison.

MARSHA HURST (PhD, political science, Columbia University). She is a member of the Master's Program faculty of the Program in Narrative Medicine at Columbia University, where she teaches courses on illness and disability narratives and on narratives of death, dying, and caregiving. At Columbia she also co-chairs the University Seminar on Narrative, Health, and Social Justice. Hurst is coeditor with Sayantani DasGupta, MD, MPH, of *Stories of Illness and Healing: Women Write Their Bodies,* an anthology of women's illness narratives, and is author of numerous articles. As a patient advocate, Hurst sits on the New York State Palliative Care Education and Training Council and is a founder and current board officer of the Westchester End-of-Life Coalition. She gives presentations, runs workshops, and writes in areas related to narrative advocacy and to narrative and end-of-life care.

CRAIG IRVINE (PhD, philosophy) is the director of the Master's Program in Narrative Medicine and director of education of the Program in Narrative Medicine at Columbia University. For more than 15 years, he has been designing and teaching cultural competency, ethics, and narrative medicine curricula for residents, medical students, physicians, nurses, social workers, chaplains, physical therapists, and other health professionals, as well as artists, writers, and thinkers from the humanities and social sciences. He has published on ethics, residency education, and narrative medicine and has presented at numerous national and international conferences on these and other topics.

DONALD JORALEMON, PhD, is professor of anthropology at Smith College. He received his BA from Oberlin College (1974) and his MA and PhD from the University of California, Los Angeles (1983). He is the author of *Exploring Medical Anthropology* (1999, third edition 2010) and the coauthor (with Douglas Sharon) of *Sorcery and Shamanism: Curanderos and Clients in Northern Peru* (1993). Among his published articles on Peruvian shamanism is the widely cited essay "The Selling of the Shaman and the Problem of Informant Legitimacy" (*Journal of Anthropological Research,* 1990). His present work focuses on the anthropology of organ transplantation and medical ethics, as well as on dying and death in America. His article "Organ Wars: The Battle for Body Parts" (*Medical Anthropology Quarterly,* 1995) won the Polgar Prize from the Society for Medical Anthropology. His most recent publications, on the medical ethics of financial compensation for organ donors, appear in the *Journal of Medical Ethics* (2001) and *The Hastings Center Report* (2003). An article on the concept of medical futility was published in the *Cambridge Quarterly of Health Care Ethics* (2002). A book manuscript, *Mortal Dilemmas: Why Is It So Hard to Die in America?,* is nearing completion.

DANIEL LIECHTY, PhD, holds graduate degrees in religious studies, ethics, counseling, and clinical social work. He practiced as a group specialist at

The Institute of Pennsylvania Hospital for a number of years and subsequently was the psychosocial coordinator for the hospice program at the Montgomery Medical Center near Philadelphia. Since 1999 he has been professor in the School of Social Work, Illinois State University. He is the vice president of The Ernest Becker Foundation, which supports exploration of issues related to death and dying in a broadly interdisciplinary context. His major books include *Transference and Transcendence* (Aronson, 1995), *Death and Denial* (Praeger, 2002), *Reflecting on Faith in a Post-Christian Time* (Cascadia, 2003), and *The Ernest Becker Reader* (University of Washington Press, 2005).

JERRY S. PIVEN, PhD, has taught at New York University, New School University, and Case Western Reserve University, where his courses have focused on the philosophy of religion, existentialism, psychoanalysis, and metaphysics. He has earned interdisciplinary graduate degrees in the fields of psychology, religion, philosophy, and literature, and has studied at the National Psychological Association for Psychoanalysis training institute. The central focus of Dr. Piven's research is on the psychology and philosophy of religion, exploring the nature of belief systems, the dynamics of dogma, faith, violence, and apocalyptic eschatologies. He is the editor of *The Psychology of Death in Fantasy and History* (2004) and *Terrorism, Jihad, and Sacred Vengeance* (2004), and author of *Death and Delusion: A Freudian Analysis of Mortal Terror* (2004), *The Madness and Perversion of Yukio Mishima* (2004), and *Nihon No Kyoki* (*Japanese Madness,* 2007). He has recently completed *Slaughtering Death: On the Psychoanalysis of Terror, Religion, and Violence.*

ROBERT POLLACK, PhD, has been professor of biological sciences at Columbia since 1978, director of the Center for the Study of Science and Religion (CSSR) since 1999, and director of University Seminars since 2011. Additionally, he is a lecturer at the Center for Psychoanalytic Training and Research, a member of the Earth Institute Faculty, and an adjunct professor at Union Theological Seminary. He was dean of Columbia College from 1982 to 1989. He has received the Alexander Hamilton Medal from Columbia University and the Gershom Mendel Seixas Award from the Columbia/Barnard Hillel. Since 2006 he has been a member of the teaching faculty of the Columbia College core course, Frontiers of Science, and he and CSSR codirector Cynthia Peabody have taught a four-day intensive course, "DNA, Evolution, and the Soul," at Union Theological Seminary. Since 2009, he has been one of four faculty teaching the EEEB 4321 "Human Identity," a senior seminar in the Human Biology major in that department. He is the author of more than a 100 research papers on the oncogenic phenotype of mammalian cells in culture. In addition, he has written as many and more opinion pieces and reviews on aspects of molecular biology, medical ethics, and science education. He has published three books since 1994: *Signs of Life; The Missing Moment;* and *The*

Faith of Biology, the Biology of Faith. His fourth book, a narration of the work of his wife, the artist Amy Pollack, *The Course of Nature,* appeared in 2012.

ANGELA RIECHERS, MA, is an award-winning design writer and educator based in Brooklyn, New York. Her work explores the intersection of memory, media, and popular visual culture, with a focus on how evolving technology affects the design of systems and objects that are created to preserve ephemeral human remembrance. Of particular interest are the ways in which digital formats and social media sites impact legacy and memorialization, and how these contemporary means of remembering coexist alongside traditional physical memorial items. In 2010, she received an AOL Artists 25 for 25 grant for Sites of Memory, a multimedia project that reattaches narrative histories of the dead to specific locations in New York City through audio-guided walking tours and map-based archives, linking separate urban sites together into a larger story about recall, mortality, and forgetting. She holds a BFA from the Rhode Island School of Design and an MFA from the School of Visual Art's Design Criticism program. She regularly speaks at design conferences and universities, and teaches at the City College of New York, New York University, and the School of Visual Arts.

CATHERINE ROGERS, MFA, is a performer and playwright whose most recent solo show, *The Sudden Death of Everyone,* has been seen in New York, Philadelphia, and Greece. Currently a graduate student in narrative medicine at Columbia University, Catherine taught writing at New York University and was a Fulbright playwright-in-residence at Aristotle University Thessaloniki and the University of Athens. She holds an MFA in playwriting from the University of Texas where she was a James A. Michener fellow.

KARLA MARIA ROTHSTEIN, RA is an architect and associate professor, living, practicing and teaching in New York City. Her areas of research span intimate spaces of metropolitan domestic life and infrastructures of death and memory, with an underlying commitment to social justice and the built environment. In both her professional work as design director at Latent Productions and through a series of studios taught at the Graduate School of Architecture Planning and Preservation at Columbia University, Rothstein is researching emerging methods of corpse disposal and developing progressive proposals of civic sanctuary and temporal urban remembrance. Since 2011, Rothstein has been a member of the Columbia University Seminar on Death. She hopes to be considered as having fostered a radical reshaping of urban public spaces, which enable us to better honor our dead.

SHERRY R. SCHACHTER, PhD, is the director of Bereavement Services for Calvary Hospital/Hospice where she develops, coordinates, and facilitates educational services for staff and develops and oversees an extensive bereavement program for families and members of the community. She is also the director of Camp Compass®, a summer camp for bereaved children and teens. For over 30 years, Dr. Schachter has worked with dying patients and their family caregivers. Dr. Schachter is a past president of the Association for Death Education and Counseling (ADEC) and is a member of the International Work Group on Death, Dying, and Bereavement.

Index

Italic page numbers indicate reference to figures.